Enhancing Sustainability Through Non-Financial Reporting

Albertina Monteiro
ISCAP, CEOS, Polytechnic of Porto, Portugal

Ana Pinto Borges
ISAG – European Business School, Portugal & CICET-FCVC, Portugal & COME-GI, Portugal

Elvira Vieira
ISAG – European Business School, Portugal & CICET-FCVC, Portugal & Polytechnic Institute of Viana do Castelo, Portugal & UNIAG, Portugal

A volume in the Advances in Finance, Accounting, and Economics (AFAE) Book Series

Published in the United States of America by
   IGI Global
   Business Science Reference (an imprint of IGI Global)
   701 E. Chocolate Avenue
   Hershey PA, USA 17033
   Tel: 717-533-8845
   Fax: 717-533-8661
   E-mail: cust@igi-global.com
   Web site: http://www.igi-global.com

Library of Congress Cataloging-in-Publication Data

Names: Monteiro, Albertina, 1974- editor. | Borges, Ana Pinto, 1980-
   editor. | Vieira, Elvira, 1977- editor.
Title: Enhancing sustainability through non-financial reporting / edited by
   Albertina Monteiro, Ana Pinto Borges, and Elvira Vieira.
Description: Hershey, PA : Business Science Reference, [2023] | Includes
   bibliographical references and index. | Summary: "The book provides a
   platform for both academics and practitioners to share their empirical
   and theoretical research on the contributions of organizations to
   sustainable development, the determinants and impacts of non-financial
   information reporting, the role of sustainability reporting standards,
   and the challenges faced by accounting, finance, management, and
   auditing. It is an essential resource for anyone seeking to enhance
   sustainability through non-financial reporting and is relevant to a wide
   range of audiences, including academics, practitioners, and other
   interested individuals and groups"-- Provided by publisher.
Identifiers: LCCN 2023024228 (print) | LCCN 2023024229 (ebook) | ISBN
   9781668490761 (hardcover) | ISBN 9781668490778 (paperback) | ISBN
   9781668490785 (ebook)
Subjects: LCSH: Sustainable development reporting. | Environmental
   reporting.
Classification: LCC HD60.3 .E54 2023 (print) | LCC HD60.3 (ebook) | DDC
   658.4/083--dc23/eng/20230623
LC record available at https://lccn.loc.gov/2023024228
LC ebook record available at https://lccn.loc.gov/2023024229

This book is published in the IGI Global book series Advances in Finance, Accounting, and Economics (AFAE) (ISSN: 2327-5677; eISSN: 2327-5685)

British Cataloguing in Publication Data
A Cataloguing in Publication record for this book is available from the British Library.

For electronic access to this publication, please contact: eresources@igi-global.com.

Advances in Finance, Accounting, and Economics (AFAE) Book Series

Ahmed Driouchi
Al Akhawayn University, Morocco

ISSN:2327-5677
EISSN:2327-5685

MISSION

In our changing economic and business environment, it is important to consider the financial changes occurring internationally as well as within individual organizations and business environments. Understanding these changes as well as the factors that influence them is crucial in preparing for our financial future and ensuring economic sustainability and growth.

The **Advances in Finance, Accounting, and Economics (AFAE)** book series aims to publish comprehensive and informative titles in all areas of economics and economic theory, finance, and accounting to assist in advancing the available knowledge and providing for further research development in these dynamic fields.

COVERAGE

- Entrepreneurship in Accounting and Finance
- Finance and Accounting in SMEs
- Economics of Migration and Spatial Mobility
- E-Accounting
- Macroeconomics
- Risk Analysis and Management
- Ethics in Accounting and Finance
- Applied Accounting
- Field Research
- E-Finance

IGI Global is currently accepting manuscripts for publication within this series. To submit a proposal for a volume in this series, please contact our Acquisition Editors at Acquisitions@igi-global.com or visit: http://www.igi-global.com/publish/.

Titles in this Series

For a list of additional titles in this series, please visit: http://www.igi-global.com/book-series/advances-finance-accounting-economics/73685

Circular Economy Implementation for Sustainability in the Built Environment
Nicoleta Cobîrzan (Technical University of Cluj-Napoca, Romania) Radu Muntean (Transilvania University of Brasov, Romania) and Raluca-Andreea Felseghi (Technical University of Cluj-Napoca, Romania)
Business Science Reference • © 2023 • 330pp • H/C (ISBN: 9781668482384) • US $250.00

Management, Technology, and Economic Growth in Smart and Sustainable Cities
Jorge A. Ruiz-Vanoye (Universidad Politécnica de Pachuca, Mexico)
Business Science Reference • © 2023 • 320pp • H/C (ISBN: 9798369303733) • US $240.00

Optimizing Energy Efficiency During a Global Energy Crisis
Meltem Okur Dinçsoy (Trakya University, Turkey) and Hamit Can (Trakya University, Turkey)
Business Science Reference • © 2023 • 408pp • H/C (ISBN: 9798369304006) • US $240.00

Theory and Practice of Illegitimate Finance
Abdul Rafay (University of Management and Technology, Pakistan)
Business Science Reference • © 2023 • 389pp • H/C (ISBN: 9798369311905) • US $295.00

The Sustainable Fintech Revolution Building a Greener Future for Finance
Kuldeep Singh (Faculty of Management Studies, CMS Business School, Jain University (Deemed), Bengaluru, India) Rebecca Abraham (Huizenga College of Business and Entrepreneurship, Nova Southeastern University, Fort Lauderdale, USA) and Prasanna Kolar (Koneru Lakshmaiah Education Foundation, India)
Business Science Reference • © 2023 • 358pp • H/C (ISBN: 9798369300084) • US $250.00

Sustainable Growth and Global Social Development in Competitive Economies
Andrei Jean Vasile (Petroleum-Gas University of Ploiesti, Romania & Romanian Academy, National Institute for Economic Research "Costin C. Kirițescu", Romania) Mile Vasić (European Marketing and Management Association, Banja Luka, Bosnia and Herzegovina) and Predrag Vukovic (Institute of Agricultural Economics, Belgrade, Serbia)
Business Science Reference • © 2023 • 331pp • H/C (ISBN: 9781668488102) • US $250.00

701 East Chocolate Avenue, Hershey, PA 17033, USA
Tel: 717-533-8845 x100 • Fax: 717-533-8661
E-Mail: cust@igi-global.com • www.igi-global.com

Table of Contents

Detailed Table of Contents

    Alice Loureiro, CICF-Research Center on Accounting and Taxation, Management School,
        Polytechnic Institute of Cávado and Ave, Portugal
    Sónia Monteiro, CICF-Research Center on Accounting and Taxation, Management School,
        Polytechnic Institute of Cávado and Ave, Portugal
    Verónica Ribeiro, CICF-Research Center on Accounting and Taxation, Management School,
        Polytechnic Institute of Cávado and Ave, Portugal

The apparent commitment of Portuguese corporations to the Sustainable Development Goals (SDGs) is still limited. Therefore, this chapter aims to address this gap by conducting a detailed descriptive analysis of SDGs reporting practices in the largest Portuguese companies over a 5-year period (2016-2020), following the approval of the 2030 Agenda. The specific objectives of this analysis are to understand how the SDGs are disclosed in non-financial reporting documents and to analyse which SDGs are referenced by companies and given priority. There has been an increasing trend in non-financial reporting over the years, and the most frequently cited SDGs in the reports are SDG12, SDG8, SDG7, and SDG13.

    Serhat Duranay, Isparta University of Applied Sciences, Turkey
    Mehmet Özsoy, Suleyman Demirel University, Turkey

The results obtained by analyzing the financial performance of sustainable investments help to break down investors' negative prejudices about this investment philosophy. Although the number of studies in this area has reached a satisfactory level in developed markets, there are serious deficiencies in emerging markets. The fund kind and methodology differentiate this study from the literature. The study examines the performance of sustainable pension funds in the Turkish market, using MCDM of entropy, TOPSIS, and GRA. Including 3 sustainable and 19 conventional pension funds, the study covers the period between 2017 and 2021. The findings reveal that TOPSIS and GRA results are consistent. Although the performance ranking of sustainable funds fluctuates, it is observed that, in general, sustainable funds do not lag behind the performance of conventional funds and may even outperform them. Moreover, they have maintained their performance and outperformed conventional funds during periods of domestic crisis. However, a similar situation was not observed during the COVID-19 period.

Chapter 3

Bianca Moraes Fernandes, Federal University of Pará, Brazil
Adriana Rodrigues Silva, Polytechnic Institute of Santarém, Portugal & CICF-Research
    Centre on Accounting and Taxation, Portugal
Risolene Alves Macena Araújo, Federal University of Pará, Brazil
Rui Costa Robalo, Polytechnic Institute of Santarém, Portugal & CICF-Research Centre on
    Accounting and Taxation, Portugal

This chapter analyses the extinction accounting within Petrobras' integrated report and its sustainability report. To accomplish this, the authors have scrutinized the disclosure of the impact of the company's operational activities on affected species and their habitats. The analysis has been conducted using the theoretical framework adapted from Maroun and Atkins, which assesses six key elements: (1) the context of extinction accounting, (2) action-focused reports, (3) partner reports, (4) analysis and reflection, (5) evaluation, and (6) disclosure. Despite encountering the general elements, it was noted that the intended objectives were not fully met. The reports under scrutiny lack information regarding the species affected by the company's operations or address the impacts generated by its activities, offering only vague references to the resources employed or the outcomes achieved by the company.

Chapter 4

Esin Bengü Ceran, İstanbul University, Turkey

Institutions have various responsibilities in terms of all the actors they interact with while carrying out their activities. At the point reached today, it is not possible to survive for an enterprise that is run only by profit maximization and by considering the needs of its shareholders. Global awareness and the rapidly developing sustainability idea in this direction are gaining importance at the businesses level as well. Both the legal obligations put forward and the social awareness that has arisen oblige businesses to take care of all stakeholders while carrying out their activities. This formation, which is widely concerned in the management organization literature, is shaped within the framework of corporate social responsibility concept. Within the scope of this chapter, the relationship of CSR with stakeholder theory, classical and modern approaches of the concept, and basic conceptual models are included.

Chapter 5

Muhammad Junaid Ahsan, University of Pisa, Italy

This chapter provides a comprehensive analysis of corporate social responsibility (CSR) practices and reporting. It begins with an overview of the history and evolution of CSR and presents different approaches to CSR. The theoretical foundations of CSR, including stakeholder, social contract, legitimacy, and resource dependence theories, are then discussed. This chapter explores the importance of CSR reporting and the different perspectives on CSR, including social accounting and social responsibility disclosure. Additionally, the impact of CSR practices and reporting on an organization's performance and reputation is examined, along with the determinants of non-financial information reporting. The roles and challenges of accounting, finance, management, and auditing professionals in CSR practices and reporting are discussed, including challenges for professionals.

Chapter 6

 Risolene Alves de Macena Araújo, Federal University of Pará, Brazil
 Adriana Rodrigues Silva, Polytechnic Institute of Santarém, Portugal & CICF-Research
  Centre on Accounting and Taxation, Portugal
 Nicoly Sousa Santos, Federal University of Pará, Brazil

The study aims to analyse the influence of contingency factors on sustainable practices in restaurants on Combú Island, Pará. A survey and interviews were conducted using a structured questionnaire that related sustainable practices to contingency factors. The main result of the research revealed that the contingency factors that most influence sustainable practices in the region are leadership and the environment. Leadership plays a crucial role in encouraging and directing employees towards environmental practices. At the same time, the environment strongly influences the environmental attitudes of managers due to the location of the businesses in an environmentally protected area. The main contribution of this study is to understand the stage of adoption of sustainable practices in local businesses on the island, which allows the development of actions that contribute to the consolidation of these practices in other companies, given the fundamental importance of sustainability in the current scenario.

Chapter 7

 Arnaldo Coelho, Faculty of Economics, University of Coimbra, Portugal
 Beatriz Lopes Cancela, ISCAC, Coimbra Business School, Portugal
 Pedro Fontoura, Faculty of Economics, University of Coimbra, Portugal
 Alexandre Rato, Faculty of Economics, University of Coimbra, Portugal

The literature on the disclosure of sustainability has been receiving increasing attention, with various studies being conducted. However, the systematic review of the literature on "sustainability disclosure" by mapping the existing research and identifying opportunities for future research is fragmented and limited, and the objectives of this investigation intend to respond to this gap. The chapter contributes to contemporary literature by carving out the importance sustainability disclosure. The methodology employed includes a systematic literature review using the Web of Science and Scopus databases (1979 and 2023), which was analyzed using the VOSviewer and RStudio software. The results of the study reveal six distinct groups of publication trends, including sustainable index and practices, corporate image and reputation, sustainability reporting, frameworks related to sustainability, corporate governance approaches, and board corporative characteristics.

Chapter 8

   Pedro Pinho, Porto Accounting and Business School, Polytechnic of Porto, Portugal
   Catarina Libório Morais Cepêda, University of Trás-os-Montes and Alto Douro, Portugal & Porto Accounting and Business School, Polytechnic of Porto, Portugal
   José Campos Amorim, Porto Accounting and Business School, CEOS, Polytechnic of Porto, Portugal
   Albertina Paula Monteiro, Porto Accounting and Business School, CEOS, Polytechnic of Porto, Portugal

Over the years, companies have not been required to disclose information about their activities, profits, and the taxes that they pay in all the countries where they operate, which has allowed them to hide their presence in many low-tax jurisdictions. For this reason, country-by-country reporting (CbCR) has emerged as one of the measures to increase organizational transparency. With a sample of the 36 largest European banks, based in 11 EU countries, in more than 90 jurisdictions around the world, this study aims to analyze the relationship between European banks' presence in tax havens, effective tax rates, performance, and productivity. Based on 3587 observations, the results reveal a tendency for European banks to move their profits to tax havens, which allows them to pay less tax or none. In addition, the results show that banks with lower effective tax rates have better performance; however, they did not prove a significant relationship with productivity. This study highlights the importance of the CbCR in the fight against tax evasion and profit shifting.

Chapter 9

   Aida Hanić, Institute of Economic Sciences, Belgrade, Serbia
   Slavica Stevanović, Institute of Economic Sciences, Belgrade, Serbia
   Petar Mitić, Institute of Economic Sciences, Belgrade, Serbia

This chapter aims to analyze the online environmental disclosure practice by big polluters in Serbia. The analysis was based on a sample of 69 companies, classified into five affiliation sectors, from the Pollutant Release and Transfer Register (PRTR). The results show that big Serbian polluters still use the traditional management approach since the level of disclosure is less than 30%. To quantify the level of disclosure, Environmental Disclosure Index was employed, containing 15 variables. Most of the analyzed companies on their websites disclosed their environmental certification, environmental policy, and waste management and reduction, while the less informed variable was pollutant types and emissions. Also, the results show that big polluters in Serbia are willing to disclose only positive environmental activities and results.

This research aims at exploring the interconnection between smart green balanced scorecard system (SGBSC) and digital environment, society, and governance performance (DESGP). Alternatively, it investigates how the effectiveness of sustainability accounting information system (ESAIS) induces a mediating impact on SGBSC and DESGP. The empirical portion of this study is based on statistical information gathered from a survey given to a cross-sectional sample of 883 SMEs in developing country. The findings from the structural equation modeling approach demonstrate that greater SGBSC implementation can result in higher DESGP. This interconnection is also partially mediated by ESAIS concurrently. The observations may provide practitioners and policymakers with fresher perspectives to develop focused strategies for SGBSC application and sustainability accounting information system implementation, which can ultimately result in beneficial outcomes in DESG establishment and operationalization.

The chapter presents a general model for constructing portfolios in which environmental, social, and governance (ESG) rating (or score) assessments are added alongside traditional risk and return objectives. The design of portfolios involves ESG scores as an additional objective. Then multiobjective optimisation models are employed to construct the corresponding efficient frontiers. Moreover, the authors introduce a technique for selecting the optimal portfolio according to the investor's preferences toward the three objectives. Six investor profiles that would position themselves in their optimal portfolio, using variance and conditional value at risk (CVaR) as risk measures, are identified for experimental analysis. Starting with Refinitiv's ESG ratings for 538 companies that are part of the STOXX Europe 600 Index from January 2016 to December 2021, the effectiveness of the proposed methodology is finally confirmed ex-post.

Preface

This book reflects about sustainability through non-financial reporting, which refers to the practice of companies and organizations disclosing information about their environmental, social, and governance (ESG) performance and impact alongside their traditional financial reporting. This approach aims to provide stakeholders, including investors, consumers, employees, regulators, and the public, with a more comprehensive view of an organization's sustainability efforts and its commitment to responsible business practices.

If we look at recent times, we realize that there has been a growing recognition of the importance of ESG factors in assessing a company's long-term value and risk and that the stakeholders are deeply concerned about the evaluation of the company's impact on society, the environment, and its governance practices. On the other hand, consumers are also more inclined to support businesses that demonstrate a commitment to sustainability.

For that reason, many countries have introduced regulations requiring companies to disclose non-financial information, such as the EU Non-Financial Reporting Directive.

International standards like the Global Reporting Initiative (GRI) and the Sustainability Accounting Standards Board (SASB) provide guidelines for reporting on ESG factors.

Stakeholder Expectations

The challenge nowadays for the companies is that they must determine which ESG issues are most relevant or material to their business and stakeholders. This involves identifying the key ESG risks and opportunities. Companies are encouraged to set targets and goals related to their ESG performance and regularly report on progress. Non-financial reporting should not be a one-time exercise but an ongoing commitment to sustainability. Ensuring the credibility and reliability of non-financial reports is essential to maintain trust with stakeholders. Making non-financial data easily accessible to the public, including through sustainability reports or corporate websites, promotes transparency and accountability.

This book comprises the recent research topic of sustainability through non-financial reporting, highlighting the challenges on enhancing this increasingly important issue related to sustainability reports. Moreover, it contributes to the emerging research themes and different methods of approach. Concretely, it constitutes a timely and relevant compendium of chapters that offer to readers relevant issues in sustainability and non-financial reports, where sustainability reports are discussed as the central theme.

Furthermore, this book contributes to the dissemination and sharing of knowledge in the area of sustainability in non-financial reporting and we really believe it could be useful among practitioners (entrepreneurs, managers, policy makers, consulting professional, among others), academics and other interested groups and individuals.

The book comprises 11 chapters covering different topics.

Chapter 1 aims to explore how the largest Portuguese companies have been reporting on the SDGs, since the approval of the 2030 Agenda. It has two objectives: understand how the Sustainable Development Goals (SDGs) are disclosed in non-financial reporting documents and analyse which SDGs are referenced by companies and which ones they consider to be priorities.

Chapter 2 studies the hypothesis that sustainable investments exhibit financial performance at least equal to that of conventional ones, as often cited in literature, is also valid in emerging markets such as Türkiye. It also intends to determine if sustainable pension funds, which are a sustainable investment instrument, can be evaluated in terms of portfolio diversification, especially in times of crisis.

Chapter 3 focus on the examination of the integration of extinction accounting within Petrobras' Integrated Report and its Sustainability Report and it contributes to increase awareness and transparency concerning biodiversity and the associated risks of extinction. Moreover, it aims to underscore the capacity of extinction accounting to inform corporate decision-making processes, enabling companies to evaluate the financial risks stemming from biodiversity depletion and to formulate strategies for risk mitigation.

Chapter 4 highlights the definition of the concept of Corporate Social Responsibility (CSR), its principles, historical development, and grounding in the context of stakeholder theory in order to form a basis for the relations to be established between concepts in the context of the book in other chapters.

Chapter 5 provides a conceptual analysis of CSR practices and reporting and explores the history and evolution of CSR, different CSR approaches, and the significance of CSR reporting. It also examines perspectives on CSR reporting, including social accounting and social responsibility disclosure, and the impact of CSR practices and reporting on an organization's performance and reputation and highlights the significant impact of global sustainability reporting standards, such as those of the Global Reporting Initiative (GRI) and the International Standards Organization (ISO), on non-financial information reporting.

Chapter 6 assesses the influence of contingency factors on sustainable practices in restaurants on Combú Island, Pará and allows the understanding of the stage of adoption of sustainable practices in local businesses on the island, which allows the development of actions that contribute to the consolidation of these practices in other companies, given the fundamental importance of sustainability in the current scenario.

Chapter 7 focus in the gaps existed in previous research on sustainability reporting by using bibliometric analysis to identify past investigations and trends, and the least explored areas of study. This research enables to develop a framework for the sustainability disclosure, identifying the main areas and current dynamics as well as to identify potential avenues for future research on sustainability disclosure.

Chapter 8 determines that the literature review identified gaps in the literature, namely the scarcity of studies focused on the relevance and effects of information reporting within the country-by-country reporting (CbCR) matter. Furthermore, the aim of the authors´ study is to highlight the CbCR value for organizational transparency and to combat tax evasion and fraud, and to analyze the impact of tax havens on the taxation and performance of the largest European banks.

Chapter 9 aims to assess the practice of online disclosure among major polluting entities in Serbia. The selected companies are drawn from the national Pollutant Release and Transfer Register (PRTR), and authors employed content analysis.

Chapter 10 intends to support the pursuit of non-financial reporting matter and seeks the understanding of sustainability through non-financial reporting as a critical aspect of modern corporate responsibility. It enables organizations to communicate their sustainability efforts, respond to stakeholder demands, and contribute to a more sustainable and transparent business environment.

Chapter 11 presents a general model for constructing portfolios in which Environmental, Social and Governance (ESG) rating (or score) assessments are added alongside traditional risk and return objectives. In this chapter the authors introduce a technique for selecting the optimal portfolio according to the investor's preferences toward the three objectives.

Thus, these chapters support the pursuit of non-financial reporting matter that plays a crucial role in addressing global sustainability challenges such as climate change, social inequality, and environmental degradation.

In conclusion, it helps the understanding of sustainability through non-financial reporting as a critical aspect of modern corporate responsibility. It enables organizations to communicate their sustainability efforts, respond to stakeholder demands, and contribute to a more sustainable and transparent business environment. As regulations, standards, and stakeholder expectations continue to evolve, non-financial reporting will remain an integral part of corporate reporting practices.

Albertina Monteiro
ISCAP, CEOS, Polytechnic of Porto, Portugal

Ana Pinto Borges
ISAG - European Business School, Portugal & CICET-FCVC, Portugal & COMEGI, Portugal

Elvira Vieira
ISAG - European Business School, Portugal & CICET-FCVC, Portugal & Polytechnic Institute of Viana do Castelo, Portugal & UNIAG, Portugal

Acknowledgment

All the chapters included in this book were double-blind reviewed. The editors would like to acknowledge the help and availability of the authors and reviewers that took part in the review process and to all people involved in this process. Without their support, the accomplishment of this book would not be possible.

First, the editors would like to express their sincere gratitude to each one of the chapter's authors, who dispensed their time and expertise to this book.

Second, the editors wish to acknowledge the valuable contributions of the reviewers regarding the improvement of quality, coherence, and content presentation of chapters. Most of the authors also served as referees; we highly appreciate their double task.

Finally, a special acknowledgement to Marta Quintas, the technical support of Research Center in Business Sciences and Tourism of Consuelo Vieira da Costa Fundation (CICET-FCVC), who help and provided assistance throughout all process.

Chapter 1
Exploring the SDGs in the Non–Financial Reporting Practices by the Largest Portuguese Companies:
A Longitudinal Analysis Since the 2030 Agenda Approval

Alice Loureiro
🆔 https://orcid.org/0009-0009-6051-7136

CICF-Research Center on Accounting and Taxation, Management School, Polytechnic Institute of Cávado and Ave, Portugal

Sónia Monteiro

CICF-Research Center on Accounting and Taxation, Management School, Polytechnic Institute of Cávado and Ave, Portugal

Verónica Ribeiro
🆔 https://orcid.org/0000-0002-9653-4116

CICF-Research Center on Accounting and Taxation, Management School, Polytechnic Institute of Cávado and Ave, Portugal

ABSTRACT

The apparent commitment of Portuguese corporations to the Sustainable Development Goals (SDGs) is still limited. Therefore, this chapter aims to address this gap by conducting a detailed descriptive analysis of SDGs reporting practices in the largest Portuguese companies over a 5-year period (2016-2020), following the approval of the 2030 Agenda. The specific objectives of this analysis are to understand how the SDGs are disclosed in non-financial reporting documents and to analyse which SDGs are referenced by companies and given priority. There has been an increasing trend in non-financial reporting over the years, and the most frequently cited SDGs in the reports are SDG12, SDG8, SDG7, and SDG13.

DOI: 10.4018/978-1-6684-9076-1.ch001

INTRODUCTION

The United Nations approved the 2030 Agenda which defines the priorities and needs a global action by governments, business, and civil society. It contains 17 Sustainable Development Goals (SDGs), and 169 targets, designed to be universal and to be applied to all countries. The 2030 Agenda represents a holist framework to analyse and measure the progress of all actors towards the SDGs achievement (Diaz-Sarachaga et al., 2021). Therefore, reporting can play an important role by disclosing the companies' contributions and progress towards the SDGs. Among the goals of the 2030Agenda, there is the target 12.6 encouraging companies to adopt sustainable practices and to integrate sustainability information into their reporting cycle. The development of sustainability reporting models in the last years leaded companies worldwide to disseminate information related to sustainable development. However, none of the sustainability/non-financial reporting frameworks (such as those of the Global Reporting Initiative (GRI) and the International Integrated Reporting Council (IIRC)) includes specific guidance on SDGs disclosure. Thus, the linkage of SDGs to corporate reporting is still at a very embryonic stage and it is, therefore, necessary to promote their progress.

In the Portuguese business context, several initiatives have been made to contribute to sustainable development evolution within organizations. Business Council for Sustainable Development (BCSD) Portugal has a series of other initiatives gathering multiple Portuguese organizations: Charter of Business Principles for Sustainability, Act4Nature Portugal, Mobility Pact, Meet 2030, ESI Europe, SINCERE and LIFE Volunteer Escapes. Such initiatives are part of a general effort to help and guide businesses toward SDGs. Portugal is ranking among the 30 most sustainable countries in the world. A concerted and effective corporate action toward Sustainable Development is, therefore, possible if Portuguese companies align their activities to incorporate the SDG. Despite the apparent commitment of Portuguese corporations to the SDGs, information about their documented contribution to the 2030 Agenda is still scarce.

In the scope of SDGs reporting, international empirical research is few and recent (Schramade, 2017; Tsalis et al. 2020; Hummel & Szekely, 2021; Haywood & Boihang, 2021; Curtó-Pagès et al., 2021; Pizzi etl al., 2022), and in Portugal even more. Most of the studies in the Portuguese context focused on listed and certified companies' SDGs-related disclosures (Monteiro et al., 2022;Carvalho et al., 2018; Carvalho, Domingues, et al., 2019; Carvalho, Santos, & Gonçalves, 2019; Fonseca & Carvalho, 2019), which represent a little part of corporate population representation.

Larger companies are increasingly concerned with improving their public image and reputation before society, considering that communicating information about their sustainable performance is a good way to legitimize themselves. According to Elalfy, Weber & Geobey (2021), larger companies are more likely to integrate the SDGs into their reporting than smaller companies. Thus, this chapter aims to explore this gap by exploring how the largest Portuguese companies have been reporting on the SDGs, since the approval of the 2030 Agenda. This chapter has the following specific objectives: a) to understand how the SDGs are disclosed in non-financial reporting documents; b) to analyse which SDGs are referenced by companies and which ones they consider to be priorities.

The chapter is organized as follows: The first section outlines the background and presents an empirical literature review regarding Business contributions to SDGs and its report. The next section develops the research design, including the sample and research methodology. The last section presents the descriptive analysis and the study's findings. Finally, solutions and recommendations, future research directions, and the main conclusions are presented.

BACKGROUND

The 2030 Agenda frames the 17 SDGs into five principles/pillars, known as 5P - People, Planet, Prosperity, Peace, and Partnerships - which provide a basis for organizing the SDGs. The SDGs cover a range of areas, which abroad multiple social, economic and environmental issues, transcribed above (UN, 2015):

Goal 1. End poverty and all its forms everywhere;

Goal 2. End hunger, achieve food security and improved nutrition and promote sustainable agriculture;

Goal 3. Ensure healthy lives and promote well-being for all at all ages;

Goal 4. Ensure inclusive and equitable quality education and promote lifelong learning opportunities for all;

Goal 5. Achieve gender equality and empower all women and girls;

Goal 6. Ensure availability and sustainable management of water and sanitation for all;

Goal 7. Ensure access to affordable, reliable, sustainable and modern energy for all;

Goal 8. Promote sustained, inclusive and sustainable economic growth, full and productive employment and decent work for all;

Goal 9. Build resilient infrastructure, promote inclusive and sustainable industrialization and foster innovation;

Goal 10. Reduce inequality within and among countries;

Goal 11. Make cities and human settlements inclusive, safe, resilient and sustainable;

Goal 12. Ensure sustainable consumption and production patterns;

Goal 13. Take urgent action to combat climate change and its impacts;

Goal 14. Conserve and sustainably use the oceans, seas and marine resources for sustainable development;

Goal 15. Protect, restore and promote sustainable use of terrestrial ecosystems, sustainably manage forests, combat desertification, and halt and reverse land degradation and halt biodiversity loss;

Goal 16. Promote peaceful and inclusive societies for sustainable development, provide access to justice for all and build effective, accountable and inclusive institutions at all levels;

Goal 17. Strengthen the means of implementation and revitalize the Global Partnership for Sustainable Development.

The Sustainable Development Agenda (SDA) 2030 emphasizes a cooperative relationship between the private sector, public sector, and civil society to commit to the SDGs. It acknowledges the critical role of the private sector in achieving these goals, given its significant influence on the global economy, advanced technologies, and management systems. The SDA challenges the private sector to align its policies, production methods, and stakeholder engagement with the SDGs to create a more sustainable world for future generations. This entails adapting practices and fostering collaboration for the successful realization of the SDGs (Rosati 2019a; Sachs 2012).

Izzo et al. (2020) argue that while the SDGs provide an opportunity for businesses to integrate sustainability into their models and engage stakeholders, there's a risk that companies might focus on appearing sustainable rather than genuinely embracing sustainability. This could reduce the SDGs to a compliance agenda, where appearance matters more than substance.

According to Heras-Saizarbitoria et al. (2022), for many stakeholders who are really concerned with environmental and social issues, including many Non-governmental Organizations (NGOs) and civil society associations, the tendency of companies towards superficial engagement with SDGs - or SDG-washing - and the lack of concrete practices to engage with Agenda 2030 targets can be used as leverage to put pressure on companies to produce more consistent CSR practices in a structured and detailed way. However, for these authors the literature based on empirical studies on the specific role of organisations in relation to the SDGs and the actual contribution of business initiatives in practice is at a very early stage.

The GRI's 2022 report on business contributions to the SDGs analyzes 206 GRI reporters' disclosure of information about their support and actions related to the SDGs in 2020-2021. While most companies in the sample demonstrate a solid grasp of the SDGs, identifying their relevance to their business, there's a notable gap in setting explicit SDG-aligned targets. This highlights a disconnect between the overarching global objectives of the SDGs and the specific goals companies are pursuing.

In Portuguese business context, several initiatives have been made to contribute to SD evolution within organizations. A recent example relies on a manifesto promoted by BCSD Portugal (2020), gathering 94 organizations committing their ambition to the construction of an SD model based on five fundamental principles (BCSD Portugal, 2020): promotion of sustainable and inclusive development (emphasizing SDGs and Paris Agreement); promotion of growth (to create indispensable value, guarantying the well-being and security of the Portuguese citizens); search for efficiency in the management of natural and financial resources; strengthening resilience and adaptive capacity of Portuguese companies; reinforcement of corporate citizenship (emphasizing the strengthening of social responsibility).

Voluntary sustainable practices among private sector have been disclosed throughout many decades before SDGs reveal. With the ascending awareness about climate change, social and environmental challenges, the business community has been rising the reporting of sustainability information, mostly due to consequent rising pressure from investors, costumers, and market competitors. Moreover, the classical financial reporting is considered incomplete and does not give a long-term useful information about business stability, potential and impacts (economic, environmental and social), still non-financial information is considered more able to complement this information (Bedenik & Barišić, 2019). In the last decades, an increasing number of organizations have begun reporting their sustainability information. This reporting takes various forms, as there are no mandatory or regulated guidelines. These reports may go by different names, including sustainability report, integrated report, corporate social responsibility report, social responsibility report, environmental report, management report, and more.

The Directive 2014/95/EU, regarding non-financial reporting, represents the main initiative developed in Europe to contribute to the 2030 Agenda actively. In the Portuguese context, this Directive was transposed by the Decree-Law n°. 89/2017, requiring that large companies that are entities of public interest with more than 500 employees (including companies listed on the stock exchange) disclose non-financial information (information related, at least, to environmental, social and worker-related issues, to respect for human rights, corruption fighting and bribery attempts). Ottenstein et al. (2022) that the Directive has improved both quantitative and qualitative characteristics of sustainability reporting by European PIEs. Thus, the European regulation positively impacts SDG reporting (Gazzola et al., 2020; Hummel & Szekely, 2022).

This Directive 2014/95/EU represents the main initiative developed in Europe to contribute to the 2030 Agenda actively. However, the Directive does not impact on the comparability of sustainability reporting in the EU. In fact, the standardization of reporting tolls is still in development and there is a general gap in reporting characterization and quality evaluation. That is why on 14th December 2022, the EU published the Directive (EU) 2022/2464, known as Corporate Sustainability Reporting Directive, for its acronym in English (CSRD). It aims to bring sustainability reporting in line with financial reporting, creating a coherent framework for the dissemination of sustainability information along the entire financial value chain in the EU. This new directive extends the scope to all large companies and all companies listed on regulated EU markets, except micro entities. Detailed specification of the sustainability information to be reported, will be in accordance with the mandatory EU standards for sustainability reporting (ESRS), that are being developing based on the ESG (Environmental, Social; Governance) criteria.

The ESRS standards are aligned with the Global Reporting Initiative (GRI) standards whenever possible, to minimize disruptions for companies already publishing their sustainability reports. The GRI intends to empower organizations transparency worldwide and encourage them to take responsibility for their impacts through the release of standards/guidelines for their reports. Since 2000, GRI has been publishing multiples guidelines for sustainability reporting.

In 2013, the GRI G4 was the last version launched before the SDGs. GRI G4 intended to give to the report a higher level of relevant and concentrated information. However, in 2016 the GRI Standards were published in response to target 12.6 (this target is part of SDG 12, which focuses on ensuring sustainable consumption and production patterns) that calls for corporate transparency mentioning the benefits of reporting sustainability actions and encouraging companies to integrate sustainability information into their reporting cycles. GRI Standards 2016 are structured as a set of modular, flexible, and interrelated reporting standards that starts with the universal standards (GRI 100) and can be completed with a variety of other topics in the economic (GRI 200), environmental (GRI 300), or social dimensions (GRI 400). The last updated of GRI standards took place in 2021.

However, the GRI framework does not provide a specific standard on SDGs disclosures. In 2015, the GRI, the United Nations Global Compact (UNGC), and the World Business Council for Sustainable Development (WBCSD) launched an innovative initiative titled "The SDG Compass: the guide for business action on the SDGs". This tool helps companies to align their strategies, measure and manage their contribution to achieving the SDGs, and places sustainability at the heart of their business strategy. It also helps companies to identify the GRI standards that can be used to disclose the actions performed to achieve the SDGs. The UN Global Compact Network, together with the GRI, developed two key documents ("Business Reporting on the SDGs: An Analysis of the Goals and Targets" and "Integrating the Sustainable Development Goals into Corporate Reporting: A Practical Guide") that should be used together as part of the regular reporting cycle of companies. The intention is to provide a structure for organizations to disclose their contribution to their prioritized SDGs and provide relevant information to stakeholders, rather than to create a new reporting framework. Later, in 2018, the GRI published the document "SDGs. Analysis of Goals and Targets", which relates all SDGs and their specific targets to GRI indicators. This document can be seen as a guide for companies to communicate their contribution to Agenda 2030 to stakeholders in their sustainability reports.

According to KPMG studies (2020, 2022), GRI is the most widely used framework for sustainability reporting in the world. And even GRI claims to be the most used standards for SD reporting on a worldwide scale (GRI, 2022a). The latest published survey explains that two-thirds and three-quarters of their research samples uses GRI guidelines or standards for their sustainability reports. Farther, the use of GRI Standards has significantly increased from only 10% for 95% between 2017 and 2020 while the use of the GRI G4 guideline has decreased from 88% for only 4% within the population of organizations using GRI framework (KPMG, 2020). However, also according to KPMG, the number of companies using integrated reports is growing in a slow, but consistent way. From 2015 to 2017, the G250 sample population (250 largest companies by revenue in Fortune 500 ranking) adopting their corporate report in an integrated manner increased 3%, from 11% to 14%, in the respective years (KPMG, 2017).

Moreover, some authors argue that the disclosure of non-financial information in separated reports does not clarifies how the sustainability is meant to be integrated in the business model and the organizational strategy. Furthermore, stakeholders are increasing in the demand of more rigours, transparent and complete information about sustainability within the organizations. For these reasons, the adoption of the integrated reporting (IR) by business community has increased (Eccles & Serafeim, 2017).

Adams et al. (2020) introduced the "Sustainable Development Goals Disclosure (SDGD) Recommendations," presenting a fresh approach for organizations to tackle sustainable development issues in alignment with the <IR> Framework, the Task Force on Climate-related Financial Disclosure (TCFD), and the GRI. These recommendations aim to set a benchmark for corporate reporting on the SDGs, fostering more effective and standardized reporting and enhancing transparency regarding climate change, social, and other environmental impacts. The recommendations were built on a suggested approach to contributing to the SDG aligned with long term value creation in Adams' (2017) report. The report set out a five-step process to align an organization's approach to the SDG with integrated thinking and long-term value creation for organizations and society as set out in the <IR> Framework.

The need for a common set of performance indicators proves to be paramount for stakeholders to compare the contributions of companies to the achievement of SDGs. The frameworks already developed for SDGs reporting are still at a very embryonic stage and it is, therefore, necessary to foster their maturing (Amey & Whooley, 2018).

Prior empirical literature in the field of SDG reporting is also very scarce. Datta and Goyal (2022) concluded that most of the studies focus on large companies from developed countries. The main studies focused on describing the companies' approach to address the SDGs in their corporate reports. Studies also focused on the contents of corporate SDG disclosure practices, standing out trends on which goals have been prioritized (Fonseca & Carvalho, 2019; Izzo et al., 2020; Nichita et al., 2020; KPMG, 2022, Nicolò et al., 2023). Findings reveal that companies have increased the SDG-related disclosure, but is still superficial (Heras-Saizarbirtoria et al., 2022) and bellow from desirable (Rosati & Faria, 2019b). Hence, SDG reporting is often unbalanced and disconnected from business goals (KPMG, 2020). Several companies worldwide still remain silent on how to incorporate SDGs in their business strategies and operation floor, suggesting that SDG reporting remains a symbolic gesture (Nicolò et al., 2023; van der Waal & Thijssens, 2020). Therefore, many companies are allocating to disclose information about the SDGs to legitimize their societal position and meet the social and political pressures arising from the 2030 Agenda approval (Zampone et al. 2022).

In the Portuguese context, Carvalho et al. (2018) stand out the scarce information about SD disclosed in certified companies' websites. Companies with greater business volume and the public limited companies (PLC) disclosure more information on sustainable development. A similar study concluded companies with higher business volume, participating in BCSD/ UNGC Portugal and regular on-line publishers of their annual reports end to provide a greater extent of SDG disclosure (Carvalho, et al., 2019; Fonseca & Carvalho, 2019).

In view of the above, major challenges are placed on organisations in identifying priority SDGs for their activities and stakeholders, incorporating them into their strategy, setting goals for their success, and measuring and reporting on their progress. Integrating the SDGs evaluation in the report implies showing to stakeholders their effective performance, resorting to the emerging non-financial reporting models. Whether through sustainability reports or through integrated reports, we understand that what is important is to align these reports with the structure and scope of the SDGs and should, therefore, be a research area to be favoured in the future.

RESEARCH DESIGN

Sample

Previous studies indicate companies' size, business volume or dimension is a positive determinant factor for SDGs disclosure or SD related information disclosure (Carvalho et al., 2018; Carvalho, Domingues, et al., 2019; Carvalho, Santos, et al., 2019; Pizzi et al., 2020). According to legitimacy and stakeholders' theories, large companies are subject to greater exposure and visibility (with regard to the media, society and regulators), and so face more pressure from different stakeholders to disclosure more information compared to small companies. On the other hand, larger companies are increasingly concerned with improving their public image and reputation before society, considering that communicating information about their sustainability performance is a good way to legitimize themselves (Datta & Goyal, 2022; van der Waal & Thijssens, 2020).

In this sense, the starting sample was selected from a special edition of Exame magazine ("500 Largest & Best Portuguese companies") published in December of 2020. Therefore, we excluded companies that do not disclose at least one non-financial report on the corporation website, between 2016 and 2020. Thus, from the 500 largest companies, only 41 companies published any type of standalone non-financial report during the period (representing 8,2% of the initial group). From the final sample were considered sustainability reports, integrated reports, corporate responsibility reports, social responsibility reports and management reports. After consulting the websites of the 41 companies included in the sample, we observed that not all of them had a standalone non-financial report for the entire analysed period. Thus, 119 valid documents were collected.

Methodology

We used a content analysis of non-financial reports, seeking to characterize the largest Portuguese companies concerned with SDG-related disclosures. Through 2016 to 2020, the data was collected respecting to: report type, number of pages, framework, level of declaration, external verification, and auditor nature. The content analysis was accomplished to answer the investigation research questions through the following terms: 'Sustainable Development Goals', 'SDG', 'priority SDG', 'priority Sustainable Development Goals'. It would be enough to find a reference to the SDGs to consider that the company disclosed about SDGs. In other words, our study did not seek to assess the quantity or quality of the disclosure made. The information intended to identify if the company mentioned SDGs in the reports, being 0 to 'no' and 1 to 'yes'. For each SDG the same dichotomous approach was accomplished to identify which SDGs were disclosed in the report and how they were disclosed: 1 – through the report and 2 – in a specific section. The same logical sequence was followed for the priority SDGs identification in the reports. The alignment of the report with the SDGs following the GRI or IIRC guidelines was examined with 0 determined for "Neither", 1 for "GRI", 2 for "IIRC" and 3 for "Both.

DESCRIPTIVE ANALYSIS AND FINDINGS

Descriptive Analysis

After consulting the websites of the 41 companies included in the sample, we observed that not all of them had a standalone non-financial report for the entire analysed period. Thus, 119 valid documents were collected (Table 1). There is a decrease in the number of reports published in 2019 and 2020, perhaps due to the pandemic circumstances.

Table 1. Non-financial reports collected by year

Year	Non-Financial Report - Frequency	Percentage of Total of Reports (%)	Percentage of Reports, Considering the Sample (41 Companies)
2016	14	11,77	34,1
2017	22	18,49	53,7
2018	31	26,05	75,6
2019	30	25,20	73,2
2020	22	18,49	53,7
Total	119	100,0	

A second and more detailed analysis was accomplished to recognize the type of reports disclosed each year. Our results indicate that Portuguese companies analysed have a general preference for sustainability reports followed by integrated reports. In all the years, the companies demonstrated a clear preference for sustainability reports, representing 68,1% of the non-financial reports published through the five years, followed by the integrated reports (20,2%) (Table 2). This result is in line with Datta & Goyal (2022), who found that sustainability reports or integrated reports are the primary sources for companies to highlight their alignment to the 2030 Agenda by reporting on SDGs. In other studies, as Monteiro, Ribeiro & Lemos, (2020) the majority of the non-financial reports published by Portuguese listed companies were sustainability reports. Haywood and Boihang (2021), on South African companies, found more integrated reports than sustainability reports. However, when analyzing the mention of SDGs, they discovered that a significantly larger proportion of sustainability reports included references to SDGs compared to integrated reports. This indicates that sustainability reports were more likely to discuss SDGs despite being less common overall.

Table 2. Type of reports published in the period 2016-2020

Type of Report	Sum of the Non-Financial Reports	% of Reports
Sustainability Report (SR)	81	68,1
Integrated Report (IR)	24	20,2
Social Responsibility Report (SRR)	5	4,2
Management Report (MR)	6	5,0
Environmental Declaration (ED)	3	2,5
Total	119	100,0

The investigation proceeded by analysing whether the SDGs were mentioned in the reports (table 3). From the 119 reports, 91 mention the SDGs (76,5%). Also, there was an increase in the number of SDG-related disclosure reports through the years. However, the year 2020 presented a decrease in published reports. But, despite that, there was an increase in the disclosure of the SDGs compared to the previous year. Moreover, 2020 presented the highest level of SDGs disclosure (90,9%): from the 22 published reports, 20 mentioned SDGs. The findings are in line with other studies, who found that Spanish companies, South African and multiple European countries that publish non-financial reports are increasingly reporting SDGs since 2016 (Curtó-Pagès et al., 2021; Haywood & Boihang, 2021; Hummel & Szekely, 2021).

Furthermore, of those 91 reports with SDG-related disclosures, 59 reports identify their priority SDGs representing 64,8% of the disclosing SDGs reports (Table 3). From 2016 to 2017 there was a decrease of reports disclosing priority SDGs. However, between 2017-2020, there is an increase of reports that disclose the priority SDGs. For example, in 2017 from 15 reports only 8 indicated their priority SDGs, corresponding to 53,3% of the disclosing SDG reports from the year. However, in 2020 from the 20 reports, 17 prioritized their SDGs, corresponding to 85%% of the reports in the mentioned year. Hummel and Szekely (2021) indicated that 61% of the reports providing information about the UN Goals, prioritize SDG a similar result obtained in our study (64,8%). Nevertheless, only 29% provide information on the process and 32% have the negative impacts in consideration.

A study involving the 2000 largest stock listed businesses found that the European companies rank highest in terms of the number of SGDs references. However, in terms of quality and discussing them within their businesses European companies had to improve (van der Waal & Thijssens, 2020). These findings are followed by Tsalis (2020), besides being a study within Greek companies, they considered, in a general aspect, the quality of the information in CSR very low. These observations emerge to understand that references to SDGs and priority SDGs studies are only the beginning of the possibilities and needs of analysis to be accomplished in this field. It is positive to record an increase in SDGs references, but it is also necessary to evaluate the quality and intentions of the references.

Table 3. SDGs mention and SDGs prioritization on non-financial reports published (2016-2020)

Year	NFR Published	A - SDGs Mention		B - SDGs Prioritization	
		NFR (SDGs Disclosure)	% (Total Reports/Year)	NFR (Priority SDG)	% (Total Reports/Year)
2016	14	6	42,9	4	66,7
2017	22	15	68,2	8	53,3
2018	31	24	77,4	14	58,3
2019	30	26	86,7	16	61,5
2020	22	20	90,9	17	85,0
Total	119	91	76,5	59	64,8

Subtitle: A - Non-financial Reports (NFR) mentioning SDGs and correspondent percentage per year and in the total of the years; B -reports with priority SDGs and correspondent percentage per year and in the total of the years.

As previously, a more detailed analysis was accomplished to understand what type of non-financial report is more prominent (in SDGs disclosure related data and in priority SDGs definition related data.

Similarly, the sustainability report remained the most entitled type of report used, 67% (Table 4). Our results indicate that companies privilege sustainability reports as a vehicle of SDG-related information communication, similar to Izzo, Ciaburri, & Tiscini (2020) and Haywood and Boihang's (2021) studies.

Table 4. SDGs mention and SDGs prioritization on non-financial reports published (2016-2020), by type of report

Type of Report	A - SDGs Mention		B - SDGs Prioritization	
	Sum of the NFR (SDG Disclosure)	NFR Percentage (%)	Sum of the NFR (Priority SDG)	NFR Percentage (%)
SR	61	67,0	39	42,9
IR	20	22,0	18	19,8
SRR	2	2,2	0	0,0
MR	5	5,5	2	2,2
ED	3	3,3	0	0,0
Total	91	100,0	59	100,0

Subtitle: Type of non-financial reports (NFR) published during the five years. A - Type of non-financial reports (NFR) published during the five years mentioning SDGs and respective proportion calculated considering the total of 119 reports published; B - Type of non-financial reports (NFR) published during the five years defining priority SDGs and respective proportion calculated considering the total of 91 reports mentioning SDGs collected.

In our analysis, we noticed a tendency among companies to mention the SDGs throughout their reports rather than confining them to a specific section. Specifically, 68.1% of the reports examined mentioned the SDGs throughout the report, while 31.9% reserved them for a specific section. This practice of mentioning SDGs throughout the report may potentially facilitate their integration into a company's strategies and business models. However, it's important to note that our observation focused solely on whether the SDGs were mentioned, without assessing their context or quality.Interestingly, our findings contrast with another study involving Italian companies, which found that the majority of these firms had a dedicated section for SDGs in their reports but did not incorporate them into their strategies and business models (Izzo, Ciaburri, et al., 2020).

Additionally, in the collection of the previous data, we also focused to understand how CEO letters to stakeholders evolved through the years regarding the SDGs approach. Table 5 shows an absence in the continuous growth of mention of SDGs. In 2016, 3,3% of the CEO letters refer to SDGs and in 2017 presented an increase to 9,9%. In 2018 there is an increase to 13,2% followed by another increase in 2019 (14,3%), however, in 2020 there was a decline (8,8%). Nevertheless, from 2016 to 2020 we observe more CEOs concerning to refer the UN Goals in their letters, which is consistent with Curtó-Pagés et al.(2021), which also detected an increase between the years 2016 and 2019. Also, van derWaal and Thijssend (2020) indicates in almost of all reports, the CEO message refers to the SDGs and the importance of the top management to be more sensitive to this initiative. In the total analyses, almost of the CEOs messages refers SDGs, however, it is still not enough, indicating a long journey to be attained in Portugal.

Table 5. SDGS mention in the CEO message

Year	NFR (Disclose SDG)	NFR (CEO Refers SDG)	%
2016	6	3	3,3
2017	15	9	9,9
2018	24	12	13,2
2019	26	13	14,3
2020	20	8	8,8
Total	**91**	**45**	**49,5**

Concerning external verification, between 2016 and 2020 there was a tendential increase of external verification of the reports, most of them by a Big Four (as demonstrated in Table 6). In the total data of the 5 years, from the 91 reports, 45 were auditing by a Big Four, representing 49,5% of the reports disclosing SDGs. The results indicate that the majority of the companies subjected to external verification choose one of the Big Four (PwC; KMPG; EY; Delloitte). These finding are in accordance with Ruiz -Barbadillo and Martínez-Ferrero (2020), where 57,7% of the total observations resorted to a Big Four for assurance.

Table 6. External assurance of the non-financial reports mentioning SDGs

Year	NFR Disclose SDG	External Verification	%	Big4 Verification	%
2016	6	3	50,0	3	50,0
2017	15	9	60,0	7	46,7
2018	24	14	58,3	12	50,0
2019	26	16	61,5	13	50,0
2020	20	12	60,0	10	50,0
Total	**91**	**54**	**59,3**	**45**	**49,5**

We also analysed which SDGs were the most referred to in the reports (table 7). SDG 12 (Responsible consumption and production) was mentioned in a larger number of reports (90.1%). Following is SDG 8 (Decent work and economic growth), SDG 7 (Affordable and clean energy) and SDG 13 (Climate action), defining 86,8% of the SDGs mentioned in the total of 91 reports. Otherwise, SDG 16 (peace, justice, and strong institutions), SDG 2 (Zero hunger) and SDG10 (Reduced inequalities) were the less mentioned. Similar results were obtained by Gazzola et al. (2020): goals like gender equity, decent work, economic growth, and responsible consumption and production were present in almost all Italian companies' non-financial information reports. Tsalis et al. (2020) concluded that firms provide more information about SDG7, SDG9 and SDG13, while SDG16 had the lowest score.

Concerning the priority SDGs (Table 8), the five most preferred and prioritized goals were SDG8 (Decent work and economic growth) and SDG12 (Responsible consumption and production) with 48,4% proceeded by SD13 (Climate action), SDG3 (Good health and well-being) and SDG7 (Affordable and clean energy) representing 42,9%, 37,4% and 36,3%, respectively, in the total of 91 reports referring

SDGs. The five less referred goals were SDG1 (No poverty) (1,1%) proceeded by SDG10 (Reduced inequalities) (6,6%), SDG14 (Life below water) and SDG2 (Zero hunger) (9,9%) and SDG16 (Peace, justice and strong institutions) (11%). Our results are aligned with Hummel and Szekely (2021)' study in European firms. The authors concluded that the most prioritized SDGs were SDG8, SDG13, SDG12, SDG3 and SDG9 and the less were SDG1, SDG14 and SDG2. Our findings can suggest that Portuguese reality is relatively aligned with European reality concerning priority SDGs. In fact, the Portuguese report on the implementation of the 2030 Agenda for Sustainable Development presented in 2017 has defined as priorities, for Portuguese context, SDGs 4, 5, 9, 10, 13 and 14 (Ministério dos Negócios Estrangeiros, 2017). The results obtained in our study indicate that, in general, the priority of companies concerning relation to the fulfilment of the SDGs is poorly aligned with the national strategy, since SDGs13 is in the most prioritized, but SDG14 is among the less mentioned as a priority for companies.

Table 7. Identification of the SDGs in the non-financial reports (2016-2020)

Sustainable Development Goal	2016	2017	2018	2019	2020	Total	%
SDG1 – No poverty	1	6	15	16	12	50	54,9
SDG2 – Zero hunger	3	7	12	13	10	45	49,5
SDG3 – Good health and well-being	5	12	21	21	17	76	83,5
SDG4 – Quality education	1	10	18	21	15	65	71,4
SDG5 – Gender equality	2	9	20	20	18	69	75,8
SDG6 – Clean water and sanitation	5	9	18	17	14	63	69,2
SDG7 – Affordable and clean energy	4	12	22	22	19	79	86,8
SDG8 – Decent work and economic growth	2	14	22	23	18	79	86,8
SDG9 – Industry, innovation and infrastructure	2	8	18	20	17	65	71,4
SDG10 – Reduced inequalities	0	7	11	14	13	45	49,5
SDG11 – Sustainable cities and communities	1	6	15	13	14	49	53,8
SDG12 – Responsible consumption and production	3	12	24	24	19	82	90,1
SDG13 – Climate action	4	13	21	23	18	79	86,8
SDG14 – Life below water	4	8	12	14	11	49	53,8
SDG15 – Life on land	4	10	18	19	15	66	72,5
SDG16 – peace, justice and strong institutions	0	6	11	13	12	42	46,2
SDG17 - Partnerships	3	6	17	19	14	59	64,8

Table 8. Identification of the priority SDGs in the non-financial reports (2016-2020)

Sustainable Development Goal	2016	2017	2018	2019	2020	Total	%
SDG1 – No poverty	0	0	0	0	1	1	1,1
SDG2 – Zero hunger	2	2	2	1	2	9	9,9
SDG3 – Good health and well-being	3	6	7	7	11	34	37,4
SDG4 – Quality education	1	3	4	7	7	22	24,2
SDG5 – Gender equality	0	0	4	3	9	16	17,6
SDG6 – Clean water and sanitation	3	3	6	5	4	21	23,1
SDG7 – Affordable and clean energy	3	5	7	7	11	33	36,3
SDG8 – Decent work and economic growth	2	5	10	12	15	44	48,4
SDG9 – Industry, innovation and infrastructure	1	3	6	8	11	29	31,9
SDG10 – Reduced inequalities	0	0	0	2	4	6	6,6
SDG11 – Sustainable cities and communities	0	1	3	4	7	15	16,5
SDG12 – Responsible consumption and production	2	4	11	13	14	44	48,4
SDG13 – Climate action	3	6	9	9	12	39	42,9
SDG14 – Life below water	2	2	1	3	1	9	9,9
SDG15 – Life on land	3	4	5	6	6	24	26,4
SDG16 – Peace, justice and strong institutions	0	2	1	1	6	10	11,0
SDG17 – Partnerships	1	3	6	5	8	23	25,3

FINDINGS

On the general analysis, we verified an increased tendency of non-financial reporting through the years and a tendency to increase the publishing of non-financial reports disclosing SDGs is uninterrupted and continuously from 2016 and 2020, the year which corresponded to the higher mentioning of SDGs in the total of non-financial reports. Our results are following other studies and leave us to the conclusion that SDGs reporting is an increasing tendency among Portuguese companies, despite being a slow and modest way. Similar findings show how Spanish companies that publish non-financial reports are increasingly reporting on the SDGs (Curtó-Pagès et al., 2021). Concerning the type of reports, we verified a clear preference for sustainability reports (representing 68,1% of the non-financial reports published through the five years), followed by the integrated reports (20,2%). This result is in line with Datta & Goyal (2022), who found that sustainability reports or integrated reports are the primary sources for companies to highlight their alignment to the 2030 Agenda by reporting on SDGs. In other studies, as Monteiro, Ribeiro & Lemos, (2022) the majority of the non-financial reports published by Portuguese listed companies were sustainability reports.

The investigation proceeded by analysing whether the SDGs were mentioned in the reports: from the 119 reports, 91 mention the SDGs (76,5%). Also, there was an increase in the number of SDG-related disclosure reports through the years. Moreover, 2020 presented the highest level of SDGs disclosure (90,9%): from the 22 published reports, 20 mentioned SDGs. The findings are in line with other studies, who found that Spanish companies, South African and multiple European countries that publish non-financial reports are increasingly reporting SDGs since 2016 (Curtó-Pagès et al., 2021; Haywood &

Boihang, 2021; Hummel & Szekely, 2021). Our results indicate that companies privilege sustainability reports as a vehicle of SDG-related information communication (67% of the disclosing SDG reports), similar to Izzo, Ciaburri, & Tiscini (2020) and Haywood and Boihang's (2021) studies.

Companies tend to mention the SDGs throughout their reports rather than confining them to a specific section. However, this observation only suggests a reporting practice and doesn't indicate the quality of disclosure or the extent of commitment to integrating SDGs into core business operations. Further analysis is needed to assess the depth of commitment and effective incorporation of SDGs into company strategies.

Based on our data, we noticed an increase in CEO letters within reports from 2016 to 2020. Interestingly, 49.5% of these CEO letters mentioned the SDGs to stakeholders. This finding aligns with a study conducted by Curtó-Pagès et al. (2021).

Concerning external verification, between 2016 and 2020 there was a tendential increase of external certification by a Big Four, representing 49,5% of the reports disclosing SDGs. The results lead to conclude that the Portuguese companies have a preference for a Big4 (PwC; KMPG; EY; Delloitte) in sustainability assurance as according to other studies (Gomes et al., 2015; Ruiz-Barbadillo & Martínez-Ferrero, 2020).

All these findings allow us to understand part the first specific objective: understand how the SDGs are disclosed in non-financial reporting practices. Furthermore, the following findings give answers to the second specific objectives: Understand which SDGs are referenced by companies and which are the priority SDGs considered.

Considering those 91 reports with SDG-related disclosures, 59 reports identify their priority SDGs representing 64,8% of the disclosing SDGs reports. From 2016 to 2017 there was a decrease of reports disclosing priority SDGs. However, between 2017-2020, there is an increase of reports that disclose the priority SDGs. For example, in 2017 from 15 reports only 8 indicated their priority SDGs, corresponding to 53,3% of the disclosing SDG reports from the year. However, in 2020 from the 20 reports, 17 prioritized their SDGs, corresponding to 85%% of the reports in the mentioned year. Hummel and Szekely (2021) indicated that 61% of the reports providing information about the UN Goals, prioritize SDG a similar result obtained in our study (64,8%). Nevertheless, only 29% provide information on the process and 32% have the negative impacts in consideration.

The most mentioned SDGs in the reports were SDG12, SDG 8, SDG7 and SDG13, which were aligned with findings from studies of other countries (Gazzola et al., 2020; Tsalis et al., 2020). Otherwise, the less mentioned were: SD16, SDG2 and SD10. Concerning the priority SDGs, the most mentioned were SD8, SDG12, SDG13, SDG3 and SDG7 and the less referred were SDG1, SDG10, SDG14, SDG2 and SDG16.

These results are aligned with a European survey, from which we suggest that Portuguese reality is relatively aligned with European reality concerning priority SDGs (Hummel & Szekely, 2021). In fact, the Portuguese report on the implementation of the 2030 Agenda for Sustainable Development presented in 2017 has defined as priorities, for Portuguese context, SDGs 4, 5, 9, 10, 13 and 14 (Ministério dos Negócios Estrangeiros, 2017). The results obtained in our study indicate that, in general, the priority of companies concerning relation to the fulfilment of the SDGs is partially aligned with the national strategy, since SDGs 9 and 13 are the most prioritized, but SDG14 is among the less mentioned as a priority for companies.

SOLUTIONS AND RECOMMENDATIONS

To improve the sustainable development practices of large companies and increase the disclosure of SDGs, we would recommend harmonizing non-financial reports through a standardized format for reporting on the Sustainable Development Goals (SDGs) within companies. This would ensure consistency and comparability among reports, enabling a more objective assessment of sustainable performance. Guidelines for the preparation of non-financial reports are necessary, with the Global Reporting Initiative (GRI) being the dominant global standard for sustainability reporting, having established the linkage between GRI disclosures and the SDGs, thereby facilitating the incorporation of SDGs into company reports. Companies should be encouraged to transparently disclose non-financial information and involve stakeholders in the non-financial reporting process. Companies should invest in programs to promote education and awareness about the value of sustainability, thereby increasing knowledge and understanding of the challenges and opportunities related to sustainable development. These solutions can help companies improve their sustainable development practices and ensure a more comprehensive and transparent disclosure of their performance in relation to the SDGs.

FUTURE RESEARCH DIRECTIONS

This study has some limitations that could be addressed in future research. One of the limitations relates to the methodology used, specifically the subjectivity involved in the content analysis. We just verified the disclosure of SDGs without assessing the extent of its content, or the quality of the information disclosed. Therefore, it would be beneficial to investigate the depth of these disclosures in future studies. Further research should aim to combine this longitudinal analysis used in this study with more refined qualitative proxies representing a company's orientation toward SDGs reporting, such as in-depth interviews with top managers. Future studies could consider the influence of corporate governance variables on SDGs disclosure (such as board size/ independency/meetings/gender diversity) as explored by other studies (Rosati & Faria, 2019b; Pizzi et al, 2020). In other future investigations, it should be used a more balanced sample between the groups to better evaluate our observations and a more diversified sample, since our initial sample characterizes only having large Portuguese companies. Moreover, content analysis where we only confirm whether or not the SDG was disclosed, but we did not analyse the extent of its content or the quality of the information disclosed, and this may add no value to its stakeholders. We did not explore if companies incorporate SDGs in the business strategy and designate specific key performance indicators for the goals. Thus, it would be an interesting complementary line of investigation in the attempt to understand the profundity of these disclosures.

Further research should also explore the linkage between the SDGs and the Environmental, Social, and Governance (ESG) approach included in the new mandatory EU standards for sustainability reporting (ESRS). Future studies could analyze the data from sustainability reports provided by European companies to identify patterns, trends, challenges, and opportunities associated with the alignment of SDGs and ESG.

CONCLUSION

Target 12.6 of Agenda 2030 encourages organizations to adopt sustainable practices and to integrate sustainability information into their reporting cycle. Thus, transparent and relevant reports on SDGs are important to communicate to stakeholders how companies are meeting their set goals. Empirical studies suggest that business interest in the SDGs has grown quickly since their launch in 2015.

Literature has been arising with diverse theoretical reviews understanding the motives and aspects related to non-financial information disclosure.

We accomplished a general descriptive analysis of SDGs reporting practices and we then compared certified from non-certified companies. On the general analysis, we verified an increased tendency of non-financial reporting through the years and a tendency to increase the publishing of non-financial reports disclosing SDGs is uninterrupted and continuously from 2016 and 2020, the year which corresponded to the higher mentioning of SDGs in the total of non-financial reports. Our results are following other studies and leave us to the conclusion that SDGs reporting is an increasing tendency among Portuguese companies, despite being a slow and modest way. The most mentioned SDGs in the reports were SDG12, SDG 8, SDG7 and SDG13, which were aligned with findings from studies of other countries (Gazzola et al., 2020; Tsalis et al., 2020). These results give answers to one of our specific objectives: Understand which SDGs are referenced by companies and which are the priority SDGs considered.

The contributions of this chapter to the literature are several. The study extends prior empirical research, introducing the certification variable. Empirically, this study provides comprehensive insights specifically on SDG-related disclosure practices over time. The chapter contributes to the country-level analysis of SDG reporting by performing a longitudinal analysis over the 5 years encompassing 2016 to 2020 after the UN Agenda 2030 was approved.

The SDGs have the potential to inform and advance research and practice on sustainability accounting and reporting. Literature states "academic investigation is needed to help understand where specific SGD-related accounting initiatives lie on the continuum between pure rhetoric and meaningful action, and to inform the most effective use of the SDGs by a broad range of organizations in developing policies and practices that will contribute toward the achievement of the SDGs" (Bebbington & Unernan, 2018, p.10).

Thus, besides the scientific contribution, our research could have practical implications. By analyzing the SDG reporting from the largest Portuguese companies, this study can help the integration of the SDGs into organizational reporting and accounting, including the adoption of the SDGs by small and medium enterprises (SMEs) to benchmark their reporting. The study could also have implications for policy formulation, namely for reporting regulatory bodies, to improve SDGs reporting quality. There is a lack of a common framework for measuring and reporting companies' contribution to the SDGs, which creates a highly fragmented and diverse information landscape and makes comparison difficult. Therefore, international framework providers and standard-setters (such as the SDG Compass, GRI, etc.) should work on the maturity of SDG reporting.

ACKNOWLEDGMENT

The authors acknowledge the financial support of FCT - Foundation for Science and Technology, I.P., within the scope of multi-annual funding UIDB/04043/2020

REFERENCES

Adams, C. A. (2017). *The Sustainable Development Goals, integrated thinking and the integrated report.* International Integrated Reporting Council & ICAS. http://integratedreporting.org/resource/sdgs-integrated-thinking-and-the-integrated-report/

Amey, M., & Whooley, N. (2018). Corporate Reporting on the SDGs: Mapping a Sustainable Future. *Advisor Perspectives,* 1–7.

Bebbington, J., & Unerman, J. (2018). Sustainable development: a review of the international development, business and accounting literature. *Accounting, Auditing, & Accountability, 31*(1), 2 – 24. . doi:10.1108/AAAJ-05-2017-2929

Bedenik, N. O., & Barišić, P. (2019). Nonfinancial Reporting: Theoretical and Empirical Evidence. *Sustainable Management Practices.* https://doi.org/http://dx.doi.org/10.5772/intechopen.87159

Carvalho, F., Domingues, P., & Sampaio, P. (2019). *Communication of commitment towards sustainable development of certified Portuguese organisations Quality, environment and occupational health and safety.* International Journal of Quality & Reliability Management. doi:10.1108/IJQRM-04-2018-0099

Carvalho, F., Santos, G., & Gonçalves, J. (2018). The disclosure of information on Sustainable Development on the corporate website of the certified portuguese organizations. *International Journal of Qualitative Research, 12*(1), 253–276. doi:10.18421/IJQR12.01-14

Carvalho, F., Santos, G., & Gonçalves, J. (2019). Critical analysis of information about integrated management systems and environmental policy on the Portuguese firms' website, towards sustainable development. *Corporate Social Responsibility and Environmental Management, 27*(2), 1069–1088. doi:10.1002/csr.1866

Curtó-Pagès, F., Ortega-Rivera, E., Castellón-Durán, M., & Jané-Llopis, E. (2021). Coming in from the cold: A longitudinal analysis of SDG reporting practices by Spanish listed companies since the approval of the 2030 agenda. *Sustainability (Basel), 13*(3), 1–27. doi:10.3390u13031178

Datta, S., & Goyal, S. (2022). Determinants of SDG Reporting by Businesses: A Literature Analysis and Conceptual Model. *Vision (Basel).* Advance online publication. doi:10.1177/09722629221096047

Diaz-Sarachaga, J. M. (2021). Shortcomings in reporting contributions towards the sustainable development goals. *Corporate Social Responsibility and Environmental Management, 28*(4), 1299–1312. doi:10.1002/csr.2129

Eccles, R. G., & Serafeim, G. (2017). Corporate and integrated reporting: A functional perspective. *Corporate Stewardship: Achieving Sustainable Effectiveness,* 156–171. doi:10.9774/GLEAF.9781783532605_10

Elalfy, A., Weber, O., & Geobey, S. (2021). The Sustainable Development Goals (SDGs): a rising tide lifts all boats? Global reporting implications in a post SDGs world. *Journal of Applied Accounting Research.* . doi:10.1108/JAAR-06-2020-0116

Fonseca, L., & Carvalho, F. (2019). The Reporting of SDGs by Quality, Environmental, and Occupational Health and The Reporting of SDGs by Quality, Environmental, and Occupational Health and Safety-Certified Organizations. *Sustainability (Basel)*, *11*(20), 5797. doi:10.3390u11205797

Gazzola, P., Pezzetti, R., Amelio, S., & Grechi, D. (2020). Non-financial information disclosure in Italian public interest companies: A sustainability reporting perspective. *Sustainability (Basel)*, *12*(15), 1–16. doi:10.3390u12156063

Gomes, S. F., Eugénio, T. C. P., & Branco, M. C. (2015). Sustainability reporting and assurance in Portugal. *Corporate Governance (Bradford)*, *15*(3), 281–292. doi:10.1108/CG-07-2013-0097

GRI. (2022). *State of progress: business contributions to the SDGs. A 2020-2021 study in support of the Sustainable Development Goals*. https://globescan.com/wp-content/up

Haywood, L. K., & Boihang, M. (2021). Business and the SDGs: Examining the early disclosure of the SDGs in annual reports. *Development Southern Africa*, *38*(2), 175–188. doi:10.1080/037683 5X.2020.1818548

Heras-Saizarbitoria, I., Urbieta, L., & Boiral, O. (2022). Organizations' engagement with sustainable development goals: From cherry-picking to SDG-washing? *Corporate Social Responsibility and Environmental Management*, *29*(2), 316–328. doi:10.1002/csr.2202

Hummel, K., & Szekely, M. (2021). Disclosure on the Sustainable Development Goals–Evidence from Europe. *Accounting in Europe*, *19*(1), 152-189. . doi:10.1080/17449480.2021.1894347

Izzo, M. F., Ciaburri, M., & Tiscini, R. (2020). The challenge of sustainable development goal reporting: The first evidence from italian listed companies. *Sustainability (Basel)*, *12*(8), 3494. Advance online publication. doi:10.3390u12083494

Izzo, M. F., Dello Strologo, A., & Graná, F. (2020). Learning from the Best : New Challenges and Trends in IR Reporters ' Disclosure and the Role of SDGs. *Sustainability (Basel)*, *12*(5545), 1–22. doi:10.3390u12145545

KPMG. (2017). The road ahead. In *Operators for Similarity Search. SpringerBriefs in Computer Science*. Springer. doi:10.1007/978-3-319-21257-9_7

KPMG. (2020). *The Time Has Come: The KPMG Survey of Sustainability Reporting 2020*. KPMG.

Monteiro, S., Ribeiro, V., & Lemos, K. (2020). Linking Corporate Social Responsibility Reporting With the UN Sustainable Development Goals: Evidence from the Portuguese Stock Market. In S. Monteiro, V. Ribeiro, & K. Lemos (Eds.), *Conceptual and Theoretical Approaches to Corporate Social Responsibility, Entrepreneurial Orientation, and Financial Performance* (pp. 134–151). IGI Global. doi:10.4018/978-1-7998-2128-1.ch007

Monteiro, S., Ribeiro, V., & Lemos, K. (2022). Linking Corporate Social Responsibility Reporting with the UN Sustainable Development Goals: Evidence from the Portuguese Stock Market. In I. Management Association (Ed.), Research Anthology on Measuring and Achieving Sustainable Development Goals (pp. 250-268). IGI Global.

Nichita, E.-M., Nechita, E., Manea, C.-L., Manea, D., & Irimescu, A.-M. (2020). Reporting on Sustainable Development Goals. A score-based approach with company-level evidence from Central-Eastern Europe economies. *Journal of Accounting and Management Information Systems*, *19*(3), 502–542. doi:10.24818/jamis.2020.03004

Nicolò, G., Zanellato, G., Tiron-Tudor, A., & Tartaglia Polcini, P. (2023). Revealing the corporate contribution to sustainable development goals through integrated reporting: A worldwide perspective. *Social Responsibility Journal*, *19*(5), 829–857. doi:10.1108/SRJ-09-2021-0373

Ottenstein, P., Erben, S., Jost, S., Weuster, C., & Zulch, H. (2022). From voluntarism to regulation: Effects of directive 2014/95/EU on sustainability reporting in the EU. *Journal of Applied Accounting Research*, *23*(1), 55–98. doi:10.1108/JAAR-03-2021-0075

Pizzi, S., Del Baldo, M., Caputo, F., & Venturelli, A. (2022). Voluntary disclosure of Sustainable Development Goals in mandatory non-financial reports: The moderating role of cultural dimension. *Journal of International Financial Management & Accounting*, *33*(1), 83–106. doi:10.1111/jifm.12139

Pizzi, S., Rosati, F., & Venturelli, A. (2020). The determinants of business contribution to the 2030 Agenda: Introducing the SDG Reporting Score. *Business Strategy and the Environment*, 1–18. doi:10.1002/bse.2628

Rosati, F., & Faria, L. G. D. (2019a). Addressing the SDGs in sustainability reports: The relationship with institutional factors. *Journal of Cleaner Production*, *215*, 1312–1326. doi:10.1016/j.jclepro.2018.12.107

Rosati, F., & Faria, L. G. D. (2019b). Business contribution to the Sustainable Development Agenda: Organizational factors related to early adoption of SDG reporting. *Corporate Social Responsibility and Environmental Management*, 1–10. . doi:10.1002/csr.1705

Ruiz-Barbadillo, E., & Martínez-Ferrero, J. (2020). Empirical analysis of the effect of the joint provision of audit and sustainability assurance services on assurance quality. *Journal of Cleaner Production*, *266*, 121943. doi:10.1016/j.jclepro.2020.121943

Sachs, J. D. (2012). From millennium development goals to sustainable development goals. *Lancet*, *379*(9832), 2206–2211. doi:10.1016/S0140-6736(12)60685-0 PMID:22682467

Schramade, W. (2017). Investing in the UN Sustainable Development Goals: Opportunities for Companies and Investors. *The Bank of America Journal of Applied Corporate Finance*, *29*(2), 87–99. doi:10.1111/jacf.12236

Tsalis, T. A., Malamateniou, K. E., Koulouriotis, D., & Nikolaou, I. E. (2020). New challenges for corporate sustainability reporting: United Nations' 2030 Agenda for sustainable development and the sustainable development goals. *Corporate Social Responsibility and Environmental Management*, *27*(4), 1617–1629. doi:10.1002/csr.1910

Van der Waal, J. W. H., & Thijssens, T. (2020). Corporate involvement in Sustainable Development Goals: Exploring the territory. *Journal of Cleaner Production*, *252*, 119625. doi:10.1016/j.jclepro.2019.119625

Zampone, G., Nicolò, G., & De Ioro, G. (2022). Gender diversity and SDG disclosure: the mediating role of the sustainability committee. *Journal of Applied Accounting Research*. doi:10.1108/JAAR-06-2022-0151

Chapter 2

Performance Evaluation of Conventional and Sustainable Pension Funds in Türkiye Before and During the COVID-19 Pandemic

Serhat Duranay

https://orcid.org/0000-0002-3090-2764

Isparta University of Applied Sciences, Turkey

Mehmet Özsoy

https://orcid.org/0000-0003-3204-7295

Suleyman Demirel University, Turkey

ABSTRACT

The results obtained by analyzing the financial performance of sustainable investments help to break down investors' negative prejudices about this investment philosophy. Although the number of studies in this area has reached a satisfactory level in developed markets, there are serious deficiencies in emerging markets. The fund kind and methodology differentiate this study from the literature. The study examines the performance of sustainable pension funds in the Turkish market, using MCDM of entropy, TOPSIS, and GRA. Including 3 sustainable and 19 conventional pension funds, the study covers the period between 2017 and 2021. The findings reveal that TOPSIS and GRA results are consistent. Although the performance ranking of sustainable funds fluctuates, it is observed that, in general, sustainable funds do not lag behind the performance of conventional funds and may even outperform them. Moreover, they have maintained their performance and outperformed conventional funds during periods of domestic crisis. However, a similar situation was not observed during the COVID-19 period.

DOI: 10.4018/978-1-6684-9076-1.ch002

INTRODUCTION

Some investors have purposes beyond increasing their financial returns and maximizing their total wealth. These investors, who are called socially responsible investors, attach great importance to the corporate policies of companies and expect their concerns on issues such as gender equality in employment, environmental protection, workplace safety, and human health to be eliminated (Goldreyer et al., 1999). Sustainable (ethic, socially responsible) investing is the process of considering social and ethical factors as well as economic criteria when making a decision to buy, sell or hold an investment instrument. In this framework, both positive and negative social screens are used when constructing sustainable investment portfolios. Firms with high corporate performance are included in these portfolios, while firms with weak social responsibility are excluded (Rivoli, 2003).

The existence of a positive relationship between the socially responsible behavior of companies and their financial returns will have positive effects on both sides of sustainable investments. In such a case, while companies tend to behave more socially responsible, investors will also be encouraged to make sustainable investments (Lozano et al., 2006). Although social, ethical, and environmental gains outweigh financial returns for socially responsible investors, these investors do not want to suffer from serious financial losses (Rivoli, 2003). It should be noted that, in addition to socially responsible investors, traditional investors may also include sustainable investments in their portfolios to reduce their risk. For them, the significance of financial losses is much higher than for socially responsible ones.

As sustainable investments have become more popular, various financial instruments have been developed in this field. One of these instruments is sustainable mutual funds. Sustainable funds are mainly based on investors' demands to include ethical, social, and environmental criteria in their investment processes (Bauer et al., 2005). These funds can be set up based on positive screens such as environmental responsibility, employee relations, and product reliability, or negative screens such as alcohol and tobacco products, gambling, and armament industry activities (Chang & Witte, 2010). Due to the rapidly gaining importance of sustainable investments, there has been a significant increase in the number of sustainable funds (Heinkel et al., 2001). In parallel with this increase occurred in the number of funds, the performance of sustainable funds has become the focus of research in the field. Performance evaluation studies generally focused on comparing the performance of sustainable funds to conventional funds (Yanık et al., 2010).

There are three hypotheses about the relative performance of sustainable and conventional investments. These are; investment portfolios have equal performances, the socially responsible investment portfolios have lower performances, and t the socially responsible investment portfolios have higher performances (Hamilton et al., 1993). The different results obtained by researchers indicate that each of these three hypotheses may be valid in different financial markets. Indeed, studies comparing the performance of sustainable investments with traditional investments reveal different results. The reasons for this difference in results may be occured due to the studies covering different periods and the comparison of the funds created according to various cultural values (Sandberg et al., 2009). Besides, the different methods used in performance calculations also have an impact on the differentiation of the results obtained (Jones et al., 2008). Early studies focusing on the performance of sustainable investments revealed that these investments underperform compared to conventional investments (Rosen et al., 1991). These findings do not contradict the structure of sustainable investments. This is because the sustainable investment philosophy, which is based on the negative screening method, leads to a narrowing of the investment universe. In this case, the risk of the portfolios naturally increases. In addition, companies that are oriented towards sustainability may sometimes face serious costs. Especially the environmental dimension of sustainability can expose companies to high conversion costs. For all these reasons, the low financial performance of sustainable funds in the early years was considered natural.

However, as the number of studies increased, it became clear that there is no difference between the performances of sustainable and conventional investments (Schröder, 2004). Studies conducted in this context support this finding (Hamilton et al., 1993; Bauer et al., 2005; Cortez et al., 2008; Fernandez-Izquierdo and Matallin-Saez, 2008). The main reason for this situation is that after a certain period of time, the majority of companies take certain steps with the pressure and responsibility to become sustainable, and the investment phase is restored to its former structure through the re-inclusion of investors in their portfolios. In addition, the financing of the costs incurred by governments and other organizations through low-cost loans provides great advantages to companies that are oriented towards greater sustainability. In short, the financial benefits of being sustainable and socially responsible compensate its costs.

Although more accurate findings on the performance of sustainable investments are available, there is still a gap in the field. In particular, the performance evaluation of different investment instruments will contribute to the literature. This study aims to determine how sustainable funds in Türkiye perform as compared to conventional ones. Moreover, this performance comparison is also examined before, during, and after the Covid-19 pandemic, and it is aimed to explore how this major global shock affected the performance characteristics. In addition, while the literature generally evaluates the performance of portfolios composed of sustainable and conventional funds, this study analyzes the performance of the funds seperately. The history of sustainable funds in Türkiye does not go back very far. This study does not only focus on the performance of sustainable and conventional funds, but also examines these performance changes before and after COVID-19, as aforementioned. Most of the existing sustainable funds were established in 2020 and after. The majority of sustainable funds for which retrospective data can be obtained are pension funds. Therefore, the analysis was conducted using data from pension funds.

This study aims to examine the hypothesis that sustainable investments exhibit financial performance at least equal to that of conventional ones, as often cited in literature, is also valid in emerging markets such as Türkiye. In addition, the question of whether sustainable pension funds, which are a sustainable investment instrument as mentioned earlier, can be evaluated in terms of portfolio diversification, especially in times of crisis, has been sought to be answered.

These analyses were carried out using Entropy, Technique for Order Preference by Similarity to Ideal Solution (TOPSIS) and Grey Relational Analysis (GRA), which are Multi-Criteria Decision Making Methods (MCDM). Annual returns, alpha, beta, Sharpe ratio, Treynor ratio, Sortino, downside risk, value at risk (VaR) are chosen as criteria for conducting MCDM to evaluate the performance. In addition to selecting the criteria for decision-making, the criteria weights are calculated with Entropy. After calculating criteria weights, TOPSIS and GRA are used for computing the orders of funds. Individual results of TOPSIS and GRA are finally utilized to confim each other's results.

In this way, it will be possible to shed light on whether sustainable pension funds offer financial incentives for socially responsible investors. Furthermore, sustainable funds that display equal or higher financial performance than conventional funds have potential portfolio diversification benefits for traditional investors. In this context, it will be revealed whether sustainable funds in Türkiye can be an investment alternative for traditional investors.

The following sections of the study are designed as follows. In the second part, information about sustainable investment philosophy and sustainable mutual funds is given and the numerical data of sustainable funds in the world and in Türkiye are mentioned. In the next section, the data set and methodology used in the analysis are introduced and the findings are presented. The study is concluded at the final section.

SUSTAINABLE INVESTINGS

Sustainable investing is an investment type where both financial and social, environmental and ethical criteria are taken into account to decide which shares or funds should be purchased (Getzner & Grabner-Krauter, 2004). The sustainable investment philosophy is rooted in ethical investing and influenced by Jewish, Christian and Islamic beliefs and traditions. According to ethical investing, investments are not made in areas that are frowned upon and forbidden in belief systems. However, modern sustainable investing is not based on religious beliefs, but rather on the personal ethical and social values of individual investors (Renneboog et al., 2008). Sometimes the concept of socially responsible investing is preferred instead of sustainable investing. However, socially responsible investing has a broader and more inclusive meaning than sustainable investing. Therefore, in order to clearly define sustainable investment, the definition made by the Global Sustainable Investment Alliance (GSIA) can be taken as a reference. In the Global Sustainable Investment Review released by GSIA, sustainable investing is defined as "An investment approach that considers environmental, social and governance (ESG) factors in portfolio selection and management" (GSIA, 2018).

Although researchers have studied in depth and addressed different factors, there are certain reasons for choosing sustainable investments. First, investors may be motivated by ethical, environmental or social concerns. Second, investors may diversify their portfolios with sustainable investment instruments based purely on their financial expectations. Third, environmental considerations may have become an integral part of investments due to legal and regulatory constraints. Finally, investors may seek to enhance their reputations by publicly disclosing their environmental and social concerns and behaviors (Tripathi & Bhandari, 2015). Whereas the first two of these reasons explain the behavior of individuals, the last two can be associated more with the behavior of institutional investors.

Sustainable investments are of great importance for the realization of sustainable development. The United Nations Conference on Trade and Development (UNCTAD) estimates that investment products that created for themes and sectors related to sustainable development reached 3.2 trillion dollars in 2020, an increase of more than 80% compared to the previous year. Sustainable funds account for over $1.7 trillion of these investment products. These are followed by green bonds at over $1 trillion, social bonds at around $212 billion and mixed sustainable bonds at $218 billion (UNCTAD, 2021). Moreover, there has been a growth in almost all sustainable financial products and markets during and after the Covid-19 pandemic. The war in Ukraine triggered the need for different energy sources, economic turmoil in countries and increased pressure on environmental issues, especially as a result of climate change commitments, accelerated the rise in sustainable investments. As a result of the growth in sustainable investments, the total value of sustainable financial assets reached 5.2 trillion dollars in 2021. Among these assets, sustainable funds have a share of 2.7 trillion dollars and sustainable bonds 2.5 trillion dollars (UNCTAD, 2022).

Such growth in sustainable investments inevitably raises the question of how these investments perform compared to conventional investments. Whether investors should sacrifice their financial expectations for their personal values has been one of the topics of research for years. In this context, the relative performance of both sustainable mutual funds and sustainability indices against their counterparts has been analyzed in depth in the literature (Gök & Özdemir, 2017).

At this point, it should be noted that these investments are longer term than conventional investments. Although the return on conventional investments may be higher in the short period, in the long period, social impact will come into play and the return on sustainable investments may be higher. The main reason for this is that social, ethical and moral practices are costly operations. For example, controlling environmental pollution, improving employee rights and the work environment, and human health practices may cause certain costs in the short term. However, at the point that can be called social impact, these practices of companies would create a positive image and sympathy among the society. This also suggests that long-term sustainable investment instruments would exhibit higher performance. Indeed, sustainable funds with a long duration can outperform funds that have been created recently (Cummings, 2000).

When the financial performances of sustainable instruments, which are basically shaped according to non-financial criteria, are analyzed, sustainable indices and sustainable mutual funds are generally focused on. For investors who are driven by social, environmental and ethical values, but cannot analyze the sustainable and financial performance of each company, the performance of sustainable funds is a matter of curiosity.

SUSTAINABLE MUTUAL FUNDS

Sustainable mutual funds may be known by different names, such as ethical mutual funds, socially responsible mutual funds and green funds. These funds are among the most popular investment instruments that have been created according to the idea of sustainable finance. Indeed, sustainable mutual funds offer great convenience to investors who are socially responsible and choose the companies they invest in accordingly. Providing the ability to invest in a professionally diversified portfolio at a reasonable cost, these funds also conduct social and ethical screening and address investors' concerns in this respect (Rodriguez, 2010).

Investors seeking to invest in an area that meets their environmental, social or ethical values may not have the time to analyze each company's socially responsible and sustainable behavior. In addition, they may feel that they may lack the necessary knowledge and experience to choose the appropriate company. They may also want to consider their financial returns as well as their non-financial values when deciding (Cummings, 2000). Sustainable mutual funds apply strategies that combine investors' financial objectives with their expectations of social concerns, such as social justice, economic development, peaceful society or environmental protection (Haigh & Hazelton, 2004). In this respect, sustainable mutual funds created and managed by professional managers will be one of the best alternatives for investors who want to focus on sustainable investing.

Even though the most common term in the literature on mutual funds is sustainable mutual funds, there are different terms used instead of this definition or that have similar meanings with these terms. In this context, the Corporate Finance Institute classifies mutual funds under four main headings. These are Socially Responsible Investing (SRI) Funds, Environmental, Social and Governance (ESG) Funds, Impact Funds and Faith-based Funds. According to this distinction, SRI funds avoid investing in controversial areas such as gambling, firearms, tobacco, alcohol and oil. In these types, the investor's moral values are at the forefront. ESG funds focus on the potential impact of environmental, social and governance risks and opportunities on a company's performance. While these funds invest in sustainability, they also aim not to sacrifice financial returns. Impact Funds place more emphasis on fund performance. Therefore, these are attractive to investors seeking high returns while acting in a socially responsible manner. Faith-based Funds, on the other hand, are created according to religious beliefs and strictly refrain from investing in activities that are considered inappropriate in their belief system (Corporate Finance Institute, 2021).

Sustainable funds invest in companies that meet their own criteria and avoid investing in companies whose activities are unacceptable to society. In this context, positive and negative screens are used in the formation of most sustainable funds. (Haigh & Hazelton, 2004). Actively changing or redirecting the policies of investee companies is generally not among the objectives of sustainable funds (Domini & Kinder, 1986). In this respect, sustainable funds are sometimes criticized. The focus of these reviews is that sustainable funds do not direct companies to increase the welfare level of the society.

It can be said that the funds established in Europe and the U.S.A. in line with the sustainable investment philosophy are mainly influenced by the views of religious groups and environmental organizations. The Pax World Fund, considered to be the first sustainable investment fund in the world, was established in 1971 by Methodists. This fund avoids investing in companies involved in armaments, alcohol and gambling (Fowler & Hope, 2007). Its opposition to armaments made the Pax World Fund attractive to investors who opposed the Vietnam War (Renneboog et al., 2008). In the UK, in the early 1900s the Methodist Church established a fund that avoided investing in specific areas, and in 1984 a Quaker insurance company established the Stewardship Fund, which is screened according to social criteria. The Church of Sweden established Ansvar Aktiefond Sverige in 1965. In France, the first socially responsible mutual fund, the Nouvelle Strategie Fund, was created in 1983 by Nicole Reille, finance officer of the Notre-Dame Order. In the Netherlands, the first one, Het Andere Beleggingsfonds, was established in 1990 with the initiatives of church groups and the environmental activists. In Germany, the first ethical funds were created by local Church banks, such as KD Fonds Ökoinvest in 1991 (Louche & Lydenberg, 2006).

Sustainable mutual funds have evolved significantly since they were first introduced in 1971. Especially as a result of accounting and environmental scandals, funds created by using ethical screens have become more popular (Abdelsalam et al., 2014). Based on Morningstar data, the number of sustainability-themed funds reached 5,932 by the end of 2021. The total value of assets under management of sustainable funds has quadrupled in the last five years, reaching approximately $2.7 trillion by the end of 2021. Interest in sustainable funds has also grown rapidly in recent years. Between 2016 and 2019, net cash flows to these funds increased from $33 billion to $159 billion. During the Covid-19 pandemic, which has affected the whole world, there have been major outflows in capital markets, especially since March 2020. However, even in this global crisis environment, total net inflows to sustainable funds continued to climb in the first half of 2020, reaching $164 billion. By the end of 2021, the total amount of cash flows into sustainable funds reached $557 billion (UNCTAD, 2021; UNCTAD 2022).

Europe is hosting the majority of sustainable funds with a share of 81%. The reason for such a large percentage of sustainable funds in Europe is the regulatory environment in the region. It is followed by the US with 13% and other regions with 6%. According to UNCTAD data, the total amount of socially responsible mutual funds and assets under management between 2010 and 2021 is presented in Figure 1. (UNCTAD, 2022).

Figure 1. Number of socially responsible funds and assets under management between 2010-2020
Source: UNCTAD - United Nations Conference on Trade and Development (2022), World Investment Report 2021, Investing in Sustainable Recovery, United Nations Publications.

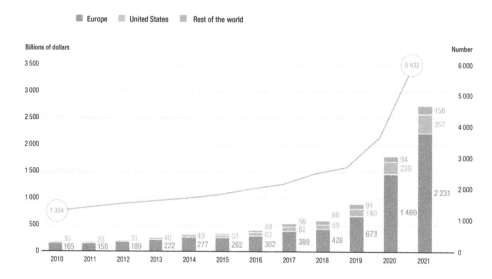

One of the reasons for the growing interest in sustainable funds in recent years is certainly the high financial performance of them. Extensive studies have revealed that sustainable funds exhibit a more stable performance, especially during periods of high volatility (Morgan Stanley, 2019a). However, considering the Covid-19 Pandemic period, which was recently overcome but its effects are still ongoing, it can be said that developing countries as well as developed countries will implement regulations to support the development of sustainable investments.

The appearance of the first sustainable mutual fund in Türkiye is much more recent than Europe and the United States. The fact that the fund was established recently caused the fund structure to reflect the change in sustainable investment philosophy. Therefore, the first sustainable fund established in Türkiye was not shaped within the framework of religious beliefs, but rather focused on environmental issues. It can be said that the new sustainable funds created in the following periods and especially in recent years have the same structure and reflect the ESG criteria. The number of sustainable mutual funds in Türkiye is relatively less than in Europe and the United States. The categories and IPO dates of these funds are presented in Table 1.

Table 1. Sustainable mutual funds in Türkiye

Fund Name	Category	IPO Date
İş Portföy TEMA Variable Fund	Variable Fund	30.05.2008
Garanti Emeklilik ve Hayat A.Ş. Sustainable Equity Pension Fund	Equity Fund	27.10.2010
Türkiye Hayat ve Emeklilik A.Ş. Sustainable Equity Pension Fund	Equity Fund	01.07.2011
Allıanz Yaşam ve Emeklilik A.Ş. Sustainable Fund of Funds Pension Fund İş Portföy Electric Vehicles Mixed Fund	Fund of Funds Mixed Fund	19.08.2011 06.06.2018
Mükafat Portföy ESG Sustainable Hedge Fund	Hedge Fund	15.09.2020
Garanti Portföy Sustainable Equity Fund Garanti Portföy Clean Energy Variable Fund	Equity Fund Variable Fund	18.01.2021 18.01.2021
Garanti Portföy ESG Sustainable Fund of Funds İş Portföy Renewable Energy Mixed Fund	Fund of Funds Mixed Fund	17.02.2021 18.03.2021
Anadolu Hayat Emeklilik A.Ş. Sustainable Equity Pension Fund	Equity Fund	01.07.2021
TEB Portföy Sustainable Fund of Funds Yapı Kredi Portföy Clean Energy Variable Fund	Fund of Funds Variable Fund	28.07.2021 27.09.2021
KT Portföy Sustainable Participation Fund	Participation Fund	14.10.2021
Agesa Hayat ve Emeklilik A.Ş. Sustainable Equity Pension Fund QNB Finans Portföy Clean Energy and Water Fund of Funds	Equity Fund Fund of Funds	19.11.2021* 01.12.2021
Deniz Portföy ESG- Sustainable Fund of Funds HSBC Portföy Sustainable Equity Fund (TL)	Fund of Funds Equity Fund	09.12.2021* 10.12.2021
Deniz Portföy Sustainable Equity Fund	Equity Fund	10.01.2022*
Yapı Kredi Portföy BIST Sustainablity Index Equity Fund Yapı Kredi Portföy Electric Vehicles Variable Fund AK Portföy Electric and Autonomous Technologies Variable Fund	Equity Fund Variable Fund Variable Fund	07.02.2022 15.03.2022 21.03.2022
ICBC Turkey Portföy Sustainable Equity Fund	Equity Fund	23.03.2022
Inveo Portföy ESG Sustainable Fund of Funds Garanti Portföy Electric and Autonomous Vehicles Variable Fund Rota Portföy Climate Change Solutions Variable Fund	Fund of Funds Variable Fund Variable Fund	25.05.2022* 20.07.2022 21.07.2022
Fiba Emeklilik Ve Hayat A.Ş ESG Sustainable Fund of Funds Pension Fund	Fund of Funds	08.08.2022
Ziraat Portföy ESG Sustainable Fund of Funds Garanti Portföy Garanti BBVA Climate Index Equity Fund Aktif Portföy Agriculture and Sustainability Fund of Funds	Fund of Funds Equity Fund Fund of Funds	05.12.2022 09.01.2023 03.03.2023

Source: KAP Public Disclosure Platform, TEFAS Türkiye Electronic Fund Trading Platform.

* For funds for which IPO dates are not available, the oldest transaction dates in TEFAS are given.

The oldest known sustainable fund in Türkiye was established in 2008. However, only 4 new funds were created for a long time afterwards, and the remaining funds were launched in 2020 and later. When the distribution of these funds is analyzed, it is seen that the majority are equity and fund of funds. Of the funds that partially date back further, 3 are pension funds and the other is a mutual fund.

The impact of pension funds on sustainable investments is actually much greater than is commonly known. As an institutional investor, pension funds are highly efficient in both shaping and growing sustainable investments. The rapid growth in sustainable funds, especially in recent years, can be attributed to the fact that institutional investors such as pension funds assess sustainability risks and shape their investment strategies according to these risks (UNCTAD, 2022).

LITERATURE REVIEW

According to the traditional portfolio theory, the construction of sustainable mutual funds leads to a restriction of the investment universe. This restriction increases the risk of the portfolio and reduces the risk-adjusted return. Therefore, the return of even the most perfectly constructed sustainable mutual fund is considered to be at most as good as the return of a conventional one. In addition, while a conventional mutual fund will be able to use the same strategies as a socially responsible fund, the opposite will not be the case (Schröder, 2003).

Today, sustainable mutual funds have been very successful in reducing the conflict between profitability and social responsibility in financial markets. In the current environment, a company can make a profit while meeting social and ethical expectations (Hellsten & Mallin, 2006). Sustainable investments may exhibit comparable performance to conventional investments and may even be more stable in periods of crises (Morgan Stanley, 2019b). However, some investors still believe that investing in sustainable assets would result in a financial loss (Morgan Stanley, 2018). U.S. asset managers consider this mindset to be the main obstacle to sustainable investment (Morgan Stanley, 2019b).

This raises the question of why investors tend towards sustainable assets. Derwall et al. (2011) categorize socially responsible investors into two groups: value-driven investors and profit-seeking investors. Value-driven investors are driven by social and sustainable values rather than purely financial benefits. Profit-seeking investors, on the other hand, consider socially responsible investments as a means to achieve high financial returns. Rivoli (2003) argues that even if they act in line with their values, investors are not willing to risk serious financial losses. Perks et al. (1992) also noted that investments with high social performance but poor financial performance are less likely to draw investor sympathy. On the other hand, for profit-seeking investors, socially responsible investments whose performance lags behind conventional investments will be out of the question. Therefore, first of all, the financial performance of sustainable investments should be analyzed well. Contrary to popular belief, if sustainable investments exhibit similar or higher financial performance than conventional ones, interest in these investments will increase rapidly.

Early studies examining the performance of sustainable funds presented results that supported the conclusions of traditional portfolio theory. However, over time, studies have emerged demonstrating that sustainable funds can provide performance on an equal or even higher level than their counterparts. Research on the performance of sustainable mutual funds, the methods used and their results are summarized below.

Luther et al. (1992) evaluated the performance of ethical funds in their study conducted in the UK. The results revealed that ethical funds outperformed, albeit to a limited extent, when the risk factor was included in the analysis. However, this result is more pronounced when compared with benchmarks that include small sized firms and disappears when the Financial Times All Share index (FTSA) is used as a benchmark.

Hamilton et al. (1993) compared the performance of 32 socially responsible mutual funds and 170 conventional funds in the United States over the period 1981 - 1990. In the study, Jensen's Alpha was used as a performance measure. According to the results, social responsibility has no effect on the expected return of stocks. Socially responsible mutual funds do not generate abnormal returns. Moreover, the performance of these mutual funds does not differ significantly from the performance of conventional ones.

Mallin et al. (1995) analyzed the monthly returns of 29 ethical and 29 non-ethical funds in the UK. The study examined average excess returns and found that ethical funds underperformed both non-ethical funds and the market average. However, when the risk factor is included in the estimation, it is concluded that ethical funds outperform non-ethical funds.

Goldreyer et al. (1999) compared the performance of 49 socially responsible mutual funds with the performance of randomly selected conventional mutual funds. The funds analyzed in the study were divided into three groups: equity, bonds and balanced weighted funds. According to the results of the study, portfolios of socially responsible funds did not underperform or outperform conventional fund portfolios. Moreover, the findings prove that funds using inclusion screens outperform funds that do not use such screens.

Statman (2000) analyzed the performance of the Domini Social Index, the S&P 500 Index, socially responsible mutual funds, and conventional funds over the period 1990-98. In the study, 31 funds that meet certain criteria among 64 funds listed by Morningstar were considered. Jensen's alpha and excess standard deviation-adjusted return were used to evaluate the performance of the funds. The results revealed that socially responsible mutual funds outperformed the Domini Social Index and the S&P 500 Index but did not outperform conventional mutual funds.

Kreander et al. (2005) investigated the performance of ethical mutual funds between 1995 and 2001. The study analyzed the performance of a total of 60 funds from four European countries and compared the performance of ethical and non-ethical funds. The findings show that there is no significant difference between the performance of ethical and non-ethical funds.

Bauer, et al. (2005) investigated the performance of 103 ethical mutual funds from Germany, the UK, and the USA through their returns. Data for the period 1990-2001 were used in the study. In order to fully compare the performance of sustainable funds and conventional ones, matching funds in terms of fund size and fund age were used. The study utilized the Carhart multi-factor model and found no significant difference between the risk-adjusted returns of ethical and conventional funds.

Bello (2005) compared socially responsible mutual funds and conventional funds to investigate the differences in fund assets, portfolio diversification, and the effects of diversification on investment performance. For this purpose, socially responsible funds with similar net assets are compared with randomly selected conventional funds. Jensen's alpha, Sharpe ratio, and excess standard deviation adjusted return were used to measure performance. The study results show that there is no difference between the performance of socially responsible and conventional funds in terms of the attributes analyzed. Moreover, both fund groups underperformed the Domini 400 Social Index and the S&P 500 during the period analyzed.

Lozano et al. (2006) evaluated the development and performance of socially responsible mutual funds in Spain during the period 1999-2003. Considering Sharpe ratios and average returns, it was found that socially responsible mutual funds performed equal to or even higher than the sector average in 2002.

Jones et al. (2008) investigated the performance of socially responsible investment funds in Australia. The return performance of 89 ethical funds between 1986 and 2005 was analyzed using a multi-factor CAPM model. Risk-adjusted returns calculated using Jensen's alpha showed that ethical funds underperformed in Australia, especially in the period between 2000 and 2005. This underperformance was 1.52% for the period 2000-2005 and 0.88% for the overall time period analyzed.

Rodriguez (2010) analyzed the risk-adjusted performance of socially responsible and conventional mutual funds between 1997 and 2005. A model developed by Graham and Harvey is used to measure risk-adjusted performance. Although socially responsible funds were found to outperform some market indices based on raw returns, this difference disappeared when the risk factor was included in the analysis. Moreover, no significant difference was found between the performance of socially responsible funds and conventional funds.

Chang and Witte (2010) examined the characteristics, risk composition, and performance of all socially responsible mutual funds in the US over the last 15 years. The study investigates whether socially responsible mutual funds as a whole perform as well as the average of all mutual funds. The results revealed that although socially responsible mutual funds have advantages such as lower expense ratios and lower tax costs, their returns are also lower. In particular, socially responsible mutual funds based on domestic equities do not provide returns on par with conventional ones. In addition, the study found that not all socially responsible mutual funds exhibit similar performance and that the performance varies according to the fund structures.

Gil-Bazo et al. (2010) examined the performance of socially responsible investment funds in the U.S. separately as before-fee performance and fees to SRI funds' performance. Using the matching estimator methodology, the study finds that before and after fees performance of socially responsible mutual funds outperformed conventional ones with similar structures between 1997 and 2005. The paper also emphasizes that socially responsible funds, which outperform conventional funds, are managed by companies specialized in this field. Socially responsible funds managed by companies that are not specialized in socially responsible investments underperform conventional funds.

Abdelsalam et al. (2014) analyzed the relative performance of socially responsible and Islamic mutual funds. The performance of the funds was first measured using partial frontier methods and then quantile regression techniques. The findings show that although there are differences in the management and screening criteria of both funds, there are no significant gaps between the performance of the funds in general. However, when the comparison is made in terms of the least efficient funds, socially responsible mutual funds are found to be superior. When the most efficient funds were analyzed, the performance of socially responsible mutual funds lagged behind that of Islamic funds.

Lean et al. (2015) analyzed and compared the performance of socially responsible mutual funds in Europe and North America. The study analyzed a sample of 500 European and 248 North American socially responsible mutual funds for the period 2001-2011. Fama-French and Carhart models are used for performance evaluation. During the period analyzed, socially responsible mutual funds outperformed their European and American benchmark markets. Moreover, the performance of North American funds outperforms that of European funds.

Becchetti et al. (2015) investigated the performance of socially responsible and conventional funds over the period 1992-2012. According to the findings, socially responsible mutual funds outperform conventional ones during the global financial crisis. This suggests that socially responsible mutual funds can play an insurance role.

Jin and Han (2018) studied the performance and sectoral distribution of green funds in China. In the research, Carhart four-factor models were used to analyze fund performances. The findings reveal that the performance of green funds is sensitive to the market factor, small cap and value stocks.

One of the most comprehensive studies in the field belongs to Morgan Stanley Institute for Sustainable Investing. Between 2004 and 2018, the performance of 10,723 mutual funds was evaluated using the Wilcoxon statistical test. The study reveals that there is no loss in the returns of sustainable funds compared to conventional ones. In addition, the risk of sustainable funds was found to be lower (Morgan Stanley, 2019). More importantly, there is strong evidence that the performance of sustainable funds was more stable during periods of extreme volatility (2008, 2009, 2015 and 2018).

Yue et al. (2020) analyzed the economic returns of 30 sustainable and 30 conventional funds in Europe. Annual returns, standard deviations, Sharpe ratios, skewness, and kurtosis were used as performance evaluation criteria. The Capital Asset Pricing Model (CAPM), Fama-French three-factor model, and

Carhart four-factor model were utilized in the study, and it was found that sustainable funds are less risky than conventional ones. However, there is no evidence that sustainable funds provide higher returns than conventional funds or benchmark indices.

Milonas et al. (2022) evaluated the performance of 80 European and 64 US funds using alpha, Sharpe ratio, Treynor ratio and excess daily return variables. The findings show that ESG funds perform slightly better than traditional funds, although there is no significant difference between them.

Ateş et al. (2022) examined the performance of sustainable-themed funds in Türkiye in comparison with conventional funds and indices. The data used in the study covers the period between 2019 and 2022. Standard Deviation, Sharpe Ratio, Jensen alpha, annual returns, and Treynor Raito were used to measure fund performance. Considering the return and systematic risks of the portfolios constructed with CAPM, it was concluded that sustainable funds outperformed their benchmarks.

Sarkar (2022) investigated the performance of ESG funds in India. The study concludes that these funds have grown very rapidly and most of them have outperformed the market portfolio according to risk-adjusted performance measures.

Kuzmina et al. (2023) examined the performance of energy sector ESG funds in the European zone. Carhart Model and statistical analyses were used to determine the performance differences between ESG funds and traditional ones. The results reveal that there is no significant difference between the performance of European ESG and conventional funds in the period analyzed.

Tampakoudis et al. (2023) researched the performance of mutual funds during COVID-19 and explored whether ESG scores have an impact on fund performance. Using data envelopment analysis, the study concluded that funds with higher ESG scores exhibited significantly higher performance.

Zhang et al. (2023) analyzed the relationship between ESG performance and downside risk of equity mutual funds in China. In the study, it was revealed that there is a positive relationship between ESG performance and downside risks of funds, but this relationship weakened during the COVID-19 pandemic.

At the time of this study, no research found that investigates the performance of sustainable mutual funds against conventional ones in Türkiye, except for the paper by Ateş et al. (2022). However, in their research examining the performance of the sustainability index, Gök & Özdemir (2017) found that the performance of the BIST Sustainability Index does not exhibit a financially significant difference from the BIST100 Index.

As seen in the literature review, several criterias are taken into account while investing in funds. In this case, the question of which mutual fund to choose becomes a multi-criteria decision-making method problem (Tsolas, 2019). In this study, the performance of sustainable funds is investigated with MCDM. Therefore, the literature on fund performance that evaluated using MCDM is also reviewed.

Lin et al. (2007), in their study evaluating the performance of Taiwanese mutual funds with TOPSIS, stated that although multi-criteria decision-making methods are not clearly more accurate than single-criteria methods, they provide a useful alternative for researchers who aim to evaluate different criteria.

Alptekin (2009) evaluated the performance of mutual and pension funds in Türkiye by using TOPSIS, one of the MCDM methods. The results revealed that TOPSIS is a preferable method among other performance measurement methods.

Chang et al. (2010) evaluated the performance of 82 Taiwanese mutual funds using TOPSIS with two different distance approaches. The outcomes revealed that the TOPSIS method gives reasonable results in measuring fund performance.

Karmakar (2018) analyzed the performance of equity funds using TOPSIS and EDAS, two MCDM methods. In the study, the Entropy was used to determine the criteria weights and it was concluded that the results obtained from TOPSIS and EDAS methods were consistent.

Tsolas (2019) proposed an approach that combines GRA and data envelopment analysis (DEA) to select among exchange-traded funds. In addition, the results obtained with this model are compared with the results obtained with other DEA models. The results indicate that this model is superior to ordinary DEA models and is more effective in fund selection.

Das (2022) analyzed the performance of mutual funds in India between 1997 and 2012 with MCDM TOPSIS and proved that this method can be successfully used to evaluate fund performance.

METHODOLOGY

In the literature, fund performances are generally analyzed based on the portfolios created. In this study, instead of creating a portfolio, the performances of sustainable and conventional funds are analyzed separately for the relevant years and a ranking based on the individual performance of these funds is aimed to be obtained. Since there are many factors to be considered in fund selection, it is basically based on a decision-making process with many criteria. Therefore, in this study, fund performances are calculated by utilizing ENTROPI-based TOPSIS and GRA methods. The methods used and their stages are briefly described below.

Entropy

Although the entropy is used in multi-criteria decision-making to determine the importance of variables in the data set, this concept was originally introduced to the literature by Clausius (1867) as one of the laws of thermodynamics. This concept used in thermodynamics was redefined in the following years by Shannon (1948) from the perspective of information theory. Entropy is used to determine the weights of criteria in multi-criteria decision making problems. The problem of calculating criterion weights has had an important place in many studies and has significantly affected the results of the analysis. In the literature, there are different weight determination methods other than this method and some of these methods are based on subjective and some on objective information, and the objectivity of the entropy method is among the advantages of this method (Ayçin, 2019). When determining entropy weights, there are 4 stages as stated in Effatpanah et al. (2022):

Step 1: Normalizing the decision matrix
Step 2: Finding the entropy value of each criterion
Step 3: Finding the degrees of differentiation
Step 4: Calculation of entropy criteria weights for each criterion

Before proceeding to the steps of the method, the decision matrix needs to be constructed. If we define the decision matrix as a matrix X with m alternatives and n criteria, the decision matrix can be constructed as in Equation 1. In Equation 1, x_{ij} is the value of alternative i for criterion j.

$$X = \begin{bmatrix} x_{i1} & x_{ij} \cdots & x_{in} \\ \vdots & \ddots & \vdots \\ x_{m1} & x_{mj} \cdots & x_{mn} \end{bmatrix} \tag{1}$$

After the decision matrix is created, if there are benefit and cost variables in the decision matrix, Equation 2 is used for benefit variables and Equation 3 for cost variables in order to standardize the variables.

$$r_{ij} = x_{ij}/max_{ij} \ (i = 1, \ldots, m; j = 1, \ldots, n) \tag{2}$$

$$r_{ij} = min_{ij}/x_{ij} \ (i = 1, \ldots, m; j = 1, \ldots, n) \tag{3}$$

Step 1: The standardized decision matrix needs to be normalized in order to convert the values that is expressed in different types into a single type. The decision matrix is normalized by Equation 4 and Pij is the normalized value of each variable for each criterion.

$$P_{ij} = \frac{r_{ij}}{\sum_{i=1}^{m} r_{ij}}; \forall_{i,j} \tag{4}$$

Step 2: After the decision matrix is normalized, the Ej value, which expresses the entropy value of each criterion, is calculated using Equation 5.

$$E_j = -k * \sum_{j=1}^{n} P_{ij} * \ln\left(P_{ij}\right) (i = 1, \ldots, m; j = 1, \ldots, n) \tag{5}$$

Step 3: After calculating the Ej values for each criterion, in order to calculate the degree of differentiation of these criteria, the Ej values are subtracted from 1 and the Dj values are calculated as shown in Equation 6.

$$D_j = 1 - E_j \ (j = 1, \ldots, n) \tag{6}$$

Step 4: Finally, the weights of the criteria (Wj) are calculated as shown in Equation 7 by deviding the degree of differentiation of each criterion to the sum of the degrees of differentiation.

$$W_j = \frac{D_j}{\sum_{j=1}^{n} D_j} \tag{7}$$

Tecniques for Order of Preferance by Smilarity to Ideal Solution (TOPSIS)

TOPSIS method, which is one of the MCDMs and is widely used in the literature, was introduced by Hwang and Yoon (1981). As the name of the method indicates, the model uses the closeness of the variables to the ideal solution while grading. When finding the ideal solution, both the proximity to the positive ideal solution and the distance to the negative ideal solution are taken into account. In the positive ideal solution, benefit variables are maximized while cost variables are minimized, and in the negative ideal solution, cost variables are maximized while benefit variables are minimized (Ayçin, 2019). TOPSIS is a method that has proven itself with studies in various fields by using its advantage in ranking problems with few alternatives (Musbah et al., 2022). The steps of the TOPSIS method are as follows.

Step 1: The decision matrix previously defined as in Equation 1 needs to be normalized in order to express the variables in the same type to increase the reliability and validity of the method. This normalization is carried out as shown in Equation 8 for TOPSIS.

$$P_{ij} = \frac{x_{ij}}{\sqrt{\sum_{i=1}^{m} x_{ij}^2}} \ (i = 1, ..., m; j = 1, ..., n) \tag{8}$$

Step 2: In this step of the method, the normalized decision matrix is weighted using the criteria weights. The normalized decision matrix obtained in the previous step is multiplied by the criteria weight matrix to obtain a weighted normalized decision matrix. Criteria weight calculation process in the TOPSIS method can be conducted using different methods. In this study, the weights are obtained with the Entropy method. The process of assigning weights is shown in Equation 9.

$$V_{mxn} = W_{mxn} * P_{mxn} \tag{9}$$

Wmxn is the weight matrix containing the weights of each variable where Vmxn is the weighted normalized decision matrix. Pij is the normalized decision matrix created in the previous step.

Step 3: After obtaining the weighted normalized decision matrix, the positive and negative ideal solutions must be found. The positive ideal solution (A*) and negative ideal solution (A⁻) are calculated as shown in Equation 10 and Equation 11 respectively.

$$A^* = \left\{ \left(\max_i v_{ij} \mid j \in J \right), \left(\min_i v_{ij} \mid j \in J' \right) \right\} A^* = \left\{ v_1^*, v_2^*, ..., v_n^* \right\} \tag{10}$$

$$A^- = \left\{ \left(\min_i v_{ij} \mid j \in J \right), \left(\max_i v_{ij} \mid j \in J' \right) \right\} A^* = \left\{ v_1^*, v_2^*, ..., v_n^* \right\} \tag{11}$$

In the above equations, J stands for maximization and J' stands for minimization. One of the important issues to consider at this stage is whether the criteria are benefit or cost. The highest values of the benefit criteria are included in the positive ideal solution, while the lowest values of the cost criteria are included. The opposite is the case for the negative ideal solution.

Step 4: After finding the positive and negative ideal solutions, the distances of the alternatives to these solutions need to be calculated. These distances are calculated with the help of Euclidean as in Equation 12 and Equation 13 for both positive and negative ideal solutions respectively.

$$S_i^* = \sqrt{\sum_{j=1}^{n} \left(v_{ij} - v_j^* \right)^2} \tag{12}$$

$$S_i^- = \sqrt{\sum_{j=1}^{n} \left(v_{ij} - v_j^- \right)^2} \tag{13}$$

In the equations above, S_i^* is the distance of each alternative from the positive ideal solution, while S_i^- is the distance of each alternative from the negative ideal solution. Since these distances include both the best and the worst case in the ranking, they contribute to researchers as a factor that increases the reliability of the method.

Step 5: In the last step of the method, the ranking among the alternatives is obtained by using the distances to the positive and negative ideal solutions calculated in the previous step. From these two distances, the ranking criterion Ci, which is calculated as the ratio of the distance to the negative ideal solution to the sum of the distances to the negative and positive ideal solutions, is calculated as in Equation 14.

$$C_i = \frac{S_i^-}{S_i^- + S_i^*} \tag{14}$$

Grey Relational Analysis (GRA)

Gray Relational Analysis is a method introduced by Julong (1989) in 1989 as a part of the Gray System approach. In this method, "gray" is defined for situations where only some of the information about the problem is available, "white" for situations where all the information is available, and "black" for situations where none is available (Karaatli et al., 2015). The steps of the GRA method are given below.

Step 1: The decision matrix defined in Equation 1 above needs to be normalized by taking into account the previously mentioned benefit and cost variables. The normalization process differs for benefit and cost criteria. In benefit criteria, normalization is calculated by subtracting the minimum value of the criterion from the relevant value and dividing it by the difference between the maximum and minimum value of the criterion. In cost criteria, the ratio value is obtained by subtracting the relevant value from the maximum value of the criterion. These calculations are given mathematically in Equation 15 and Equation 16 for the benefit and cost criteria, respectively.

$$x_i^* = \frac{x_i(j) - \min_j x_i(j)}{\max_j x_i(j) - \min_j x_i(j)} \tag{15}$$

$$x_i^* = \frac{\max_j x_i(j) - x_i(j)}{\max_j x_i(j) - \min_j x_i(j)} \tag{16}$$

Step 2: After normalizing the decision matrix, a reference series containing the best values of all criteria (the highest values of the benefit criteria and the lowest values of the cost criteria) is created. Using this reference series (Δ_{oi}), the absolute value decision matrix is obtained from the normalized decision matrix. This is done by subtracting the relevant values from the reference series as in Equation 17.

$$\Delta_i = x_0^*(j) - x_i^*(j) \tag{17}$$

$x_o^*(j)$ in the equation represents the best value of the jth criterion in the reference series. Δ_i is the decision matrix and contains all values differenced from the reference values.

Step 3: In this step of the GRA method, the data is now ready to find the gray relational coefficients. Gray relational coefficients are calculated as stated in Equation 18. Equation 19 and Equation 20 are used to calculate the gray relational coefficients by calculating the maximum and minimum values of the Δ_i matrix.

$$\gamma_i(j) = \frac{\Delta_{min} + \zeta.\Delta_{max}}{\Delta_i(j) + \zeta.\Delta_{max}} \tag{18}$$

$$\Delta_{max} = \max_i \max_j \Delta_i(j) \tag{19}$$

$$\Delta_{min} = \min_i \min_j \Delta_i(j) \tag{20}$$

In the equation, $\gamma_i(j)$ denotes the gray relational coefficients and ζ is the discriminant coefficient that can take values between [0,1]. This coefficient is usually used as 0.5 in studies.

Step 4: In the last step of the method, gray relational degrees need to be calculated. These degrees are calculated by multiplying and summing the gray relational coefficients of each alternative with the weights of the criteria. This process is expressed mathematically as shown in Equation 21.

$$`` _i = \sum_{j=1}^{n}[W_i(j).\gamma_i(j)] \tag{21}$$

Γ_i expressed in the equation represents the gray relational degree of each alternative. Wi(j) shows the weights of the criteria. After calculating Γ_i for all alternatives, it becomes possible to rank and decide between alternatives.

Data

In this study, the 5-year financial performance of sustainable and conventional funds for the period 2016 - 2021 is analyzed. However, most of the sustainable funds in Türkiye were established after 2020. There are 4 funds whose data are available before 2020. Three of these funds are sustainable pension funds and the other is a sustainable mutual fund. The mutual fund was excluded from the analysis in order to ensure the homogeneity of the data and to interpret the results more accurately. The sustainable pension funds included in the analysis are equity funds and fund of funds. Therefore, it was decided that the conventional pension funds used for comparison purposes are also equity funds and fund of funds. As a result, the analyses were conducted on a total of 22 funds, including 3 sustainable pension funds and 19 pension funds. The names of the funds used in the study and their codes are given in Table 2.

Table 2. Fund names and codes

Code	Name	Fund Type
ZHB	Türkiye Hayat ve Emeklilik Sustainable Equity Pension Fund	Sustainable
GHH	Garanti Emeklilik ve Hayat A.Ş. Sustainable Equity Pension Fund	Sustainable
APG	Allianz Yaşam ve Emeklilik Sustainable Fund of Funds Pension Fund	Sustainable
ANS	Viennalife Emeklilik ve Hayat Equity Pension Fund	Conventional
VEH	Türkiye Hayat ve Emeklilik Equity Pension Fund	Conventional
HHB	Türkiye Hayat ve Emeklilik Other Than BIST30 Equity Pension Fund	Conventional
IEH	NN Hayat ve Emeklilik Equity Pension Fund	Conventional
MHH	MetLife Emeklilik ve Hayat Equity Pension Fund	Conventional
GEG	Garanti Emeklilik ve Hayat Equity Group Pension Fund	Conventional
GEH	Garanti Emeklilik ve Hayat Equity Pension Fund	Conventional
EIH	Fiba Emeklilik ve Hayat Oyak Portföy Equity Pension Fund	Conventional
BEH	Fiba Emeklilik ve Hayat Equity Pension Fund	Conventional
BBH	Fiba Emeklilik ve Hayat Equity Group Pension Fund	Conventional
CHH	Cigna Sağlık Hayat ve Emeklilik First Equity Pension Fund	Conventional
BPH	BNP Paribas Cardif Emeklilik Equity Pension Fund	Conventional
HES	Axa Hayat ve Emeklilik Equity Pension Fund	Conventional
AHB	Anadolu Hayat Emeklilik Second Equity Pension Fund	Conventional
AG3	Anadolu Hayat Emeklilik Equity Group Pension Fund	Conventional
AH5	Anadolu Hayat Emeklilik Equity Pension Fund	Conventional
AZH	Allianz Hayat Emeklilik Equity Pension Fund	Conventional
AEB	AgeSA Hayat ve Emeklilik Equity Group Pension Fund	Conventional
AEH	AgeSA Hayat ve Emeklilik Equity Pension Fund	Conventional

The data of the funds were obtained from fonbul.com. Various criteria have been used in the literature to compare the financial performance of funds (Ateş et al., 2022; Bello, 2005; Lozano et al., 2006; Yue et al., 2020). Researchers have generally included a few of these performance criteria in line with the objectives and scope of their projects. In this study, however, considering the contribution to the literature on the effects of other criteria on performance, a broader number of criteria were included. All criteria used in the research are presented in Table 3 below.

Table 3. Performance criteria and descriptions

Criteria	Description
Annual Return	The annual returns of the fund.
Sharpe	The level of return to be obtained for each unit of risk incurred. High Sharpe Ratio is preferred.
Alpha	The average return difference between the selected benchmark and the fund. High Alpha is preferred.
Beta	The direction and level of the relationship between the returns of the selected benchmark and the fund returns. Minimum Beta is preferred.
Treynor	The ratio of the fund's return to the Beta of the selected benchmark. High Treynor is preferred.
Sortino	The level of return to be obtained for each unit of negative risk incurred. High Sortino is preferred.
VaR	The highest probability of loss if the fund is held for a certain period of time. Low VaR value is preferred.
Maximum Loss	The largest rate of decline realized in the period under consideration. Low Maximum Loss rate is preferred.
Downside Risk	The loss value of the fund that may be observed in the worst case scenario that may be encountered during the selected period. Low Downside Risk is preferred.

RESULTS

In this study, the performance of sustainable and conventional funds between 2017-2021 is calculated and compared using entropy-based TOPSIS and GRA methods. In order to calculate the performance of the relevant funds, besides variables such as annual return, Sharpe, Alpha, Treynor, and Beta, which are frequently cited in the literature, Sortino, downside risk, VaR, and maximum loss variables are used to enrich the calculations and increase the reliability. A total of 9 different variables were used to analyze the performance of 22 funds separately for 5 years.

Entropy method was used to estimate the weights of these 9 different criteria, and after the weights were determined, the performance was evaluated first for TOPSIS and then for GRA by following the steps of the methods, and rankings were obtained.

Results of TOPSIS Method

Table 4 below shows the ranking of each alternative according to the C_i values obtained by TOPSIS method for 5 years. The funds marked in bold (ZHB, GHH, APG) are sustainable pension funds and the others are conventional ones.

Table 4. TOPSIS rankings of fund performances for 2017-2021

Funds	Rankings				
	2017	2018	2019	2020	2021
ZHB	2	11	22	15	21
GHH	11	15	20	21	1
APG	1	1	16	22	9
ANS	13	20	18	8	10
VEH	14	14	19	16	20
HHB	21	19	21	17	17
IEH	22	18	15	19	14
MHH	6	8	14	20	15
GEG	7	7	5	10	5
GEH	8	10	9	14	8
EIH	20	12	4	7	11
BEH	17	21	2	1	16
BBH	15	16	17	2	2
CHH	4	6	10	3	3
BPH	19	9	11	18	13
HES	12	13	13	9	12
AHB	10	5	8	6	7
AG3	3	4	6	4	4
AH5	5	17	12	11	22
AZH	9	3	7	5	6
AEB	16	2	1	12	18
AEH	18	22	3	13	19

According to the TOPSIS method, while APG maintained its leading position among other funds in 2017 and 2018, it faced a significant performance loss in 2019 and 2020 but recovered this performance loss in 2021 and performed above average. In addition, although ZHB was the second-highest-performing pension fund in 2017, it failed to maintain this performance in the following years. On the other hand, while GHH had an average performance, it exhibited extremely low performance in 2019 and 2020 but became the best-performing pension fund in 2021.

Based on the TOPSIS results, it can be concluded that sustainable pension funds are resilient to regional crises but experience a noticeable performance decline in the event of a global health crisis. Such a situation can only be explained by an in-depth analysis of the companies and sectors in which the funds invest and the fluctuations in these sectors during COVID-19 pandemic.

Results of GRA Method

Similar to the TOPSIS, the Entropy method was used to determine the weights in the GRA. The rankings obtained by following the steps of the method are given in Table 5 below.

Table 5. GRA rankings of fund performances for 2017-2021

Funds	Rankings				
	2017	2018	2019	2020	2021
ZHB	4	10	22	15	21
GHH	12	18	20	21	1
APG	1	1	16	22	11
ANS	14	19	18	8	9
VEH	17	14	19	16	18
HHB	21	20	21	17	14
IEH	22	17	15	19	15
MHH	10	8	14	20	16
GEG	8	7	5	10	5
GEH	9	11	9	13	8
EIH	20	13	3	7	10
BEH	16	21	2	1	19
BBH	15	15	17	2	2
CHH	2	6	10	3	3
BPH	19	9	11	18	13
HES	11	12	13	9	12
AHB	7	4	8	6	7
AG3	3	5	6	4	4
AH5	5	16	12	11	22
AZH	6	3	7	5	6
AEB	13	2	1	12	17
AEH	18	22	4	14	20

According to the GRA method, APG decreased from the leading position to the lower ranks, reaching an average performance and achieving its current position. The same was the case for ZHB and GHH sustainable pension funds, which achieved almost similar performances with the TOPSIS method. The TOPSIS and GRA results are presented together in Table 6 below for easier comparison.

Table 6. TOPSIS and GRA rankings of fund performances

	2016		2017		2018		2019		2020		2021	
	TOPSIS	GRA	TOPSIS	GRA	TOPSIS	GRA	TOPSIS	GRA	TOPSIS	GRA	TOPSIS	GRA
ZHB	18	17	2	4	11	10	22	22	15	15	21	21
GHH	10	11	11	12	15	18	20	20	21	21	1	1
APG	1	1	1	1	1	1	16	16	22	22	9	11
ANS	6	6	13	14	20	19	18	18	8	8	10	9
VEH	19	19	14	17	14	14	19	19	16	16	20	18
HHB	21	21	21	21	19	20	21	21	17	17	17	14
IEH	20	20	22	22	18	17	15	15	19	19	14	15
MHH	12	10	6	10	8	8	14	14	20	20	15	16
GEG	5	5	7	8	7	7	5	5	10	10	5	5
GEH	11	12	8	9	10	11	9	9	14	13	8	8
EIH	22	22	20	20	12	13	4	3	7	7	11	10
BEH	8	9	17	16	21	21	2	2	1	1	16	19
BBH	7	7	15	15	16	15	17	17	2	2	2	2
CHH	2	2	4	2	6	6	10	10	3	3	3	3
BPH	9	8	19	19	9	9	11	11	18	18	13	13
HES	14	14	12	11	13	12	13	13	9	9	12	12
AHB	16	16	10	7	5	4	8	8	6	6	7	7
AG3	13	13	3	3	4	5	6	6	4	4	4	4
AH5	17	18	5	5	17	16	12	12	11	11	22	22
AZH	15	15	9	6	3	3	7	7	5	5	6	6
AEB	3	3	16	13	2	2	1	1	12	12	18	17
AEH	4	4	18	18	22	22	3	4	13	14	19	20

TOPSIS and GRA results are similar and consistent. This supports the conclusions given under the TOPSIS results. Although sustainable pension funds are resilient to local crises and financial fluctuations, they are more sensitive to global health crises. This suggests that the investment portfolios of pension mutual funds in Türkiye are from sectors that have been severely affected by the COVID-19 pandemic. However, in order to support this conclusion, the structures of these funds need to be analyzed in depth.

CONCLUSION

The destructive power of the capitalist system has caused a gap between society and corporations. As companies struggle to survive in the financial markets, they are increasingly ignoring their responsibilities to humanity and the environment. Sustainable investments are therefore perhaps the last hope of integration for humanity and corporations.

A sustainable financial system orients companies towards meeting human expectations, supporting social life, and protecting the environment. Companies share their commitments with society through their non-financial reports. Individual and institutional investors, on the other hand, reward companies that achieve a certain sustainable performance by investing in them and support the creation of a system in line with their values.

Today, the sustainable financial system is developing rapidly. However, in order to create a fully sustainable financial system globally, all investors need to be oriented toward this area. In a paradox with social, ethical, and cultural expectations, some investors expect a financial performance equivalent to their existing investments in order to invest in a sustainable way. The philosophy of sustainable finance has basically emerged as a result of people's expectations and pressures in this direction and focuses on prioritizing financial gain. However, a large part of society still refuses financial losses. Therefore, while sustainable investments generate positive environmental, social, and governance impacts, they must also exhibit high financial performance. Indeed, contrary to early perceptions, sustainable investments today perform as well as, and sometimes even better than, conventional investments. Especially in developed countries, this financial performance has been clearly demonstrated both in normal periods and in times of crisis. However, the situation is not quite clear in developing countries that have not yet taken the necessary steps in the field of sustainable finance.

In this study, the performance of sustainable investments in Türkiye, whose initiatives in the field of sustainable finance have only started to gain maturity in recent years, is analyzed. In this direction, sustainable and conventional pension funds were compared with Entropy, TOPSIS, and GRA, which are among the Multi-Criteria Decision Making Models, over financial performance indicators. The performances between 2017 and 2021 were analyzed in the study. These years are valuable as they reflect the effects of two different crisis periods in Türkiye. 2017 reflects the effects of a political crisis. 2019 and beyond reflect a global pandemic crisis environment. In addition, there is an ongoing economic volatility in Türkiye after 2016 and the effects of this volatility have been felt in financial markets in recent years.

As a result of the analyses, it was observed that TOPSIS and GRA models provided consistent results. This indicates that the findings are highly accurate and consistent. When the results of both methods are considered together, it is clear that sustainable pension funds generally perform at the top or in the middle of the performance rankings. In other words, the financial performance of sustainable funds has not only remained behind conventional funds but even surpassed them in certain periods. This finding supports the studies of Ateş et al. (2022) for Türkiye. Bello (2005), Lozano et al. (2006), Gil-Bazo et al. (2010) and Lean et al. (2015) also present similar results on the performance of sustainable funds. Based on the findings, it can be concluded that sustainable funds in Türkiye are created and managed in a similar manner to funds in developed markets, and accordingly, they perform similarly well against traditional funds. This helps to alleviate the concerns of investors who are considering investing according to the sustainability philosophy but have financial worries in their minds.

Considering the crisis periods, the attempted coup in Türkiye in 2016 and the subsequent political crisis did not have a negative impact on the performance of sustainable funds. In 2016 and the following 2017, APG maintained its first place in the performance ranking, ZHB rose to the top, and GHH maintained its current position in the middle ranking. In this context, as shown by Becchetti et al. (2015) and Morgan Stanley (2019), sustainable funds in Türkiye have also managed to maintain their financial performance compared to conventional funds during a political crisis. However, it is difficult to state a similar situation for the pandemic period. In 2019, when the Covid-19 pandemic broke out, and then in 2020, there was a noticeable decline in the performance ranking of sustainable pension funds. Even in

2021, ZHB ranked at the bottom, while APG and GHH's financial performance improved. Thus, it can be argued that sustainable funds, while being a preferable investment instrument in a domestic crisis, still experience significant financial performance declines in global crisis environments.

Although local crises in different markets need to be analyzed, the results show that sustainable financial instruments, which are subject to more stringent sanctions and scrutiny than their counterparts, provide a good hedging mechanism in regional crises. In addition, these funds also exhibit high financial performance in normal periods, making them a good choice for both conventional and socially responsible investors. However, the financial decline faced by these funds in a global crisis brings to mind another area of scrutiny. What financial instruments make up the structure of these funds and how resilient will this financial structure be against a possible global crisis? For example, a sustainable fund, which is largely based on the health sector in order to be sustainable, may suffer serious losses in a crisis similar to the COVID-19 pandemic.

As mentioned in the results, sustainable funds in Türkiye experienced a significant performance decline in a global crisis environment. The main reason for this situation is that Türkiye has not yet taken serious action in the field of sustainable investments. Although there has been an increase in the number of sustainable funds in recent years, this number is far behind its counterparts in Europe and the US. There are also serious deficiencies in the regulatory and supervisory practices in the field of sustainable finance. The lack of sustainability indices based on different themes, the failure to clearly set out the practices that will guide companies to be sustainable, and the inability to provide adequate financial support in this area negatively affect sustainable investments. However, besides all these, the biggest deficiency is the societal lack of knowledge and awareness of sustainable investments. Therefore, individual investors hesitate to engage in sustainable investments.

The results of this research prove that sustainable funds perform well despite these limitations. Although the performance of sustainable funds fluctuates, if the demand for these funds increases, all funds will perform much better and more robustly. But even as it stands, sustainable funds offer a good investment alternative for both socially responsible and traditional investors. Given the lack of financial information in Türkiye, socially responsible investors who are oriented towards sustainable investments can overcome potential difficulties in company selection by turning to these funds. Traditional investors, on the other hand, can diversify their portfolios with these funds to avoid any financial losses.

This study was conducted in a limited universe due to both the recent establishment of other funds and the inaccessibility of their historical data and the desire to obtain findings directly on the performance of sustainable pension funds. However, it would be useful to reproduce the study with more comprehensive data in the future. In this way, broader findings on the performance of all sustainable investment funds can be obtained. Moreover, analyzing the relative performance of sustainable mutual and sustainable pension funds will also contribute to the literature. In addition, it would be useful to repeat the analysis with different multi-criteria decision-making methods in order to obtain more robust and reliable results and to support the results reached in this study.

REFERENCES

Abdelsalam, O., Fethi, M. D., Matallín, J. C., & Tortosa-Ausina, E. (2014). On the comparative performance of socially responsible and Islamic mutual funds. *Journal of Economic Behavior & Organization*, *103*, 108–128. doi:10.1016/j.jebo.2013.06.011

Alptekin, N. (2009). Performance evaluation of Turkish type a mutual funds and pension stock funds by using TOPSIS method. *International Journal of Economics and Finance Studies, 1*(2), 11–22.

Ateş, M. H., Çakan, C. D., & Koç, İ. Ö. (2022). Türkiye'de sürdürülebilir temalı fonların geleneksel fonlarla karşılaştırmalı performans analizi. *Ekonomi Politika & Finans Araştırmaları Dergisi, 7*, 123-139. doi:10.30784/epfad.1148841

Ayçin, E. (2019). *Çok kriterli karar verme: Bilgisayar uygulamalı çözümler.* Nobel Akademik Yayıncılık.

Bauer, R., Koedijk, K., & Otten, R. (2005). International evidence on ethical mutual fund performance and investment style. *Journal of Banking & Finance, 29*(7), 1751–1767. doi:10.1016/j.jbankfin.2004.06.035

Becchetti, L., Ciciretti, R., Dalò, A., & Herzel, S. (2015). Socially responsible and conventional investment funds: Performance comparison and the global financial crisis. *Applied Economics, 47*(25), 2541–2562. doi:10.1080/00036846.2014.1000517

Bello, Z. Y. (2005). Socially responsible investing and portfolio diversification. *Journal of Financial Research, 28*(1), 41–57. doi:10.1111/j.1475-6803.2005.00113.x

Chang, C. E., & Witte, H. D. (2010). Performance evaluation of U.S. socially responsible mutual funds: Revisiting doing good and doing well. *American Journal of Business, 25*(1), 9–24. doi:10.1108/19355181201000001

Chang, C. H., Lin, J. J., Lin, J. H., & Chiang, M. C. (2010). Domestic open-end equity mutual fund performance evaluation using extended TOPSIS method with different distance approaches. *Expert Systems with Applications, 37*(6), 4642–4649. doi:10.1016/j.eswa.2009.12.044

Corporate Finance Institute. (2023). *Ethical Investing.* https://corporatefinanceinstitute.com/resources/knowledge/trading-investing/ethical-investing/

Cortez, M. C., Silva, F., & Areal, N. (2009). The performance of European socially responsible funds. *Journal of Business Ethics, 87*(4), 573–588. doi:10.100710551-008-9959-x

Cummings, L. S. (2000). The financial performance of ethical investment trusts: An Australian perspective. *Journal of Business Ethics, 25*(1), 79–92. doi:10.1023/A:1006102802904

Das, L. (2022). Evaluation of mutual funds using TOPSIS method, *REST Journal on Banking. Accounting and Business, 1*(2), 34–43. doi:10.46632/jbab/1/2/6

Derwall, J., Guenster, N., Bauer, R., & Koedijk, K. (2005). The eco-efficiency premium puzzle. *Financial Analysts Journal, 61*(2), 51–63. doi:10.2469/faj.v61.n2.2716

Diltz, J. D. (1995). Does social screening affect portfolio performance? *Journal of Investing, 4*(1), 64–69. doi:10.3905/joi.4.1.64

Domini, A. L., & Kinder, P. D. (1986). *Ethical investing, how to make profitable investments without sacrificing your principles* (1st ed.). Addison Wesley.

Effatpanah, S. K., Ahmadi, M. H., Aungkulanon, P., Maleki, A., Sadeghzadeh, M., Sharifpur, M., & Chen, L. (2022). Comparative analysis of five widely-used multi-criteria decision-making methods to evaluate clean energy technologies: A case study. *Sustainability (Basel), 14*(3), 1403. Advance online publication. doi:10.3390u14031403

Fernandez-Izquierdo, A., & Matallin-Saez, J. C. (2008). Performance of ethical mutual funds in Spain: Sacrifice or premium? *Journal of Business Ethics, 81*(2), 247–260. doi:10.100710551-007-9492-3

Fowler, S. J., & Hope, C. (2007). A critical review of sustainable business indices and their impact. *Journal of Business Ethics, 76*(3), 243–252. doi:10.100710551-007-9590-2

Getzner, M., & Grabner-Krauter, S. (2004). Consumer preferences and marketing strategies for 'green shares': Specifics of the Austrian market. *International Journal of Bank Marketing, 22*(4), 260–278. doi:10.1108/02652320410542545

Gil-Bazo, J., Ruiz-Verdú, P., & Santos, A. A. P. (2010). The performance of socially responsible mutual funds: The role of fees and management companies. *Journal of Business Ethics, 94*(2), 243–263. doi:10.100710551-009-0260-4

Global Sustainable Investment Alliance. (2018). *Global Sustainable Investmet Review*. https://www.google.com/url?sa=t&rct=j&q=&esrc=s&source=web&cd=&cad=rja&uact=8&ved=2ahUKEwiH7OWh_uHwAhUYgf0HHdgnBxgQFjABegQIBhAD&url=http%3A%2F%2Fwww.gsi-alliance.org%2Fwpcontent%2Fuploads%2F2019%2F03%2FGSIR_Review2018.3.28.pdf&usg=AOvVaw3A7tZh80HJW6ZAqMQ_zGe7

Gök, İ. Y., & Özdemír, O. (2017). Borsa İstanbul Sürdürülebilirlik Endeksinin performans karakteristiği. *Sosyoekonomi, 25*(34), 87–105.

Goldreyer, E. F., Ahmed, P., & Diltz, J. D. (1999). The performance of socially responsible mutual funds: Incorporating sociopolitical information in portfolio selection. *Managerial Finance, 25*(1), 23–36. doi:10.1108/03074359910765830

Haigh, M., & Hazelton, J. (2004). Financial markets: A tool for social responsibility? *Journal of Business Ethics, 52*(1), 59–71. doi:10.1023/B:BUSI.0000033107.22587.0b

Hamilton, S., Jo, H., & Statman, M. (1993). Doing well while doing good? The investment performance of socially responsible mutual funds. *Financial Analysts Journal, 49*(6), 62–66. doi:10.2469/faj.v49.n6.62

Heinkel, R., Kraus, A., & Zechner, J. (2001). The effect of green investment on corporate behavior. *Journal of Financial and Quantitative Analysis, 36*(4), 431–449. doi:10.2307/2676219

Hellsten, S., & Mallin, C. (2006). Are "ethical" or "socially responsible" investments socially responsible? *Journal of Business Ethics, 66*(4), 393–406. doi:10.100710551-006-0001-x

Hussein, K., & Omran, M. (2005). Ethical investment revisited: Evidence from Dow Jones Islamic indexes. *Journal of Investing, 14*(3), 105–126. doi:10.3905/joi.2005.580557

Hwang, C. L., & Yoon, K. P. (1981). *Multiple attribute decision making: Methods and applications* (Vol. 186). Springer-Verlag., doi:10.1007/978-3-642-48318-9

Jin, J., & Han, L. (2018). Assessment of Chinese green funds: Performance and industry allocation. *Journal of Cleaner Production, 171,* 1084–1093. doi:10.1016/j.jclepro.2017.09.211

Jones, S., Van der Laan, S., Frost, G., & Loftus, J. (2008). The investment performance of socially responsible investment funds in Australia. *Journal of Business Ethics, 80*(2), 181–203. doi:10.100710551-007-9412-6

Julong, D. (1989). Introduction to grey system theory. *Journal of Grey System, 1*(1), 1–24.

KAP Public Disclosure Platform. (2021). *Yatırım Fonları.* https://www.kap.org.tr/tr/YatirimFonlari/YF

Karaatlı, M., Ömürbek, N., Budak, İ., & Dağ, O. (2015). Çok kriterli karar verme yöntemleri ile yaşanabilir illerin sıralanması. *Selçuk Üniversitesi Sosyal Bilimler Enstitüsü Dergisi, 33,* 215–228.

Karmakar, P., Paromita, D., & Biswas, S. (2018). Assessment of mutual fund performance using distance based multi-criteria decision making techniques: An Indian perspective. *Research Bulletin (International Commission for the Northwest Atlantic Fisheries), 44*(1), 17–38. doi:10.33516/rb.v44i1.17-38p

Kreander, N., Gray, R. H., Power, D. M., & Sinclair, C. D. (2005). Evaluating the performance of ethical and non-ethical funds: A matched pair analysis. *Journal of Business Finance & Accounting, 32*(7-8), 1465–1493. doi:10.1111/j.0306-686X.2005.00636.x

Kurtz, L. (1997). No effect, or no net effect? Studies on socially responsible investing. *Journal of Investing, 6*(4), 37–49. doi:10.3905/joi.1997.37

Kuzmina, J., Atstaja, D., Purvins, M., Baakashvili, G., & Chkareuli, V. (2023). In search of sustainability and financial returns: The case of ESG energy funds. *Sustainability (Basel), 15*(3), 1–16. doi:10.3390u15032716

Lean, H. H., Ang, W. R., & Smyth, R. (2015). Performance and performance persistence of socially responsible investment funds in Europe and North America. *The North American Journal of Economics and Finance, 34,* 254–266. doi:10.1016/j.najef.2015.09.011

Lin, J. J., Chiang, M. C., & Chang, C. H. (2007). A comparison of usual indices and extended TOPSIS methods in mutual funds' performance evaluation. *Journal of Statistics and Management Systems, 10*(6), 869–883. doi:10.1080/09720510.2007.10701289

Louche, C., & Lydenberg, S. (2006). Socially responsible investment: Differences between Europe and the United States. *Vlerick Leuven Gent Working Paper Series,* 2006/22.

Lozano, J. M., Albareda, L., & Balaguer, M. R. (2006). Socially responsible investment in the Spanish financial market. *Journal of Business Ethics, 69*(3), 305–316. doi:10.100710551-006-9092-7

Luther, R. G., Matatko, J., & Corner, D. C. (1992). The investment performance of U.K. "ethical" unit trusts. *Accounting, Auditing & Accountability Journal, 5*(4), 57–70. doi:10.1108/09513579210019521

Mallin, C. A., Saadouni, B., & Briston, R. J. (1995). The financial performance of ethical investment funds. *Journal of Business Finance & Accounting, 22*(4), 483–496. doi:10.1111/j.1468-5957.1995.tb00373.x

Milonas, N., Rompotis, G., & Moutzouris, C. (2022). The Performance of ESG Funds vis-à-vis Non-ESG Funds. *The Journal of Impact and ESG Investing, 2*(4), 96–115. doi:10.3905/jesg.2022.1.041

Morgan, S. (2018). *Sustainable Signals: New Data from the Individual Investor*. https://www.morganstanley.com/pub/content/dam/msdotcom/ideas/sustainablesignals/pdf/Sustainabl_Signals_Whitepaper.pdf

Morgan Stanley. (2019a). *Sustainability Reality: Analyzing Risks and Returns of Sustainable Funds*. https://www.morganstanley.com/content/dam/msdotcom/ideas/sustainable-investing-offers-financial-performance-lowered risk/Sustainable_Reality_Analyzing_Risk_and_Returns_of_Sustainable_Funds.pdf

Morgan Stanley. (2019b). *Sustainable Signals: Growth and Opportunity in Asset Management*. https://www.morganstanley.com/assets/pdfs/2415532_Sustainable_Signals_Asset_Mgmt_L.pdf

Musbah, H., Ali, G., Aly, H. H., & Little, T. A. (2022). Energy management using multi-criteria decision making and machine learning classification algorithms for intelligent system. *Electric Power Systems Research*, *203*, 107645. Advance online publication. doi:10.1016/j.epsr.2021.107645

Perks, R. W., Rawlinson, D. H., & Ingram, L. (1992). An exploration of ethical investment in the UK. *The British Accounting Review*, *24*(1), 43–65. doi:10.1016/S0890-8389(05)80066-6

Renneboog, L., Horst, J. T., & Zhang, C. (2008). Socially responsible investments: Institutional aspects, performance, and investor behavior. *Journal of Banking & Finance*, *32*(9), 1723–1742. doi:10.1016/j.jbankfin.2007.12.039

Rivoli, P. (2003). Making a difference or making a statement? Finance research and socially responsible investment. *Business Ethics Quarterly*, *13*(3), 271–287. doi:10.5840/beq200313323

Rodriguez, J. (2010). The performance of socially responsible mutual funds: A volatility-match approach. *Review of Accounting and Finance*, *9*(2), 180–188. doi:10.1108/14757701011044189

Rosen, B. N., Sandler, D. M., & Shani, D. (1991). Social issues and socially responsible investment behavior: A preliminary empirical investigation. *The Journal of Consumer Affairs*, *25*(2), 221–234. doi:10.1111/j.1745-6606.1991.tb00003.x

Sandberg, J., Juravle, C., Hedesström, T. M., & Hamilton, I. (2009). The heterogeneity of socially responsible investment. *Journal of Business Ethics*, *87*(4), 519–533. doi:10.100710551-008-9956-0

Sarkar, S. (2022). Performance evaluation of ESG funds in India – A study. *The Management Accountant*, *57*(3), 40–47. doi:10.33516/maj.v57i3.40-47p

Sauer, D. A. (1997). The impact of social-responsibility screens on investment performance: Evidence from the Domini 400 social index and Domini Equity Mutual Fund. *Review of Financial Economics*, *6*(2), 137–149. doi:10.1016/S1058-3300(97)90002-1

Schröder, M. (2003). *Socially responsible investments in Germany, Switzerland and the United States - an analysis of investment funds and indices*. ZEW Discussion Paper, 03–10. doi:10.2139/ssrn.421462

Schröder, M. (2004). The performance of socially responsible investments: Investment funds and indices. *Financial Markets and Portfolio Management*, *18*(2), 122–142. doi:10.100711408-004-0202-1

Shannon, C. E. (1948). A note on the concept of entropy. *The Bell System Technical Journal*, *27*(3), 379–423. doi:10.1002/j.1538-7305.1948.tb01338.x

Statman, M. (2000). Socially responsible mutual funds. *Financial Analysts Journal, 56*(3), 30–39. doi:10.2469/faj.v56.n3.2358

Tampakoudis, I., Kiosses, N., & Petridis, K. (2023). The impact of mutual funds' ESG scores on their financial performance during the COVID-19 pandemic. A data envelopment analysis. *Corporate Governance (Bradford)*. Advance online publication. doi:10.1108/CG-12-2022-0491

TEFAS Türkiye Electronic Fund Trading Platform. (2021). *Fon Detaylı Analiz.* https://www.tefas.gov.tr/FonAnaliz.aspx

Tripathi, V., & Bhandari, V. (2015). Socially responsible stocks: A boon for investors in India. *Journal of Advances in Management Research, 12*(2), 209–225. doi:10.1108/JAMR-03-2014-0021

Tsolas, I. E. (2019). Utility exchange traded fund performance evaluation. A comparative approach using grey relational analysis and data envelopment analysis modelling. *International Journal of Financial Studies, 7*(4), 1–9. doi:10.3390/ijfs7040067

United Nations Conference on Trade and Development. (2021). *World Investment Report 2021, Investing in Sustainable Recovery.* United Nations Publications. https://unctad.org/system/files/official-document/wir2021_en.pdf

United Nations Conference on Trade and Development. (2022). *World Investment Report 2022, International Tax Reforms and Sustainable Investment.* United Nations Publications. https://unctad.org/system/files/official-document/wir2022_en.pdf

Yanık, S., Içke, B. T., & Aytürk, Y. (2010). Sosyal sorumlu yatırım fonları ve performans özellikleri. *İstanbul Üniversitesi Siyasal Bilgiler Fakültesi Dergisi, 43*, 109-134.

Zhang, N., Zhang, Y., & Zong, Z. (2023). Fund ESG performance and downside risk: Evidence from China. *International Review of Financial Analysis, 86*, 1–20. doi:10.1016/j.irfa.2023.102526

KEY TERMS AND DEFINITIONS

Alpha: Alpha shows the average return difference between the selected benchmark and the fund.

Annual Return: Represents the annual returns of the fund.

Beta: Beta indicates the direction and level of the relationship between the returns of the selected benchmark and the fund returns.

Downside Risk: Downside risk expresses the loss value of the fund that may be observed in the worst-case scenario that may be encountered during the selected period.

Entropy: Entropy method is used to determine the weights of criteria in multi-criteria decision-making problems.

GRA: Gray relational analysis method is a method that provides meaningful results as a rating, classification and decision-making technique in cases where there is insufficient, incomplete or imprecise data.

Maximum Loss: Maximum loss refers to the largest rate of decline realized in the period under consideration.

Multi-Criteria Decision-Making Methods: Multi-criteria decision-making techniques consist of approaches and methods that try to reach the "best/appropriate" possible solution that meets multiple conflicting criteria.

Pension Funds: The pension fund is an asset created by the pension company for the purpose of managing the contributions within the framework of the pension contract and monitored in the Private Pension System accounts according to the principles of risk distribution and fiduciary ownership.

Sharpe: Sharpe ratio expresses the level of return to be obtained for each 1 unit of risk incurred.

Sortino: Sortino ratio expresses the level of return to be obtained for each 1 unit of negative risk incurred.

Sustainable Funds: Sustainable funds invest in the shares and lease certificates of companies that give importance to the environment, society, and corporate governance in accordance with ESG criteria.

TOPSIS: The TOPSIS method uses the proximity of the variables to the ideal solution when ranking. When finding the ideal solution, both the proximity to the positive ideal solution and the distance to the negative ideal solution are taken into account.

Treynor: The ratio of the fund's return to the Beta of the selected benchmark.

VaR: VaR indicates the highest probability of loss if the fund is held for a certain period of time.

Chapter 3
Extinction Accounting:
An Analysis of Petrobras' Voluntary Disclosure

Bianca Moraes Fernandes
Federal University of Pará, Brazil

Adriana Rodrigues Silva
https://orcid.org/0000-0003-1538-6877
Polytechnic Institute of Santarém, Portugal & CICF-Research Centre on Accounting and Taxation, Portugal

Risolene Alves Macena Araújo
https://orcid.org/0000-0001-6423-6299
Federal University of Pará, Brazil

Rui Costa Robalo
Polytechnic Institute of Santarém, Portugal & CICF-Research Centre on Accounting and Taxation, Portugal

ABSTRACT

This chapter analyses the extinction accounting within Petrobras' integrated report and its sustainability report. To accomplish this, the authors have scrutinized the disclosure of the impact of the company's operational activities on affected species and their habitats. The analysis has been conducted using the theoretical framework adapted from Maroun and Atkins, which assesses six key elements: (1) the context of extinction accounting, (2) action-focused reports, (3) partner reports, (4) analysis and reflection, (5) evaluation, and (6) disclosure. Despite encountering the general elements, it was noted that the intended objectives were not fully met. The reports under scrutiny lack information regarding the species affected by the company's operations or address the impacts generated by its activities, offering only vague references to the resources employed or the outcomes achieved by the company.

DOI: 10.4018/978-1-6684-9076-1.ch003

INTRODUCTION

While profit-seeking motives often drive the intensified exploitation of available resources (Gupta et al., 2022), there is a mounting recognition of the imperative to acknowledge the escalating environmental repercussions on species and their habitats (Roberts et al., 2021). In response to this evolving context, the concept of extinction accounting is gaining prominence as a novel approach for companies to comprehensively assess and quantify the ecological impacts stemming from their operations (Roberts et al., 2021; Hassan et al., 2020). Simultaneously, it empowers stakeholders to gain a deeper understanding of the environmental footprint associated with a company's financial outcomes (Schaltegger et al., 2023). In this chapter, we propose to analyze how extinction accounting is included in the Integrated Report and in the Sustainability Report of an important Brazilian company, Petrobras.

Animals endure the loss of their natural habitats and disruptions in their food chains, often resulting in extinction. The Chico Mendes Institute for Biodiversity Conservation (ICMBio), and many other institutions like, the International Union for Conservation of Nature (IUCN), the Worldwide Fund for Nature (WWF), etc., maintains a list of endangered species. Nevertheless, the actual count of threatened species may surpass this figure, given the challenge of estimating the total number of existing species. Additionally, many species may have already gone extinct even before their discovery, as exemplified by the scientific survey "Mapping the Biosphere" (Wheeler et al., 2012).

The rising rates of species extinction have raised grave concerns among researchers. For instance, Ceballos et al. (2017) assert that planet Earth is currently grappling with a crisis of species extinction and a profound decline in populations, triggering a cascade of detrimental impacts on ecosystem functioning and essential societal services. While mass extinctions are a natural part of the planet's historical cycle, it is undeniable that the extent of extinction attributed to human activities - estimated to be approximately 1,000 to 10,000 times higher than previously recorded (World Wildlife Fund - WWF) - stands as an unprecedented event in human history and an anomaly in Earth's evolutionary record (Ceballos et al., 2015). In the past 65 million years, there has been no such accelerated decimation of fauna as witnessed today, sparking speculation that human overexploitation of the biosphere may trigger the planet's sixth mass extinction event (Barnosky et al., 2011; Ceballos et al., 2015; Jones, 2014; Kolbert, 2014).

Preserving ecosystems and promoting biodiversity are of paramount importance and should be treated as urgent matters. As highlighted by De Boer and Van Bergen (2012), ecosystem degradation ranks among the top ten anticipated challenges for the next two decades, underscoring the critical role that ecosystem preservation and biodiversity promotion play in ensuring the survival of both humanity and businesses. Furthermore, the report recommends that companies should increase their focus on assessing their reliance on natural resources.

Preventing extinction is a shared responsibility, and academia should utilize its resources to contribute to this effort. Extinction accounting has emerged as a burgeoning subject in accounting research, yet a singular concept to define it remains elusive. Atkins and Maroun (2018) describe it as an evolution of sustainability and biodiversity reporting, transcending the mere documentation of what a company consumes or achieves to encompass a deeper understanding of the ecological, economic, social, and ethical impacts stemming from its activities. Given that ecological losses may not always influence stakeholder decisions, it becomes imperative for companies to communicate the recognition that the absence of a particular species or ecosystem directly (or indirectly) affects their operations (Atkins & Maroun, 2018; Gaia & Jones, 2017; Russell et al., 2017).

Research in the field of extinction accounting holds the potential to provide substantial practical and theoretical contributions. This chapter's primary contributions are centered on increasing awareness and transparency concerning biodiversity and the associated risks of extinction. Moreover, it aims to underscore the capacity of extinction accounting to inform corporate decision-making processes, enabling companies to evaluate the financial risks stemming from biodiversity depletion and to formulate strategies for risk mitigation. Additionally, this study can foster stakeholder engagement, facilitate the formulation of public policies pertaining to conservation and corporate environmental responsibility, enhance corporate sustainability practices, and promote public education and awareness concerning biodiversity. Furthermore, this chapter extends the existing body of literature on extinction accounting by scrutinizing an entity from a developing country, Brazil. Its objective is to analyze how extinction accounting is included in Petrobras' Integrated Report and Sustainability Report. To achieve this, the study will employ the theoretical framework adapted from Maroun and Atkins (2018) to assess the disclosure of the impact of the company's operational activities on affected species and their habitats.

This study is organized into several sections. The following section conducts a literature review encompassing Brazilian biodiversity, endangered species, and extinction accounting. It also furnishes background information on Petrobras and its integrated reporting practices. Subsequently, in section 3, the research methods are elaborated upon. Section 4 presents and discusses the empirical results obtained in the context of the adopted theoretical framework. Finally, in section 5, the study offers conclusions, highlights its contributions, acknowledges limitations, and proposes directions for future research.

LITERATURE REVIEW

Brazilian Biodiversity and Endangered Species

Brazil is renowned for its vast array of fauna and flora species. With over 120 thousand species of invertebrates and approximately 8,930 species of vertebrates, including 734 mammals, 1,982 birds, 732 reptiles, 973 amphibians, 3,150 continental fish, and 1,358 marine fish, the country boasts the world's richest biodiversity. Regrettably, 1,173 of these species are classified as endangered (Ministério do Meio Ambiente, 2014; 2014a). Among 17 countries, Brazil houses an astonishing 70% of the planet's species diversity, making it a global biodiversity hotspot (Scarano & Ceotto, 2016).

The responsibility and obligation to avert the threat of further species extinction fall upon society, public authorities, and the private sector. The unsustainable exploitation of the biosphere poses risks to both animals and humans. Scarano and Ceotto (2016) underscore the significance of biodiversity in ecosystem functioning, emphasizing that each animal plays a pivotal role on our planet. Biodiversity is indispensable for human survival and well-being, as it ensures a wide array of ecosystem services, including food security, water quality and quantity, climate stability, cultural diversity, and more.

Numerous studies (e.g., Atkins & Maroun, 2018; Baillie et al., 2004; Scarano & Ceotto, 2016; Diamond, 1989; Thomas et al., 2004) endeavor to comprehend the primary contributors to mass extinctions. Among these factors, the most frequently cited include habitat loss, monoculture, global warming, and climate change (Atkins & Maroun, 2018); invasions by exotic species; the use of pesticides and herbicides; excessive human hunting and fishing; and pollution (Adler et al., 2018). While all of these factors are highly detrimental, some authors regard ecosystem conversion (Adler et al., 2018) and habitat destruction (Atkins & Maroun, 2018) as the most severe.

Institutions such as the International Union for the Conservation of Nature (IUCN) and the Chico Mendes Institute for Biodiversity Conservation (ICMBio) conduct research on habitats and biomes to monitor endangered species and assess their level of threat. The IUCN oversees the Red List, which serves as a global indicator of biodiversity health. Beyond being a comprehensive report on species and their status, the Red List serves as a crucial tool for raising awareness and galvanizing efforts to conserve biodiversity and drive policy changes necessary for safeguarding natural resources. It provides information on species' geographic range, population size, habitat and ecology, utilization or trade, threats, and conservation measures, all of which assist in making informed conservation decisions (IUCN)[1].

ICMBio is entrusted with the management of Federal Conservation Units in Brazil, with a mission to safeguard the country's natural heritage and promote the socio-environmental development of traditional communities. The institute maintains the Biodiversity Portal, an extensive repository of data and information pertaining to Brazilian biodiversity. This repository encompasses data generated by the institute itself, as well as information received from the Ministry of Environment and other affiliated institutions. Through this portal, users can access information on endangered species, categorized by taxonomy, geographic distribution, time frame, and data source.

A query of the public records available in this portal, focusing solely on the animal category, reveals a total of 619,312 records, with 42,848 corresponding to threatened species, while 576,464 belong to non-threatened species. Among the group of 42,848 threatened species, 21,785 are classified as vulnerable, 14,849 as endangered, 6,211 as critically endangered, and 3 as extinct in the wild.

These figures underscore the existence of a significant number of species facing the imminent threat of extinction, which places a considerable responsibility on society at large, as well as on companies, academics, and the scientific community. These stakeholders must actively mobilize their resources and expertise to contribute to the reversal of this alarming trend. The subsequent subsection of this literature review section will explore the contributions made by accounting researchers to this vital discourse.

Extinction Accounting

Companies incorporate non-financial data into their annual reports; however, there is a noticeable variation in both the quality and quantity of such information. Companies often prioritize the disclosure of information related to Sustainable Development Goals (SDGs) associated with health, education, and gender equality (Gazolla et al., 2020). Regarding extinction accounting, there is an ongoing debate concerning the initial shortcomings of environmental accounting in the ecological context (Russell et al., 2017). Certain studies (e.g., Jones & Solomon, 2013; Mansoor & Maroun, 2016; Gaia & Jones, 2017) have critiqued early efforts in biodiversity reporting and accounting, contending that these reports were primarily descriptive and posed challenges in aligning with the goals of emancipatory accounting and species reporting. This agenda can be challenging to grasp, may appear overly scientific, and might not effectively convey the concept of accountability towards species and wildlife, nor does it effectively communicate the urgency of addressing species extinction (Jones & Solomon, 2013).

Some criticisms of biodiversity reporting have been presented by several researchers (e.g., Adler et al., 2018; Gray & Milne, 2018; Weir, 2018). These researchers have explored the concept of extinction accounting as a solution. This new perspective on environmental accounting allows entities to present in their report's descriptions of the environments in which they operate, as well as the consequences of habitat exploitation and the consequences of species extinction (Atkins & Maroun, 2018; Jones, 2010; Jones & Solomon, 2013).

From accountants' perspective, Gray and Milne (2018) have proposed an accounting narrative that delves into not only the symptoms associated with species extinction but also its underlying causes, with human activity being a primary factor. The authors contend that humans are not external to nature but are, in fact, responsible for extinctions, habitat loss, environmental degradation, and climate change, among other ecological challenges. They caution that these catastrophic events are not external issues but rather internal problems stemming from society's economic and capitalist system. Consequently, it is imperative for accounting and accountability reports to convey the message that nature is an integral component of the system, not an isolated entity.

Equally concerned about species extinction, Adler et al. (2018) emphasize the significance of publicizing both its manifestations and underlying causes. Their research involved an examination of the annual ranking of the world's 500 largest companies by gross revenue, as published by Fortune magazine. Focusing on the top 150 companies, they applied an index developed by Adler et al. (2017) to assess the extent to which these companies disclosed information pertaining to biodiversity and their practices related to species conservation. The authors also investigated how collaborations between these companies and partners in biodiversity and industry influenced their reporting on biodiversity and endangered species. Their findings revealed that fewer than 15 companies produced substantial reports detailing the impacts of their operations, indicating a limited level of concern among these corporations regarding the factors contributing to species extinction and its observable consequences.

Cuckston (2018) examines the utility of the IUCN Red List as a tool for species conservation and the prevention of extinction. This study scrutinizes the mechanisms and classifications employed by the Red List, ultimately concluding that the categorization of extinction risk represents a simplification of intricate information. The author contends that it is imperative to integrate both quantitative calculations and qualitative assessments, bridging the gap between the Red List's historical development and construction and the concepts from the "social studies of finance literature." Cuckston posits that accounting can serve as a liberating instrument, possessing the potential for transformation and advancement. Moreover, the Red List can function in an emancipatory capacity within the realms of accounting or extinction auditing, potentially averting extinction when applied judiciously.

In the context of the UK public sector and its endeavors to embrace extinction-related accounting practices, Weir (2018) adopted a unique perspective. His approach highlights that the prevention of future extinctions relies more on the willingness of stakeholders than on the availability of funding initiatives. Nevertheless, the author contends that the absence of financial investments in species protection necessitates difficult choices, as there are insufficient resources to avert extinctions. This challenge arises from the complexities associated with researching biodiversity and implementing nature accounting within the public sector.

Amidst the escalating discourse in the field of accounting, innovative ideas aimed at mitigating species extinction are emerging. For instance, Atkins et al. (2018) advocate for the establishment of an extinction accounting framework, building upon the foundation of the Global Reporting Initiative (GRI) standards and extending its scope to encompass the interplay with species featured on the IUCN Red List. Their objective is to illustrate the transformative potential of such reporting. The researchers conducted an analysis of disclosures made by South Africa's largest companies, with a specific focus on initiatives aimed at conserving South African rhinos. By interpreting disclosures across integrated reports, sustainability reports, and company websites, they unearthed a profound commitment to ethical conduct and a genuine dedication to rhino conservation.

The key takeaway from their study is that extinction accounting emerges as a product of evolving societal norms and heightened ecological awareness, driven by a growing recognition of the threats to biodiversity and the stark reality of extinction. Notably, the disclosure of information concerning rhinos can be construed as emancipatory, signifying that companies are not merely reporting for managerial purposes but, rather, to combat the decline of species that hold cultural and biological significance.

Another theoretical framework for extinction accounting was introduced by Atkins and Maroun (2018). This framework highlights the assessment of the value associated with the loss of plant and animal species. It proposes an unconventional approach to valuation, wherein the measurement focuses on the impact of a species' extinction on its ecosystem, rather than valuing natural capital per se. This discussion prompts critical inquiries, including: "What is the significance of species extinction?", "What are the financial implications for companies in the event of extinction?", and "What is the financial value at risk in the face of potential extinction?" The ultimate aim is to underscore the urgency of averting species extinction.

In the paper authored by Maroun and Atkins (2018), an analysis is conducted on the treatment of extinction prevention within integrated reporting, and a practical approach to implementing the authors' theoretical framework of extinction accounting is presented. The primary objective is to ascertain whether "biodiversity accounting" holds emancipatory potential or remains a surface-level approach to nature and wildlife, primarily centered around the principles of extinction from the Global Reporting Initiative (GRI).

The authors conclude that by employing Atkins and Maroun's (2018) framework in conjunction with existing literature and the GRI, it becomes feasible to formulate statements, reports, and narratives that comprehensively depict the species impacted by business operations, both in terms of geographic distribution and operational aspects. This can, in turn, foster greater awareness regarding the biodiversity impact generated. Nevertheless, Atkins and Maroun (2018), alongside Romi and Longing (2017) and Tregidga (2013), engage in discussions about how corporate initiatives aimed at preventing extinction may inadvertently exhibit hegemonic and anthropocentric attitudes toward nature, consequently diminishing the emancipatory potential of extinction accounting.

Maroun and Atkins (2018) contend that if extinction accounting fails to be emancipatory or, at the very least, progressive in its approach to nature, it could result in further declines in populations or species.

As previously mentioned, the interconnectedness of species underscores the significance of each organism in preserving the natural balance of the ecosystem. Nevertheless, accurately quantifying the risk associated with the loss of individual species, such as flebotomíneos or "*tocandiras*" ants, proves challenging. Nonetheless, scientists can evaluate the global impact of the loss of ecosystem services. The objective of the theoretical framework in extinction accounting is not to assign costs to companies or items within financial statements but rather to illustrate the enormity of the consequences resulting from the extinction of a species (Atkins & Maroun, 2018). Moreover, it's crucial to emphasize that companies should focus on disclosing non-financial information that is materially relevant to their businesses and sustainability, rather than attempting to report everything requested by stakeholders (Tsagas & Villiers, 2020).

Furthermore, Petrobras primarily operates with a profit-oriented approach, which could potentially contribute to increased exploitation of the biosphere. As a result, the objective of this chapter is to closely examine the incorporation of extinction accounting into Petrobras' Integrated Report and Sustainability Report. The goal is to understand how Petrobras discloses information related to the impact on biodiversity resulting from its operations and its proposed strategies for mitigating associated risks. In contrast to previous research that has concentrated on developed country-specific cases (Roberts et al., 2021), this study aims to investigate these aspects within the Brazilian context, using one of the largest corporations in the country. Due to its prominent position, Petrobras attracts significant attention from the media, the public, NGOs, governmental entities, and the private sector (Adler et al., 2018).

Petrobras

As one of Brazil's foremost companies, Petrobras exerts influence across economic, social, and environmental dimensions (Voss, 2016). Its primary focus lies in energy generation, and its scope of operations encompasses oil and gas exploration and production, power generation, oil and gas refining, petrochemicals, distribution, biofuel production, transportation, and marketing[2].

In the Fact Sheet dated August 12, 2019 (Petrobras), it is stated that Petrobras, boasting 48 years of experience in developing Brazilian offshore basins, holds a global leadership position in this sector. The company ranks among Latin America's largest publicly traded corporations, with a market value of $94.4 billion as of July 31, 2019. Petrobras' common and preferred shares are listed on prominent stock exchanges, including the São Paulo Stock Exchange (B3), New York Stock Exchange, Madrid Stock Exchange, and Buenos Aires Stock Exchange, with a collective shareholder base exceeding 600,000 individuals and entities.

The shareholder composition is divided, with the controlling block, inclusive of the Federal Union, BNDES, BNDESPar, Social Participation Fund, and Caixa Econômica Federal, holding 43% of the voting shares. In contrast, foreigners on the B3 account for 21%, Brazilians on the B3 hold 19%, and 17% of shares are listed on the New York Stock Exchange. In 2018, Petrobras reported a net income of R$25.8 billion and a Last Twelve Months (LTM) income of R$31.6 billion.

Petrobras places a significant emphasis on sustainability, notably through its Commitment to Life program, which seeks to enhance safety standards throughout its operational processes. Additionally, the company actively works towards reducing greenhouse gas emissions, resulting in an 8% reduction from 2017 to 2018.

On its website[iii], Petrobras provides information regarding its socio-environmental programs, highlighting investments exceeding R$1 billion, the involvement of more than 2 million hectares in productive reconversion activities, efforts in the restoration of degraded areas, and forest conservation/management. Moreover, the company engages with over 975 thousand individuals through educational initiatives and has produced approximately 90,039 specialized publications. Their initiatives directly impact around 470 fauna species and involve work with approximately 1,000 species of flora. However, this information is presented solely in numerical terms, without specifying the particular species or biomes undergoing these initiatives.

There are criticisms regarding the information released by Petrobras. Voss (2016) argues that the company's overwhelming emphasis on economic development tends to overshadow sustainability, which should be at the heart of Petrobras' operations. This underscores how the construction of social and environmental accounting within the company contributes minimally, if at all, to the transition toward sustainability. Additionally, Voss cites the case of corruption within the company, where issues such as contract overbilling and unsustainable fossil fuel practices demonstrate a misalignment between the company's actions and its information disclosure. Furthermore, Voss contends that the presentation of social and environmental accounting distorts the connotations associated with sustainability, confining this accounting to serving the interests and representing the perspectives of the most influential groups.

Integrated Reporting

Commencing in South Africa in 1994, the King Code of Corporate Governance Principles, often referred to as King I, incorporated corporate governance indicators known for their inclusivity in providing information to a broader spectrum of stakeholders, rather than solely catering to shareholders' interests (Dumay et al., 2016; Gibassier, 2015). Subsequently, in 2013, the International Integrated Reporting Council (IIRC) published a proposed framework for Integrated Reporting (IIRC, 2013), which solicited input from various interested stakeholders (Dumay et al., 2016). Within this framework, the IIRC articulated its objective as follows:

Improve the quality of information available to providers of financial capital to enable a more efficient and productive allocation of capital. Promote a more cohesive and efficient approach to corporate reporting that draws on different reporting strands and communicates the full range of factors that materially affect the ability of an organization to create value over time. Enhance accountability and stewardship for the broad base of capitals (financial, manufactured, intellectual, human, social and relationship, and natural) and promote understanding of their interdependencies. Support integrated thinking, decision-making and actions that focus on the creation of value over the short, medium and long term. (IIRC, 2013, p. 2)

Supporting Integrated Reporting, Flower (2015) contends that conventional accounting reports fall short in offering a comprehensive view of a company's historical and prospective performance. Meanwhile, there is growing societal scrutiny surrounding corporations' raison d'être, as the existing information primarily elucidates their wealth generation mechanisms, omitting the broader spectrum of value creation encompassing individuals, society, and the environment (Gray, 2010). Integrated Reporting, in turn, offers an innovation by demonstrating value creation over time, considering the interconnectedness between different types of capital, and including specific biodiversity data in reports (Eccles & Krzus, 2010; Eccles et al., 2011; Solomon & Maroun, 2012). Thus, biodiversity should be adequately portrayed in reports, given its importance as environmental or natural capital for the corporation's activities.

Brazilian legislation, as outlined in Law no. 6.404 of December 15, 1976 (Brazil, 1976), as subsequently amended by Law no. 11.638 of December 28, 2007 (Brazil, 2007), mandates that companies are required to furnish a range of obligatory financial statements. These encompass the balance sheet, statement of retained earnings, statement of income for the year, statement of cash flows, and, in the case of publicly traded companies such as Petrobras, the statement of added value. Furthermore, in accordance with the Technical Pronouncement CPC 26 (R1) from the Accounting Pronouncements Committee, companies are also obligated to provide the statement of comprehensive income for the period, statements of changes in equity, explanatory notes, and the balance sheet from the earliest available period.

Integrated reporting is not currently mandatory in Brazil; however, its significance has been duly acknowledged. The RIO+20 Declaration, emanating from the United Nations Conference on Sustainable Development held in Brazil in 2012, underscores the importance of incorporating sustainable information into corporate reporting. Governments, industries, and stakeholders are encouraged to foster best practice models and facilitate the integration of sustainable reporting, with the support of the UN system. Furthermore, the recognition of Integrated Reporting gained additional ground on December 9, 2020, when the Securities and Exchange Commission (CVM) issued Resolution No. 14. This resolution mandates that publicly-held companies, when choosing to prepare and disclose an Integrated Report, must adhere to CPC Guideline 09 – Integrated Report.

Given the visibility and impact of Petrobras' activities in Brazil, the Integrated Report and Sustainability Report for the year 2018 were selected for analysis. Integrated Reporting was chosen due to its integrated thinking process, which results in periodic reports that present data on value creation over time and other communications related to value creation. (IIRC, 2013)

RESEARCH METHOD

This study has adopted a qualitative approach to comprehend the integration of extinction accounting within Petrobras' 2018 Integrated Report and Sustainability Report. The years 2017 and 2018 are the only periods that featured the integrated report. We selected the year 2018 due to its status as the most recent publication of the integrated report and Petrobras' prior experience in producing the report for the year 2017. Updating the data would necessitate an analysis of distinct documents related to the year 2018.

Consequently, this research relies on pertinent documentary data made available by the company. The analysis primarily seeks information pertaining to biodiversity, the environment, species, and threats to extinction. Additionally, to enhance the analysis, the websites of projects mentioned in the 2018 Sustainability Report were scrutinized, including *"Projeto Golfinho Rotador," "Projeto Albatroz Brasil,"* and *"Projeto Mantas Brasil."* The analytical framework employed is based on adaptations from Maroun and Atkins (2018) (Table 1).

Maroun and Atkins (2018) present a theoretical framework comprising six elements for the analysis of disclosures related to extinction or impacted species within integrated reports. This interpretive analysis, in certain aspects, adopts a critical perspective to evaluate its alignment with the extinction accounting concepts proposed in the existing literature. A theoretical framework for extinction accounting should encompass the following objectives: (i) provision of sufficient information regarding impacted species; (ii) elucidation of the rationale for concerns about extinction; and (iii) presentation of policies, plans, and actions taken to address potential extinctions consistently and through ongoing revision (Jones, 1996; Jones & Solomon, 2013; Tregidga, 2013). The criteria employed for evaluating the results were as follows:

- Element 1 presents information in tables, graphs, images, or descriptions, in accordance with GRI304 recommendations for disclosing impacted species, habitats, geographic areas, and species listed on the IUCN Red List, among other details. Nonetheless, Maroun and Atkins' (2018) theoretical framework for extinction accounting broadens the range of disclosure options with the objective of enhancing the likelihood of comprehension and implementation of the proposed accounting approach. This becomes particularly significant given the constraints of the GRI framework and the imperative to establish an emancipatory and efficient extinction accounting system.
- Elements 2 and 3 center on the company's collaborations with non-governmental organizations or other institutions engaged in biodiversity conservation. These collaborations underscore the company's acknowledgment of its impact on biodiversity and its efforts to mitigate these effects by working in tandem with established organizations to fulfill its environmental responsibilities. This information is pertinent for comprehending the directives outlined in corporate codes that underscore the significance of having comprehensive policies and plans to underpin strategic objectives.

- Elements 4 and 5 are designed to grasp the strategies put into effect subsequent to their implementation, aligning with the integrated reporting approach that evaluates management and disclosure post-implementation by managers (IIRC, 2013; IOD, 2016). Within the context of extinction accounting, the reporting should furnish details concerning the risks confronting the company in relation to species extinction, the actions taken to rectify this situation, and the outcomes, both positive and negative (Atkins et al., 2016). Consequently, the analysis incorporates elements of self-critique, introspection, and the reevaluation of strategies.

Finally, with regard to Element 6, an assessment is conducted to determine whether all the elements and components of the theoretical framework are integrated into the opinions, reports, and other information disseminated to users. The company is expected to provide a clear and objective explanation of the interrelation between the risk of species loss and the strategies implemented, alongside information about the outcomes and their level of success (IIRC, 2013).

Table 1. Elements in an extinction accounting framework

Elements	Purposes	Items
Extinction accounting context (1)	Describe the extinction risk in the context of the company's business and the diverse reasons for wanting to address this risk.	1.1 Record a list of plant and animal species, identified as endangered by the IUCN Red List, whose habitats are affected by the company's activities. 1.2 Report where, geographically, the company's activities pose a threat to endangered plant and animal species, as identified by the IUCN Red List. 1.3 Report potential risks/impacts on these specific species arising from the company's operations (equivalent to the existing GRI principles to this point). 1.4 Incorporate images (photos or drawings, for example) of threatened species which are affected by the company's operations and which the company needs to protect. 1.5 Report full details (narrative as well as financial figures) relating to any fines or ongoing claims relating to endangered species legislation. 1.6 Report corporate expressions of moral, ethical, emotional, financial and reputational motivations for preserving species and preventing extinction (to respond to diverse needs and requirements of different stakeholders/readers).
Action-focused reporting (2)	Explain the actions the company takes and plans to take to reduce extinction risk.	2.1 Report actions/initiatives taken by the company to avoid harm to, and to prevent extinction of, endangered plant and animal species.
Partnership reporting (3)	Complement action-focused reporting by explaining broader partnerships/initiatives formed to combat/reverse extinction trends.	3.1 Report partnerships/engagement between wildlife/nature/conservation organizations and the company which aim to address corporate impacts on endangered species and report the outcome/impact of engagement/partnerships on endangered species.
Analysis and reflection (4)	Evaluation of extinction prevention initiatives against aims/targets to inform changes to actions and partnerships.	4.1 Report assessment and reflection on outcome/impact of engagement/partnerships and decisions taken about necessary changes to policy/initiatives going forward.
Assessment (5)	Audit of affected species/populations/biomes.	5.1 Report regular assessments (audit) of species populations in areas affected by corporate operations.
Reporting (6)	Provide an account of the progress made to date on preventing or mitigating extinction, planned future actions and risk exposure.	6.1 Report assessment of whether or not corporate initiatives/actions are assisting in prevention of species extinction. 6.2 Report strategy for the future development and improvement of actions/initiatives: an iterative process. 6.3 Ensure that the whole process of 'extinction accounting' is integrated into corporate strategy and is incorporated into the company's integrated report, the company's business plan, corporate strategy and risk management/internal control system not resigned to separate sustainability reports or websites. 6.4 Potential liabilities relating to future possible legal fines/claims relating to endangered species impacts. 6.5 Discussion of ways in which the company is working to prevent future liabilities related to harming endangered species. 6.6 Provide pictorial representation of success in conservation – and of failure (i.e., habitat loss).

Source: Adapted from Maroun and Atkins (2018)

RESULTS

To exemplify the information that characterizes the six elements, some of the main clippings, by elements, from Petrobras' Integrated Report and Sustainability Report were selected for illustration in the following subsections.

Extinction Accounting Context (Element 1)

It is possible to observe corporate expressions by Petrobras, in its Integrated Report, to preserve species and prevent extinction in the way that item 1.6 proposes, exemplified by the following extract:

In 2018, we recorded 31 events with confirmed or probable impacts on fauna, flora or habitat, such as, for example, the suppression of vegetation, erosion and accidental death of animals in units. For all these events, we adopted measures to **mitigate, treat or recover the environmental impact***, such as replacing protected species and revegetation, treatment and recovery of degraded areas, adaptation of facilities and other measures. Aiming to prevent and mitigate the risks and impacts to fauna, as well as to human health, the safety of our employees and operational safety, we developed and started implementing 2018 corporate guidelines for fauna management in our operational units. (Integrated Report, 2018, p.49, emphasis added)*

It is possible to recognize that the information presented in the clipping can be related to items 1.3 and 2.1. However, there is no detail on the species affected, geographic areas, and biomes. What can be perceived is a generic statement by the Petrobras about its intention to preserve or avoid extinction.

In its Sustainability Report, the Petrobras makes available a wide range of information related to the environment, which provides some relevant information. However, it presents some deficiencies. For example, it complies with item 1.1 of the theoretical extinction accounting framework, providing the number of threatened species in national and international lists (IUCN), but does not specify which plant and animal species are included. Petrobras only lists the number of threatened species as you could see in the following extract:

Based on the national and international lists of threatened species, several species present in the areas of influence of our activities were identified. Number of Threatened Species - National List: **Vulnerable 136; Endangered 58; Critically endangered 35**. *Number of Threatened Species - International List (IUCN):* **Vulnerable 100; Endangered 42; Critically endangered 13**. *(Sustainability Report, 2018, p. 57, adapted, emphasis added)*

The mentioned descriptions are useful to raise stakeholders' awareness of important ecosystems and highlight that the company is aware of the impacts of its operations (Maroun & Atkins, 2018).

More detailed information on the species, their conservation status and habitats can be found on the projects' websites, with images incorporated into the Sustainability Report. However, although Petrobras has partnered with or sponsored them via the Petrobras Socio-environmental Program, none of the projects mentions the company's activities as a threat or interference with the animals. An example is the '*Projeto Golfinho Rotador*'s website, which registers the threatened species according to item 1.1 of the proposed theoretical framework as follows:

Stenella longirostris is classified as "insufficiently known" by the International Union for Conservation of Nature. . . . The ICMBio /MMA Action Plan for Aquatic Mammals of Brazil, which classifies the `golfinho rotador` in the category of "insufficient data", proposes the development of studies on the population dynamics and natural history of the dolphins of Fernando de Noronha, aiming to provide subsidies for *their conservation and management, such as the researches of the `Projeto Golfinho Rotador`. (Projeto Golfinho Rotador, 2019, conservation, adapted)*

Action-Focused and Partnership Reporting (Elements 2 and 3)

Concerning the measures implemented to mitigate the risk of extinction, it is evident that Petrobras outlines in its reports various plans and actions aimed at both risk mitigation and preventing species loss. In addition to its partnerships and initiatives, the company is actively addressing the risks associated with species loss.

However, within the entire Integrated Report, there are only two mentions of animal species in need of protection to prevent extinction. These references can be found in the Sustainability Report, which describes environmental projects aimed at contributing to conservation. Specifically, the company's Forest and Climate sector encompasses 15 projects focused on productive reconversion, reforestation of degraded areas, and the preservation of forests and natural habitats.

The description of the *"No Clima da Caatinga"* project, falling under item 2.1, is provided in Petrobras' 2018 Sustainability Report. This project aims to "contribute to the conservation of the caatinga and the protection of water resources in the forests of Ceará and Piauí, as well as the preservation of the *"tatu-bola"* species" (Petrobras, 2018, p. 86, emphasis added). It represents one of the company's efforts to prevent extinction. Additionally, another project known as *"Uruçu Capixaba"* focuses on "forest restoration and the protection of 'Melipona capixaba,' a bee species endemic to the Espírito Santo region, of significant importance for pollination, with a reduced risk of extinction" (Sustainability Report, 2018, p. 86). Maroun and Atkins (2018) argue that this type of reporting on specific species represents a preliminary step toward emancipatory extinction accounting.

Item 3.1 is related to item 2.1, as partnerships with organizations dedicated to species conservation also contribute to preventing extinction. While there are mentions of projects and commitments at various points in the Sustainability Report, there are limited references to fauna and flora, as illustrated in the following statement:

*We developed corporate criteria for the identification and prioritization of degraded areas to support better actions to recover these areas. Together with the Monteiro Lobato Gas Treatment Unit (UTGCA), in Caraguatatuba (SP), with the Research and Development Center (CENPES), and with the Ecology Laboratory of Tropical Forests of the University of São Paulo (Labtrop/USP), we conducted a Remotely Piloted Aircraft Systems (RPAS) flight in a 76,000 m2 area where **20,000 seedlings of native Atlantic Forest** species were planted to map and assess the results of the forest restoration project in the Permanent Preservation Area (APP) of the Camburu River. (Sustainability Report, 2018, p. 55, adapted, emphasis added)*

While no performance measures, costs, or timelines are provided, the disclosures indicate that the company acknowledges its impacts on biodiversity and is actively working to mitigate these risks through partnerships with organizations known for their environmental responsibility (Maroun & Atkins, 2018).

Analysis, Reflection and Assessment (Elements 4 and 5)

Throughout the analysis, reflection, and assessment stage, limited information was directly identified within the components of the Integrated Report. Some information was discovered, but it was categorized under different elements as it comprised general data. However, specific data concerning the outcomes of initiatives, partnerships, and other pertinent details were sourced from the project websites, complete with integrated images that were part of the Sustainability Report. When assessing the impact on species and ecosystems, it was solely on the project websites that records of variations in these values could be located, a detail notably absent in the Integrated Report.

For example, in the Sustainability Report, it is possible to observe item 4.1, in which the disclosure of the result of partnerships/commitments is disclosed as follows:

In Bolivia and Colombia, we prioritize social and environmental investment projects agreed upon with communities in the area of influence. In 2018, we conducted 11 pieces of training that benefited more than 3,780 people in activities such as industrial textiles and conservation and protection of coastal ecosystems. (Sustainability Report, 2018, p. 57, adapted)

The projects *"Golfinho Rotador", "Albatroz Brasil"*, and *"Mantas Brasil"* have scientific disclosure in which it is possible to observe the monitoring of species populations. However, differently from what was proposed by item 5.1, there is no addressing of species impacts to the corporation's activities as you could see in the following extract:

Albatrosses and petrels are birds extremely adapted to ocean life. They spend months and years roaming vast expanses of the oceans, seeking land only to nest, usually on remote islands. They represent a particularly threatened group of birds, affected by the introduction of exotic predators and habitat destruction at nesting sites, overfishing and incidental catch at sea, and climate change. Of the 29 albatross and petrel species covered by the International Agreement for the Conservation of Albatrosses and Petrels (ACAP), 19 (66%) are at risk of extinction and 11 (38%) are in decline. Bycatch in surface, bottom longline, and bottom trawl fisheries is the main cause of population declines that currently threaten 15 of the 22 albatross species with extinction. (Projeto Albatroz Brasil, Boletim Técnico Científico do Projeto Albatroz, 2019, p. 8)

Reporting (Element 6)

Certain pieces of information that could be classified as updates on progress, planned actions, or potential future risks are notably absent from Petrobras' Integrated Report. This absence stems from the fact that these actions or initiatives are not linked to the prevention of species extinction. Item 6.4 specifically addresses potential contingent liabilities pertaining to future credits and sanctions related to the impacts on endangered species. However, the Integrated Report fails to clarify whether these credits pertain specifically to endangered species.

In the scientific disclosures provided by the projects, certain data are presented to illustrate the progress of actions undertaken with Petrobras' support. However, these disclosures do not encompass all the aspects that item 6.1 suggests, which involve explaining whether the initiative is effective or not. Instead, they solely indicate that the initiative is currently in operation:

Among the main actions carried out in the period, research related to Goal 2 of PLANACAP stands out. For example, action 2.15 "Develop new technologies to mitigate incidental capture and improve existing ones", has been fully developed by the 'Projeto Albatroz' with support from Petrobras, the Albatross Task Force Program and through a project supported by ACAP to test the HookPod-mini in pelagic longline vessels in southern Brazil. (Projeto Albatroz Brasil, Boletim Técnico Científico do Projeto Albatroz, 2019, p. 14)

Overall, the six proposed elements are present in the reports. However, the intended objectives are not fully realized as suggested by Maroun and Atkins (2018). It is evident that there is no direct correlation between the species affected by the company's activities. Additionally, Petrobras does not disclose information about the affected species, as indicated in the study conducted by Adler et al. (2018). There is minimal information provided regarding the impacts on ecosystems. Considering that current literature aims to not only highlight the symptoms associated with species extinction but also to identify its underlying causes (Gray & Milne, 2018), the findings of this research indicate that Petrobras should make more substantial efforts in its future disclosures related to extinction accounting.

Simultaneously, it became evident that the most comprehensive information regarding the animals, their habitats, and the risks of extinction was solely available on the projects' websites, established through partnerships with environmental and research organizations. This aligns with the findings of Adler et al. (2018), who also emphasized the greater significance of disclosures through partnerships, underscoring the importance of cooperation and collaboration (Adler et al., 2018; Atkins & Maroun, 2018).

For companies and organizations looking to disclose voluntary information related to extinction, it is advisable to carry out an in-depth analysis of the impacts of their activities on species and ecosystems, identifying relevant risks and opportunities (Roberts et al., 2021). Subsequently, it is crucial to set measurable targets, define key indicators and adopt recognized international standards to transparently report on conservation efforts (Maroun & Atkins, 2018). The active involvement of stakeholders, the incorporation of sustainability into business decisions and the continuous search for innovation all play a key role. The consistent practice of reporting progress and learning from experience is key to driving both environmental responsibility and sustainable success for companies (Gazolla et al., 2020).

CONCLUSION

Extinction accounting has been devised to harness its emancipatory potential and prevent the indiscriminate exploitation of species, habitats, and biomes, all while considering ecological factors. Maroun and Atkins (2018) highlight how extinction accounting represents a considerably more advanced form of disclosure compared to the current "for biodiversity" accounting approach. This novel accounting framework draws inspiration from principles found in the GRI, integrated reporting, and previous literature on emancipatory accounting, creating a theoretical structure for revealing the risks associated with species extinction and illustrating prevention strategies. Atkins and Maroun (2018) outline it as a process encompassing the following elements: articulating the risk of extinction, divulging the measures implemented to counteract extinction, scrutinizing the outcomes, both positive and negative, of these measures, and reporting on each facet of extinction accounting.

This study reveals that the Integrated Report and Sustainability Report do not adhere to the level of detail advocated by the authors as a model for extinction accounting. Petrobras' approach to ecosystem preservation primarily centers around greenhouse gas emissions reduction and biofuel generation. However, this strategy largely overlooks actions directed toward biomes, ecosystems, and endangered species, which are the primary focus of the theoretical framework. In contrast, the partner projects' websites provide a significantly more comprehensive range of elements, offering detailed information about species under threat of extinction, including their characteristics, habitats, and activities, among other enriching details that contribute to their projects. These websites also provide a greater depth of user engagement. Within the integrated report, these projects are only briefly mentioned without delving into further detail.

This study advances the discourse on extinction accounting by employing a framework for disclosure elements that establish a direct link between actions conducted at the geographical or operational level, thereby enabling both managers and information users to comprehensively assess the magnitude of impact that specific activities or companies exert on particular species or habitats. This holistic approach is pivotal, regardless of whether the outcomes are financial, as it serves as a catalyst for the necessary measures to counteract the alarming trends of species extinction. Despite criticisms surrounding the exclusive analysis of the Integrated Report, potentially limiting its scope, the interpretation was also rendered feasible by the analyses of the Sustainability Report, the theoretical foundation and the alignment between the data and the theoretical framework. The primary contributions of this chapter are manifold, principally revolving around heightening awareness and transparency pertaining to biodiversity and the concomitant risks of extinction. Additionally, this study possesses the potential to invigorate stakeholder engagement, streamline the formulation of public policies concerning conservation and corporate environmental responsibility, foster advancements in corporate sustainability practices, and advance public education and awareness concerning biodiversity.

We recommend that future research explores diverse sectors of activity, extends its investigation to encompass various types of corporate reports, delves into digital media platforms, and considers any other forms of corporate disclosures. Furthermore, we encourage the examination of extended timeframes to gain deeper insights into the longitudinal adoption of practices by corporations. Expanding the scope of analysis in these dimensions will provide a more comprehensive and nuanced understanding of corporate practices over time.

As previously discussed, it is crucial to recognize the interconnectedness of fauna, flora, biomes, and ecosystems, as development cannot occur in isolation from these interconnections. Accounting, being a highly relevant management tool, can play a vital role in the decision-making process by highlighting the aspects of extinction. By rendering this data more visible to stakeholders, thoughtful analysis may contribute to the mitigation of impacts and the prevention of species loss on a global scale.

ACKNOWLEDGMENT

This work is financed by national funds through FCT - Foundation for Science and Technology, I.P., within the scope of multi-annual funding UIDB/04043/2020.

REFERENCES

Adler, R., Mansi, M., & Pandey, R. (2018). Biodiversity and threatened species reporting by the top Fortune Global companies. *Accounting, Auditing & Accountability Journal, 31*(3), 787–825. doi:10.1108/AAAJ-03-2016-2490

Adler, R., Mansi, M., Pandey, R., & Stringer, C. (2017). United Nations Decade on Biodiversity: A study of the reporting practices of the Australian mining industry. *Accounting, Auditing & Accountability Journal, 30*(8), 1711–1745. doi:10.1108/AAAJ-04-2015-2028

Atkins, J., Barone, E., Maroun, W., & Atkins, B. (2016). Bee accounting and accountability in the UK. In J. Atkins & B. Atkins (Eds.), *The Business of Bees: An Integrated Approach to Bee Decline and Corporate Responsibility* (pp. 198–211). Greenleaf Publishers. doi:10.9774/GLEAF.9781783534340_12

Atkins, J., & Maroun, W. (2018). Integrated extinction accounting and accountability: Building an ark. *Accounting, Auditing & Accountability Journal, 31*(3), 750–786. doi:10.1108/AAAJ-06-2017-2957

Atkins, J., Maroun, W., Atkins, B. C., & Barone, E. (2018). From the Big Five to the Big Four? Exploring extinction accounting for the rhinoceros. *Accounting, Auditing & Accountability Journal, 31*(2), 674–702. doi:10.1108/AAAJ-12-2015-2320

Baillie, J., Hilton-Taylor, C., & Stuart, S. N. (2004). *2004 IUCN Red List of Threatened Species: A Global Species Assessment.* IUCN Publications., doi:10.2305/IUCN.CH.2005.3

Barnosky, A. D., Matzke, N., Tomiya, S., Wogan, G. O., Swartz, B., Quental, T. B., Marshall, C., McGuire, J. L., Lindsey, E. L., Maguire, K. C., Mersey, B., & Ferrer, E. A. (2011). Has the Earth's sixth mass extinction already arrived? *Nature, 471*(7336), 51–57. doi:10.1038/nature09678 PMID:21368823

Brasil. (1976). *Lei 6.404, de 15 de dezembro de 1976. Dispõe sobre as sociedades por ações. Diário Oficial [da] República Federativa do Brasil, Brasília, DF.* http://www.planalto.gov.br

Brasil. (2007). *Lei 11.638, de 28 de dezembro de 2007. Diário Oficial [da] República Federativa do Brasil, Brasília, DF, 28 de dez. 2007.* http://www.planalto.gov.br

Ceballos, G., Ehrlich, P. R., Barnosky, A. D., García, A., Pringle, R. M., & Palmer, T. M. (2015). Accelerated modern human–induced species losses: Entering the sixth mass extinction. *Science Advances, 1*(5), e1400253. doi:10.1126ciadv.1400253 PMID:26601195

Ceballos, G., Ehrlich, P. R., & Dirzo, R. (2017). Biological annihilation via the ongoing sixth mass extinction signaled by vertebrate population losses and declines. *Proceedings of the National Academy of Sciences of the United States of America, 114*(30), E6089–E6096. doi:10.1073/pnas.1704949114 PMID:28696295

CPC 26 (R1) (2019). *Apresentação das demonstrações contábeis.* Brasília. https://www.cpc.org.br/CPC/Documentos-Emitidos/Pronunciamentos/Pronunciamento?Id=57

Cuckston, T. (2018). Making extinction calculable. *Accounting, Auditing & Accountability Journal, 31*(3), 849–874. doi:10.1108/AAAJ-10-2015-2264

De Boer, Y., & Van Bergen, B. (2012). *Expect the unexpected: building business value in a changing world*. KPMG International.

Diamond, J. M. (1989). Quaternary megafaunal extinctions: Variations on a theme by Paganini. *Journal of Archaeological Science, 16*(2), 167–175. doi:10.1016/0305-4403(89)90064-2

Dumay, J., Bernardi, C., Guthrie, J., & Demartini, P. (2016). Integrated reporting: A structured literature review. *Accounting Forum, 40*(3), 166–185. doi:10.1016/j.accfor.2016.06.001

Eccles, R. G., & Krzus, M. P. (2010). One report: Integrated reporting for a sustainable strategy. John Wiley & Sons.

Eccles, R. G., Saltzman, D., Muniandy, B., Ali, M. J., Today, A., Team, E., ... Dêclaration, L. (2011). Achieving Sustainability Through Integrated Reporting. *Stanford Social Innovation Review*. Advance online publication. doi:10.1016/j.sbspro.2013.08.672

Flower, J. (2015). The international integrated reporting council: A story of failure. *Critical Perspectives on Accounting, 27*, 1–17. doi:10.1016/j.cpa.2014.07.002

Gaia, S., & Jones, M. J. (2017). UK local councils reporting of biodiversity values: A stakeholder perspective. *Accounting, Auditing & Accountability Journal, 30*(7), 1614–1638. doi:10.1108/AAAJ-12-2015-2367

Gazzola, P., Pezzetti, R., Amelio, S., & Grechi, D. (2020). Non-financial information disclosure in Italian public interest companies: A sustainability reporting perspective. *Sustainability (Basel), 12*(15), 6063. doi:10.3390u12156063

Gibassier, D. (2015). Six Capitals–The Revolution Capitalism Has to Have–Or Can Accountants Save the Planet? *Social and Environmental Accountability Journal, 35*(3), 204–205. doi:10.1080/096916 0X.2015.1093782

Gray, R. (2010). Is accounting for sustainability actually accounting for sustainability… and how would we know? An exploration of narratives of organisations and the planet. *Accounting, Organizations and Society, 35*(1), 47–62. doi:10.1016/j.aos.2009.04.006

Gray, R., & Milne, M. J. (2018). Perhaps the Dodo should have accounted for human beings? Accounts of humanity and (its) extinction. *Accounting, Auditing & Accountability Journal, 31*(3), 826–848. doi:10.1108/AAAJ-03-2016-2483

Gupta, H., Nishi, M., & Gasparatos, A. (2022). Community-based responses for tackling environmental and socio-economic change and impacts in mountain social–ecological systems. *Ambio, 51*(5), 1123–1142. doi:10.100713280-021-01651-6 PMID:34784008

Hassan, A. M., Roberts, L., & Atkins, J. (2020). Exploring factors relating to extinction disclosures: What motivates companies to report on biodiversity and species protection? *Business Strategy and the Environment, 29*(3), 1419–1436. doi:10.1002/bse.2442

IIRC - International Integrated Reporting Council (2013). *The International Framework Integrated Reporting*. Author.

IOD. (2016). *King IV report on corporate governance in South Africa Johannesburg.* Lexis Nexus South Africa.

Jones, M. (2014). Ecosystem and natural inventory biodiversity frameworks. In M. Jones (Ed.), *Accounting for biodiversity* (pp. 39–61). Routledge. doi:10.4324/9780203097472-13

Jones, M. J. (1996). Accounting for biodiversity: A pilot study. *The British Accounting Review, 28*(4), 281–303. doi:10.1006/bare.1996.0019

Jones, M. J. (2010). Accounting for the environment: Towards a theoretical perspective for environmental accounting and reporting. *Accounting Forum, 34*(2), 123–138. doi:10.1016/j.accfor.2010.03.001

Jones, M. J., & Solomon, J. F. (2013). Problematising accounting for biodiversity. *Accounting, Auditing & Accountability Journal, 26*(5), 668–687. doi:10.1108/AAAJ-03-2013-1255

Kolbert, E. (2014). *The Sixth Extinction. An Unnatural History.* Henry Holt and Company.

Mansoor, H., & Maroun, W. (2016). An initial review of biodiversity reporting by South African corporates: The case of the food and mining sectors. *Suid-Afrikaanse Tydskrif vir Ekonomiese en Bestuurswetenskappe, 19*(4), 592–614. doi:10.4102ajems.v19i4.1477

Maroun, W., & Atkins, J. (2018). The emancipatory potential of extinction accounting: Exploring current practice in integrated reports. *Accounting Forum, 42*(1) 102-118. doi:10.1016/j.accfor.2017.12.001

Ministério do Meio Ambiente. (2014). *Portaria 444.* http://www.icmbio.gov.br/portal/images/stories/docs-plano-de-acao/00-saiba-mais/04_PORTARIA_MMA_N%C2%BA_444_DE_17_DE_DEZ_DE_2014.pdf

Ministério do Meio Ambiente. (2014a). *Portaria 445.* http://www.icmbio.gov.br/cepsul/images/stories/legislacao/Portaria/2014/p_mma_445_2014_lista_peixes_amea%C3%A7ados_extin%C3%A7%C3%A3o.pdf

Ministério do Meio Ambiente. (2019). *Biodiversidade – Fauna.* http://www.mma.gov.br/mma-em-numeros/biodiversidade

Rio+20 Declaration. (2012). *United Nations: Rio+20 - The future we want.* Rio+20 United Nations Conference on Sustainable Development.

Roberts, L., Hassan, A., Elamer, A., & Nandy, M. (2021). Biodiversity and extinction accounting for sustainable development: A systematic literature review and future research directions. *Business Strategy and the Environment, 30*(1), 705–720. doi:10.1002/bse.2649

Romi, A. M., & Longing, S. D. (2017). Accounting for bees: Evidence from disclosures by US listed companies. In *The Business of Bees* (pp. 226–244). Routledge.

Russell, S., Milne, M. J., & Dey, C. (2017). Accounts of nature and the nature of accounts: Critical reflections on environmental accounting and propositions for ecologically informed accounting. *Accounting, Auditing & Accountability Journal, 30*(7), 1426–1458. doi:10.1108/AAAJ-07-2017-3010

Scarano, F. R., & Ceotto, P. (2016). *A importância da biodiversidade brasileira e os desafios para a conservação, para a ciência e para o setor privado. Floresta Atlântica de Tabuleiro: Diversidade e Endemismo na Reserva Natural Vale.*

Schaltegger, S., Gibassier, D., & Maas, K. (2023). Managing and accounting for corporate biodiversity contributions. Mapping the field. *Business Strategy and the Environment, 32*(5), 2544–2553. doi:10.1002/bse.3166

Solomon, J., & Maroun, W. (2012). Integrated reporting: The new face of social, ethical and environmental reporting in South Africa? ACCA. The Association of Chartered Certified Accountants.

Thomas, C. D., Cameron, A., Green, R. E., Bakkenes, M., Beaumont, L. J., Collingham, Y. C., Erasmus, B. F. N., de Siqueira, M. F., Grainger, A., Hannah, L., Hughes, L., Huntley, B., van Jaarsveld, A. S., Midgley, G. F., Miles, L., Ortega-Huerta, M. A., Townsend Peterson, A., Phillips, O. L., & Williams, S. E. (2004). Extinction risk from climate change. *Nature, 427*(6970), 145–148. doi:10.1038/nature02121 PMID:14712274

Tregidga, H. (2013). Biodiversity offsetting: Problematisation of an emerging governance regime. *Accounting, Auditing & Accountability Journal, 26*(5), 806–832. doi:10.1108/AAAJ-02-2013-1234

Tsagas, G., & Villiers, C. (2020). Why "less is more" in non-financial reporting initiatives: Concrete steps towards supporting sustainability. *Accounting, Economics, and Law Convivium, 10*(2), 20180045. doi:10.1515/ael-2018-0045

Voss, B. (2016). *Discursive constructions of social and environmental accounting in Brazil: the case of Petrobras* [Doctoral dissertation]. Universidade de São Paulo.

Weir, K. (2018). The purposes, promises and compromises of extinction accounting in the UK public sector. *Accounting, Auditing & Accountability Journal, 31*(3), 875–899. doi:10.1108/AAAJ-03-2016-2494

Wheeler, Q. D., Knapp, S., Stevenson, D. W., Stevenson, J., Blum, S. D., Boom, B. M., Borisy, G. G., Buizer, J. L., De Carvalho, M. R., Cibrian, A., Donoghue, M. J., Doyle, V., Gerson, E. M., Graham, C. H., Graves, P., Graves, S. J., Guralnick, R. P., Hamilton, A. L., Hanken, J., ... Woolley, J. B. (2012). Mapping the biosphere: Exploring species to understand the origin, organization and sustainability of biodiversity. *Systematics and Biodiversity, 10*(1), 1–20. doi:10.1080/14772000.2012.665095

ADDITIONAL READING

Atkins, J., & Atkins, B. (Eds.). (2017). *The business of bees: An integrated approach to bee decline and corporate responsibility.* Routledge. doi:10.4324/9781351283922

De Villiers, C., Rinaldi, L., & Unerman, J. (2014). Integrated Reporting: Insights, gaps and an agenda for future research. *Accounting, Auditing & Accountability Journal, 27*(7), 1042–1067. doi:10.1108/AAAJ-06-2014-1736

Vinnari, E., & Vinnari, M. (2022). Making the invisibles visible: Including animals in sustainability (and) accounting. *Critical Perspectives on Accounting, 82*, 102324. doi:10.1016/j.cpa.2021.102324

KEY TERMS AND DEFINITIONS

Biodiversity: The variety of life on Earth, including the diversity of species, ecosystems, and genetic diversity within species.

Endangered Species: Species that are at risk of extinction due to human activities such as habitat destruction, pollution, and climate change.

Extinction Accounting: A novel approach for companies to comprehensively assess and quantify the ecological impacts stemming from their operations, encompassing a deeper understanding of the ecological, economic, social, and ethical impacts stemming from its activities.

Habitat Loss: The destruction or degradation of natural habitats, which can lead to the loss of biodiversity and the extinction of species.

Integrated Report: A report that provides a holistic and integrated representation of a company's performance, including financial and non-financial information, such as environmental and social performance.

Red List: A global indicator of biodiversity health overseen by the International Union for the Conservation of Nature (IUCN), which provides information on species' geographic range, population size, habitat and ecology, utilization or trade, threats, and conservation measures, all of which assist in making informed conservation decisions.

Sustainability Report: A report that provides information on a company's environmental, social, and governance performance, including its efforts to address sustainability challenges.

ENDNOTES

[1]   Available at: https://www.iucnredlist.org/
[2]   Available at: https://www.petrobras.com.br/pt/nossas-atividades/areas-de-atuacao/
[3]   Available at: https://projetoalbatroz.org.br/pesquisas/publicacoes-cientificas

Chapter 4
Conceptual Framework of Corporate Social Responsibility and Its Basic Roots

Esin Bengü Ceran
İstanbul University, Turkey

ABSTRACT

Institutions have various responsibilities in terms of all the actors they interact with while carrying out their activities. At the point reached today, it is not possible to survive for an enterprise that is run only by profit maximization and by considering the needs of its shareholders. Global awareness and the rapidly developing sustainability idea in this direction are gaining importance at the businesses level as well. Both the legal obligations put forward and the social awareness that has arisen oblige businesses to take care of all stakeholders while carrying out their activities. This formation, which is widely concerned in the management organization literature, is shaped within the framework of corporate social responsibility concept. Within the scope of this chapter, the relationship of CSR with stakeholder theory, classical and modern approaches of the concept, and basic conceptual models are included.

INTRODUCTION

The production capacity, which has increased rapidly with the industrial revolution, and the production that has accelerated with the point that technology has reached today, and the damages caused by the consumption habits that develop along with it, appear in different aspects every day. In a sense, our planet, which sends us warnings with various signals, wants us to see how much this increase in production and consumption increases resource consumption. The awareness created in this direction is gaining importance day by day under the concept of sustainability and it is observed that it permeates our daily activities. Within the scope of this section, the sustainability concept of enterprises, which are important parts of society and which are the locomotive of societies in the context of production and consumption, has been examined within the framework of CSR. CSR covers the responsibilities of businesses towards all their stakeholders. In the period of the beginnings of the history of business, the responsibility of

DOI: 10.4018/978-1-6684-9076-1.ch004

the companies was taken into consideration only in order to satisfy the shareholders, but today they are obliged to create value for all stakeholders, whom they directly or indirectly affect and are affected by.

CSR applications have obtained a vital place in business life at this stage, serving as the primary driving force for short, medium and long-term activities, primarily in large enterprises. On the other hand, important studies within the scope of CSR are included in the academic literature, especially in the context of business management practices. In line with the increasing awareness about CSR, the importance of the concept is increasing visibly. Within the scope of this study, it is aimed to contribute to the book "Enhancing Sustainability Through Non-Financial Reporting", which tries to base the relationship between non-financial reporting and sustainability, by gathering the conceptual framework of CSR.

Nonfinancial reporting is the reporting of non-financial social activities of institutions and presenting them to the relevant people (Özbay, 2019). Increasing the awareness of sustainability and the activities that will come with it are related to the awareness and implementation of the responsibilities of the institutions in this sense. The realization of non-financial reporting is possible with the adoption of CSR practices by institutions. First, CSR activities must be carried out so that a report can be created in this direction. In this sense, the concept of CSR appears as a prerequisite for the realization of financial reporting and the enhancement of sustainability in this direction.

The relationship between CSR applications and social activity reports has been mentioned in many studies and its importance has been emphasized (Perrini, 2006; Di Vaio et al, 2022, Ortiz-Martínez et al, 2022). Establishing a relationship between concepts in academic studies is possible by first revealing the conceptual framework of the concepts to be associated. This chapter has a unique value in terms of the definition of the concept of CSR, its principles, historical development, and grounding in the context of stakeholder theory in order to form a basis for the relations to be established between concepts in the context of the book in other chapters.

Within the scope of the chapter, firstly, definitions of the concept of CSR were given, and then the evolution of the concept from the Middle Ages to the present was revealed. Within the scope of its theoretical framework, the intricate relationship with stakeholder theory, classical and modern approaches to the concept, and basic models for framing the concept of CSR are included.

LITERATURE REVIEW

Defining the CSR Concept

Corporate social responsibility is a concept that is gaining more relevance with each passing day. In particular, almost every large-scale institution carries out activities for social responsibility awareness and declares them. However, it is still not clear which activities can be called corporate social responsibility. In this direction, first of all, it is necessary to define the concept of corporate social responsibility (CSR).

The definition of CSR is based on a relationship between the institution and its stakeholders (Crowther & Aras, 2008). Bowen's book "Social Responsibilities of the Businessman" is one of the first and most important sources that draw attention to the impact of companies on other stakeholders of society (Aktan & Börü, 2007). Bowen emphasizes that large enterprises have tangible effects on society and that they should regulate their decision mechanisms accordingly (Bowen, 1953). Along with this connection established in the literature regarding the relationship between society and business decisions, many definitions of the concept of CSR have been made until today, and today's theoretical foundations of the concept of CSR have been established. When we look deeper into the concept of CSR we realize its dimensions first. The three dimensions that are thought to constitute the concept of CSR are accepted in the literature as sustainability, accountability, and transparency. Sustainability is related to the effects of an action taken today in future years. Sustainability; emphasizes the responsibility towards future generations in the use of resources. Accountability means institutions are aware of an environment affected by their activities and that they take responsibility for their actions with this awareness. Transparency means that institutions continue to conduct their activities so as to allow each person involved in the process to have access to the required information, whether they are internal or external, and to use the data.

The concept of corporate social responsibility is evaluated in the context of the relationship and interaction of the activities of commercial enterprises with social needs and social goals (UNCTAD, 1999). The European Union defines Corporate Social Responsibility as a management concept in which companies integrate social and environmental concerns into their business activities and interactions with their stakeholders. The European Union has proposed that Corporate Social Responsibility is the result of companies striving to harmonize economic, environmental, and social aspects, while simultaneously keeping in mind the needs of their shareholders and stakeholders (UNIDO, 2023).

The Organisation for Economic Co-operation and Development (OECD) defines corporate Social Responsibility as a core business value and strategy integrated into all aspects of company operations, from research and development to purchasing, manufacturing, and supply (OECD, 2001). In addition to this comprehensive definition, it was also noted that businesses have problems protecting and supporting their corporate identities and social environmental standards. The difference between corporate social responsibility and philanthropy gains importance at this point.

In addition to the CSR definitions of international institutions, CSR has been defined with different dimensions in the academic literature. Different sources have adopted different perspectives while defining the concept of CSR since its first appearance. Initially, the idea that companies should solely focus on making a profit to fulfill their social responsibility was suggested; however, it has since become evident that solely profit maximization does not always benefit all stakeholders, and can even result in harm in some cases. In this direction, the dimensions in the definition of liability have changed over time. Freidman's definition of CSR was sufficient only to make a profit (Latapí Agudelo et al. 2019); Davis referred to the need for CSR activities to go beyond making profit (Davis, 1960).

Davis (1960), who is regarded as the second pioneer of the CSR literature after Bowen, who is described as the father of the concept of CSR, defines CSR as "a management context that expresses the decisions and actions taken by businessmen for reasons beyond the direct economic or technical interests of the firm".

CSR defines the economic, legal, ethical, and discretionary obligations of businesses towards society. In terms of being the most basic economic unit in society (basic economic unit), the first and most important responsibility of the enterprises towards society is to continue their activities with an awareness of economic responsibility. Along with the social contract with society, businesses have to establish a legal basis while carrying out their activities. Legal responsibility covers social contracts as well as laws. In addition to legal obligations, ethical obligations are among the expectations that businesses must meet within the scope of social responsibility. Although it is relative and difficult to determine the boundaries of ethical responsibilities, there are also ethical obligations that have become commonplace. In addition to these, there are optional obligations that change in line with personal perceptions and judgments. These discretionary obligations, which are not legally enforceable and whose requirements vary by people, are shaped in line with the expectations of the environment in which the enterprise is located and its adaptation preference. This four-dimensional definition, detailed by Carroll, has become even richer over time.

Corporate social responsibility is the idea that companies have obligations to groups of society other than shareholders, even if they are not by law or by union agreement. Two aspects of this definition are important. The first is that the obligation must be accepted voluntarily; Behavior affected by the coercive forces of law or union contract is not voluntary. Second, the obligation is a broad one that goes beyond the traditional duty to shareholders and encompasses other social groups such as customers, employees, suppliers, and neighboring communities (Jones, 1980).

Murray and Montanary (1986), who see social responsibility awareness as the management of exchanges between the company and its environment and approach the concept from a marketing management perspective. They argue that for a business to be socially responsible, it is expected to meet the moral, economic, legal, ethical, and discretionary expectations of society.

While examining the CSR concept in management literature it is also mentioned that the decisions regarding CSR are the decisions to be made by the top management from a strategic management point of view. Another definition of the concept is that both internal, as well as acting "ethically" and "responsibly" towards all stakeholders in its external environment, taking and implementing decisions in this direction (Aktan & Börü, 2007). With this definition, it has been revealed that the concept is related not only to the internal but also to the social stakeholders in the external environment.

To make a summary definition based on all the definitions made during the development process of the concept; CSR is the obligation of enterprises to operate with the aim of benefiting all present and future internal and external stakeholders, while still carrying out their activities. Furthermore, they should be aware of other expectations of the stakeholders, and not just focus on profits. As a concise description of CSR includes the consideration of social, economic and environmental objectives that are beneficial to all stakeholders.

The Historical Development Process of the Concept

With the conceptual definition of CSR in the academic literature, the historical development of the concept can be observed more clearly. However, the social development of institutions' social responsibility goes back much further. It is possible to come across findings on the concept of CSR when it is examined in terms of the effects of small businesses in the middle ages on society in line with the religious point of view, the industrial revolution in the 12th-18th centuries, and the mercantilism in the 16th century, in terms of their relations with institutions and society (Aktan & Börü 2007). Some sources position the existence of institutions with examples such as the elderly, the mentally ill, and orphanages in the ancient Roman empire based on the CSR perspective (Chaffe 2017).

The transformation of the concept, which is seen to be integrated with strategic and corporate management perspectives in the activities of businesses, over the years will be discussed in this section. Within the scope of the industrial revolution, James Watt's discovery of the Steam engine in 1765 and the change in the usual factory order, the invisible hand metaphor for commercial life in the book of Adam Smith's (1776) Wealth of Nations, the French Revolution of 1789; take place in the literature as historical turning points associated with the concept of corporate social responsibility.

When the 1800s are examined, it is seen that businesses focus on the productivity of their employees. It was noted that the factory system adopted in production in this period caused various social problems, and it was argued that problems such as child labor, slums, and poverty were accompanied by factorization. To address these issues, certain industrialists stepped up and implemented various improvement initiatives, which were seen as pioneering instances of CSR. Some of these improvements are hospitals, clinics, cafeterias, etc., which are established in line with the welfare schemes created in the factory areas (Wren, 2009). In addition to what Daniel Wren conveyed about the period, Morrell Heald (1957) mentions some practices that were thought to have the character of CSR in the pre-World War I period. As Reported by Heald; while Colorado Fuel and Iron company declared its corporate purpose as the solution to social problems at that time, the YMCA (Young Men's Christian Associations) movement brought solutions to social problems with the support it received from institutions. In this period, it was observed that institutions had practiced for society, which were seen as philanthropy at that time but could be included in the scope of CSR today, and it was noted that these practices continued increasingly after the First World War.

The development of the concept of CSR continued to accelerate after the First World War. During this period, Chester Barnard's The Functions of the Executive (1938), JM Clark's Social Control of Business (1939), and Theodore Kreps's Measurement of the Social Performance of Business (1940) can be examined as the main works that include applications related to the development of the CSR. Again in the same period, the results of the survey published by Fortune (1946) in line with the questions about the CSR practices for companies are also seen as an important step in the development of CSR (Carroll, 2008). While these survey studies increased the awareness of those who participated in the survey and those who evaluated the results of these studies as readers, they also caused companies to take a closer look at their practices in this direction. In addition, it could be argued that the concept of responsibility for that period was molded in this way.

Along with the introduction of the concept of CSR into the academic literature in the 1950s, definitions of the concept were made in the 60s, an increase in the number of definitions was observed in the 70s, a decrease in the definitions, and an increase in empirical studies existed in the 80s.

Table 1. Key actions involved in CSR during its conceptual development process

Period	Key Actions Involved in Corporate Social Responsibility
Before The İndustrial Revolution -Illustrations of Corporate Social Responsibility	In the Middle Ages-regulations through a religious perspective, for the effects of small businesses on society In the Ancient Roman Empire- the existence of the institutions on behalf of the elderly, the mentally ill and orphanages
After The Industrial Revolution (18-19th century)	1776 Adam Smith's The Wealth of Nations- The invisible hand metaphor for commercial life 1789 French Revolution
Period Before The 1st World War -Recognition of social responsibilities	Discussions about the problems such as child labor, squatting, poverty and factory life as their reason Industrialists who carry out improvement practices regarding the social problems that brought about by factoryization Practices such as hospitals, clinics, cafeterias, etc., established in line with the welfare schemes created in the factory areas Colorado Fuel and Iron company -CSR practices Y.M.C.A. (Young Men's Christian Associations) movement
Period After The 1st World War (20th century) - Increasing importance about the concept	1938 Chester Barnard's The Functions of the Executive 1939 J. M. Clark's Social Control of Business 1940 Theodore Kreps's Measurement of the Social Performance of Business 1946 The results of the survey published by Fortune magazine in line with the questions about the CSR practices of the companies.
1950s- The introduction of the concept of CSR into the academic literature	1953 Bowen's Social Responsibilities of the Businessman
1960s - Defining the CSR concept	Davis (1960), who pioneered the academic definition of the concept of CSR, also touched upon different dimensions of CSR. Davis dimensions social responsibility as socio-economic and socio-human obligations.
1970s- Increase in the number of definitions and association with other variables	Relations with various other concepts in corporate practices and academic literature. Eilbirt and Parket (1973) studied the concepts that CSR was related to at that period.
1980s- Decrease in definitions increase in empirical studies, and increase businesslife practices	1981 Establishment of the General Directorate of Environment of the European Commission 1983 Establishment of the World Commission on Environment and Development 1986 Chernobyl nuclear disaster 1987 Publication of the "Our Common Future" report, presented by the Brundtland Commission and providing the definition of sustainable development 1987 The United Nations' (UN) acceptance of the Montreal Protocol 1988 Establishment of the Intergovernmental Panel on Climate Change (IPCC)
1990s -The expansion of activities at the international platforms	1992 UN Conference on Environment and Development (Rio Conference), held in Rio de Janeiro- the Agenda 21 Action plan, 1997 The UN Climate Change Environment Convention (UNFCCC) and the Kyoto Protocol for nations to adopt environmentally responsible management styles
2000s, increase in awareness-oriented practices at the international platforms, clarifiyng the definition and dimensions of the concept in academic terms	Schwartz and Carroll's (2003) transformation of the corporate social responsibility concept into a model in which Carroll (1979, 1991) reduced the four CSR categories to three areas. The model presented in the form of a venn diagram and detailed with its economic, legal and ethical dimensions. 2000 The Millennium Declaration and the Millennium Development Goals, adopted by governments at the UN Millennium Summit 2002 "World Sustainable Development Summit" in Johannesburg 2012 UN Conference on Sustainable Development Rio+20 Summit in Rio de Janeiro -"The Future We Want" 2015, UN Summit in New York- Agenda 2030: UN Sustainable Development Goals (SDGs)
After 2015- on going progress towards the goals set in implementation and development within the framework of CSV in academic literature	Currently ; Corporate social responsibility practices continue to be standardized at the international level in line with the UN Sustainable Development Goals. In the academic literature, strategic corporate social responsibility (SCSR) develops in the context of shared value creation (CSV) and stakeholder theory.

As of the 1950s, the literature and business practices related to CSR began to form primarily in the USA. Literature and business practices on the subject developed in Europe and Asian countries at the end of the 90s (Carroll, 2008). Bowen's Social Responsibilities of the Businessman (1953), published in this period, is a fundamental resource for social responsibility (Aktan & Börü, 2007). Carroll(2008) stated that in this period, the concept of social responsibility was more 'talk' than 'action' and still needs time to be put into practice.

In the 1960s, Davis included different dimensions of the concept in his work. Davis first referred to business people's awareness of their responsibilities to the public, such as full employment, inflation, and the maintenance of competition. On the other hand, the existence of human values such as morale, cooperation, motivation, and self-actualization in the workplace, which the employer needs to nurture individually, was also in question. Davis defines the concept in two dimensions as socio-economic and socio-human obligations. He also states that the literature and practices related to gender have yet to underestimate the socio-human dimension. In this respect, it is seen that the author had foresight before the period. Although it was not noticed at that time, it can easily be said that the first and most important point of view regarding the dimensions of the concept of social responsibility was put forward by Davis.

By the 1970s, the concept was associated with various other concepts in corporate practices and academic literature. Minority hiring, ecology, minority training, contributions to education, contributions to the arts, hard-core hiring, hard-core training, urban renewal, and civil rights were the concepts associated to CSR in those days which listed within the study conducted by Eilbirt and Parket (1973). In addition to these, developing understandable accounting statements, truth in advertising, product defects, consumer complaints, consumer-oriented label changes, and guarantees and warranties were also discussed as concepts related to CSR in the 70s (Carroll,2008).

The 80's are mentioned as the period of the CSR concept was put into practice. Important steps were taken in this period to support CSR argument. The establishment of the European Commission's Directorate General for Environment (1981), the establishment of the World Commission for Environment and Development (1983), the Chornobyl Nuclear Disaster (1986), the publication of the report 'Our Common Future' presented by the Brundtland Commission and providing the definition of sustainable development (1987), United Nations' adoption of the Montreal Protocol (1987) and the establishment of the Intergovernmental Panel on Climate Change (IPCC) (1988) are important events that took place during this period (Latapí Agudelo et al. 2019).

In the 90s, the concept began to be mentioned in the global media, and activities were carried out on the subject at the international level. The most important ones are; the adoption of a set of principles with the Agenda 21 Action Plan, the UN Climate Change Environment Convention (UNFCCC), and the Kyoto Protocol (1997) for nations to adopt environmentally responsible management styles. It is known that after these international steps, the awareness of the public has increased significantly and the sanctions are increasing day by day.

In the 2000s, it accelerated its development into two separate branches in terms of CSR's conceptual framework and applications. In this period; Schwartz and Carroll (2003) transformed the concept of corporate social responsibility into a model in which Carroll (1979, 1991) reduced the four CSR categories to three areas. The model is presented in the form of a Venn diagram and detailed with its economic, legal, and ethical dimensions. This triple model has been widely accepted in the literature and has formed an important basis in framing the concept with its current form by doing a lot of work on it. In addition to this, international applications of CSR have become increasingly important in the 2000s. The Millennium Declaration and the Millennium Development Goals, adopted by governments at the UN Millennium Summit in 2000 and targeting 2015, are accepted as a tool that enables developing countries to work in cooperation with developed countries for our common future. In 2002, the

'World Sustainable Development Summit' was held in Johannesburg. In 2012, the UN Conference on Sustainable Development (Rio+20) was held in Rio de Janeiro. As a result of the Rio+20 Summit, a final document named 'The Future We Want' was adopted as a roadmap for development. On September 27, 2015, 'Agenda 2030: UN Sustainable Development Goals (SDGs)' was adopted as 17 goals and 169 sub-goals in New York. By drawing a new global development framework with the 2030 Sustainable Development Goals, environmental issues such as sustainable cities, climate change, combating drought, and protecting biological diversity were included in the sustainable development agenda (Tc Ministry of Foreign Affairs website, 2023,online).

In addition to the international standardization of corporate social responsibility practices, it continues to develop in the academic literature in the context of strategic corporate social responsibility (SCSR), shared value creation (CSV), and stakeholder theory (Chandler, 2016; Porter & Kramer, 2011, Chandler and Werther, 2013). At the point where the literature has reached today, with the support received from the practice, companies are expected to incorporate the sustainability perspective into their strategic processes by considering the needs of all stakeholders, and it is observed that the conceptual framework has developed in this direction.

Stakeholder Theory and Corporate Social Responsibility

As in classical social responsibility perspective, the aim of the enterprises was shaped as profit maximization for shareholder satisfaction, and in this direction, profitable indicators were considered sufficient in financial reporting. Currently, the purpose of firms has evolved beyond just pleasing shareholders to providing advantages for all stakeholders; thus, the requirement for reporting that considers non-financial, social, and environmental elements has arisen. The concept of CSR is of key importance in ensuring sustainability at the point reached today, as it has a quality that is formed by the combination of economic, social, and environmental elements. By making non-financial reports, a party is able to exhibit its non-financial activities and interact with its stakeholders. (García-Sanchez et al., 2019). While non-financial reports are the way of disclosure of sustainability activities, CSR practices cover the practices of these activities before disclosure.

If companies do not transparently disclose their claims that they have adopted CSR practices, it cannot be determined at this point whether the practices are implemented (Watson et al.,2002) In this respect, reports that transparently disclose CSR applications have become a demand of all stakeholders today. Compromising on transparency undermines stakeholder trust, and this reflects negatively on various parameters. Voluntary disclosure and transparent reporting provide significant advantages to companies and contribute to the creation of long-term sustainable competitive advantages (Madhani, 2007). Accountability, another important principle of corporate social responsibility, is another important principle in terms of reporting. The tendency to evaluate reports that adopt more transparency with the principle of accountability in terms of reporting quality is increasing day by day (Gold et al., 2020). reporting standards are evolving more and more into transparency in order to promote social and environmental norms and maximize the interests of all stakeholders. Standardization activities developed for all reporting activities that develop in the context of stakeholder theory are also associated with the sustainability principle of CSR (Martínez-Ferrero, 2015).

Stakeholder theory suggests that the essence of business is primarily to build relationships and create value for all its stakeholders. Non-financial reporting activities also have an important place among the practices that businesses will implement for an understanding of CSR based on the principles of transparency, accountability, and sustainability. It is possible to address not only the profit of the shareholders, but also the maximization of the expectations of all stakeholders, with a transparent, accountable, and perspective that attaches importance to the understanding of sustainability in reporting processes. In this direction, the relationship between the concept of CSR and stakeholder theory will be discussed in the following section.

Many studies on stakeholder theory or CSR deal with these two concepts' relations to each other, and some sources directly associate the concept of corporate social responsibility with stakeholder theory. The basis for establishing such a strong relationship between the two concepts is that they both relate social interests to commercial interests. Stakeholder theory shows an approach from the perspective of all stakeholders in the immediate and general environment, from competitors to employees, from the government to customers, who are affected by the activities of business enterprises. The CSR, on the other hand, takes a broad perspective on the impact of businesses' activities on society. In other words, stakeholder theory supports Adam Smith's invisible hand theory and believes that the interests of some stakeholders will create benefits for each stakeholder, while the CSR perspective focuses on the necessity of certain activities for the benefit of society (Donaldson and Preston, 1995; Freeman & Dmytriyev, 2017).

To establish the relationship between the stakeholder theory and the public sector, first of all, the stakeholders of the business must be correctly identified. Although stakeholder identification has been done with various methods and models in the literature, it is difficult to make a standardized stakeholder identification. In this direction, first of all, 'the involved' and 'the affected' stakeholders should be determined and borders should be established accordingly (Vos, 2003).The two basic questions asked in the definition of stakeholder are 'What are the responsibilities of an organization?' and the second question is 'To whom is the organization responsible?'(Vos,2003). The answer to these questions is a guide for determining the stakeholders of the organization. However, the level of responsibility that each business feels towards its stakeholders varies. At this point, CSR differs from stakeholder theory. According to Smith, when the perfect right of primary stakeholders is provided, these evolve into results that will meet social expectations, so institutions should turn to their primary stakeholders and keep philanthropy in the background (Brown & Forster, 2013). Stakeholder management is of great importance for businesses, from a strategic management perspective; while maximizing the interests of shareholders is the primary responsibility of top management, it is a moral obligation to look after the interests of other stakeholders. Here, relations between stakeholders are differentiated in the context of obligation and moral responsibility. According to this approach, companies have fiduciary obligations to stakeholders other than shareholders, in other words, these responsibilities are not optional but mandatory as moral obligations (Freeman, 1994).

While examining the concept of CSR, it is difficult to determine what businesses do to increase productivity and maximize profits, and what they do with the concern of providing social benefits (Carroll, 2008). The approach nurtured in the Adam Smith doctrine focused on shareholder maximization with a narrow perspective, while striving to meet human needs, increase productivity, create employment and create wealth, preventing the system from using its full potential to meet the needs of the wider society. With the help of Creating Shared Value perspective, with the paradigm shift, the focus of companies is broadened and the business world is enabled to implement applications for the benefit of wider audiences. In this direction, companies are stripped of their philanthropic perspective and redesigned as their aim is not only profit but also creating shared value (Porter and Kramer, 2011).

When the academic literature is observed we can see that the relationship between businesses and society has been examined in the context of social responsibility and stakeholder theories (Brown & Forster, 2013). According to the post-positivist approach arising from Adam Smith's theory, decisions have economic and moral components. In this manner, companies can only engage in philanthropic activities after meeting the expectations and needs of all primary stakeholders. In Adam Smith's doctrine on justice and rights, it is seen that there is an approach that supports and guides the doctrines of CSR and stakeholder theory. Addressing the competition among stakeholders, Smith has taken important fundamental steps to establish a relationship between CSR and stakeholder theory. However, it required much more arguments to be able to reveal the relationship between these two theories. Parmar et al. (2010) put forward the distinction between stakeholder theory and CSR by noting that; "Although CSR is critical to helping academics identify the 'social obligations of business'...the issue of value creation and trade is not within the scope of CSR." (Brown & Forster, 2013).

Freeman and Dmytriyev (2017) criticize perspectives such as that corporate social responsibility practices are made without the consent of the shareholders, that some unethical situations can turn into an effort to cover up, and that they have an opposing stance with profitability. They evaluate CSR within the scope of stakeholder theory in response to these criticisms.

According to the authors, profitability and social responsibility should not be evaluated as two mutually exclusive concepts. At the point reached today, it can be observed that CSR is sometimes turned into an effort to hide some unethical issues that the managers add to their practices as an obligation without the request of the shareholders. However, CSR should be seen as activities carried out in an ethical framework that can benefit all stakeholders. The relationship between companies and their stakeholders is a dynamic one and has different levels of influence on local governments (Friedman and Miles, 2002).

Despite a stakeholder perspective that binds shareholders and other stakeholders with moral obligations, today CSR has turned into a value-creation approach and has prioritized putting all stakeholders at the same distance. Adam Smith's point of view, which attaches secondary importance to other primary shareholders, has to become history at the point reached in line with the evolution of the concept. Today, the concepts of CSR and stakeholder identification, which are discussed within the scope of creating shared value, adopt shared interest maximization instead of shareholder-oriented senior management. Successful collaborations with the CSV approach include practices that are linked to data-driven defined results, linked to the goals of all stakeholders, and can be monitored with clear metrics (Porter and Kramer, 2011).

While talking about business ethics, it is possible to come across the concepts of stakeholder theory and CSR a lot. These two theories are generally associated with each other within the scope of "business ethics". Freeman and Dmytriyev (2017) see stakeholder theory and CSR as slightly overlapping different concepts, the main similarity between the two concepts is noted as they emphasize the importance of involving social interests in business activities (Figure 1). Stakeholder theory suggests that the essence of business is primarily to build relationships and create value for all its stakeholders. Although it varies by industry and business model, stakeholders are generally employees, customers, communities, suppliers, and financiers. All these stakeholders are equally important to the company. CSR, on the other hand, does not prioritize the situation of other stakeholders by focusing specifically on social awareness. CSR has a structure that includes philanthropy, volunteering, environmental efforts, and ethical work practices that focus on social benefit. CSR focuses on ensuring that the business fulfills its responsibilities to local communities and society at large. The concept neglects other stakeholders by giving priority to the orientation of business toward the general public over other commercial responsibilities (Freeman & Dmytriyev, 2017).

Figure 1. The relation between stakeholder theory and CSR
Source: Freeman and Dmytriyev (2017)

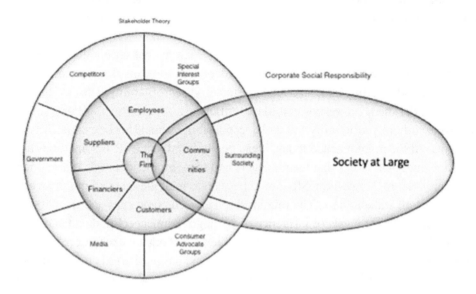

Another important difference between stakeholder theory and CSR is where both theories look at the company. Stakeholder theory looks at the company from the perspective of the company itself and the perspective of the company's immediate stakeholders. From this point of view, the company is responsible to all its stakeholders while carrying out its activities. Furthermore, stakeholder theory assumes that stakeholders are interconnected and that creating value for one stakeholder creates value for others (Freeman et al., 2010). CSR looks at the company from a societal perspective. CSR prioritizes the company's social responsibilities over its responsibilities to other stakeholders. When both perspectives are evaluated in terms of 'Purpose, Value Creation, and Stakeholder Interdependence' elements, their commonalities become clearer. A morally determined purpose by companies will save an organization from being embroiled in situations where false dichotomy arises, such as economic and social, business and ethical, or stakeholder interests and societal interests. The transformation of purpose into practice is defined as creating value for everyone. It is possible to create value by realizing that the main purpose of the company's emergence is to serve all stakeholders. On the other hand, it is not possible to separate the stakeholders from each other. Stakeholders are interdependent, creating value for one stakeholder also means creating value for others. Helping communities can improve shareholders in many ways, and satisfying suppliers or employees is also beneficial for customers (Freeman & Dmytriyev, 2017).

Therefore, although both of these perspectives seem distinct, they overlap. Although stakeholder theory seems to have a larger umbrella, all stakeholders whose importance is emphasized within the scope of stakeholder theory can also be included in the CSR perspective, since they are a part of society. In this sense, it would not be false to say that the two theories represent each other intricately.

CSR APPROACHES (CLASSICAL-MODERN)

The concept of CSR, which has been examined under various approaches in the literature, has been examined within the framework of classical and modern approaches in this section. In the early periods when the concept emerged, an approach focused only on shareholder satisfaction was observed, but today we can observe that it has evolved into value creation in the context of all stakeholders. While financial reporting is seen as sufficient and important in line with the shareholder-oriented perspective in the classical approach, in the modern approach, it is the case that institutions focus on all potential internal and external stakeholders, and non-financial reporting gains importance in this direction.

Classical Social Responsibility Approach

The classical approach, based on Adam Smith's invisible hand theory, suggests that the routine activities of businesses will already benefit society and reveals that commercial institutions working for profit maximization will not need to make an additional social benefit effort (Sancar, 2021; Özcan, 2021). According to this point of view, while businesses provide profit for themselves by successfully carrying out economic activities, they also create social benefits and thus fulfill their social responsibilities. There is no social benefit that institutions need to pay special attention to other than their economic activities, and the effort to be made for this is rejected due to the potential to harm their activities.

The classical CSR approach argues that businesses realize their social obligations if they work efficiently. Transferring the revenues of the companies to philanthropic projects will reduce their income and reduce the efficiency of their economic activities, which will primarily support social benefits. With this indirect effect, while the income of the companies will decrease, the social benefit they will create, will also decrease. Thus, it is considered that primarily the companies and the society will suffer (Çelik, 2007).

The classical approach is based on the relationship that Adam Smith has established between justice and goodness. According to this view, which defines justice as perfect rights and imperfect rights, justice should be prioritized and benevolence should be encouraged. However, it is thought that it is not possible to observe this fine distinction at the level of enterprises. According to this view, if society imposes benevolence, it violates the perfect rights of others in favor of the imperfect rights of some. From this point of view, it is important to determine whether managers violate any rights (perfect or faulty) during exchanges between stakeholders. Some CSR activities benefit all stakeholders and therefore do not violate any rights, but some activities may require a compromise between stakeholder groups. Concerning the former, an attempt to increase employee pay can help the company (and its shareholders) by increasing employee well-being while also increasing employee productivity. Similarly, donations to local charities can also be considered to support a company's community image and increase sales. From Smith's point of view, the displacement of benefits between stakeholder groups is questioned at the point where it benefits competitors and harms shareholder rights (Brown & Forster, 2013).

Until the 1929 economic crisis, while the classical public sector approach was adopted by business life, it was understood that giant enterprises did not create social welfare as advocated in the invisible hand theory in this period. Along with this, businesses started to be questioned in terms of CSR. In addition to the fact that businesses only engage in philanthropic activities, the damage they cause to the environment and society has begun to draw attention. To prevent this destruction, laws regulating the environment, human rights, and commercial issues have been started to be regulated. Through these laws, the business world has started to act following the idea that these issues are at least as important as profit and efficiency (Alparslan and Aygün, 2013). Thus, the foundations of the modern approach to CSR were laid.

Modern Social Responsibility Approach

Despite the business-oriented perspective in the classical approach, in the modern CSR approach, businesses need to provide benefits not only on behalf of their shareholders but also on behalf of all stakeholders while carrying out their activities. According to this approach, it is possible for businesses working with a focus on the social benefit to earn profits at the same time. However, the focus should not be on profit maximization, but also on creating social benefit (Özcan 2021).

The modern CSR approach is also called the socio-economic view. According to this view, businesses aim to make a profit in addition to the purpose of providing the social benefit (Şahin, 1996). In other words, according to this view, the primary goal of businesses is not to maximize shareholder profit but to create social benefit. The evolution of the classical management perspective and the definition of business made within the framework of the contemporary management approach also support this argument. According to the definition of modern management, businesses are established to meet social needs, and they also offer the opportunity to earn profits to their shareholders with the activities they carry out in line with this purpose.

Non-profit-oriented practices such as cleaning the lake polluted during the production activities of the enterprise, creating training opportunities to increase the expertise of the employees, and making improvements in the economic conditions of the employees can be given as examples of the modern CSR understanding. With the environmental pollution in the 1980s and the increase in the awareness in society in this direction, the damage caused by the enterprises to the environment has attracted even more reactions, and there has been a public demand for the enterprises to carry out improvement activities in this direction (Şahin, 1996).

Modern organizations should continue their activities not only on production and profitability goals but also on the premise that they influence the development of society with the awareness that they are a part of society. Social responsibility is the manager's obligation to take actions that protect and improve both the welfare of society as a whole and the interests of the organization. According to the modern CSR understanding, managers have to take care of the social outputs while making efforts to realize the social goals and interests of the organization. Within the framework of the modern management approach, the interest shown by both the managers and the society in social responsibility continues to increase for many years (Petrescu, 2018).

At the point reached in the social expectations and the new business world, there is no longer an order in which only economic interests are considered and social destruction is ignored. Earning profits by damaging public resources is no longer an acceptable situation today. Quality expert Kaoru Ishikawa says, "A company's first concern is the happiness of its people. If people don't feel happy, . . . that company does not deserve to exist," and reveals today's way of doing business and the understanding of CSR (Sharma & Talwar, 2005).

At the point reached today, CSR is associated with the vision of creating value. Value creation is viewed from a strategic point of view in two ways; when approached from the classical point of view, the goal of creating profit-oriented value emerges. However, the profitability of businesses focusing on this outdated value understanding is likely to be temporary and end in the short term. Today's equivalent of creating value is that a business carries out its activities by focusing on the benefit of all the stakeholders it affects and is affected by. In this way, sustainable value creation is possible. Trade-offs between economic efficiency and social progress over the years have harmed all stakeholders and rendered value creation sterile. It is pointless to expect it to be possible to create sustainable value by ignoring the well-being of its customers, the depletion of vital natural resources, the viability of key suppliers, or the economic hardship of communities (Porter & Kramer, 2011). Sustainability of value creation will be possible with shared value creation. Today, with the vision of creating shared value, it is aimed to provide the long-term sustainable benefit to all interest groups and it is observed that the practices are shaped in this direction.

Basic Corporate Social Responsibility Models

Within the scope of this chapter, a conceptual framework regarding corporate social responsibility has been tried to be established, and for this purpose, the definition of the concept, its historical development process, its relationship with financial reporting, which is the subject of the book, and its conceptual basis are supported with stakeholder theory. This section features critical models that are essential for the advancement and ultimate definition of the concept in the academic literature. The concept of CSR, which we define on the basis that businesses adopt the principles of CSR and act by considering the benefit of all present and future internal and external stakeholders, first appears as social sensitivity in its progress in the literature. Ackerman's social responsiveness model revealed the characteristics of the concept in its most basic form. Later, in the 60s, the social responsibility model was formed with the compilation of Davis. In 1991, Carroll's pyramid was a crucial milestone in the progression of the concept. In the end, the model of the triple bottom line of Elginkton has narrowed the definition of the CSR into three dimensions. In this section you will find the detail of the models mentioned.

Ackerman's Social Responsiveness Model

Increasing expectations such as clean air, fair employment, honesty in packaging by the society force companies to realize these expectations and act accordingly (Ackerman, 1973).Based on this argument, Ackerman developed the corporate responsiveness model, which is staged as the way companies view and act on social problems in the context of their management level. Ackerman argues that the goal of corporate social effort should be responsiveness. In the model, it is seen that companies operate in three different stages, usually at the Top management, Staff Specialists, and Divisional Management levels, to develop a response to social issues (Sharma & Talwar, 2005).

Figure 2. Conversion of social responsiveness from policy to action
Source: Robert W. Ackerman, "How Companies Respond to Social Demands", Harvard Business Review, July-August 1973 p. 96.

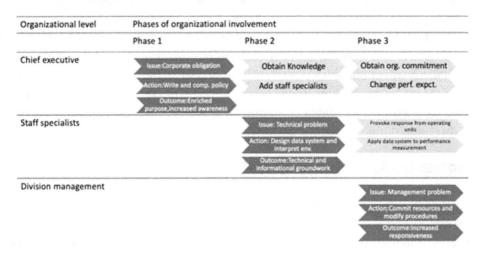

The figure describes the process of institutionalizing a social problem by the Ackerman model. The first stage is; the realization of a social problem by the top management, in the second stage; staff specialists are appointed for the company to look at the problem in more detail and produce a solution, and the third stage is the implementation of the strategy determined by the specialists by the institution. It has gradually revealed the sensitivity and action of model institutions toward social problems (Srivastava et al., 2012). In the first stage, there is a social problem, but its relationship with the institution has not been established. In the third stage, the action to be taken by the institution is determined. The problem that has been brought to the organization and awareness at the senior management (chief executive) level reaches the division manager in the process, and an operational solution is created for the situation, which is a social problem in the first place. In this way, it is ensured that institutions internalize social problems and bring solutions. This is what Ackerman calls the social sensitivity of institutions (Ackerman, 1973).

The Ackerman model is characterized as a strategy that guides the implementation of CSR activities. This model provides strategies for dealing with problems with social consequences. Other parameters and restrictions of CSR activities are not covered by this model (Kanji & Agrawal, 2016).

Davis' Social Responsibility Model

Defining the concept of corporate social responsibility as "expressing the decisions of the managers and the actions of the businesses outside of their direct economic or technical interests", Davis reveals that businesses are responsible to society because they operate by using the resources they receive from the society (Davis, 1960). According to Davis (1975), businesses have more than one reason to be socially responsible. While the institutions operate in the society they are in, they are also exposed to many direct and indirect effects. In this direction, he modeled social responsibility through five propositions. The propositions in the model are called the guidelines of social responsibility. According to the model;

Social responsibility arises from social power; due to the power they hold, businesses have responsibilities towards society. To create a fair relationship in line with the power held, businesses should also take responsibility for their actions.

- Open system interface; businesses must operate with inputs open to the public and open to the public, this is a two-way open system. Businesses should act following this two-way open system.
- Calculation of social costs; according to the classical understanding, while it is sufficient to question the technical feasibility and economic profitability to start a business, it is now necessary to calculate the social cost. It is one of the factors that businesses should pay attention to not only the profitability or technical competence of an activity to be carried out but also the social situations that will result.
- The user pays; in the pricing of a good or service, social costs should be included in addition to the production costs. In this way, it will be ensured that the end user will pay for the social costs that will occur during the production and use of the product.
- Social citizenship of businesses; with this proposition, businesses are accepted as a part of society as legal entities and it is revealed that they will be affected by the activities they carry out as a part of society and outside their fields. Businesses are affected by the results of commercial activities as much as each individual in society. In this respect, they also have the quality of being social citizens. Businesses will enjoy a societal benefit from commercial activities outside their field, just as any citizen would; Therefore, the business community has a responsibility to actively use its capabilities to recognize social problems and help to solve them.

Carroll's Corporate Social Responsibility Pyramid

In Carroll's CSR model, companies have four types of social responsibility; economic, legal, ethical, and philanthropic responsibilities. Institutions are considered socially responsible at different levels under these components.

Figure 3. The pyramid of corporate social responsibility

Economic component: The profit motive is the primary objective of entrepreneurship, companies are first and foremost business entities and are defined as the basic economic units of society. In this direction, the main role of companies is to produce goods and services that will meet the needs of society. However, this should not mean that the company's management only focuses on profit maximization and neglects other responsibilities. The responsibility of making profits for companies, which are the basic economic unit of society, brings other responsibilities. If the economic responsibility is not fulfilled, the survival of the companies will not be possible, and other responsibilities will lose their meaning. For this reason, economic responsibility (profit-making) is defined as the main variable in the model.

Legal component: Carroll refers to the existence of a social contract between companies and society. In line with this contract, businesses are expected to maintain their economic mission within the framework of the law. While society accepts the responsibility of making profits, expects the social framework in which it is located to comply with its legal responsibilities. Companies have to comply with legal procedures in the context of all the activities they carry out and all the products they offer.

Ethical component: Although the legal component includes the norms that must be followed about fairness and justice to some extent, it is lacking in terms of social expectations that are not regulated by law. Ethical responsibilities encompass activities and practices that are expected or prohibited by members of the community. Ethical responsibilities correspond to the expectation that companies act fairly and equitably towards all stakeholders while carrying out their activities. Expectations within the ethical component lead to the formation of new laws and procedures over time. At first glance, ethical expectations are likely to be questioned and found out of place, but in fact, these expectations have the potential to guide the change of laws over time. In this direction, taking into account the ethical elements will also facilitate the adaptation to the legal obligations that will be created soon.

The philanthropic component has been defined as corporate actions taken by society in response to businesses' expectations of being good corporate citizens. Activities carried out by companies to increase social welfare are included in the philanthropy component. Such practices are based on the voluntary basis of companies, there is no obligation for businesses to engage in philanthropic activities. Although the perception in society seems to be the equivalent of philanthropy, which is the highest component of corporate social responsibility other obligations carried out by businesses before this stage are also included in the scope of CSR. The philanthropy component is the one at the top of the pyramid, which is entirely voluntary.

According to the model, economic responsibilities are at the root of the other three components. It is the responsibility of companies to fulfill economic responsibility, in other words, to make a profit, to continue their activities legally, to choose the fairway, and to engage in activities that will benefit other stakeholders. Businesses that fulfill all these components are deemed to have fulfilled their corporate social responsibilities at different levels. The fact that a business that fulfills its economic and legal responsibilities does not engage in ethical and philanthropic activities should not mean that it is completely devoid of social responsibilityObviously, Caroll has fashioned a model that is inclusive and cascades the expectations of institutions in a pyramidal form. In this way, institutions can be considered socially responsible in line with the component they are compatible with.

Triple Bottom Line Theory

Triple bottom line theory was developed by Elkington when he realized that the social and economic dimensions of the agenda in the 1987 Brundtland Report needed to be addressed in a more integrated way for real environmental progress. At the heart of the model is the 3P formulation (people, planet, and profits) first used by Shell as the 3P (Figure 4). With TBL, the context of corporate social responsibility is revealed in three dimensions. With this triple perspective companies should focus not only on the economic value they add but also on the environmental and social values they add or destroy (Elkington, 2004). CSR is based on all stakeholders, has three dimensions: Human (People), Universe (Planet), and Profit (Profit), as opposed to the classical social responsibility perspective that focuses only on shareholders.

Figure 4. Triple bottom line

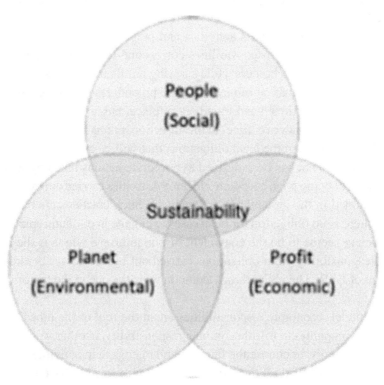

Elkington states 7 sustainability revolutions which are needed by institutions to put this model into practice. According to the author, there are 7 types of revolutions to achieve triple performance: markets, values, transparency, lifecycle technology, partnership, time, and corporate governance (Table 2) (Elkington, 2004).

Table 2. Seven sustainability revolutions

	Old Paradigm → New Paradigm
1 Market	Compliance → Competition
2 Values	Hard → Soft
3 Transparency	Closed → Open
4 Lifecycle technology	Product → Function
5 Partnerships	Subversion → Symbiosis
6 Times	Wider → Longer
7 Corporate governance	Exclusive → Inclusive

1. Revolution will be driven largely by competition through markets. Markets operating in compliance will be replaced by a more aggressive market where competition is accelerating. The business world will operate more in markets that are more open to competition, both locally and internationally.

With the radical change occurring at the level of the markets, changes are expected at the global level.

2. Revolution is driven by the worldwide change in human and societal values. With the revolution that will take place in line with values, the business world will have to keep up with the new order. Institutional crises in the context of values allowed this revolution to accelerate.

3. Revolution is taking place in line with increased international transparency. With the development of technology, the demand for increased transparency is intensifying. In the corporate context, the opening of the Global Reporting Initiative (GRI) in 2001 is one of the strongest symbols of this trend. With this revolution, institutions are evolving from closed systems to open systems.

4. Revolution, with the change in life-cycle technology, a transformation is taking place in which companies have to change the focus of the final product and oversee the whole process, from the extraction of raw materials to recycling or disposal. With this revolution, the perspective of focusing on the function of the production material at each stage rather than the product is gained.

5. Revolution will establish various partnerships with companies and other organizations. The rate of emergence of new forms of partnerships, including various campaign groups, will accelerate.

6. Revolution will occur in the way we understand and manage time. In addition to short and medium-term interests, the perspective of thinking for future generations will spread in the long term. The perception of time extends at the level of companies in this sense.

7. Revolution is realized with the internalization of corporate governance by getting stronger with the support of other revolutions. It will be possible to establish a sustainable business world with widespread institutionalization not only in process and product design but also in the entire value chain and evolution to a corporate life based on the triple bottom line model.

It is emphasized that the transition to the TBL model can be fully achieved with the 7-stage revolution process. Sustainability revolutions in these 7 steps, which Elkington put forward as possible revolutions in those years, seem to have been achieved to a large extent today. Although it seems that the integration of the TBL model into corporate life and its grounding in almost all processes has been achieved to a large extent, efforts are continuing at the international level to further internalize and expand the model.

CONCLUSION

In today's world, where the importance of a sustainable life for all the stakeholders of the society has become undeniable, the obligations and contributions of businesses at this point are also being examined to a great extent. From this point of view, the concept of corporate social responsibility, which continues its development, emerges as the most critical concept in which businesses can be evaluated in the context of the goal of creating a sustainable planet. Using today's resources with future generations in mind is the main goal of the social responsibilities of businesses.

Within the scope of this section, the concept of CSR of enterprises is examined in the context of its theoretical framework. How the obligations of businesses to enhance sustainability are defined within the framework of the CSR concept, the evolution that businesses have undergone throughout history, from the approach that only takes care of their shareholders to the understanding of value creation that we have reached today; its relationship with stakeholder theory, its similarities and differences; Theoretical approaches to the concept and the main basic models developed for the CSR concept are discussed in the chapter.

At the point at which we are today, we can see that the businesses have moved to focusing on sustainability activities in order to create a real value, not just to gain social support. Many businesses that engage in activities that harm the interests of stakeholders with the concern of profit maximization and that carry out sustainability dynamics only within the framework of their obligations still continue their activities. However, at this point, it is seen that there is a direction in the direction of decreasing the practices that will harm the sustainability dynamics, regardless of the basic motivation. At this point, in addition to the common goals created at the international level, the general awareness and social consciousness formed in this direction, the regulations that are increasing day by day have a great effect. It is important that this study reveals the theoretical framework of the positive evolution observed in the sustainability activities of businesses in the context of CSR.

As a result of the literature review made within the scope of this chapter, the development process of the concept throughout history has been revealed. The roots of the concept, which trace back to the Middle Ages, long before the phrase corporate social responsibility was coined, are now being developed within the boundaries of strategic corporate social responsibility (SCSR) and shared value creation (CSV). With the increasing awareness of the concept of corporate social responsibility, it is observed that stakeholders demand reporting on social and environmental activities, apart from financial activities, from businesses.

It is foreseen that the concept will continue to progress in the direction shared value creation (CSV), and the supply of non-financial reporting is expected to increase gradually in this direction. While it is observed that the companies that go public share their reports on social and environmental activities more widely today, it is expected that this report, which is based on voluntariness, will increase over the years by small businesses and other large enterprises that are not offered to the public. The reason for this is the principle of legitimacy, in the eyes of the stakeholders (Beck et al, 2017). It is expected that businesses that have these concerns will participate in non-financial reporting in the name of sustainability, with the understanding of creating value for stakeholders becoming widespread in the coming period.

From an academic point of view, it is important to carry out studies in three dimensions in the future direction; (1) The theoretical deepening of the studies on the concept of CSR on the basis of stakeholder theory, (2) Contributing to the process by making various analyzes in line with the data obtained from non-financial reports, (3) within the framework of this newly developed reporting system, identifying the parts identified in the CSR literature but missing in the reporting and conveying them to the relevant parties.

This book discusses the evolution of sustainability in line with non-financial reporting. This chapter presents the CSR conceptual framework, which forms the basis of non-financial reporting, in the context of stakeholder theory. With the classical point of view, the understanding that focuses only on shareholder profit and considers financial reporting sufficient has evolved into a modern understanding that takes care of all stakeholders and adopts transparent disclosure of non-financial activities. This study has a unique value in terms of presenting the theoretical conceptual framework in a way that will form the basis for the relations between the concepts to be established in the other chapters of the book.

REFERENCES

Ackerman, R. W. (1973). How companies respond to social demands. *Harvard Business Review*, *51*(4), 88–98.

Aktan, C. C., & Börü, D. (2007). Kurumsal sosyal sorumluluk. Kurumsal sosyal sorumluluk. *İşletmeler ve sosyal sorumluluk*, 11-36.

Alparslan, A. G. A., & Aygün, M. (2013). Kurumsal Sosyal Sorumluluk ve Firma Performansı. *Süleyman Demirel Üniversitesi İktisadi ve İdari Bilimler Fakültesi Dergisi*, *18*(1), 435–448.

Beck, C., Dumay, J., & Frost, G. (2017). In pursuit of a 'single source of truth': From threatened legitimacy to integrated reporting. *Journal of Business Ethics*, *141*(1), 191–205. doi:10.100710551-014-2423-1

Bowen, H. R. (1953). Graduate education in economics. *The American Economic Review*, *43*(4), iv-223.

Brown, J. A., & Forster, W. R. (2013). CSR and stakeholder theory: A tale of Adam Smith. *Journal of Business Ethics*, *112*(2), 301–312. doi:10.100710551-012-1251-4

Carroll, A. B. (1979). A three-dimensional conceptual model of corporate performance. *Academy of Management Review*, *4*(4), 497–505. doi:10.2307/257850

Carroll, A. B. (1991). The pyramid of corporate social responsibility: Toward the moral management of organizational stakeholders. *Business Horizons*, *34*(4), 39–48. doi:10.1016/0007-6813(91)90005-G

Carroll, A. B. (2008). A history of corporate social responsibility: Concepts and practices. The Oxford handbook of corporate social responsibility.

Çelik, A. (2007). Şirketlerin Sosyal Sorumluluklari. Kurumsal sosyal sorumluluk. *İşletmeler ve sosyal sorumluluk*, 43-58.

Chaffee, E. C. (2017). The origins of corporate social responsibility. *University of Cincinnati Law Review*, *85*, 347–373.

Chandler, D. (2016). *Strategic corporate social responsibility: Sustainable value creation*. SAGE Publications.

Chandler, D., & Werther, W. B. Jr. (2013). *Strategic corporate social responsibility: Stakeholders, globalization, and sustainable value creation*. Sage Publications.

Crowther, D., & Aras, G. (2008). *Corporate social responsibility*. Bookboon.

Davis, K. (1960). Can business afford to ignore social responsibilities? *California Management Review*, *2*(3), 70–76. doi:10.2307/41166246

Davis, K. (1975). Five propositions for social responsibility. *Business Horizons*, *18*(3), 19–24. doi:10.1016/0007-6813(75)90048-8

Di Vaio, A., Varriale, L., Di Gregorio, A., & Adomako, S. (2022). Corporate social performance and non-financial reporting in the cruise industry: Paving the way towards UN Agenda 2030. *Corporate Social Responsibility and Environmental Management*, *29*(6), 1931–1953. doi:10.1002/csr.2292

Donaldson, T., & Preston, L. E. (1995). The stakeholder theory of the corporation: Concepts, evidence, and implications. *Academy of Management Review*, *20*(1), 65–91. doi:10.2307/258887

Eilbirt, H., & Parket, I. R. (1973). The practice of business: The current status of corporate social responsibility. *Business Horizons*, *16*(4), 5–14. doi:10.1016/0007-6813(73)90043-8

Elkington, J. (2004). Enter the triple bottom line. In *The Triple Bottom Line* (pp. 1–16). Routledge.

Freeman, R. E. (1994). The politics of stakeholder theory: Some future directions. *Business Ethics Quarterly*, *4*(4), 409–421. doi:10.2307/3857340

Freeman, R. E., & Dmytriyev, S. (2017). Corporate Social Responsibility and Stakeholder Theory: Learning From Each Other. *Symphonya. Emerging Issues in Management*, 7-15. https://doi.org/. doi:10.4468/2017.1.02

Freeman, R. E., Harrison, J. S., Wicks, A. C., Parmar, B. L., & De Colle, S. (2010). *Stakeholder theory: The state of the art*. Academic Press.

Friedman, A. L., & Miles, S. (2002). Developing stakeholder theory. *Journal of Management Studies*, *39*(1), 1–21. doi:10.1111/1467-6486.00280

García-Sánchez, I. M., Gómez-Miranda, M. E., David, F., & Rodríguez-Ariza, L. (2019). Board independence and GRI-IFC performance standards: The mediating effect of the CSR committee. *Journal of Cleaner Production*, *225*, 554–562. doi:10.1016/j.jclepro.2019.03.337

Gold, A., Heilmann, M., Pott, C., & Rematzki, J. (2020). Do key audit matters impact financial reporting behavior? *International Journal of Auditing*, *24*(2), 232–244. doi:10.1111/ijau.12190

Heald, M. (1957). Management's responsibility to society: The growth of an idea. *Business History Review*, *31*(4), 375–384. doi:10.2307/3111413

Jones, T. M. (1980). Corporate social responsibility revisited, redefined. *California Management Review*, *22*(3), 59–67. doi:10.2307/41164877

Kanji, R., & Agrawal, R. (2016). Models of Corporate Social Responsibility: Comparison, Evolution and Convergence. *IIM Kozhikode Society & Management Review*, *5*(2), 141–155. doi:10.1177/2277975216634478

Latapí Agudelo, M. A., Jóhannsdóttir, L., & Davídsdóttir, B. (2019). A literature review of the history and evolution of corporate social responsibility. *International Journal of Corporate Social Responsibility*, *4*(1), 1–23. doi:10.118640991-018-0039-y

Madhani, P. M. (2008). Role of voluntary disclosure and transparency in financial reporting. In D. Alagiri & K. Mallela (Eds.), *Corporate financial reporting - changing scenario* (pp. 75–81). ICFAI University Press.

Martínez-Ferrero, J., Garcia-Sanchez, I. M., & Cuadrado-Ballesteros, B. (2015). Effect of financial reporting quality on sustainability information disclosure. *Corporate Social Responsibility and Environmental Management*, *22*(1), 45–64. doi:10.1002/csr.1330

Murray, K. B., & Montanari, J. B. (1986). Strategic management of the socially responsible firm: Integrating management and marketing theory. *Academy of Management Review*, *11*(4), 815–827. doi:10.2307/258399

OECD. (2001). *Corporate Social Responsibility: Partners for Progress.* OECD.

Ortiz-Martínez, E., Marín-Hernández, S., & Santos-Jaén, J. M. (2022). Sustainability, corporate social responsibility, non-financial reporting and company performance: Relationships and mediating effects in Spanish small and medium sized enterprises. *Sustainable Production and Consumption.*

Özbay, D. (2019). Türkiye'de finansal olmayan raporlama ve gelişim trendi. *Uluslararası Yönetim İktisat ve İşletme Dergisi*, *15*(2), 445–462.

Özcan, G. (2021). *Yeni tüketici açısından kurumsal sosyal sorumluluk yaklaşımının kurumsal itibar ve tüketicilerin tavsiye etme niyetine etkisi üzerine bir araştırma* [PhD thesis].

Perrini, F. (2006). The practitioner's perspective on non-financial reporting. *California Management Review*, *48*(2), 73–103. doi:10.2307/41166339

Petrescu, I. (2018). Social responsibility in modern management. *Review of General Management*, *28*(2), 5–15.

Porter, M. E., & Kramer, M. R. (2011). Creating shared value. *Harvard Business Review.*

Şahin, E. (1996). *İşletme-çevre etkileşimi ve işletmelerin sosyal sorumluluğu* [Master thesis]. Selçuk University SBE.

Sancar, O. (2021). *Hastane Çalışanlarının Kurumsal Sosyal Sorumluluk Algısının Ekstra Rol Davranışlarına Etkisi* [Doctoral dissertation]. Marmara Universitesi.

Schwartz, M. S., & Carroll, A. B. (2003). Corporate social responsibility: A three-domain approach. *Business Ethics Quarterly*, *13*(4), 503–530. doi:10.5840/beq200313435

Sharma, A. K., & Talwar, B. (2005). Corporate social responsibility: Modern vis-à-vis Vedic approach. *Measuring Business Excellence*, *9*(1), 35–45. doi:10.1108/13683040510588828

Srivastava, A. K., Negi, G., Mishra, V., & Pandey, S. (2012). Corporate social responsibility: A case study of TATA group. *IOSR Journal of Business and Management*, *3*(5), 17–27. doi:10.9790/487X-0351727

Turkish Ministry of Foreign Affairs. (2023). *Política Externa Empreendedora e Humanitária.* https://www.mfa.gov.tr/surdurullenen-kalkinma.tr.mfa

UNCTAD. (1999). *Preparing for future multilateral trade negotiations: issues and research needs from a development perspective.* UNCTAD.

UNIDO. (2023). *Definition of CSR.* https://www.unido.org/our-focus/advancing-economic-competitiveness/competitive-trade-capacities-and-corporate-responsibility/corporate-social-responsibility-market-integration/what-csr

Vos, J. F. (2003). Corporate social responsibility and the identification of stakeholders. *Corporate Social Responsibility and Environmental Management, 10*(3), 141–152. doi:10.1002/csr.39

Watson, A., Shrives, P., & Marston, C. (2002). Voluntary disclosure of accounting ratios in the UK. *The British Accounting Review, 34*(4), 289–313. doi:10.1006/bare.2002.0213

Wren, D. A., & Bedeian, A. G. (2009). *The evolution of management thought.* John Wiley & Sons.

KEY TERMS AND DEFINITIONS

Accountability: Means that organizations are aware of the environment affected by their activities and they accept responsibility for their actions with this understanding.

Classic CSR Approach: Supports the idea that corporations are only responsible to satisfy their shareholders' benefit, and it expects the other parties' benefits will be satisfied indirectly by the way.

Corporate Social Responsibility: Is the concern and motivation of businesses to take care of the benefit of all stakeholders and create value for each of them while carrying out their activities.

Modern CSR Approach: Supports the idea that corporations should work for creating value for all parties they interact with and shareholders' benefit will be satisfied automatically by the way.

Stakeholder Theory: Is the theory based upon the assumption that business is an open system, and should be able to do its activities in order to satisfy the needs of all actors with whom it interacts.

Sustainability: Puts emphasis on our obligation to future generations in the consumption of resources.

Transparency: Means that institutions continue to conduct their activities so as to allow each person involved in the process to have access to the required information.

Chapter 5
Corporate Social Responsibility Practices and Reporting:
A Conceptual Analysis

Muhammad Junaid Ahsan

https://orcid.org/0000-0002-5754-8187

University of Pisa, Italy

ABSTRACT

This chapter provides a comprehensive analysis of corporate social responsibility (CSR) practices and reporting. It begins with an overview of the history and evolution of CSR and presents different approaches to CSR. The theoretical foundations of CSR, including stakeholder, social contract, legitimacy, and resource dependence theories, are then discussed. This chapter explores the importance of CSR reporting and the different perspectives on CSR, including social accounting and social responsibility disclosure. Additionally, the impact of CSR practices and reporting on an organization's performance and reputation is examined, along with the determinants of non-financial information reporting. The roles and challenges of accounting, finance, management, and auditing professionals in CSR practices and reporting are discussed, including challenges for professionals.

INTRODUCTION

Corporate Social Responsibility (CSR) has gained significant attention in recent years as organizations strive to create a positive impact on society and the environment. CSR refers to organizations' voluntary actions to address the social and environmental impacts of their operations (Battisti, Nirino, Leonidou, & Thrassou, 2022). As stakeholder expectations and concerns continue to evolve, CSR practices and reporting are becoming increasingly important. CSR practices and reporting are becoming increasingly important, as organizations strive to meet stakeholders' expectations and create a positive impact on society (Carroll, 2021). CSR practices include initiatives such as energy efficiency, community engagement, diversity, and inclusion. These practices are intended not only to minimize negative impacts but also to create positive contributions to society and the environment (Yasir et al., 2021).

DOI: 10.4018/978-1-6684-9076-1.ch005

CSR has emerged as a focal point of attention in both the academic and business spheres, prompting extensive discussions and debates to unravel its scope and implications (Ahsan, 2023; Swanson, 2021; Wesselink & Osagie, 2020; Yasir et al., 2021). The evolving nature of CSR and its multifaceted dimensions pose a formidable challenge to establishing a universally accepted definition. Scholars and experts from diverse fields have proposed various definitions of CSR, reflecting the dynamic and contextual nature of the concept (Matten & Moon, 2020; Zhao, Yang, Wang, & Michelson, 2023).

Defining CSR constitutes a significant conundrum in the literature because it encompasses the economic, social, and environmental aspects. Attempts to confine CSR within rigid frameworks have proven challenging because their essence transcends traditional boundaries (Du & Xie, 2021). Scholars have sought to capture the essence of CSR through various lenses, resulting in a plethora of perspectives (Dwivedi et al., 2022).

For some researchers, CSR embodies the voluntary actions that organizations undertake to address social and environmental impacts that surpass their legal obligations (Carroll, 1979; Szőcs & Schlegelmilch, 2020). This perspective emphasizes that responsible organizations proactively engage in initiatives that extend beyond legal mandates, reflecting their commitment to societal and environmental well-being. However, (Lu et al., 2021); Moon (2007) underscores the significance of CSR in contributing to broader societal welfare and sustainable development. In this view, CSR is not merely a reactive response, but an integral part of a company's mission to create positive impacts on society and the environment.

Moreover, the CSR literature transcends geographical boundaries and presents contextual variations across different industries and regions. The diverse array of definitions underscores that CSR's meaning is not fixed, but rather influenced by the socio-cultural, economic, and environmental contexts within which organizations operate. Understanding how difficult it is to define CSR is vital to advancing the field and fostering a comprehensive understanding of its significance.

This chapter provides a conceptual analysis of CSR practices and reporting and explores the history and evolution of CSR, different CSR approaches, and the significance of CSR reporting. The theoretical foundations of CSR, including stakeholder, social contract, legitimacy, and resource dependence theories, are discussed to provide a comprehensive understanding of the conceptual framework of CSR.

Furthermore, this chapter addresses CSR adoption between developed and developing countries. Additionally, this chapter examines perspectives on CSR reporting, including social accounting and social responsibility disclosure, and the impact of CSR practices and reporting on an organization's performance and reputation. Determinants of non-financial information reporting, the role and challenges of accounting, finance, management, and auditing professionals in CSR practices and reporting, and challenges for professionals are also discussed.

Finally, this chapter highlights the significant impact of global sustainability reporting standards, such as those of the Global Reporting Initiative (GRI) and the International Standards Organization (ISO), on non-financial information reporting. Overall, this chapter provides valuable insights into the concept of CSR and its importance to organizations in the modern business landscape.

HISTORY OF CSR

The history and evolution of CSR can be traced back to the early 20th century, when organizations began to recognize their social and environmental responsibilities. In the 1950s and the 1960s, CSR focused mainly on philanthropy and charitable activities (Latapí Agudelo, Jóhannsdóttir, & Davídsdóttir, 2019). In the 1970s, there was a significant shift in the focus of CSR towards environmental and social issues. This is mainly because of growing concerns over environmental degradation and social injustice. Organizations began to take a more proactive approach to addressing these issues and started to develop policies and practices to reduce their negative impacts on society and the environment (Latapí Agudelo et al., 2019).

The 1980s and the 1990s saw the evolution of CSR as a strategic function of organizations. Companies have begun to view CSR as a way to improve their reputation and create a competitive advantage (Wesselink & Osagie, 2020). CSR has become more closely linked to business strategy, and organizations have started to integrate social and environmental considerations into their decision-making processes.

Today, CSR is considered an integral part of an organization's operations, and companies are expected to consider the social and environmental impacts of their actions in all areas of their business. CSR practices and reporting have become increasingly important as organizations strive to meet stakeholder expectations and create a positive impact on society.

Sustainability is another important aspect of CSR. Sustainability refers to the ability of organizations to meet present needs without compromising the ability of future generations to meet their own needs (Verma, 2019). CSR practices and reporting can help organizations identify and mitigate social and environmental risks and improve their long-term performance.

In summary, the history and evolution of CSR are complex subjects that have undergone significant changes over the years. CSR has come a long way from its early roots in philanthropy to its current role as a strategic function of organizations. Today, CSR is a vital part of an organization's operations, and it is essential for companies to incorporate social and environmental considerations into their decision-making processes. By doing so, companies can create a positive impact on society and the environment while also improving their long-term performance.

APPROACHES OF CSR

There are different approaches to CSR, including philanthropic, moral, and strategic. The **philanthropic approach** to CSR, also known as the charitable approach, involves organizations engaging in charitable activities and donating a portion of their profits to charitable causes (Hack, Kenyon, & Wood, 2014). Philanthropic CSR can take the form of donations, sponsorships, or other forms of charitable giving. This approach is often seen as a way for organizations to return to the community and build a positive reputation (Awan, Khattak, & Kraslawski, 2019). However, critics argue that philanthropic CSR can be superficial and may not address underlying social and environmental issues (Haydon, Jung, & Russell, 2021).

The **moral approach** to CSR is based on the belief that organizations have ethical and moral responsibilities towards their stakeholders, including employees, customers, suppliers, and the wider society (Schmeltz, 2012). This approach is often associated with the concept of corporate citizenship, which refers to the idea that organizations have a duty to contribute to the well-being of the society in which they operate (Tamvada, 2020). The moral approach to CSR emphasizes the importance of ethical behavior, transparency, and accountability in all areas of an organization's operations.

The **strategic approach** to CSR, also known as the business case approach, focuses on the idea that CSR can create a competitive advantage for organizations (McElhaney, 2009).. This approach is based on the belief that CSR can help organizations build trust and credibility with stakeholders, attract and retain talent, and improve their reputations (Nave & Ferreira, 2019). The strategic approach to CSR emphasizes the importance of integrating CSR into an organization's overall business strategy and aligning CSR initiatives with its goals and values.

There are also other approaches to CSR, including stakeholder and sustainability approaches. The **stakeholder approach** to CSR emphasizes the importance of considering the interests and needs of all stakeholders, including employees, customers, suppliers, shareholders, and wider society, in an organization's decision-making processes (Freeman & Velamuri, 2021). The sustainability approach to CSR focuses on the long-term environmental and social impacts of an organization's operations, and emphasizes the importance of sustainable development.

Organizations can adopt one or more of these approaches to CSR depending on their goals, values, and priorities. However, it is important for organizations to understand the different approaches to CSR and develop a clear CSR strategy that aligns with their overall business strategies and values.

In recent years, there has been growing recognition that CSR should not be viewed as a separate function within an organization, but rather as an integral part of an organization's operations and decision-making processes. This has led to the emergence of the concept of **shared value approach**, which refers to the idea that organizations can create value for themselves and society by addressing social and environmental issues in their operations. The shared-value approach to CSR emphasizes the importance of creating sustainable business models that deliver both economic and social benefits (Menghwar & Daood, 2021).

In recent years, researchers have delved into understanding the nuances of CSR adoption in both developed and developing countries, uncovering distinct patterns and motivations that guide CSR practices in these diverse contexts. Notably, the emphasis on CSR differs significantly between developed and developing economies, reflecting the unique socio-economic and cultural landscapes in which companies operate (Abdelhalim & Eldin, 2019).

In developed economies, CSR initiatives are often driven by consumer demand for ethical and sustainable products and services (He & Harris, 2020). Consumers in these regions are increasingly conscious of the environmental and social impacts of their purchasing decisions, leading companies to integrate CSR practices into their business models as a means to appeal to this growing market segment. Companies in developed countries place significant importance on addressing environmental issues, such as carbon emissions and waste reduction, to meet the expectations of environmentally conscious consumers (Nguyen, Parker, Brennan, & Lockrey, 2020).

On the other hand, in developing countries, CSR tends to be more closely tied to social development goals and community welfare (Khaled, Ali, & Mohamed, 2021). Given the pressing challenges faced by these regions, including poverty, lack of access to education, and inadequate healthcare, CSR initiatives in developing economies often prioritize community engagement and social upliftment. For instance, companies may invest in local infrastructure development, support education and skill-building programs, and address pressing societal issues to positively impact the communities they serve (Jamali, Zanhour, & Keshishian, 2009; Jones, Edwards, Bocarro, Svensson, & Misener, 2020).

Organizations operating in diverse regions must be cognizant of the unique challenges and priorities of the communities they serve. This understanding is important in designing CSR initiatives that are not only effective in achieving social and environmental goals but also resonate with the expectations and values of stakeholders in different regions.

Overall, the different approaches to CSR reflect an evolving understanding of the role of organizations in society and the importance of considering social and environmental impacts in business decision-making. While there is no one-size-fits-all approach to CSR, organizations that adopt a clear and strategic approach are more likely to create positive social and environmental impacts while also achieving their business goals.

THEORETICAL FOUNDATIONS OF CSR AND ITS RELATIONSHIP WITH NON-FINANCIAL INFORMATION REPORTING

The theoretical foundations of CSR are rooted in various disciplines, including business ethics, sociology, and environmental management. The concept of CSR has evolved over time and several theories have been proposed to explain its nature and purpose.

Stakeholder theory is one of the most influential theories in the field of CSR as it provides a framework for understanding the social and environmental responsibilities of organizations. The theory was first introduced by Edward Freeman, a business scholar at the University of Virginia, in 1984 in his book "Strategic Management: A Stakeholder Approach." (Freeman, 1984, 2010).

According to stakeholder theory, organizations are responsible for all stakeholders, including shareholders, employees, customers, suppliers, and the community. This means that organizations should not only consider the interests of their shareholders but also take into account the interests of other stakeholders who are affected by their actions. Stakeholder theory recognizes that stakeholders have different interests and expectations and that organizations must balance these interests to create long-term value for all stakeholders.

Stakeholder theory proposes that organizations should be managed in a way that maximizes the interests of all stakeholders rather than just the interests of shareholders. This means that organizations should consider the social and environmental impacts of their operations and take steps to mitigate any negative impacts. For example, a company may invest in renewable energy to reduce its carbon footprint or implement diversity and inclusion programs to promote a more equitable workplace. The stakeholder theory emphasizes the importance of stakeholder engagement, which involves communicating with stakeholders and understanding their needs and expectations. By engaging with stakeholders, organizations can build trust and credibility, and develop more effective CSR strategies that align with stakeholder interests.

One of the key strengths of stakeholder theory is that it recognizes that organizations operate within a broader social and environmental context and that they have a responsibility to contribute to the well-being of society as a whole. The theory also recognizes that organizations can create long-term value by investing in CSR initiatives that benefit all stakeholders rather than just focusing on short-term financial gains.

However, stakeholder theory has also been criticized for being too broad and vague and for failing to provide specific guidance on how organizations should balance the interests of different stakeholders (Goyal, 2022). Critics have also argued that this theory does not provide a clear framework for measuring the social and environmental impacts of CSR initiatives (Eizaguirre, García-Feijoo, & Laka, 2019; Goyal, 2022).

Despite these criticisms, stakeholder theory remains an important framework for understanding organizations' social and environmental responsibilities. The theory has influenced the development of CSR reporting standards and guidelines and has helped to shape the way organizations think about their relationships with stakeholders. Recognizing the importance of stakeholder engagement and considering the interests of all stakeholders, organizations can create more sustainable and responsible business practices that benefit society as a whole.

Another theory of CSR is the **social contract theory**, which suggests that organizations have a moral obligation to society (Muldoon, 2016; Rosenfeld, 1984). This theory argues that organizations have a social contract with society and that they have the responsibility to act in the best interests of society. Social contract theory emphasizes the importance of organizations fulfilling their moral obligations to society and has been used to justify the inclusion of non-financial information in CSR reporting.

Social contract theory has its roots in political philosophy, particularly in the work of 17th-century philosopher John Locke, who argued that individuals form societies and create governments to protect their natural rights. In the business context, social contract theory suggests that organizations have an obligation to act in the best interests of society because they benefit from operating within it.

Social contract theory has been used to justify the inclusion of non-financial information in CSR reporting. This is because non-financial information, such as a company's impact on the environment or its treatment of employees, is an important part of fulfilling an organization's moral obligations to society. By disclosing this information, organizations can demonstrate their commitment to fulfilling their social contracts with society.

One potential criticism of the social contract theory is that it is difficult to define and measure an organization's obligations to society. This can make it challenging for organizations to determine what actions should be taken to fulfill their moral obligations. Additionally, critics argue that social contract theory places an undue burden on organizations to act in the best interests of society, rather than simply pursuing profit (Rothstein, 2021).

Despite these criticisms, social contract theory has had a significant impact on CSR development. It has helped shift the focus of CSR from solely economic and legal obligations to broader social and environmental concerns. It has also influenced the way organizations report on their CSR activities, with many companies now including nonfinancial information in their CSR reports.

Overall, social contract theory provides a framework for understanding the moral obligations of organizations to society. While it may not provide a definitive answer to what organizations should do to fulfill these obligations, it has helped shape the way that CSR is understood and practiced today.

The third theory of CSR is **legitimacy theory**, which suggests that organizations are responsible for maintaining their legitimacy (Deegan, 2006; Preston, 1975). According to this theory, organizations must meet the expectations of society to be perceived as legitimate and must demonstrate their social responsibility in order to maintain their social license to operate. Legitimacy theory emphasizes the importance of organizations being responsive to the expectations of society and transparent about their social and environmental performance. Legitimacy theory is rooted in institutional theory, which suggests that organizations are influenced by the norms, values, and expectations of the broader social and cultural context in which they operate. Legitimacy theory suggests that organizations must be seen as legitimate in the eyes of society to be successful over the long term.

One way that organizations can maintain their legitimacy is to be transparent about their social and environmental performance. This includes disclosing information about CSR practices and policies, and being responsive to stakeholder concerns. By doing so, organizations can build trust and credibility with stakeholders, which can enhance their legitimacy.

In addition to transparency, legitimacy theory emphasizes the importance of responsiveness. This means that organizations must be responsive to the expectations of society and must demonstrate their social responsibility through their actions. Organizations that fail to do so may face criticism or backlash from stakeholders, which can damage their legitimacy. Legitimacy theory has been used to justify the inclusion of non-financial information in CSR reporting. Organizations can demonstrate their commitment to social responsibility and maintain their legitimacy by providing stakeholders with information about their social and environmental performance.

In summary, the legitimacy theory of CSR suggests that organizations have the responsibility to maintain their legitimacy by being socially responsible and meeting the expectations of society. This theory emphasizes the importance of transparency and responsiveness in maintaining legitimacy and has been used to justify the inclusion of non-financial information in CSR reporting.

Finally, the fourth theory of CSR is the **resource dependence theory**, which suggests that organizations are responsible for managing their relationships with stakeholders to maintain their access to resources (Davis & Cobb, 2010; Hillman, Withers, & Collins, 2009). This theory was first proposed in the 1970s by Pfeffer and Salancik and has since been expanded by scholars such as Hillman and Davis.

According to this theory, organizations must manage their relationships with stakeholders to maintain access to resources such as capital, talent, and raw materials. Resource dependence theory emphasizes the importance of organizations being responsive to the expectations of stakeholders and transparent about their social and environmental performance.

In this theory, CSR is seen as a way for organizations to manage their relationships with stakeholders and maintain their access to key resources. By engaging in socially responsible practices, organizations can build trust and credibility with their stakeholders and ensure their continued support.

For example, a company that engages in sustainable sourcing practices for raw materials can build a positive reputation with its suppliers and ensure a reliable supply chain. By treating employees well and providing a safe and healthy work environment, a company can attract and retain its top talent. By engaging with and giving back to the community, a company can build its goodwill and support its business.

The resource dependence theory also highlights the importance of transparency and accountability in CSR reporting. By reporting on their social and environmental performance, organizations can build trust with stakeholders and demonstrate their commitment to responsible business practices.

Overall, the resource dependence theory provides a framework for understanding the importance of CSR in managing stakeholder relationships and ensuring access to key resources. By engaging in socially responsible practices and reporting their CSR efforts, organizations can build trust, credibility, and long-term success.

CSR REPORTING STANDARDS

CSR reporting is an important aspect of CSR as it enables organizations to communicate their CSR efforts and impacts on stakeholders. CSR reporting is the process of disclosing information about an organization's CSR practices, policies, and performance. CSR reporting helps organizations build trust and credibility with stakeholders as it provides transparency and accountability for their CSR activities. Additionally, CSR reporting can help organizations identify areas for improvement in their CSR practices and set goals for future performance.

For implementation of CSR reporting, an significant aspect is Section 135 of the 2013 Companies Act, an important legislative provision that addresses companies' CSR practices (Gatti, Vishwanath, Seele, & Cottier, 2019). Enshrined within the legal framework of the Act, this provision mandates that certain qualifying companies allocate a specified portion of their profits to CSR initiatives. Under this provision, qualifying companies are required to establish a CSR committee comprising board members and other stakeholders to formulate and oversee the company's CSR policies and initiatives. The Act further outlines the specific areas in which CSR activities can be undertaken, such as promoting education, ensuring environmental sustainability, supporting healthcare initiatives, and empowering marginalized communities. This legislative provision not only imparts a sense of social responsibility to corporations, but also encourages them to contribute meaningfully to the well-being of society and the environment.

The **Global Reporting Initiative** (GRI) is a widely recognized and used framework for CSR reporting. It was established in 1997 and has become one of the most widely adopted standards for CSR reporting, with over 10,000 organizations using its reporting guidelines. The GRI provides a comprehensive framework for reporting a range of sustainability issues including environmental, social, and governance (ESG) factors. GRI standards are updated regularly to ensure that they remain relevant to the changing business landscape and stakeholder expectations.

The **Sustainability Accounting Standards Board** (SASB) is another widely used CSR reporting framework. The SASB provides a set of industry-specific standards for ESG reporting that are designed to be comparable across companies within the same industry. SASB standards cover a range of issues, including environmental, social, and governance factors, and are designed to be integrated with financial reporting.

The **Carbon Disclosure Project** (CDP) is a framework for reporting environmental performance, including carbon emissions. The CDP is a global initiative that provides a platform for companies to disclose their environmental impacts and performance to investors and stakeholders. The CDP provides a standardized questionnaire for companies to complete that covers a range of environmental factors, including carbon emissions, water usage, and waste management.

The **Integrated reporting** framework is a relatively new framework for CSR reporting, which was established in 2013. The framework provides guidance on how organizations can report their value creation over time, including their financial, environmental, and social performance. The Integrated Reporting Framework is designed to help organizations communicate how they create value in the short, medium, and long term and to help stakeholders understand how the organization is managing its risks and opportunities.

While there are many different frameworks for CSR reporting, no single standard or framework is universally accepted. However, the GRI is considered the most comprehensive and widely used standard for CSR reporting. Many organizations choose to use multiple frameworks for their reporting, depending on their industry, stakeholder expectations, and the specific issues they are addressing.

In addition to using frameworks for CSR reporting, many organizations participate in external assurance processes, such as audits and reviews, to validate their CSR reporting. Assurance provides stakeholders with additional confidence in the accuracy and reliability of the information reported by the organization. External assurance can also help organizations identify areas for improvement in their CSR practices and reporting.

Overall, CSR reporting is an important tool for organizations to communicate their CSR efforts and impact stakeholders. While there are many different frameworks for CSR reporting, GRI is widely considered the most comprehensive and widely used standard. External assurance can provide additional confidence in the accuracy and reliability of CSR reports. By communicating their CSR efforts and impacts through CSR reporting, organizations can build trust and credibility with stakeholders and demonstrate their commitment to sustainable business practices.

DIFFERENT ORIENTATIONS OF CSR REPORTING

Social accounting, social responsibility accounting, socioeconomic accounting, social reporting, and social responsibility disclosure were among the initial names given to procedures for assessing and disclosing the effects of corporations' operations on natural and social environments (Parker, 1986, p. 3). Various authors have used phrases such as social responsibility reporting and sustainability reporting (Amran, Lee, & Devi, 2014; Bouten, Everaert, Van Liedekerke, De Moor, & Christiaens, 2011; Friedman & Miles, 2001). A social audit is a procedure that is used to "identify, analyze, measure (if practicable), assess, and monitor the influence of an organization's activities on society (that is, on certain social groups) and on the public (Blake, Frederick, & Myers, 1976, p. 3).

According to Mathews (1984), "voluntary disclosure of information, both qualitative and quantitative, provided by organizations to enlighten or influence a range of audiences" is what social reporting, social responsibility disclosure, and social responsibility accounting are all defined as. These two definitions show two very different perspectives on CSR reporting. While Mathews is interested in the voluntary character of CSR reporting and its capacity to influence audiences, Blake et al. are concerned with public well-being and analysis and monitoring. The disparity between management and stakeholder perspectives may help us understand this. The perspective offered by Blake et al. is a governance perspective that reflects stakeholders' desire to monitor and evaluate CSR performance. Mathews' managerial perspective focuses on managing a company's interaction with its stakeholders.

Stakeholders' Promotion of CSR Reporting: A Governance Orientation

Many corporate stakeholders promoted CSR, which was a call for businesses to "protect and improve the welfare of society as a whole along with [their] own interests," in response to concerns about how business and its activities affected the natural and social environments that emerged in the early 1950s (Blomstrom & Davis, 1975, p. 6). Some stakeholders believed that corporations had a duty to uphold "economic, legal, ethical, and discretionary expectations" (Carroll, 1979, p. 500). Corporations are under increasing pressure to fulfil these duties and provide tangible results in terms of "internal stakeholder impacts, external stakeholder effects, and external institutional effects"'(Wood & Jones, 1995, p. 230) that can be evaluated externally (Wood, 1991, p. 711).

A regulatory mechanism that can monitor and evaluate CSR performance is recognized as necessary by stakeholders because of these changes in the interaction between businesses and society. They understand that an alternative to "conventional command-and-control regulatory systems" is a "system of corporate disclosure and responsibility" that makes extensive, intelligible, standardized, and audited CSR performance information public (Hess, 2008, p. 448). Stakeholders urged that businesses "take account of the social repercussions of their operation in a more precise, timely and lasting way" as a result (Antal, Dierkes, MacMillan, & Marz, 2002, p. 25).

Between the late 1960s and the late 1980s, there were small and varying stakeholder demands for CSR reporting (Antal et al., 2002). Following the 1989 Exxon Valdez oil catastrophe, these needs became more pressing. Some nations have passed laws demanding a certain amount of information (Peak, 1990). More importantly, several non-governmental organizations (NGOs) started operating with the aim of promoting ethical business conduct and the disclosure of CSR performance data through CSR reporting. Examples include the Global Reporting Initiative (GRI), Account Ability, and the Coalition for Environmentally Responsive Economies (CERES). The establishment of the UN Global Compact (UNGC

2008), the publication of four generations of reporting standards by GRI, the publication of updates to Account Ability's AA1000 standard, and the creation of the Sustainability Accounting Standards Board are all examples of how stakeholders continue to promote CSR reporting today. From a low point in the late 1960s and early 1970s, when less than 7% of companies operating in high environmental impact industries participated in CSR reporting (Accounting Review 1973), to a high point in 2011, where 95% of the 250 largest global companies participated in CSR reporting, these actions by governments and NGOs were successful in raising the level of participation of corporations in CSR reporting (KPMG International Cooperative 2011).

Strategic Alignment via CSR Reporting: A Managerial Orientation

According to the open systems theory, an organization's ability to adapt to its environment determines whether it will survive and operate well (Scott & Davis, 2015, pp. 28-30). The "fundamental alignment mechanism" of an organization, which always strives to preserve congruence between the organization and its environment, serves as the process by which adaptation takes place. Organizational strategies must evolve in the same way as the external environment does. (Miles & Snow, 1984, p. 11). As a result, efficient management of the corporate social environment has grown in importance to the survival and success of businesses as CSR has evolved and established itself as a reality of the business world. Businesses must now "integrate a social viewpoint into the key frameworks [they] [use] to assess competitiveness and guide their commercial strategy" (Porter & Kramer, 2006, p. 84).

Through stakeholder engagement, which is the process of "consultation, communication, conversation, and exchange" between the organization and its stakeholders, corporations deliberately build their CSR operations to match their strategy and satisfy their stakeholders' expectations. By doing this, these businesses obtain positive CSR performance, which reflects their broad duties of being profitable, adhering to rules and regulations, upholding moral principles, and participating in charitable endeavors (Carroll, 1979). Companies with positive CSR performance may profit from CSR initiatives in a number of ways, including by lowering costs and risks, managing legitimacy and reputation, enhancing or strengthening competitive advantages, and fostering synergistic interactions among stakeholders (Kurucz, Colbert, & Wheeler, 2008).

However, obtaining these advantages "depends on stakeholders' understanding of a company's CSR initiatives" (Du, Bhattacharya, & Sen, 2010). Therefore, businesses employ CSR reporting to inform their stakeholders or alter their incorrect impressions of their positive CSR performance (Lindblom, 1983). In contrast, businesses with negative CSR performance struggle with legitimacy and are consequently worried about improving their corporate image. Some of them might decide to improve their CSR performance, while others might decide not to make any adjustments. Instead, they merely manage their perceptions by seeking to alter the expectations of their stakeholders or by faking environmental benefits. Reports on "business misinformation" using greenwashing (Laufer, 2003, p. 253). These reports' revelation of CSR performance is "selective," "self-serving," and "self-laudatory" (Antal et al., 2002).Hooghiemstra (2000) the purpose of these reports is to provide the impression that corportions "conform to societal standards without really changing their organizational actions" (Rodrigue, Magnan, & Cho, 2013).

Substantive and Symbolic CSR Reporting

Organizational acts may be either practical or decorative. The purpose of substantive actions is to advance the organization toward certain objectives, and they frequently coordinate closely with other organizational structures and activities (Meyer & Allen, 1997). By contrast, symbolic behaviors are responses to external constraints that allow internal autonomy to be retained (Oliver, 2010). Organizations safeguard their internal objectives by symbolically adopting behaviors decoupled from other organizational structures and activities (Meyer & Allen, 1997). For instance, in response to pressure from organizational stakeholders to implement a buyback strategy, "top managers may disconnect real financial investments from nominally declared stock repurchase plans to protect free cash flow for themselves" (Westphal & Zajac, 2001).

When it comes to CSR reporting, reports that seek to inform corporate stakeholders on CSR performance developments and those that seek to alter their perceptions of the corporation's CSR performance are substantial and closely associated with the latter. Disclosure is important because it "implies actual, concrete adjustments in organizational behavior to conform to prevailing social norms" or draws attention to the fact that business actions follow these prevailing social norms (Rodrigue et al., 2013). On the other hand, reports attempt to deceive and alter the impressions of business stakeholders. They are independent of the CSR Performance of the company and assist it in seeming to "conform to societal standards without really changing organizational actions" (Rodrigue et al., 2013, p. 109).

IMPACT OF CSR PRACTICES AND REPORTING ON ORGANIZATIONS

How Do CSR Practices and Reporting Impact an Organization's Performance and Reputation?

Corporate Social Responsibility (CSR) practices and reporting can have a significant impact on an organization's performance and reputation (Singh & Misra, 2021). CSR practices refer to the voluntary actions organizations take to address the social and environmental impacts of their operations. CSR reporting is the process of disclosing information regarding an organization's CSR practices, policies, and performance. One of the key impacts of CSR practices and reporting on an organization's performance is the potential for cost savings (Melo & Garrido-Morgado, 2012). Organizations that engage in CSR practices, such as energy efficiency or waste reduction, can often realize significant cost savings by reducing resource consumption and increasing productivity (Ahsan & Ahmed, 2023). Additionally, CSR practices such as supply chain management and stakeholder engagement can help organizations identify and mitigate risks and improve their operations.

CSR practices and reporting can also positively impact an organization's reputation. Organizations that engage in CSR practices and report their social and environmental performance transparently are often viewed more favorably by stakeholders (Ahsan & Khalid, 2023; Reynolds, Schultz, & Hekman, 2006). This can lead to increased trust and credibility and can help organizations differentiate themselves from their competitors. Additionally, CSR practices and reporting can help organizations build stronger relationships with their stakeholders, including employees, customers, suppliers, and the community (Kolk, 2004). One of the ways CSR practices and reporting can impact an organization's reputation is by aligning it with consumers' expectations and values. Consumers are becoming increasingly aware of the social and environmental impacts of the products and services they consume, and they are looking for organizations that share their values (Roberts, 1996). By engaging in CSR practices and reporting transparently on their social and environmental performance, organizations can demonstrate their commitment to social and environmental issues and align themselves with consumer expectations. Alternatively, CSR practices and reporting can impact an organization's reputation by attracting and retaining talent. Employees are increasingly looking for organizations that share their values and are committed to positively impacting society. By engaging in CSR practices and reporting transparently on their social and environmental performance, organizations can attract and retain talent, and create a positive work environment (Sokro, 2012).

This is often attributed to the positive impact of CSR practices and reporting on an organization's reputation, which can lead to increased trust and credibility and help organizations differentiate themselves from their competitors (Narayanan & Das, 2022; Rawlins, 2008; Richey & Ponte, 2021).

CSR practices and reporting can positively impact an organization's financial performance. For instance, a study by Bahta, Yun, Islam, and Bikanyi (2021) found that companies that actively engage in CSR initiatives such as environmental sustainability and community development projects experience higher profitability and increased shareholder value. This highlights the financial benefits of effective CSR practices. Moreover, research conducted by Phillips, Thai, and Halim (2019) demonstrates a significant correlation between transparent CSR reporting and improved financial performance. Organizations that disclose comprehensive and reliable information about their social and environmental initiatives tend to attract socially conscious investors and consumers, leading to enhanced brand reputation and market competitiveness. As a result, these companies often experience higher stock prices and enhanced financial returns than their counterparts who do not prioritize CSR reporting.

Several other studies support the notion that CSR practices positively influence financial performance. McWilliams and Siegel (2001) examined a large sample of companies and found that those with strong CSR practices tend to have higher financial performance measures such as return on assets and return on equity. Their positive reputation for social responsibility attracts more investors and customers, thus contributing to their financial success. Additionally, Boakye, TIngbani, Ahinful, Damoah, and Tauringana (2020) revealed that companies implementing environmental sustainability practices, such as waste reduction and energy efficiency, experienced significant cost savings over time, positively impacting profitability and financial performance.

Case studies of successful CSR initiatives provide valuable insights into how multinational corporations have effectively implemented CSR practices to achieve positive financial outcomes and enhance their brand reputation. One notable example is Unilever's Sustainable Living Plan, which has been implemented in both developed and developing countries. Unilever's CSR initiatives focus on the sustainable sourcing of raw materials, reducing environmental impacts, and improving social conditions in the communities where they operate. A company's commitment to sustainability and responsible business practices has resulted in significant financial benefits. Studies have shown that Unilever's focus on sustainability has led to increased sales and brand loyalty, with sustainable brands growing 69% faster than the rest of the business, accounting for 75% of Unilever's overall growth (Narayanan & Das, 2022).

Another compelling case study is Starbucks' CSR initiatives, which have been implemented globally in both developed and developing countries. Starbucks has made significant efforts to promote ethical sourcing, environmental sustainability and community engagement. Their commitment to CSR has attracted socially conscious consumers and investors, leading to positive financial outcomes. Research shows that companies with strong CSR reputations, such as Starbucks, tend to outperform their peers in terms of stock market performance and financial returns (Richey & Ponte, 2021).

By building a strong CSR reputation through their initiatives, Unilever and Starbucks have effectively positioned itself as a socially responsible and trustworthy brand, attracting a loyal customer base and investors who align with their values. These examples from literature highlight the vital role of CSR practices and reporting in enhancing financial performance and strengthening an organization's position in the market.

What Are the Determinants of the Extent and Quality of Non-Financial Information Reporting in Organizations?

The extent and quality of non-financial information reporting in organizations are determined by a number of factors (Sierra-Garcia, Garcia-Benau, & Bollas-Araya, 2018). These factors can be broadly grouped into three categories: organizational, regulatory, and societal (La Torre, Sabelfeld, Blomkvist, & Dumay, 2020). Organizational factors are internal factors that determine the extent and quality of non-financial information reporting. One of the key organizational factors is the level of management commitment to non-financial information reporting (Bhimani & Langfield-Smith, 2007). Organizations with a high level of management commitment to non-financial information reporting are more likely to engage in more extensive and higher-quality non-financial information reporting. Additionally, organizations with a strong corporate culture that values social and environmental responsibility are more likely to engage in more extensive and higher-quality non-financial information reporting.

Another important organizational factor is resource availability. Organizations that have the resources to invest in non-financial information reporting are more likely to engage in more extensive and higher-quality non-financial information reporting. This includes both financial and human resources, such as the availability of skilled personnel to collect and report nonfinancial information (Bhimani & Langfield-Smith, 2007).

Regulatory factors are external factors that determine the extent and quality of non-financial information reporting. One of the key regulatory factors is the level of legal and regulatory requirements for non-financial information reporting (Venturelli, Caputo, Leopizzi, & Pizzi, 2018). Organizations that operate in jurisdictions with strong legal and regulatory requirements for non-financial information reporting are more likely to engage in more extensive and higher-quality non-financial information reporting (Wyatt, 2008). Additionally, organizations that are subject to the reporting requirements of organizations, such as the Global Reporting Initiative (GRI) or the Sustainability Accounting Standards Board (SASB), are more likely to engage in more extensive and higher-quality non-financial information reporting.

Societal factors refer to external factors that shape societal expectations and attitudes towards non-financial information reporting. One of the key societal factors is the level of stakeholder engagement and expectations (Stolowy & Paugam, 2018). Organizations that have a high level of engagement with stakeholders, particularly those with a strong interest in social and environmental issues, are more likely to engage in more extensive and higher-quality non-financial information reporting. Additionally, organizations operating in sectors or industries where societal expectations for non-financial information reporting are high, such as the extractive or energy sectors, are more likely to engage in more extensive and higher-quality non-financial information reporting.

How Do Global Sustainability Reporting Standards, Such as Those of the Global Reporting Initiative (GRI) and the International Standards Organization (ISO), Impact the Extent and Quality of Non-Financial Information Reporting?

Global sustainability reporting standards, such as those of the Global Reporting Initiative (GRI) and the International Standards Organization (ISO), can have a significant impact on the extent and quality of non-financial information reporting (Skouloudis, Evangelinos, & Kourmousis, 2010). These standards provide organizations with a framework for reporting their social and environmental performance, and they help ensure consistency and comparability across different organizations. One of the key impacts of global sustainability reporting standards is that they help increase the extent of non-financial information reporting (Kolk, 2003). Organizations that use these standards are required to report a wide range of social and environmental issues, such as energy consumption, greenhouse gas emissions, and water use. These standards provide organizations with guidance on how to report their social and environmental performance, and they help ensure that the information is accurate, reliable, and comparable. This helps ensure that organizations report a comprehensive range of non-financial information, and it helps to increase transparency and accountability (Brown & Deegan, 1998). Additionally, these standards require organizations to provide assurance on their non-financial information, which helps to further increase the credibility and reliability of the information (Clarkson, Li, Richardson, & Vasvari, 2008).

Furthermore, global sustainability reporting standards can help organizations identify areas for improvement in their social and environmental performance. By reporting a wide range of social and environmental issues, organizations can identify areas where they perform well and areas where they can improve. Additionally, by comparing their performance to the standards, organizations can identify areas where they are outperforming their peers and areas where they need to improve.

Moreover, global sustainability reporting standards can also help organizations align with societal expectations and values. As consumers, investors, and other stakeholders become increasingly interested in the social and environmental impacts of products and services, organizations are under pressure to report their performance transparently. Adopting global sustainability reporting standards helps organizations meet these expectations and demonstrate their commitment to sustainability.

CHALLENGES FOR PROFESSIONALS

Accounting, finance, management, and audit professionals play key roles in CSR practices and reporting. These professionals play a vital role in ensuring that organizations engage in responsible CSR practices and transparently report their social and environmental performance (Babiak & Trendafilova, 2011). However, these professionals may face several challenges to fulfilling this role.

Accounting professionals are responsible for the financial reporting of an organization, which includes reporting non-financial information such as social and environmental performance. They play a key role in the measurement and management of CSR performance by providing data and information required for CSR reporting. Additionally, accounting professionals are responsible for ensuring that the reported information is accurate, reliable, and comparable and for providing assurance on the reported information (Godfrey, Hodgson, Tarca, Hamilton, & Holmen, 2010).

Finance professionals are responsible for managing an organization's financial resources, including the allocation of resources for CSR activities. They play an important role in strategic planning and implementation of CSR activities by providing the financial analysis required to identify the costs and benefits of CSR activities. Additionally, finance professionals are responsible for ensuring that CSR activities are financially sustainable and that they create value for the organization (Tilt, 2010).

Management professionals are responsible for the overall management of an organization, including the management of CSR activities (Forray & Leigh, 2012). They play a pivotal role in the strategic planning and implementation of CSR activities by setting the direction of the organization's CSR activities and ensuring that they align with its overall strategy. Additionally, management professionals are responsible for ensuring that CSR activities are integrated into the overall operations of the organization and that they are aligned with the expectations of stakeholders.

Auditing professionals are responsible for ensuring the accuracy and reliability of the reported information (Pflugrath, Roebuck, & Simnett, 2011). They play a vital role in the assurance of non-financial information by providing an independent assessment of the reported information and assurance of the internal controls of the organization. Additionally, auditing professionals are responsible for ensuring that the reported information complies with relevant laws and regulations, and that it is transparent and comparable.

A major challenge is the lack of clear and consistent guidelines for CSR reporting. While there are global sustainability reporting standards, such as GRI and ISO, they are not mandatory, and not all organizations follow them. This can make it difficult for accounting, finance, management, and auditing professionals to ensure consistency and comparability in the reporting process.

Another challenge is the complexity and subjectivity of CSR performance measurements. CSR performance is often multifaceted and difficult to quantify, which can make it challenging for professionals to accurately measure and report an organization's CSR performance. Furthermore, there is often a lack of consensus on what constitutes good CSR performance, making it difficult for professionals to ensure that their reported information is transparent and comparable.

A third challenge is that many organizations lack the resources necessary to effectively implement and report CSR practices. This can include a lack of financial resources, skilled personnel, and technology to collect and report non-financial information. This can make it challenging for professionals to effectively engage in CSR practices and reporting.

The fourth challenge is the lack of integration between CSR practices and the overall operations of organizations. CSR practices are often seen as separate from the organization's core operations, which can make it difficult for professionals to ensure that CSR practices are aligned with the organization's overall strategy and integrated into the organization's operations.

The fifth challenge is the lack of engagement and participation from stakeholders. Many organizations struggle to engage their stakeholders in the CSR reporting process, which can make it difficult for professionals to ensure that their reported information aligns with stakeholders' expectations.

In summary, accounting, finance, management, and auditing professionals play a key role in CSR practices and reporting by providing the data and information needed for CSR reporting, ensuring that CSR activities are financially sustainable, creating value for the organization, setting the direction for the organization's CSR activities, ensuring that they align with the organization's overall strategy, and ensuring that the reported information is accurate, reliable, and comparable. However, professionals in these roles may face challenges, such as a lack of clear and consistent guidelines, complexity and subjectivity of CSR performance measurements, lack of resources, lack of integration, and lack of engagement and participation from stakeholders.

CONCLUSION

In conclusion, CSR practices and reporting are becoming increasingly important, as organizations strive to meet stakeholders' expectations and create a positive impact on society. The history and evolution of CSR shows that it is an integral part of an organization's operations, and organizations are expected to consider the social and environmental impacts of their actions in all areas of their business. CSR reporting is an important aspect of CSR as it enables organizations to communicate their CSR efforts and impacts on stakeholders. The importance of CSR reporting lies in the fact that it enables organizations to build trust and credibility with stakeholders and identify areas for improvement in their CSR practices.

The relationship between CSR and non-financial information reporting is closely linked to the concepts of transparency and accountability. Organizations that engage in CSR activities are expected to be transparent about their social and environmental performance and to be accountable for the impacts of their actions. Non-financial information reporting is an important aspect of transparency and accountability, because it enables organizations to communicate their CSR efforts and impacts to stakeholders.

Non-financial information reporting is closely linked to the concepts of performance measurement and management. Organizations that engage in CSR activities are expected to measure and manage their social and environmental performance. Non-financial information reporting is an important aspect of this process. By providing information about social and environmental performance, organizations can identify areas for improvement and set goals for future performance.

Additionally, CSR practices and reporting can significantly affect an organization's performance and reputation. CSR practices can lead to cost savings, improved operations, and increased stakeholder engagement. CSR reporting can help organizations build trust and credibility with stakeholders and align themselves with consumers' expectations and values. Additionally, CSR practices and reporting can help organizations attract and retain talent and have a positive impact on their financial performance. As a result, organizations that engage in CSR practices and report transparently on their social and environmental performance are often viewed more favorably by stakeholders, which can lead to increased trust and credibility and help organizations differentiate themselves from their competitors.

Additionally, global sustainability reporting standards such as those of the Global Reporting Initiative (GRI) and International Standards Organization (ISO) can have a significant impact on the extent and quality of non-financial information reporting. These standards help organizations increase the extent of non-financial information reporting, improve the quality of non-financial information reporting, identify areas for improvement in their social and environmental performance, and align themselves with societal expectations and values. Organizations that adopt these standards are more likely to report a comprehensive range of non-financial information, which is more likely to be accurate, reliable, and comparable.

The practical implications of this chapter on CSR practices and reporting are vast and encompass various aspects that can benefit organizations and society as a whole. First, the emphasis on CSR practices and reporting enables organizations to proactively address social and environmental impacts beyond their legal obligations. By doing so, organizations can build stronger relationships with their stakeholders and gain trust and credibility (Syakur, Susilo, Wike, & Ahmadi, 2020). Disclosing CSR efforts and impacts through CSR reporting fosters transparency and accountability, further reinforcing stakeholders' confidence in an organization's commitment to responsible business practices (Heras-Saizarbitoria, 2022).

The societal contributions of this study are noteworthy. By highlighting the benefits of CSR practices and reporting, this chapter encourages organizations to adopt responsible business practices, leading to broader positive impacts on society and the environment. As organizations embrace CSR, they contribute to sustainable development goals, promote social welfare, and address pressing environmental issues. This could lead to a more sustainable and equitable future, benefiting communities and society as a whole.

Furthermore, the article's emphasis on global sustainability reporting standards, such as those of the Global Reporting Initiative (GRI) and the International Standards Organization (ISO), promotes a consistent and comprehensive approach to non-financial information reporting (Global Reporting Initiative, 2023). Adopting these standards can facilitate better comparisons between organizations' CSR performance and enable more informed decision making by stakeholders, including investors, consumers, and policymakers.

REFERENCES

Abdelhalim, K., & Eldin, A. G. (2019). Can CSR help achieve sustainable development? Applying a new assessment model to CSR cases from Egypt. *The International Journal of Sociology and Social Policy*, *39*(9/10), 773–795. doi:10.1108/IJSSP-06-2019-0120

Ahsan, M. J. (2023). The role of emotional intelligence in effective corporate social responsibility leadership. *The International Journal of Organizational Analysis*, *31*(8), 75–91. doi:10.1108/IJOA-02-2023-3615

Ahsan, M. J., & Ahmed, R. (2023). Green-Lean Practices and Production Performance: Evidence From SMEs of an Emerging Economy. In Emerging Trends in Sustainable Supply Chain Management and Green Logistics (pp. 75-97). IGI Global.

Ahsan, M. J., & Khalid, M. H. (2023). Laissez-Faire Leadership. In *Leadership Approaches in Global Hospitality and Tourism* (pp. 61–72). IGI Global. doi:10.4018/978-1-6684-6713-8.ch004

Amran, A., Lee, S. P., & Devi, S. S. (2014). The influence of governance structure and strategic corporate social responsibility toward sustainability reporting quality. *Business Strategy and the Environment*, *23*(4), 217–235. doi:10.1002/bse.1767

Antal, A. B., Dierkes, M., MacMillan, K., & Marz, L. (2002). Corporate social reporting revisited. *Journal of General Management*, 28(2), 22–42. doi:10.1177/030630700202800202

Awan, U., Khattak, A., & Kraslawski, A. (2019). Corporate social responsibility (CSR) priorities in the small and medium enterprises (SMEs) of the industrial sector of Sialkot, Pakistan. *Corporate social responsibility in the manufacturing and services sectors*, 267-278.

Babiak, K., & Trendafilova, S. (2011). CSR and environmental responsibility: Motives and pressures to adopt green management practices. *Corporate Social Responsibility and Environmental Management*, *18*(1), 11–24. doi:10.1002/csr.229

Bahta, D., Yun, J., Islam, M. R., & Bikanyi, K. J. (2021). How does CSR enhance the financial performance of SMEs? The mediating role of firm reputation. *Ekonomska Istrazivanja*, *34*(1), 1428–1451. doi:10.1080/1331677X.2020.1828130

Battisti, E., Nirino, N., Leonidou, E., & Thrassou, A. (2022). Corporate venture capital and CSR performance: An extended resource based view's perspective. *Journal of Business Research*, *139*, 1058–1066. doi:10.1016/j.jbusres.2021.10.054

Bhimani, A., & Langfield-Smith, K. (2007). Structure, formality and the importance of financial and non-financial information in strategy development and implementation. *Management Accounting Research, 18*(1), 3–31. doi:10.1016/j.mar.2006.06.005

Blake, D. H., Frederick, W. C., & Myers, M. S. (1976). *Social auditing: evaluating the impact of corporate programs.* Greenwood.

Blomstrom, R., & Davis, K. (1975). *Business and society: Environment and responsibility.* McGraw-Hill.

Boakye, D. J., TIngbani, I., Ahinful, G., Damoah, I., & Tauringana, V. (2020). Sustainable environmental practices and financial performance: Evidence from listed small and medium-sized enterprise in the United Kingdom. *Business Strategy and the Environment, 29*(6), 2583–2602. doi:10.1002/bse.2522

Bouten, L., Everaert, P., Van Liedekerke, L., De Moor, L., & Christiaens, J. (2011). *Corporate social responsibility reporting: A comprehensive picture?* Paper presented at the Accounting forum. 10.1016/j.accfor.2011.06.007

Brown, N., & Deegan, C. (1998). The public disclosure of environmental performance information—A dual test of media agenda setting theory and legitimacy theory. *Accounting and Business Research, 29*(1), 21–41. doi:10.1080/00014788.1998.9729564

Carroll, A. B. (1979). A three-dimensional conceptual model of corporate performance. *Academy of Management Review, 4*(4), 497–505. doi:10.2307/257850

Carroll, A. B. (2021). Corporate social responsibility (CSR) and the COVID-19 pandemic: Organizational and managerial implications. *Journal of Strategy and Management.*

Clarkson, P. M., Li, Y., Richardson, G. D., & Vasvari, F. P. (2008). Revisiting the relation between environmental performance and environmental disclosure: An empirical analysis. *Accounting, Organizations and Society, 33*(4-5), 303–327. doi:10.1016/j.aos.2007.05.003

Davis, G. F., & Cobb, J. A. (2010). Resource dependence theory: Past and future. *Stanford's organization theory renaissance, 1970–2000.*

Deegan, C. (2006). Legitimacy theory. In *Methodological issues in accounting research: theories, methods and issues* (pp. 161–181). Spiramus Press Ltd.

Du, S., Bhattacharya, C. B., & Sen, S. (2010). Maximizing business returns to corporate social responsibility (CSR): The role of CSR communication. *International Journal of Management Reviews, 12*(1), 8–19. doi:10.1111/j.1468-2370.2009.00276.x

Du, S., & Xie, C. (2021). Paradoxes of artificial intelligence in consumer markets: Ethical challenges and opportunities. *Journal of Business Research, 129*, 961–974. doi:10.1016/j.jbusres.2020.08.024

Dwivedi, Y. K., Hughes, L., Baabdullah, A. M., Ribeiro-Navarrete, S., Giannakis, M., Al-Debei, M. M., ... Cheung, C. M. (2022). Metaverse beyond the hype: Multidisciplinary perspectives on emerging challenges, opportunities, and agenda for research, practice and policy. *International Journal of Information Management, 66*, 102542. doi:10.1016/j.ijinfomgt.2022.102542

Eizaguirre, A., García-Feijoo, M., & Laka, J. P. (2019). Defining sustainability core competencies in business and management studies based on multinational stakeholders' perceptions. *Sustainability (Basel)*, *11*(8), 2303. doi:10.3390u11082303

Forray, J. M., & Leigh, J. S. (2012). A primer on the principles of responsible management education: Intellectual roots and waves of change. *Journal of Management Education*, *36*(3), 295–309. doi:10.1177/1052562911433031

Freeman, R. E. (1984). Strategic Management: A Stakeholder Approach, Boston, Pitman. In L. Janina (Ed.), *Ethik als Standard in der Beschaffung. Werte und Normen als Gestaltungsausgangspunkt von Nicht-Regierungs-Organisationen*. Springer Gabler.

Freeman, R. E. (2010). *Strategic management: A stakeholder approach*. Cambridge university press. doi:10.1017/CBO9781139192675

Freeman, R. E., & Velamuri, S. R. (2021). A New Approach to CSR: Company Stakeholder Responsibility 1. In The Routledge Companion to Corporate Social Responsibility (pp. 203-213). Routledge.

Friedman, A. L., & Miles, S. (2001). Socially responsible investment and corporate social and environmental reporting in the UK: An exploratory study. *The British Accounting Review*, *33*(4), 523–548. doi:10.1006/bare.2001.0172

Gatti, L., Vishwanath, B., Seele, P., & Cottier, B. (2019). Are we moving beyond voluntary CSR? Exploring theoretical and managerial implications of mandatory CSR resulting from the new Indian companies act. *Journal of Business Ethics*, *160*(4), 961–972. doi:10.100710551-018-3783-8

Godfrey, J., Hodgson, A., Tarca, A., Hamilton, J., & Holmen, S. (2010). *Accounting*. John Wiley & Sons, Inc.

Goyal, L. (2022). Stakeholder theory: Revisiting the origins. *Journal of Public Affairs*, *22*(3), e2559. doi:10.1002/pa.2559

Hack, L., Kenyon, A. J., & Wood, E. H. (2014). A critical corporate social responsibility (CSR) timeline: How should it be understood now. *International Journal of Management Cases*, *16*(4), 46–55.

Haydon, S., Jung, T., & Russell, S. (2021). 'You've been framed': A critical review of academic discourse on philanthrocapitalism. *International Journal of Management Reviews*, *23*(3), 353–375. doi:10.1111/ijmr.12255

He, H., & Harris, L. (2020). The impact of Covid-19 pandemic on corporate social responsibility and marketing philosophy. *Journal of Business Research*, *116*, 176–182. doi:10.1016/j.jbusres.2020.05.030 PMID:32457556

Hess, D. (2008). The three pillars of corporate social reporting as new governance regulation: Disclosure, dialogue, and development. *Business Ethics Quarterly*, *18*(4), 447–482. doi:10.5840/beq200818434

Hillman, A. J., Withers, M. C., & Collins, B. J. (2009). Resource dependence theory: A review. *Journal of Management*, *35*(6), 1404–1427. doi:10.1177/0149206309343469

Hooghiemstra, R. (2000). Corporate communication and impression management–new perspectives why companies engage in corporate social reporting. *Journal of Business Ethics, 27*(1), 55–68. doi:10.1023/A:1006400707757

Jamali, D., Zanhour, M., & Keshishian, T. (2009). Peculiar strengths and relational attributes of SMEs in the context of CSR. *Journal of Business Ethics, 87*(3), 355–377. doi:10.100710551-008-9925-7

Jones, G. J., Edwards, M. B., Bocarro, J. N., Svensson, P. G., & Misener, K. (2020). A community capacity building approach to sport-based youth development. *Sport Management Review, 23*(4), 563–575. doi:10.1016/j.smr.2019.09.001

Khaled, R., Ali, H., & Mohamed, E. K. (2021). The Sustainable Development Goals and corporate sustainability performance: Mapping, extent and determinants. *Journal of Cleaner Production, 311*, 127599. doi:10.1016/j.jclepro.2021.127599

Kolk, A. (2003). Trends in sustainability reporting by the Fortune Global 250. *Business Strategy and the Environment, 12*(5), 279–291. doi:10.1002/bse.370

Kolk, A. (2004). A decade of sustainability reporting: Developments and significance. *International Journal of Environment and Sustainable Development, 3*(1), 51–64. doi:10.1504/IJESD.2004.004688

Kurucz, E. C., Colbert, B. A., & Wheeler, D. (2008). The business case for corporate social responsibility. In The Oxford handbook of corporate social responsibility (pp. 83-112). doi:10.1093/oxfordhb/9780199211593.003.0004

La Torre, M., Sabelfeld, S., Blomkvist, M., & Dumay, J. (2020). Rebuilding trust: Sustainability and non-financial reporting and the European Union regulation. *Meditari Accountancy Research, 28*(5), 701–725. doi:10.1108/MEDAR-06-2020-0914

Latapí Agudelo, M. A., Jóhannsdóttir, L., & Davídsdóttir, B. (2019). A literature review of the history and evolution of corporate social responsibility. *International Journal of Corporate Social Responsibility, 4*(1), 1–23. doi:10.118640991-018-0039-y

Laufer, W. S. (2003). Social accountability and corporate greenwashing. *Journal of Business Ethics, 43*(3), 253–261. doi:10.1023/A:1022962719299

Lindblom, B. (1983). Economy of speech gestures. In *The production of speech* (pp. 217–245). Springer. doi:10.1007/978-1-4613-8202-7_10

Lu, J., Liang, M., Zhang, C., Rong, D., Guan, H., Mazeikaite, K., & Streimikis, J. (2021). Assessment of corporate social responsibility by addressing sustainable development goals. *Corporate Social Responsibility and Environmental Management, 28*(2), 686–703. doi:10.1002/csr.2081

Mathews, M. R. (1984). A suggested classification for social accounting research. *Journal of Accounting and Public Policy, 3*(3), 199–221. doi:10.1016/0278-4254(84)90017-6

Matten, D., & Moon, J. (2020). Reflections on the 2018 decade award: The meaning and dynamics of corporate social responsibility. *Academy of Management Review, 45*(1), 7–28. doi:10.5465/amr.2019.0348

McElhaney, K. (2009). A strategic approach to corporate social responsibility. *Leader to Leader, 52*(1), 30–36. doi:10.1002/ltl.327

McWilliams, A., & Siegel, D. (2001). Corporate social responsibility: A theory of the firm perspective. *Academy of Management Review, 26*(1), 117–127. doi:10.2307/259398

Melo, T., & Garrido-Morgado, A. (2012). Corporate reputation: A combination of social responsibility and industry. *Corporate Social Responsibility and Environmental Management, 19*(1), 11–31. doi:10.1002/csr.260

Menghwar, P. S., & Daood, A. (2021). Creating shared value: A systematic review, synthesis and integrative perspective. *International Journal of Management Reviews, 23*(4), 466–485. doi:10.1111/ijmr.12252

Meyer, J. P., & Allen, N. J. (1997). *Commitment in the workplace: Theory, research, and application.* Sage Publications. doi:10.4135/9781452231556

Miles, R. E., & Snow, C. C. (1984). Fit, failure and the hall of fame. *California Management Review, 26*(3), 10–28. doi:10.2307/41165078

Moon, J. (2007). The contribution of corporate social responsibility to sustainable development. *Sustainable Development (Bradford), 15*(5), 296–306. doi:10.1002d.346

Muldoon, R. (2016). *Social contract theory for a diverse world: Beyond tolerance.* Routledge. doi:10.4324/9781315545882

Narayanan, S., & Das, J. R. (2022). Can the marketing innovation of purpose branding make brands meaningful and relevant? *International Journal of Innovation Science, 14*(3/4), 519–536. doi:10.1108/IJIS-11-2020-0272

Nave, A., & Ferreira, J. (2019). Corporate social responsibility strategies: Past research and future challenges. *Corporate Social Responsibility and Environmental Management, 26*(4), 885–901. doi:10.1002/csr.1729

Nguyen, A. T., Parker, L., Brennan, L., & Lockrey, S. (2020). A consumer definition of eco-friendly packaging. *Journal of Cleaner Production, 252*, 119792. doi:10.1016/j.jclepro.2019.119792

Oliver, R. L. (2010). *Satisfaction: A behavioral perspective on the consumer.* ME Sharpe. Inc.

Parker, L. D. (1986). Polemical themes in social accounting: a scenario for standard setting. *Advances in Public Interest Accounting, 1*, 67-93.

Peak, M. H. (1990). The Alaskan oil spill: Lessons in crisis management. *Management Review, 79*(4), 12–22.

Pflugrath, G., Roebuck, P., & Simnett, R. (2011). Impact of assurance and assurer's professional affiliation on financial analysts' assessment of credibility of corporate social responsibility information. *Auditing, 30*(3), 239–254. doi:10.2308/ajpt-10047

Phillips, S., Thai, V. V., & Halim, Z. (2019). Airline value chain capabilities and CSR performance: The connection between CSR leadership and CSR culture with CSR performance, customer satisfaction and financial performance. *The Asian Journal of Shipping and Logistics*, *35*(1), 30–40. doi:10.1016/j.ajsl.2019.03.005

Porter, M. E., & Kramer, M. R. (2006). The link between competitive advantage and corporate social responsibility. *Harvard Business Review*, *84*(12), 78–92. PMID:17183795

Preston, L. E. (1975). Corporation and society: The search for a paradigm. *Journal of Economic Literature*, 434–453.

Rawlins, B. (2008). Give the emperor a mirror: Toward developing a stakeholder measurement of organizational transparency. *Journal of Public Relations Research*, *21*(1), 71–99. doi:10.1080/10627260802153421

Reynolds, S. J., Schultz, F. C., & Hekman, D. R. (2006). Stakeholder theory and managerial decision-making: Constraints and implications of balancing stakeholder interests. *Journal of Business Ethics*, *64*(3), 285–301. doi:10.100710551-005-5493-2

Richey, L. A., & Ponte, S. (2021). Brand Aid and coffee value chain development interventions: Is Starbucks working aid out of business? *World Development*, *143*, 105193. doi:10.1016/j.worlddev.2020.105193

Roberts, J. A. (1996). Green consumers in the 1990s: Profile and implications for advertising. *Journal of Business Research*, *36*(3), 217–231. doi:10.1016/0148-2963(95)00150-6

Rodrigue, M., Magnan, M., & Cho, C. H. (2013). Is environmental governance substantive or symbolic? An empirical investigation. *Journal of Business Ethics*, *114*(1), 107–129. doi:10.100710551-012-1331-5

Rosenfeld, M. (1984). Contract and justice: The relation between classical contract law and social contract theory. *Iowa Law Review*, *70*, 769.

Rothstein, B. (2021). *Controlling corruption: The social contract approach*. Oxford University Press. doi:10.1093/oso/9780192894908.001.0001

Schmeltz, L. (2012). Consumer-oriented CSR communication: Focusing on ability or morality? *Corporate Communications*, *17*(1), 29–49. doi:10.1108/13563281211196344

Scott, W. R., & Davis, G. F. (2015). *Organizations and organizing: Rational, natural and open systems perspectives*. Routledge. doi:10.4324/9781315663371

Sierra-Garcia, L., Garcia-Benau, M. A., & Bollas-Araya, H. M. (2018). Empirical analysis of non-financial reporting by Spanish companies. *Administrative Sciences*, *8*(3), 29. doi:10.3390/admsci8030029

Singh, K., & Misra, M. (2021). Linking corporate social responsibility (CSR) and organizational performance: The moderating effect of corporate reputation. *European Research on Management and Business Economics*, *27*(1), 100139. doi:10.1016/j.iedeen.2020.100139

Skouloudis, A., Evangelinos, K., & Kourmousis, F. (2010). Assessing non-financial reports according to the Global Reporting Initiative guidelines: Evidence from Greece. *Journal of Cleaner Production*, *18*(5), 426–438. doi:10.1016/j.jclepro.2009.11.015

Sokro, E. (2012). Impact of employer branding on employee attraction and retention. *European Journal of Business and Management*, *4*(18), 164–173.

Stolowy, H., & Paugam, L. (2018). The expansion of non-financial reporting: An exploratory study. *Accounting and Business Research*, *48*(5), 525–548. doi:10.1080/00014788.2018.1470141

Swanson, D. L. (2021). CSR Discovery Leadership: A Multilevel Framework in Historical Context. In The Routledge Companion to Corporate Social Responsibility (pp. 43-55). Routledge.

Syakur, A., Susilo, T. A. B., Wike, W., & Ahmadi, R. (2020). Sustainability of communication, organizational culture, cooperation, trust and leadership style for lecturer commitments in higher education. Budapest International Research and Critics Institute (BIRCI-Journal): Humanities and Social Sciences, 3(2), 1325-1335.

Szőcs, I., & Schlegelmilch, B. B. (2020). Embedding CSR in corporate strategies. In Rethinking business responsibility in a global context: Challenges to corporate social responsibility, sustainability and ethics (pp. 45-60). doi:10.1007/978-3-030-34261-6_4

Tamvada, M. (2020). Corporate social responsibility and accountability: A new theoretical foundation for regulating CSR. *International Journal of Corporate Social Responsibility*, *5*(1), 1–14. doi:10.118640991-019-0045-8

Tilt, C. A. (2010). *Corporate responsibility, accounting and accountants*. Springer.

Venturelli, A., Caputo, F., Leopizzi, R., & Pizzi, S. (2018). The state of art of corporate social disclosure before the introduction of non-financial reporting directive: A cross country analysis. *Social Responsibility Journal*.

Verma, A. K. (2019). Sustainable development and environmental ethics. *International Journal of Environmental Sciences*, *10*(1), 1–5.

Wesselink, R., & Osagie, E. R. (2020). Differentiating CSR managers roles and competencies: taking conflicts as a starting point. In *Research handbook of responsible management*. Edward Elgar Publishing. doi:10.4337/9781788971966.00044

Westphal, J. D., & Zajac, E. J. (2001). Decoupling policy from practice: The case of stock repurchase programs. *Administrative Science Quarterly*, *46*(2), 202–228. doi:10.2307/2667086

Wood, D. J. (1991). Corporate social performance revisited. *Academy of Management Review*, *16*(4), 691–718. doi:10.2307/258977

Wood, D. J., & Jones, R. E. (1995). Stakeholder mismatching: A theoretical problem in empirical research on corporate social performance. *The International Journal of Organizational Analysis*, *3*(3), 229–267. doi:10.1108/eb028831

Wyatt, A. (2008). What financial and non-financial information on intangibles is value-relevant? A review of the evidence. *Accounting and Business Research*, *38*(3), 217–256. doi:10.1080/00014788.2008.9663336

Yasir, M., Majid, A., Yasir, M., Qudratullah, H., Ullah, R., & Khattak, A. (2021). Participation of hotel managers in CSR activities in developing countries: A defining role of CSR orientation, CSR competencies, and CSR commitment. *Corporate Social Responsibility and Environmental Management*, *28*(1), 239–250. doi:10.1002/csr.2045

Zhao, L., Yang, M. M., Wang, Z., & Michelson, G. (2023). Trends in the dynamic evolution of corporate social responsibility and leadership: A literature review and bibliometric analysis. *Journal of Business Ethics*, *182*(1), 135–157. doi:10.100710551-022-05035-y

Chapter 6
Contingent Factors and Sustainable Practices in the Amazon:
An Analysis of Riverside Restaurants on Ilha do Combu/PA

Risolene Alves de Macena Araújo
ⓘ https://orcid.org/0000-0001-6423-6299
Federal University of Pará, Brazil

Adriana Rodrigues Silva
ⓘ https://orcid.org/0000-0003-1538-6877
Polytechnic Institute of Santarém, Portugal & CICF-Research Centre on Accounting and Taxation, Portugal

Nicoly Sousa Santos
Federal University of Pará, Brazil

ABSTRACT

The study aims to analyse the influence of contingency factors on sustainable practices in restaurants on Combú Island, Pará. A survey and interviews were conducted using a structured questionnaire that related sustainable practices to contingency factors. The main result of the research revealed that the contingency factors that most influence sustainable practices in the region are leadership and the environment. Leadership plays a crucial role in encouraging and directing employees towards environmental practices. At the same time, the environment strongly influences the environmental attitudes of managers due to the location of the businesses in an environmentally protected area. The main contribution of this study is to understand the stage of adoption of sustainable practices in local businesses on the island, which allows the development of actions that contribute to the consolidation of these practices in other companies, given the fundamental importance of sustainability in the current scenario.

DOI: 10.4018/978-1-6684-9076-1.ch006

INTRODUCTION

The growing concern for environmental sustainability has become paramount within the business landscape. Both developed and underdeveloped nations have faced criticism for their involvement in environmental degradation, leading to economic, social, and environmental challenges (Windolph et al., 2014). This criticism is further underscored by Motta et al. (2019), who asserts that sustainability remains an evolving theme in the business world, emphasizing that companies must articulate and internalize sustainable principles. These authors contend that adopting sustainable practices can contribute significantly to environmental preservation by reducing the consumption of raw materials, electricity, and water.

As society becomes increasingly attuned to social and environmental issues, organizations are increasingly pressured to embrace sustainable development practices (Treptow et al., 2019). Consequently, companies are now factoring environmental considerations into their decision-making processes (Latif et al., 2020). This heightened corporate interest in environmental matters is primarily instigated by external stakeholders, such as government bodies, communities, and customers, who exert substantial pressure on companies to adopt a sustainable stance (Feitosa et al., 2014). This sustainable orientation is driven by external forces such as government policies, environmental regulations, market competition, and economic dynamics. It is further compounded by warnings from scientists, multilateral organizations, civil society, and environmental activists about the perils of environmental degradation and global warming, which have direct implications for businesses (Cecato & Marines, 2015).

Within the literature, numerous perspectives exist concerning the influence of internal factors on companies. Research by Robin et al. (2019) highlights how specific regions' cultures can substantially impact environmental practices. Deliberal et al. (2016) assert that an environmental strategy can confer a competitive advantage upon companies, as it emanates from administrative routines intertwined with organizational culture. This combination is complex for competitors to replicate. While somewhat underrepresented in research, leadership also plays a pivotal role in shaping an organization's mission, vision, and collective efforts towards including sustainable practices (Dallabona et al., 2019).

Considering this, applying Contingency Theory to sustainability can unveil numerous factors that influence the implementation and configuration of sustainable practices. This theory operates on the premise that there is no one-size-fits-all model for managing companies, as they are influenced by their unique contingency factors, including structure, strategy, technology, size, and environment (Picchiai & Ferreira, 2019).

Pryshlakivsky and Searcy (2015) leveraged Contingency Theory to develop a heuristic model for assessing trade-offs in corporate sustainability performance measurement systems, underlining the importance of incorporating contingency factors in addressing sustainability issues. However, Maletic et al. (2017) noted that empirical research on the interplay between contingency theory, corporate sustainability, and its performance implications is still evolving. To address this research gap, the current study poses the following question: What contingency factors influence sustainable practices in gastronomic enterprises operating on Combu Island in Pará, Brazil?

Combu Island, situated 1.5 kilometers from Belém - PA, is legally protected as an Environmental Protection Area under law 6.083/97. The island's economy thrives on businesses engaged in extractive activities and tourism. Tourism, in particular, has led to a surge in micro and small businesses (MSBs), including restaurants (Rosa & Cabral, 2017). Aiming to examine the internal and external contingency factors shaping sustainable practices in gastronomic enterprises on Combu Island, the motivation for this study is rooted in the island's significance in preserving its environmental resources and ensuring the well-being of its population (De Carvalho et al., 2019). The region exhibits characteristics of traditional riverside communities, evident in its social organization, subsistence activities, utilization of natural resources, and intergenerational knowledge transfer. The region's gastronomic sector has witnessed significant growth due to the influx of visitors, particularly on weekends, as the area is primarily oriented towards tourism (De Carvalho et al., 2019). Additionally, according to NBR 15.401, organizations across the tourism sector, including gastronomy, express a keen interest in demonstrating their commitment to sustainability by managing the impacts of their activities and aligning their objectives with sustainability goals (ABNT, 2014). Lastly, this research is warranted by the absence of studies exploring the influence of contingency factors on sustainable practices, especially within gastronomic enterprises.

The primary contribution of this study lies in its exploration of how riverside enterprises in the Amazon region have seamlessly integrated sustainable practices into their operations. This understanding can be a blueprint for fostering similar practices in other local companies. Furthermore, by expanding our comprehension of Contingency Theory within this context, the study facilitates the evaluation of the factors that wield the most influence in adopting sustainable practices, thereby promoting the development and consolidation of these methods.

This study is structured in five different sections. After this introduction, the next section will deal with the theoretical framework of the research, explaining contingency theory and environmental sustainability in small and medium-sized companies. The third section will detail the methodology used to fulfil our research objective. The fourth section will analyze and discuss the data obtained. Finally, in the fifth and last section, we will present the conclusions of this study.

THEORETICAL FRAMEWORK

Contingency Theory

The use of Contingency Theory in studies related to Managerial Accounting is based on the premise that there are no universally appropriate accounting practices that apply to all companies in all circumstances, as they depend on contextual factors (Otley, 1980), reinforcing the assumption that each organization has its peculiarities (Otley, 2016).

In the Brazilian context, studies have used diverse elements to capture contingency factors, such as environment and organizational structure - mechanistic and organic (Fagundes et al., 2010); environment, technology, structure, strategy, and organizational size (Beuren & Fiorentin, 2014); environment and managerial practices (Kuzma et al., 2016); and external environment, size, strategy, structure, technology, organizational culture, and leadership (Oliveira & Callado, 2018). However, empirical studies on applying contingency theory to sustainability are scarce (Maletic et al., 2017), although there is an understanding that sustainability practices may be context-dependent (Campbell, 2007).

The literature points to several contingency factors, as elucidated in Table 1.

Table 1. Definition and variables of contingency factors

References	Factors	Definition and Variables
Chenhall (2007); Espejo (2008); Wadongo (2014)	Environment	The contingency factor environment can present instability and uncertainties for the organization. Considered an external factor, as it undergoes changes, it affects the internal framework of the entity. Examples of external environmental factors include the attitude of the competition and the likes and preferences of customers.
Chenhall (2003); Espejo (2008)	Structure	A formal arrangement of different functions to members of the organization aimed at ensuring that structural arrangements influence work efficiency, for example, employee participation in decision-making.
Chenhall (2003); Espejo (2008)	Strategy	A means by which managers can influence the nature of the external environment, the organization's technologies in structural mechanisms, culture, and managerial control systems. One variable of this factor can be the attractive price of the product/service and the development of unique product/service characteristics.
Chenhall (2003); Crozatti (1998)	Culture	The representation of characteristics such as knowledge, beliefs, values, morals, laws, customs, and other capacities and habits that people acquire from civil society that are considered, directly or indirectly, at all times of the entity's existence. There are several elements that influence its formation, such as the community, interacting with the organization by providing and acquiring resources, the customer who has expectations about the quality of the product, the size of the organization, and the way it impacts culture regarding the delegation of power and responsibilities.
Dallabona et al. (2019); Wadongo (2014)	Leadership	Leadership is defined as the ability to interpret objectives, establish priorities, plan activities, delegate responsibilities, solve problems, and guide people. Leadership arises in the form of values, ideas, and teachings. We can cite task assignment and the decision of what and how to perform such tasks as leadership variables.

According to Espejo (2008), the environment is considered an external factor outside the organization's control, while the other factors are internal and influenced by it, subject to the company's control. An example of this can be seen in the coronavirus (Covid-19) pandemic, which changed companies' attitudes regarding hygiene standards.

Based on the factors outlined above, aligning the contingent characteristics of the organization with sustainability is necessary, considering the uniqueness of each organization.

Environmental Sustainability and Micro and Small Enterprises (MSEs)

The concept of sustainable development broadly encompasses the environment, considering the presence of humans within it. This challenges traditional forms of production, human behavior, city organization and operation, demanding new standards for societies' socio-environmental and economic development (Temoteo et al., 2018; Rocha et al., 2019). Therefore, given that sustainable development is composed of economic development combined with environmental concern (Seramim et al., 2018), it becomes necessary to adopt sustainable practices to enhance the performance of companies (Amankwah-Amoah et al., 2018).

It is important to note that the term "sustainability" was first defined in the Brundtland Report (Brundtland, 1987), which coined and explained the meaning of sustainability as the process of economic growth, environmental protection, and social equality. When applied to businesses, sustainability refers to how companies manage their business risks (economic, environmental, and social) and their obligations and opportunities (Jan et al., 2019).

Sustainable entrepreneurs directly link their business success to positive effects on the natural environment and humanity, creating value for various stakeholders (Freudenreich et al., 2020). The increasing appreciation for environmental and social issues, coupled with new legal requirements, has characterized the unique responsibilities of companies, becoming a determining factor in business success (Rocha et al., 2019). In this context, Fernandes et al. (2016) mention that sustainability implemented in small and medium-sized enterprises (SMEs) creates opportunities for these companies to negotiate with larger organizations due to the heightened concern for sustainability among stakeholders.

The specific management characteristics and extreme heterogeneity of SMEs make it challenging for researchers to focus on smaller companies and develop appropriate theories distinct from those applied to larger corporations (Leone, 1999). However, Martins et al. (2016) explain that large companies are better equipped to meet stakeholder requirements, whereas SMEs, due to their unique management characteristics, cannot employ the same mechanisms as large organizations. Consequently, small businesses cannot implement solutions developed for large companies, and their sustainable practices need better dissemination in the environmental context.

The number of studies on environmental sustainability in the organizational scope is more closely related to large companies because of their significant societal impact. Nevertheless, according to Revell et al. (2010), SMEs contribute approximately 60 to 70% of the estimated global pollution. Studies conducted in the United States, Thailand, and European countries highlight the importance of small businesses for the economy and social issues in the regions where they operate. These companies are primarily responsible for job creation, resource utilization, and waste production (Barbosa et al., 2020).

Barbosa et al. (2020) caution that, despite the significant number of small businesses, the planning and operationalization required to transform them into sustainable organizations present a considerable challenge. This underscores the need for more sustainable management models in the literature. Some challenges stem from the need for additional financial resources or a lack of knowledge in implementing sustainable practices (Motta et al., 2019). Furthermore, the efforts to drive changes in organizational culture that promote environmental awareness are more within reach of large companies (Fonseca & Martins, 2010), representing a more distant reality for SMEs.

This study focuses on small gastronomic enterprises. Zaro et al. (2013) clarify that sustainability in gastronomy requires the attention of managers, organizers, and employees to drive significant behavioral changes, particularly in reducing food waste and solid waste production, ultimately leading to cost reduction. Additionally, Minasse (2015) corroborates that gastronomic tourism can be a strategic element in promoting and valuing various culinary activities, making them more widely known and fostering a greater understanding of the geographical and cultural diversity among the Brazilian population.

Furthermore, it is worth noting that "green" practices in restaurants are a globally discussed topic. In South Korea, Hwang and Lee (2019) studied people's satisfaction when dining at restaurants that implement this type of management. Another study conducted in the United States concluded that the public prefers restaurants that adopt sustainable initiatives (Hu et al., 2010). However, in other contexts, the perspective of end customers may not directly affect day-to-day management practices but rather the regulations enforced by Responsible Organizations, as seen in Taiwan (Wang et al., 2013) and Brazil (Pospischek et al., 2014).

Kim and Hall (2020) assert that adopting sustainable practices in restaurants significantly affects consumers. Their research indicates that when restaurants involve customers in sustainability practices, there is an increase in customer loyalty and a reduction in restaurant waste. Finally, Cantele and Cassia (2020) found that when sustainability is implemented in restaurants, several positive effects occur, including customer satisfaction and improved competitiveness, which can mediate the indirect relationship between sustainability and company performance.

METHODOLOGICAL PROCEDURES

Research Classification

The research was conducted in the Combu Island region, specifically in the food sector, due to the high number of restaurants operating in the area and their relevance to the local economy. This relevance is due to the large flow of tourists to the island, which generates income for both the local and Belém residents. In addition, Yurtseven (2011) confirms that gastronomy has great weight within cultural and economic tourism, so these endeavours must be developed sustainably (Krause & Bahls, 2013).

This study is classified as descriptive and quantitative; descriptive, as it aims to describe the characteristics of restaurants regarding the contingent factors that interfere with sustainable practices and quantitative, for using statistical methods (such as mean and percentage frequency) in the analysis of results.

Sample, Data Collection and Analysis

The technical procedure used was the Survey, using a structured questionnaire adapted from the research of Amazonas, Silva and Andrade (2018) and Ferreira (2016). The adaptations refer to the transformation of questions according to the activity segment and the use of part of the questionnaire that explores the contingency variables that interfere with the management process and decision-making of restaurants.

Data collection initially took place by applying the questionnaire via the WhatsApp social network over two weeks between January and February 2021, from which eight responses were obtained. Before the practical application of the questionnaire, a visit to Combu Island was made to verify the number of restaurants. The result showed a total of 32 restaurants. However, due to the low response rate, on February 27, 2021, a visit to the restaurants was made to apply the questionnaire in person, following Covid-19 safety protocols. It was even possible to obtain more information beyond the questionnaire. On both occasions, a structured questionnaire containing 33 questions divided into three blocks was used: (1) Respondent Profile, consisting of 4 open-ended questions to find out the age, position, length of service in the company, and education level of the restaurant managers and owners; (2) Company Profile, consisting of only two open-ended questions to find out the length of activity and how many people work in the company; and (3) Contingency Factors, consisting of 27 questions divided into the following sub-blocks: a) 5 Likert-scale questions about the contingency factor of structure, b) 4 questions about leadership, with 3 in a Likert scale and one open-ended question, c) 5 Likert-scale questions about the environment, d) 5 strategy questions, with 4 in a Likert scale and one open-ended question, e) 4 culture questions and four technology questions in a Likert scale. The Likert scale of the questions about the contingency factors ranges from 1 to 5, varying between Strongly Disagree, Somewhat Disagree, Neither Agree nor Disagree, Somewhat Agree and Strongly Agree. The questionnaire also contained two open-ended questions, one question in the leadership contingency factor to find out what sustainable practices are implemented at the initiative of managers and owners, and another in the strategy contingency factor to check which social networks the restaurants use to publicize the sustainable practices developed in the workplace.

The questionnaire underwent a pre-test with three researchers, including one biologist, one forest engineer, and one geographer, all specializing in environmental management. The purpose was to validate the content covered and the accessibility of the question format, and some changes were suggested in response. With the acceptance of the suggestions, the questionnaire received a positive evaluation from the three researchers. During the data collection, 31 responses were obtained. However, nine questionnaires were excluded because they were not answered by the managers or owners of the restaurants, who were the target audience for the sample. Therefore, a total of 22 valid questionnaires were analyzed.

The data were first processed using RStudio software version 4.1, which allows for data treatment on the Likert scale. The Likert package was used to generate the contingency factor graphs. Excel 2020 was used to create the table of respondent and company profiles. Descriptive analysis was performed based on weighted averages and the percentage frequency of responses. The Likert scale values of 1 to 5 were used to calculate the standards, and the percentages found were used as weights for the respective values. Finally, the most common practices in the restaurants were identified, allowing for the research problem to be answered.

DATA ANALYSIS AND DISCUSSION

Profile of Respondents and Companies

Table 1 presents some information about the profile of managers and owners who responded on Combu Island. Regarding the number of employees, 54.55% of the restaurants operate with up to nine employees, classified according to SEBRAE for trade and service companies, where up to 9 employees are characterized as a microenterprise (ME); 45.46% of the establishments have from 10 to 49 employees, described as a small-sized company (EPP).

Table 2. Profile of the managers and owners who responded in Combu Island

Category	Quantity	Percentage
Age		
Up to the age of 30	3	13,64%
31 to 60 years old	18	81,82%
Above 60 years old	1	4,55%
Total	22	100%
Job Position		
Manager	14	64%
Owner	8	36%
Total	22	100%
Education		
Elementary School	2	9,09%
High School	12	54,55%
College degree	5	22,73%
Technical degree	3	13,64%
Total	22	100%
Work Experience		
0 to 2 years	10	45,45%
2 to 5 years	8	36,37%
Above 5 years	4	18,18%
Total	22	100%
Company activity time		
0 to 2 years	9	40,90%
2 to 5 years	8	36,37%
Above 5 years	5	22,73%
Total	22	100%
Number of Employees		
up to 9 (ME)	12	54,55%
10 to 49 (EPP)	10	45,46%
Total	22	100%

Such characteristics did not show significant variance in most points of the profiles of respondents and are like those found in the work of Picchiai et al. (2019), which focuses on micro and small enterprises in the food sector as a target audience, where the average age of respondents was 42 years and high school was the most common educational level. The characteristic that stood out the most was the size of the companies in the study, where the percentage of microenterprises was 88%, and only 10% were small businesses (EPP).

Analysis of Contingent Factors and Sustainable Practices

Considering the information presented in Figure 1 regarding the relationship between a company structure and sustainable practices in the establishment, it is observed that 10 (45.5%) fully agree that half of the employees are qualified to perform their function. In comparison, 4 (18.2%) completely disagree with this statement. These data reflect the actions of the National Commercial Learning Service (Senac) in partnership with the Brazilian Service of Support for Micro and Small Enterprises (Sebrae) Pará on Combu Island in the project "Sebrae present in Tourism". Due to the pandemic, this project has aimed to attract customers to the space, ensuring that the professionals who receive them receive training courses in gastronomy to serve customers more safely about personal hygiene, food hygiene, and the environment (SENAC, 2020).

It is also noted that 15 (68.2%) respondents agree that the place where meals are prepared meets sanitary standards, while only 1 (4.5%) completely disagree. This result is consistent with the research by Picchiai et al. (2019), which identified that 75% of restaurants in the metropolitan region of Campinas comply with legal and sanitary regulations. Respondents in this study reported difficulty in fully complying with the regulations due to their bureaucratic nature, but they always strive to meet them. This situation is also reported by Treptow et al. (2019), who points out that legislation is complex for most companies and is seen by managers as an obstacle for incubated companies in Santa Maria, mainly due to the excessive bureaucracy required for their operation. Therefore, the legislation does not present itself as an opportunity or provide incentives for adopting sustainable practices in business management.

In the analysis, it was identified that 8 (36.4%) respondents disagree entirely, meaning they have not taken any training courses to develop their management skills, but 12 (54.5%) of the respondents wholly or partially agree that they have taken some management training courses to run the establishment. This is a divergent characteristic from that of Picchiai et al. (2019), whose 70% of respondents in the same field did not take any training courses to develop management skills. Although the result is negative in terms of the level of training course completion, the author argues that taking training courses is a resource to improve knowledge in areas related to the improvement of establishment functioning, such as regulations and resolutions, and thus improve business performance, being essential in the development of a company.

However, it should be noted that 8 (36.4%) respondents fully agree that improvement courses are offered to restaurant employees once a year, followed by 5 (22.7%) who disagree entirely with this statement. These data differ from Picchiai et al.'s (2019) research, as these authors found that 74% of owners still need to offer improvement or training courses to their employees.

Furthermore, it is observed that 19 (86.4%) fully agree that the company seeks to implement ideas and suggestions from employees aimed at environmental sustainability, while 3 (13.6%) partially agree. This result supports the finding of Fagundes et al. (2010), whose study aimed to analyze the organizational structure and management of an industrial equipment manufacturing and assembly company from the perspective of contingency theory and found mixed characteristics in terms of work centralization, always reaching a consensus or communication with top management. In addition, other authors argue that employee participation generates individual motivation and contributes to the organization's development (Beuren & Fiorentin, 2013; Chenhall, 2007).

Figure 1. Distribution of responses to questions about the company's structure and relationship with sustainable practices
Note: Strongly disagree (1); Somewhat disagree (2); Neither agree nor disagree (3); Somewhat agree (4); Strongly agree (5).

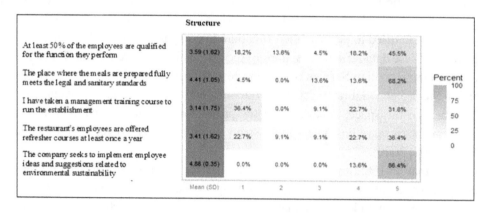

Figure 2 presents data on the relationship between company leadership and sustainable practices. It was found that 21 (95.4%) of the respondents partially or fully agree that the establishment's leadership encourages employees to apply sustainable practices, corroborating with the research by Nor-Aishah et al. (2020), which demonstrated that leadership has a positive effect on environmentally sustainable performance. Nor-Aishah et al. (2020) signaled entrepreneurial leadership as positively affecting socially sustainable performance. This coincides with this research's results that 19 (86.3%) respondents consider the leader's role fundamental in implementing sustainable practices.

Motta et al. (2019) consider that today, regardless of their size and business line, companies are required by the dynamic environment in which they operate, where innovation is part of high-value quality, added to products and an environmentally responsible posture. In this perspective, 19 (86.3%) leaders partially or fully agree that they always seek to bring innovations to the company. This percentage is close to the results of Dallabona et al. (2019), who obtained 86% consensus on the referred question.

Figure 2. Distribution of responses to questions about company leadership and its relationship with sustainable practices
Note: Strongly disagree (1); Somewhat disagree (2); Neither agree nor disagree (3); Somewhat agree (4); Strongly agree (5).

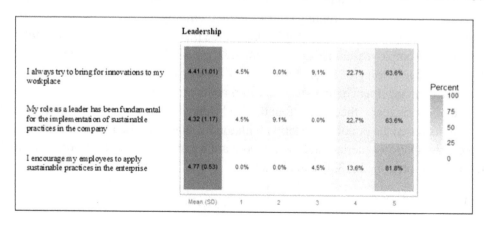

Figure 3 displays data on the relationship between the company's environment and the sustainable practices of the establishment. Similar to the leading factor, the environment strongly influenced this study. It can be observed that 15 (68.18%) of the respondents partially or fully agree with the statement that they implement practices that contribute to reducing the prices of the products offered to customers while gaining a competitive advantage over competitors.

Sustainable practices can be used as a competitive advantage by enabling the entrepreneur to reduce costs, benefiting the company. Innovation can be a way to reduce operational costs in providing services to these establishments, providing a competitive differential in the segment, as perceived by Spezamiglio, Galina, and Calia (2016).

It was also identified that 20 (90.9%) respondents partially or fully agree that customers feel more satisfied knowing that the restaurant they visit is concerned with sustainability. This result is like that presented by Fernandes et al. (2016). Approximately 73% of respondents partially or fully agree that customers demand a socially and environmentally responsible posture from the researched companies. Another aspect that deserves attention is that 11 (50%) respondents partially or fully disagree that the restaurant has sustainable practices just because others do. This result diverges from the study conducted by Latif et al. (2020), where one of the research hypotheses was confirmed, the positive relationship of mimetic pressure in adopting environmental management accounting in manufacturing companies in Pakistan.

All respondents partially or fully agree that restaurant management is concerned with complying with local environmental laws, showing that legislation influences the company's environmental practices. This result corroborates Robin et al. (2019), who conclude that implementing environmental measures provides a robust external motivation. In the study by Martins et al. (2019), the topic of business sustainability is discussed with the manager's awareness, reflecting on Law 6.938/81 - the National Environmental Policy - which seeks to prevent depredatory actions carried out by entrepreneurs in the name of socio-economic development, but which violate national security interests and ecosystem balance.

A Deliberal et al. (2016) study shows that environmental management becomes a competitive advantage. It can be considered a strategic organizational capability and a way to improve companies' environmental and economic performance. Furthermore, it was observed that 18 (81.8%) respondents partially or fully agree that competition is intense in their segment.

Figure 3. Distribution of responses to questions about the company's environment and its relationship with sustainable practices
Note: Strongly disagree (1); Somewhat disagree (2); Neither agree nor disagree (3); Somewhat agree (4); Strongly agree (5).

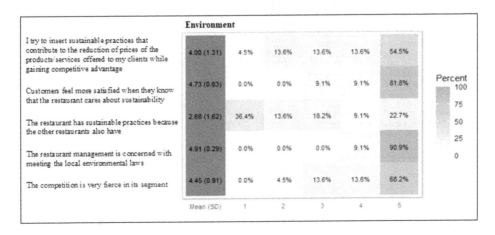

Figure 4 shows data on the relationship between the company's strategy and sustainable practices in the establishment. It can be noted that 11 (50%) respondents agree, partially or entirely, that they use sustainable practices as a competitive advantage, while 4 (18.2%) neither agree nor disagree with this statement. This result is consistent with the study by Treptow et al. (2019), whose investigated companies that balance sustainability with innovation gain a competitive advantage.

The intention to promote sustainable practices is seen as a competitive strategy. Still, regarding Figure 4, it is possible to observe that 19 (86.3%) respondents wholly or partially agree that they have a communication channel (Instagram, WhatsApp, and Facebook) with their customers to promote sustainable activities developed in their workspace. This result reflects the finding of Rocha et al. (2019), in which preventive companies show that they are motivated by image, market value, and the environment, having a flatter hierarchical structure and high customer dependence. However, when consulting the social media accounts of the analyzed companies in this research, they appeared to be much less representative in promoting sustainable actions than the percentage reported in this survey.

To complement the analysis, it was identified that 18 (81.8%) of the managers and owners partially or fully agree that they seek to develop characteristics focused on sustainable practices in the provision of services and products. This index can be attributed to the pandemic scenario of COVID-19, where many respondents affirm that with the safety norms for COVID-19 prevention, many changes were made in the establishments' routine, generating more plastic and disposables.

Although only half of the respondents said they use sustainable practices as a competitive advantage, 20 (90.9%) respondents partially or fully agree that restaurants are concerned with maintaining the island's biodiversity through sustainable practices to attract customers. This result may be contradictory, as only 11 respondents stated that they use sustainable practices as a competitive advantage. At the same time, 20 agree they maintain the island's biodiversity through sustainable practices to attract customers. The analysis of Deliberal et al. (2016) supports this study by presenting results in which stakeholders, such as customers, have a moderate correlation with environmental orientation, suggesting that stakeholders can influence companies in developing strategies related to environmental aspects.

Figure 4. Distribution of responses to questions about company strategy and its relationship with sustainable practices
Note: Strongly disagree (1); Somewhat disagree (2); Neither agree nor disagree (3); Somewhat agree (4); Strongly agree (5).

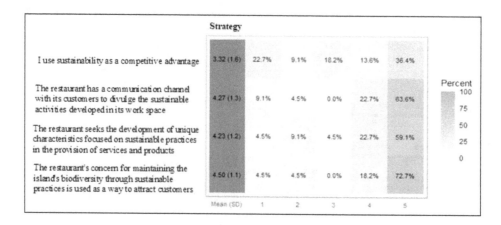

Figure 5 presents the data on the relationship between culture and sustainable practices in the establishment. The figure shows that 15 (68.2%) respondents agree, partially or totally, that some of their employees are from the island, contributing to the concern for sustainable practices. According to respondents, even people from other regions are concerned about the sustainable practices carried out on the island. About 19 (86.3%) respondents agree, partially or totally, that restaurants are concerned with passing on their environmental values to visitors so that they adopt a consciousness of the preservation of the island. This item also has a relationship with the contingency factor of leadership since, according to Crozatti (1998), organizational culture is defined by the company's leaders who impose their way of doing things. One example of practices related to culture that is passed on to visitors is the encouragement of reducing disposable items. Therefore, culture positively influences sustainable practices and is linked to company leadership.

Another point observed is that 16 (72.7%) respondents agree, partially or totally, that the handicrafts used for commercializing and decorating the environment are part of the local culture and are made sustainably. Regarding this item, the on-site handicrafts come from both the island and other regions. Finally, 17 (77.2%) respondents agree, partially or totally, that the region's values, customs, and habits contribute to sustainable restaurant practices. This may be due to the region where they are located having specific legislation, as it is an Environmental Protection Area. According to the research by Morais, Oliveira, and Souza (2014), many environmental sustainability practices carried out by organizations' result from external pressures, such as the government, in such a way that they become consolidated in companies. Thus, the practices may have become a habit of the region.

Figure 5. Distribution of responses to questions related to the company's culture and its relationship with sustainable practices
Note: Strongly disagree (1); Somewhat disagree (2); Neither agree nor disagree (3); Somewhat agree (4); Strongly agree (5).

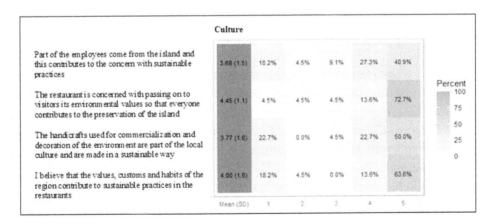

Figure 6 presents the data on the company's technology and its relation to sustainable practices in the establishment. It was found that half of the respondents partially or fully agree that some sustainable practice is adopted in the restaurant's energy use. However, 7 (31.8%) respondents disagree entirely with this statement. The fact that energy consumption in restaurants has a lower percentage of interference in sustainable practices can be justified by the constant power outages in the region, which leads restaurants to opt for generators, causing higher energy consumption. It was noted during the research that some restaurants in the region also consider using solar energy to reduce electricity consumption.

In addition, it is noted that about 20 (90.9%) respondents partially or fully agree that services offered to customers are developed in a way that minimizes the impacts generated on the environment. As in Chenhall's (2003) research, it was possible to verify that one of the motivations for environmentally focused technological practices is cost savings. One of the examples of practices carried out by some companies surveyed in this study is the proper disposal of cooking oil used in food preparation, cultivation of vegetables for use in restaurants, and adoption of cups to reduce the use of disposables.

Figure 6. Distribution of responses to questions about the company's technology and its relationship with sustainable practices
Note: Strongly disagree (1); Somewhat disagree (2); Neither agree nor disagree (3); Somewhat agree (4); Strongly agree (5).

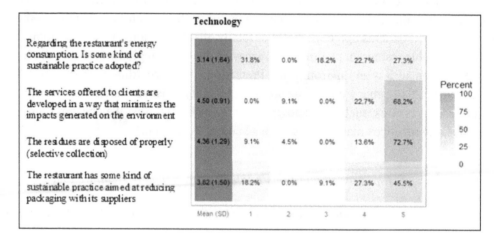

It should be added that 19 (86.3%) respondents emphasised that these establishments properly dispose of the generated waste (selective collection). Despite the response average being closer to fully agreeing, it was observed that some restaurants stopped performing this activity because the boat that collects the waste no longer passed by the location. Both in the research of Nascimento et al. (2010) and in the research of Rosa and Cabral (2017), the environmental impacts generated on Combu Island were analyzed. Despite the different dates on which the works were published, the same problem was found on the island: waste burning. This problem was also observed in the present research. According to the respondents, it is due to the absence of the boat that collected the garbage that interferes with the local fauna and flora, bringing damage even to the island's residents.

Finally, it is noted that 16 (72.8%) respondents agree, partially or entirely, that the restaurant has some sustainable practices aimed at reducing packaging with its suppliers. It is believed that this practice is stimulated by the fact that the region regularly suffers from the scarcity of collection by the municipality, a factor reported by some respondents who claimed to carry out movements in partnership with cooperatives to have garbage collection performed in the region.

CONCLUSION

The objective of this study was to investigate the contingency factors (internal and external) that influence sustainable practices in gastronomic businesses on Combu Island. It was verified that environmental practices are adopted in the region, mainly because it is an area protected by law. In addition, there is an incentive from local organizations' such as Sebrae, which directly guides entrepreneurs towards sustainable restaurant practices. The research problem was answered through the percentage frequency and mean of the responses obtained by the Likert scale.

The results showed that the factor most influencing sustainable practices is the environment, mainly due to local legislation. Regarding the contingency factor environment, an inconsistency in the responses was identified. The question with higher averages stated that the restaurant seeks to include sustainable practices while gaining a competitive advantage over competitors. However, in another question, one of the lowest averages was obtained in the contingency factor strategy, affirming that the restaurant uses sustainability as a competitive advantage. From this inconsistency, managers and owners are reluctant to state that they only have sustainable practices because of the competitive advantage. This can also be seen from the low frequency of restaurants that claim to have sustainable practices because their competitors do.

Another contingent factor that most influence sustainable practices is leadership, confirmed by situations that influence and depend on the decision of company leaders, such as technology, where the organization's leaders determine the process of developing products and services offered. Within the contingent factor of technology, selective waste collection is a regular practice, obtaining the second highest mean, which depends on the leader's role in its implementation. Thus, leadership's importance in applying sustainable practices in gastronomic enterprises in the investigated region is evident.

The factor with the lowest mean of responses was structure due to the low qualification of managers, owners, and employees regarding their function. The importance of Senac and Sebrae in expanding the knowledge of the enterprise's employees is observed.

Therefore, this study provides knowledge about each contingent factor, indicating those that most influence the sustainable practices of restaurants in Combu Island, allowing for a clearer understanding of how they affect the company and bringing empirical results about the influence of legislation and stakeholders on sustainable practices. Another aspect raised in the research is using sustainable practices as a competitive advantage for companies, as predicted in the literature, where its relevance is attested.

The study also contributes to future research in the region, primarily related to the management of companies in environmental protection areas, allowing for a broader understanding of the topic. Given the importance of environmental and sustainable practices for organizations', this is a relevant discussion for society since how they operate directly impacts a region's social and natural context.

Among the limitations presented in this research is the sample with 22 questionnaires, having to exclude another 9 for not being answered by managers, which consequently affected the result. Another area for improvement was the need for similar themes related to contingency factors, specifically sustainable practices, and the questionnaire format, limiting some responses to pre-established statements. Future research could explore contingency factors related to sustainability practices in other environmental preservation regions. Moreover, they could also use other methodological strategies, such as data collection through interviews and content analysis.

ACKNOWLEDGMENT

This work is financed by national funds through FCT - Foundation for Science and Technology, I.P., within the scope of multi-annual funding UIDB/04043/2020.

REFERENCES

ABNT – Associação Brasileira de Normas Técnicas. (2014). *Associação Brasileira de Normas Técnicas*. http://www.abnt.org.br/m2.asp?cod_pagina=963

Amankwah-Amoah, J., Adomako, S., & Danso, A. (2018). Entrepreneurial orientation, environmental sustainability and new venture performance: Does stakeholder integration matter? *Business Strategy and the Environment*, *28*(1), 79–87. doi:10.1002/bse.2191

Amazonas, S. (2018). Gestão ambiental hoteleira: Tecnologias e práticas sustentáveis e práticas sustentáveis aplicadas a hotéis. *Ambiente & Sociedade*, *21*, 1–20.

Barbosa, M., Castañeda-Ayarza, J. A., & Ferreira, D. H. L. (2020). Sustainable strategic management (GES): Sustainability in small business. *Journal of Cleaner Production*, *258*, 120880. doi:10.1016/j.jclepro.2020.120880

Beuren, I. M., & Fiorentin, M. (2014). Influência de fatores contingenciais nos atributos do Sistema de Contabilidade Gerencial: Um estudo em empresas têxteis do Estado do Rio Grande do Sul. *Revista de Ciências da Administração*, *16*(38), 195–212. doi:10.5007/2175-8077.2014v16n38p195

Campbell, J. (2007). Why Would Corporations Behave in Socially Responsible Ways? An Institutional Theory of Corporate Social Responsibility. *Academy of Management Review*, *32*(3), 946–967. doi:10.5465/amr.2007.25275684

Cantele, S., & Cassia, F. (2020). Sustainability implementation in restaurants: A comprehensive model of drivers, barriers, and competitiveness-mediated effects on firm performance. *International Journal of Hospitality Management*, *87*, 102510. doi:10.1016/j.ijhm.2020.102510

Cecato, V. M. (2015). *A contribuição do processo de comunicação para a construção da cultura da sustentabilidade: um estudo de micro, pequenas e médias empresas brasileiras* [Dissertação de Mestrado]. Escola de Comunicações e Artes, Universidade de São Paulo, São Paulo. doi:10.11606/D.27.2016.tde-01022016-153822

Chenhall, R. H. (2003). Management control systems design within its organizational context: Findings from contingency-based research and directions for the future. *Accounting, Organizations and Society*, *28*(2–3), 127–168. doi:10.1016/S0361-3682(01)00027-7

Crozatti, J. (1998). Modelo de gestão e cultura organizacional: conceitos e interações. *Caderno de estudos*, (18), 01-20. https://doi.org/ doi:10.1590/S1413-92511998000200004

Dallabona, L., Silva, D. & Lavarda, C. (2019). Contingent Variables, leadership styles and organizational slack predominant in a Santa Catarina textile industry. *Revista Capital Científico – Eletrônica*, *17*(1). . doi:10.5935/2177-4153.20190002

Danso, A., Adomako, S., Owusu-Agyei, S., & Konadu, R. (2019). Environmental sustainability orientation, competitive strategy and financial performance. *Business Strategy and the Environment*, *28*(5), 885–895. doi:10.1002/bse.2291

De Carvalho, S. S., da Silva Pimentel, M. A., & de Lima, A. M. M. (2019). Desafios da área de proteção ambiental em território insular: Proposição de planejamento para gestão de recursos hídricos sob a perspectiva dos moradores da ilha do Combu, Belém, Pará. *Brazilian Journal of Environmental Sciences*, *51*(51), 62–78. doi:10.5327/Z2176-947820190446

Deliberal, J. P., Tondolo, V. A. G., Camargo, M. E., & Tondolo, R. R. P. (2016). Gestão Ambiental como uma Capacidade Estratégica: Um Estudo no Cluster Fabricação de Móveis no Sul do Brasil. *Brazilian Business Review*, *13*(4), 124–147. doi:10.15728/bbr.2016.13.4.6

Espejo, M. M. S. B. (2008). Perfil dos Atributos do Sistema Orçamentário sob a Perspectiva Contingencial: uma Abordagem Multivariada. Tese Doutoramento em Ciências Contábeis, Programa de Pós-Graduação em Ciências Contábeis, Faculdade de Economia, Administração e Contabilidade da Universidade de São Paulo.

Fagundes, J. A., Petri, M., Lavarda, R. B., Rodrigues, M. R., Lavarda, C. E. F., & Soller, C. C. (2010). Estrutura Organizacional E Gestão Sob A Ótica Da Teoria Da Contingência. *Gestão & Regionalidade*, *26*(78). Advance online publication. doi:10.13037/gr.vol26n78

Fernandes, C. C., Mazzola, B. G., Esteves, K., & Oliveira, M. M. (2016). Práticas e indicadores de sustentabilidade em incubadoras de empresa: um estudo no Estado de São Paulo. *Revista de administração, contabilidade e economia da FUNDACE*, *7*(3), 34-50.

Ferreira, A. O. (2016). Gestão de micro e pequenas empresas na perspectiva da teoria da contingência: um estudo em restaurantes da Região Metropolitana de Campinas – RMC [Tese de mestrado]. Faculdade Campo Limpo Paulista, Campo Limpo Paulista, SP, Brasil.

Fonseca, S. A., & Martins, P. S. (2010). Gestão ambiental: uma súplica do planeta, um desafio para políticas públicas, incubadoras e pequenas empresas. Production, 20(4). https://doi.org/ doi:10.1590/S0103-65132010005000056

Freire, J. C. S. (2002). *Juventude Ribeirinha: Identidade e Cotidiano* [Dissertação de Mestrado em Planejamento do Desenvolvimento – PLADES]. Núcleo de Altos Estudos Amazônicos, Universidade Federal do Pará, Belém, Brasil.

Freudenreich, B., Lüdeke-Freund, F., & Schaltegger, S. A. (2020). Stakeholder Theory Perspective on Business Models: Value Creation for Sustainability. *Journal of Business Ethics*, *166*(1), 3–18. doi:10.100710551-019-04112-z

Hu, H. H., Parsa, H. G., & Self, J. (2010). The dynamics of green restaurant patronage. *Cornell Hospitality Quarterly*, *51*(3), 344–362. doi:10.1177/1938965510370564

Hwang, K., & Lee, B. (2019). Pride, mindfulness, public self-awareness, affective satisfaction, and customer citizenship behaviour among green restaurant customers. *International Journal of Hospitality Management*, *83*, 169–179. doi:10.1016/j.ijhm.2019.05.009

Jan, A., Marimuthu, M., & Bin, P. M. (2019, August 10). The nexus of sustainability practices and financial performance: From the perspective of Islamic banking. *Journal of Cleaner Production, 228,* 703–717. doi:10.1016/j.jclepro.2019.04.208

Kim, M. J., & Hall, C. M. (2020). Can sustainable restaurant practices enhance customer loyalty? The roles of value theory and environmental concerns. *Journal of Hospitality and Tourism Management, 43,* 127–138. doi:10.1016/j.jhtm.2020.03.004

Krause, R. W., & Bahls, Á. A. (2013). Orientações gerais para uma gastronomia sustentável. *Turismo: visão e ação, 15*(3), 434-450. . doi:10.14210/rtva.v15n3.p434-450

Kuzma, E. L., Doliveira, S. L. D., Gonzaga, C. A. M., & Novak, M. A. L. (2016). A Inserção da Sustentabilidade na Formação de Administradores. *Revista de Gestão Ambiental e Sustentabilidade, 5*(2), 146–165. doi:10.5585/geas.v5i2.430

Latif, B., Mahmood, Z., San, O. T., Mohd, S. R., & Bakhsh, A. (2020). Coercive, Normative and Mimetic Pressures as Drivers of Environmental Management Accounting Adoption. *Sustainability (Basel), 12*(11), 4506. doi:10.3390u12114506

Leone, N. M. C. P. G. (1999). As especificidades das pequenas e médias empresas. *RAUSP Management Journal, 34*(2), 91-94. http://www.spell.org.br/documentos/ver/18123/as-especificida des-das-pequenas-e-medias-empresas/i/pt-br

Maletič, M., Maletič, D., & Gomišček, B. (2017). The role of contingency factors on the relationship between sustainability practices and organizational performance. *Journal of Cleaner Production, 171*(10), 423–433. Advance online publication. doi:10.1016/j.jclepro.2017.09.172

Martins, M. A. M. D. M., Costa, K. C., Martins, S. D. M., Formigoni, A., & Rossini, A. M. (2017). Crimes ambientais e sustentabilidade: discussão sobre a responsabilidade penal dos gestores e administradores de empresas. *Revista Metropolitana de Sustentabilidade, 7*(3), 143-158. http://revistaseletronicas.fmu.br/index.php/rms/article/view /1575

Minasse, M. H. (2015). *Eu como cultura? Notas sobre políticas de valorização da gastronomia no Brasil.* Seminário Nacional de Pesquisa e Pós-Graduação em Turismo, Universidade Federal do Rio Grande do Norte.

Morais, D. O. C., da Silva Oliveira, N. Q., & de Souza, E. M. (2014). As práticas de sustentabilidade ambiental e suas influências na nova formatação institucional das organizações. *Revista de Gestão Ambiental e Sustentabilidade, 3*(3), 90-106. http://www.spell.org.br/documentos/ver/39221/as-praticas-de-sustentabilidade-ambiental-e-suas-influencias-na-nova-format acao-institucional-das-organizacoes/i/pt-br

Motta, S. D., Bianchi, R. C., Zonatto, P. A. F., Silva, A. C. C. J., & Boligon, J. A. R. (2019). Análise Das Práticas Sustentáveis. In *Microempresas Do Setor Industrial Da Região Central Do Estado Do Rio Grande Do Sul* (pp. 1127–1144). Revista de Administração da UFSM. doi:10.5902/1983465939047

Nascimento, N. S., Farias, M. S., de Lima, N. G., & Miranda, R. S. (2010). *Um estudo dos problemas ambientais da área de proteção ambiental da ilha do Combú Belém-PA.* https://www.ibeas.org.br/congresso/Trabalhos2010/V-002.pdf

Nor-Aishah, H., Ahmad, N. H., & Ramayah, T. (2020). Entrepreneurial Leadership and Sustainable Performance of Manufacturing SMEs in Malaysia: The Contingent Role of Entrepreneurial Bricolage. *Sustainability (Basel), 12*(8), 3100. doi:10.3390u12083100

Oliveira, A. S. de, & Callado, A. A. C. (2018).Fatores contigenciais e o controle gerencial: uma avaliação em organizações não governamentais (ONGS) brasileiras. *Advances in Scientific and Applied Accounting, 11*(1), 92–109.

Otley, D. T. (1980). The contingency theory of management accounting: Achievement and prognosis. *Accounting, Organizations and Society, 5*(4), 413–428. doi:10.1016/0361-3682(80)90040-9

Otley, D. T. (2016). The contingency theory of management accounting and control:1980–2014. *Management Accounting Research, 31*, 45–62. doi:10.1016/j.mar.2016.02.001

Picchiai, D., & Ferreira, A. O. (2019). Gestão de micro e pequenas empresas: estudo em restaurantes da região metropolitana de Campinas. *DRd - Desenvolvimento Regional Em Debate, 9*, 454-477. . doi:10.24302/drd.v9i0.2117

Pospischek, V. S., Spinelli, M. G. N., & Matias, A. C. G. (2014). Avaliação de ações de sustentabilidade ambiental em restaurantes comerciais localizados no município de São Paulo. *Demetra: Food, Nutrition & Health/Alimentação Nutrição & Saúde, 9*(2). Advance online publication. doi:10.12957/demetra.2014.8822

Pryshlakivsky, J., & Searcy, C. A. (2017). Heuristic Model for Establishing Trade-Offs in Corporate Sustainability Performance Measurement Systems. *Journal of Business Ethics, 144*(2), 323–342. doi:10.100710551-015-2806-y

Revell, A., Stokes, D., & Chen, H. (2010). Small businesses and the environment: Turning over a new leaf? *Business Strategy and the Environment, 19*(5), 273–288.

Robin, C. F., Pedroche, M. S. C., Astorga, P. S., & Almeida, M. M. A. (2019). Green Practices in Hospitality: A Contingency Approach. *Sustainability (Basel), 11*(13), 3737. doi:10.3390u11133737

Rocha, R. T., Introvini, R. F., Caldana, A. C. F., Krauter, E., & Liboni, L. B. (2019). Gestão sustentável – motivadores, barreiras e percepção de micro e pequenos empresários. *Gestão & Regionalidade, 35*(106). Advance online publication. doi:10.13037/gr.vol35n106.5121

Rodrigues, E. T. (2006). *Organização comunitária e desenvolvimento territorial: O contexto ribeirinho em uma ilha da Amazônia* [Dissertação **de** Mestrado em Planejamento do Desenvolvimento]. Núcleo de Altos Estudos Amazônicos. Universidade Federal do Pará.

Rosa, C. C., & Cabral, E. R. (2017). Os impactos socioambientais e econômicos do turismo: O caso da ilha do Combú, no entorno da cidade de Belém–PA. *Colóquio Organizações. Desenvolvimento e Sustentabilidade, 7*, 364–383.

Serviço Nacional de Aprendizagem Comercial. (2020). *Formação em Boas Práticas para profissionais da Ilha do Combú*. https://www.pa.senac.br/noticia/formacao-em-boas-praticas-para-profissionais-da-ilha-do-Combú

Spezamiglio, B. S., Galina, S. V. R., & Calia, R. C. (2016). Competitividade, Inovação E Sustentabilidade: Uma Inter- Relação Por Meio Da Sistematização Da Literatura. *Revista Eletrônica de Administração (Porto Alegre), 22*(2), 363-393. https://doi.org/ doi:10.1590/1413-2311.009162016.62887

Treptow, I., Kneipp, J., Müller, L., Frizzo, K., & Gomes, C. (2019). Práticas de inovação sustentável em empresas incubadas da cidade de Santa Maria, RS. *Revista Metropolitana de Sustentabilidade, 9*(1), 69. https://revistaseletronicas.fmu.br/index.php/rms/article/view/1649

Wang, Y. F., Chen, S. P., Lee, Y. C., & Tsai, C. T. S. (2013). Developing green management standards for restaurants: An application of green supply chain management. *International Journal of Hospitality Management, 34*, 263–273. doi:10.1016/j.ijhm.2013.04.001

Yurtseven, H. R. (2011). Sustainable gastronomic tourism in Gokceada (Imbros): Local and authentic perspectives. *International Journal of Humanities and Social Science, 1*(18), 17–26.

Zaro, M., Pistorello, J., Pereira, G. S., Nery, C. H. C., & Conto, S. M. D. (2013). Geração de resíduos sólidos em eventos gastronômicos: o Festiqueijo de Carlos Barbosa, RS. *Revista Rosa dos Ventos, 5*(2), 264-279.

ADDITIONAL READING

Higgins-Desbiolles, F., Moskwa, E., & Wijesinghe, G. (2019). How sustainable is sustainable hospitality research? A review of sustainable restaurant literature from 1991 to 2015. *Current Issues in Tourism, 22*(13), 1551–1580. doi:10.1080/13683500.2017.1383368

Kusa, R., Suder, M., & Duda, J. (2023). Impact of greening on performance in the hospitality industry: Moderating effect of flexibility and inter-organizational cooperation. *Technological Forecasting and Social Change, 190*, 122423. doi:10.1016/j.techfore.2023.122423

TM, A., Kaur, P., Ferraris, A., & Dhir, A. (2021). What motivates the adoption of green restaurant products and services? A systematic review and future research agenda. *Business Strategy and the Environment, 30*(4), 2224–2240. doi:10.1002/bse.2755

Chapter 7
Sustainability Disclosure:
A Literature Review and Bibliometric Analysis

Arnaldo Coelho
Faculty of Economics, University of Coimbra, Portugal

Beatriz Lopes Cancela
 https://orcid.org/0000-0003-0167-1714
ISCAC, Coimbra Business School, Portugal

Pedro Fontoura
Faculty of Economics, University of Coimbra, Portugal

Alexandre Rato
Faculty of Economics, University of Coimbra, Portugal

ABSTRACT

The literature on the disclosure of sustainability has been receiving increasing attention, with various studies being conducted. However, the systematic review of the literature on "sustainability disclosure" by mapping the existing research and identifying opportunities for future research is fragmented and limited, and the objectives of this investigation intend to respond to this gap. The chapter contributes to contemporary literature by carving out the importance sustainability disclosure. The methodology employed includes a systematic literature review using the Web of Science and Scopus databases (1979 and 2023), which was analyzed using the VOSviewer and RStudio software. The results of the study reveal six distinct groups of publication trends, including sustainable index and practices, corporate image and reputation, sustainability reporting, frameworks related to sustainability, corporate governance approaches, and board corporative characteristics.

DOI: 10.4018/978-1-6684-9076-1.ch007

INTRODUCTION

The world has undergone significant changes in recent times, with technological advancements and globalization leading to a shift in consumer behavior (Farooq et al., 2019). This shift can be attributed to a growing awareness of the need to care for and preserve the planet, as well as increased pressure from stakeholders for organizations to improve their results and actions (Tran and Beddewela, 2020). The main objective of this research is to identify strategies and mechanisms that do not negatively impact companies' commercial sector, while also promoting organizations' loyalty and transparency towards society (Dwekat et al., 2020). Sustainability reporting has emerged as a tool that companies use to disclose and communicate their environmental, social and economic results and goals (Pham and Tran, 2020). There is evidence to suggest that promoting and communicating a company's commitment to responsible behavior can help to retain and attract customers (Berne-Manero and Marzo-Navarro, 2020).

Given the importance of sustainability reporting, several studies have been conducted to explore how it can create value for organizations and society. Channuntapipat (2021) made a significant contribution by examining the reliability and transparency of sustainability reports and how they can lead to increased corporate sustainability actions. Aureli et al. (2020) analyzed the reactions of investors and markets to the relationship between sustainability practices and financial performance. Baier et al. (2021) highlighted the importance of accurate communication in sustainability reports, as misleading information can undermine the credibility of these reports. Ruiz-Barbadillo and Martinez-Ferrero (2020) studied the potential influence of culture and country on corporate disclosures. Finally, Antonio et al. (2020) recognized the importance of stakeholder engagement in understanding the perception and importance of social, cultural, and political aspects, and adopted a transnational approach.

Previous research on sustainability reporting has identified several gaps that provide opportunities for future investigations. One suggestion is to develop more robust theoretical frameworks that allow for a more rigorous and accurate analysis (Traxler et al., 2020). Vieira and Radonjič (2020) suggest changing the method of analysis of disclosed information, focusing on quality over quantity, and exploring mechanisms that facilitate the creation of sustainable value (Manning et al., 2019). According to Mahmood et al. (2018), it is also important to study how to improve sustainable disclosure in order to capture organizational value more comprehensively. Additionally, Dwekat et al. (2020) emphasized the importance of new areas of research to support the evolution and development of sustainability reporting, emphasizing the importance of evaluating report value from a holistic perspective that takes into account various dimensions of firm performance.

This study aims to address the gaps in previous research on sustainability reporting by using bibliometric analysis to identify past investigations and trends, as well as the least explored areas of study. This methodology, which is replicable and transparently described (Paoloni et al., 2020), allows for the identification and systemization of different areas of investigation.

Specifically, our research aims to develop a framework for the sustainability disclosure, identifying the main areas and current dynamics. The second objective is to identify potential avenues for future research on sustainability disclosure. In addressing these goals, we will address the following research questions:

RQ1: Who are the most notable and influential contributors (e.g., journals, articles, authors, institutions, countries) in the field of business administration that study sustainability disclosure?

RQ2: What is the different research (or knowledge) clusters that have emerged in the field?

RQ3: What are the main investigation opportunities in this area?

The conclusions of this study are based on a thorough review of the literature, addressing the limitations of previous research in this field. Through the use of bibliometric analysis, this study identifies and analyzes the main topics related to sustainability disclosure, highlighting new opportunities for research in this field. Additionally, this study contributes to the literature by identifying key themes for future research and gaps in the literature. Furthermore, this study examines the main practices advocated to help companies improve their sustainability reports. Finally, bibliometric maps are used to identify the most commonly studied themes in the literature and those that have received less attention, highlighting potential opportunities for future research.

The structure of this article is as follows: Chapter Two presents a theoretical background on sustainability disclosure. Chapter Three describes the methodology adopted in this analysis. In Chapter Four, the results are presented, along with a brief overview of the literature, identified gaps, and future research opportunities. Finally, Chapter Five presents the conclusion of the research, its contributions, and limitations.

THEORETICAL BACKGROUND

Sustainability is a multifaceted and complex concept that encompasses various perspectives and theories. The idea of focusing on the three dimensions of sustainability - economy, environment, and society - in the business context, emerged in the late 20th century (Elkington, 2020; Hussain, Rigoni, & Orij, 2018). In recent years, sustainability has been approached strategically, as a means to combine short-term survival and long-term socially responsible development. As a result, companies are increasingly aligning their goals with the three dimensions of sustainability and are considering environmental and social issues in addition to creating economic value (Lueg et al., 2019; Holt et al., 2020). Evaluation of companies now includes not only the results and strategies they adopt, but also how they implement them (Haney et al., 2020). Literature highlights the importance of reforming current production systems, creating more sustainable organizations (Shang et al., 2020), reducing environmental impact, developing sustainable projects, and engaging with local communities as key challenges (Plieninger et al., 2021). Where corporate social responsibility is essentially based on the "responsibilities of a company towards society and the environment, deriving from the idea that business and society are truly interlinked" (Torelli et al., 2020, pp. 471), and on the practices they may adopt, sustainability ir rather concentrated on the achievements of these policies and practices (Bai et al., 2023; Cancela et al., 2022).

Sustainability reporting is a common practice among companies, and it has become mandatory to demonstrate the company's commitment to social, environmental, and economic development. Although relatively new, these reports vary in their content and lack the necessary rigor (Muslu et al., 2019). They provide stakeholders with insight into the efforts and commitments of companies (Wolff et al., 2020), the strategies they adopt to achieve desired results (Corciolani et al., 2020) and serve as an important source of analysis information (Schiehll and Kolahgar, 2021).

Sustainability reports can also be seen as a link between the company and other market players (Orazalin and Mahmood, 2018). According to Masoud and Vij (2020), these reports should contain two types of content: factors that influence sustainable disclosure, such as financial performance, management size, and gender diversity, and mandatory factors related to the environment, human resources, products and services, and relationships with local communities. Some authors, such as Kouaib et al. (2020), highlight the importance of women in management positions, as the information presented becomes more stable, transparent, and reliable, but also less accurate and clear (Garcia-Sanchez et al., 2019).

The stakeholder theory is a fundamental tool for company management (Freeman et al., 2021) and promotes social responsibility and policies as a means of generating value and fostering business development. This theory is characterized by high levels of trust, cooperation, and information sharing between both parties (Jones et al., 2018), ensuring long-term organizational survival (Hickman and Akdere, 2019). Currently, the size of the company does not influence the achievement of sustainable objectives, as any person or organization can create value in society and contribute to a more sustainable and beneficial future for future generations (Elkington, 2020).

Sustainability reports make it possible to communicate effectively with all stakeholders and at the same time seek economic benefits for companies. These benefits can be extensive when well exploited, and the following are considered as main points:

1. Risk management: Adopting a risk management mindset enables companies to identify and seize opportunities for positive impact on society and markets where they operate. According to Cheng et al. (2021), risk management is a philosophy that integrates social, economic, and environmental aspects to manage them effectively, safeguarding organizations and communities.
2. Financial benefits: Companies strive to achieve financial benefits, as they are crucial for their long-term survival. However, to achieve these benefits, companies need to convince and attract stakeholders that believe in their policies and strategies. Financial performance and investments tend to grow in companies that enhance disclosure and dissemination of their results in reports. However, it also serves as a motivation to improve and increase their performance (Wasara and Ganda, 2019).
3. Better quality: One of the biggest criticisms of sustainability reports is the lack of required quality and, in some cases, the omission of negative aspects that could damage the image and reputation of companies. According to Reverte (2020), companies that structure their reports based on standards issued by international organizations tend to achieve better financial benefits.
4. Image and reputation: When a consumer thinks of a brand, they associate it with an image and reputation. Even though these are intangible things, they provide a huge competitive advantage (Martin-Miguel et al., 2020). Brands nowadays strive to convey a positive image to consumers. This perception can be changed according to the signals that the company transmits about sustainable aspects (Cowan and Guzman, 2020), increasing its reputation and recognition.

Sustainability reporting is a crucial component of corporate transparency and responsibility in today's business landscape, even if it comes with its own set of challenges and complexities (Chantziaras et al., 2020). Sustainability reporting is essential for organizations to demonstrate their commitment to environmental and social responsibility, build trust with stakeholders (Fontoura & Coelho, 2022; Teixeira et al., 2022), and contribute to a more sustainable future (Elkington, 2020). The studies conducted on sustainability are crucial for companies to understand how markets and societies react to the strategies they are implementing. Corporate awareness and responsibility have grown as researchers included this factor in their decisions (Garcia-Sanchez et al., 2019), leading companies to change their strategies, perspectives, goals, and most importantly, mindsets (Bastas and Liyanage, 2019). It is now widely acknowledged that sustainability is a necessity for companies.

Jacobsen et al. (2020) identified four groups of sustainable practices: (1) inspirational and informational practices, (2) productive practices, (3) creative practices, and (4) system-building practices, which have a positive and immediate effect on organizational reputation and image (Al-Amin et al., 2018) and on financial performance. Sustainability reduces business risk (Lueg et al., 2019), increases business opportunities while respecting societies and local communities (Chantziaras et al., 2020).

However, there are still differences in sustainability reporting between small and large companies. As one would expect, more reputable companies are more prone to scrutiny from society. Nevertheless, small companies are now starting to promote corporate responsibility in their strategies, devoting some effort to combating environmental problems (Chi et al., 2020).

The biggest gap identified in these reports is the absence of a general guideline that helps organizations to disclose their information equally and fairly, making it easier to compare and study across companies (Tsalis et al., 2018). However, the GRI guidelines are the most commonly used for standardizing criteria. Many companies use them to provide information about their environmental, social and economic (de Villiers and Sharma, 2020) strategies and outcomes. Khan et al. (2020) highlighted that image and reputation in the eyes of society and stakeholders are the main drivers of such strategies and outcomes (Karaman et al., 2021).

From another perspective, company performance against the Environmental, Social, and Governance (ESG) indicator has also been used in company analysis. ESG encompasses social, environmental, and governance dimensions (Chiaramonte et al., 2020), with the first two dimensions being regarded as the most relevant to stakeholders (Qureshi et al., 2020). Regardless of size, structure, or area of operation, companies should use this indicator in the medium and long-term (Oncioiu, et al., 2020). In addition to the aspects mentioned above, companies are evaluated through indices that analyze and rank companies based on the topics they consider most important (Hehenberger-Risse et al., 2019), as well as perspectives and projects for the future of sustainable development (Slišāne Dzintra et al., 2020). These indices are seen as a pretext for companies to fulfill their commitments in a reliable and objective manner (Chen et al., 2019), conveying a transparent image of reliability and truthfulness (Beekaroo et al., 2019). Thus, companies that do not use sustainability indexes as a tool to reach out to stakeholders are at a significant disadvantage compared to their direct competitors (Ates, 2020).

In short, sustainability reports have yet to achieve the necessary level of perfection; they have strengths, but also some imperfections. These shortcomings are studied in the literature to find ways to eliminate them. Their main weaknesses include lack of consistency, issues with data collection and analysis (Domingues et al., 2017), low legitimacy (Nazari et al., 2017) and the concealment of negative information arising during the reporting period (Albertini, 2019). However, the advantages for organizations are also notable, such as strengthening society and shareholder trust (Gazzola et al., 2019), setting up new communication mechanisms (Yáñez et al., 2019), and increasing the value of organizations (Ting, 2021).

METHODOLOGY

This paper employs a two-step approach to deepen our understanding of the studies on sustainability disclosure. In the first step, we conducted a bibliometric analysis. In the second step, we conducted a literature review to examine the studies developed in this area. All findings were supported by relevant literature. To create a published study map, the WoS and Scopus was searched using the PRISMA 2020 flow diagram, as shown in Figure 1.

Figure 1. PRISMA 2020 flow diagram

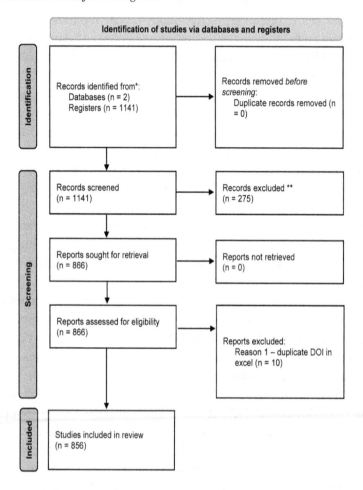

*The research began with articles on corporate social responsibility and reports. In order to capture all of the important articles on the topics, we choose to use several keywords/topics. Thus, the keywords used in the search databases were: (1) "Sustainability disclosure", (2) "Sustainability report", (3) "CSR disclosure", (4) "Social report" and, (5) "Social responsibility disclosure"

**Duplicates were excluded through Software R, through the Bibliometrix (275).

The data used for this article was sourced from the Web of Science and Scopus databases, platforms that enable the acquisition, analysis, and dissemination of information across different academic disciplines. By conducting a search using keywords, this tool automatically generates information related to the study topic. As a result, we were able to generate sufficient and credible data to obtain essential information for our research work, based on citations, articles, authors, and departments (Meho and Yang, 2007).

This review paper adapted the method developed by David and Han (2004) as follows: (1) The sample articles used were limited to published scholarly journal articles written in English (excluding book chapters and unpublished works) to ensure quality (David and Han, 2004; Newbert, 2007); (2) Only major databases (Scopus and Web of Science) used in previous literature review studies in similar fields (Engert et al., 2016) were used; (3) Empirical sustainability-related studies in the broad area of Management were searched using keywords such as "Sustainability disclosure", "Sustainability report",

"CSR disclosure", "Social responsibility report", and "Social responsibility disclosure", through these databases; (4) The two databases were joined using RStudio, and duplicate articles were excluded as shown in Figure 1; (5) The identified articles were then checked for relevance within the current topic, and (6) the data considered for this article was collected in January 2023, taking years 1979 to 2023 as the study period.

Bibliometric research is a quantitative methodology that allows for the analysis of bibliographic content through network analysis based on the most relevant documents, keywords, authors, or journals. By using mapping techniques, these analyses aim to provide insight into the structure of the network, enabling the analysis of its contents and drawing important conclusions for the development of the discipline studied (Waltman et al., 2010). This author also argues that the technique should solve the following problems: (1) identify the main topics covered by the academic literature, (2) understand and analyze the different relationships between the most recurrent keywords and themes, and (3) discuss their evolution. In this study, the VOSviewer program was used to build the respective bibliometric maps, classified by authors, articles, and journals (Merigó and Yang, 2017).

The decision to use only one database, the Web of Science (WoS), was made after considering a range of options. WoS is considered the oldest, widest, and most reliable database in the research world (Birkle et al., 2020). The tool has many advantages, which supported our choice, such as the largest record of articles and citations, the most authentic and reliable source for research papers (Khan et al., 2020), the possibility of extracting relevant information (Luo et al., 2020), the delivery of solutions that enable research in emerging areas, and the international collaboration with cities and world leaders in scientific production and development (Csomos *et al.,* 2020). Other databases were consulted and no relevant additional publications were found.

RESULTS

Evolution and Data Analysis

In summary, this analysis used bibliometric research and the Web of Science database to examine the trend of publications and citations on the topic of sustainability disclosure between 1979 and 2020. The results showed a steady increase in the number of publications starting in 2005 and a similar increase in citations beginning in 2008. The field of study with the most representation in the research sample was "Environmental Studies," followed by "Business," "Management," "Ethics," "Economics," and "Engineering Environmental." Additionally, the analysis was carried out in January 2023, and it should be considered that the data is not updated after that date.

Figure 2. Annual scientific production

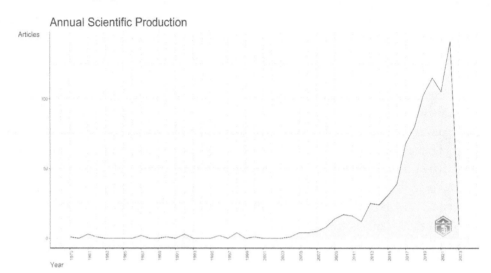

Table 1. General research data of number of articles and citations

Keywords	Number of Articles	Number of Citations
Sustainability disclosure OR Sustainability report OR CSR disclosure OR Social Responsibility Report OR Social Responsibility Disclosure OR	866	26,394

Table 1 reveals that there are 866 articles and 26,394 citations pertaining to Sustainability Disclosure. The number of articles and citations identified in this analysis is notably lower when compared to other bibliometric studies. Utilizing the RStudio Software, specifically the Bibliometrix and Biblioshiny tools, several key results were obtained. (References should be added accordingly).

Using the VOS viewer software and implementing the "full counting" method with a minimum threshold of seven entries per term, after excluding "thesaurus terms," a total of 162 items were obtained. These items were analyzed to identify clusters of higher density and to examine the relationships between the various items (as depicted in Figure 3).

As shown in Figure 4, six main areas are evident. The first cluster comprises thirteen study areas, the second cluster comprises ten study areas, the third and fourth clusters comprise seven study areas each, the fifth cluster comprises six study areas, and the sixth cluster comprises eight study areas. In total, 51 possible research areas were identified. Among the identified research areas, the most frequently mentioned were "Social Responsibility Disclosure," "Social Responsibility Report," "Agency Theory," "Assessment," "Firm Value," "Board Size," and "Empirical Result." In contrast, less frequently mentioned research areas included "Corporate Transparency," "Forecast Accuracy," "Family Firm," "ESG Disclosure," "Women Directors," "SME," and "Biodiversity".

Figure 3. Density of the most relevant areas of study

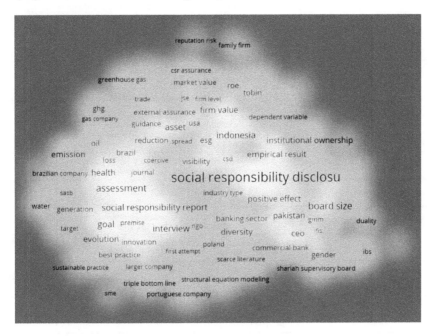

Sustainability Disclosure: Publications and Intellectual Knowledge

Table 2 provides a summary of the most cited and relevant scientific publications pertaining to the terms mentioned above. Purani et al. (2014) reported that only 2% of articles published in 10 well-ranked marketing journals were dedicated to the topic of Sustainability. The subject of sustainability has increasingly been incorporated into the discourse and curriculum of various disciplines, including marketing. An analysis conducted by Gamerschlag et al. (2011) revealed that companies tend to integrate Corporate Social Responsibility (CSR) aspects into their annual or financial reports, provide data on financial, environmental, social, and human capital, and utilize various media such as press releases to disseminate this information.

Table 2. Top 20 most cited scientific articles on SCM

Author	Journal	Title	Year	Citation
Roberts	Accounting, Organizations and society	"Determinants of corporate social responsibility disclosure: an application of stakeholder theory"	1992	1054
Neu *et al.*	Accounting, Organizations and society	"Managing Public impressions: Environmental disclosures in annual reports"	1998	793
Revert C.	Journal of Business Ethics	"Determinants of corporate social responsibility disclosure ratings by spanish listed firms"	2009	644
Cowen *et al.*	Accounting organizations and society	"The impact of corporate characteristics on social Responsibility disclosure – a typology and frequency – based analysis"	1987	608
Khan *et al.*	Journal of business ethics	"Corporate Governance and Corporate Social Responsibility disclosures: evidence from na emerging Economy"	2013	587
Branco and Rodrigues	Journal of business ethics	"Factors influencing Social Responsibility Disclosure by Portuguese Companies"	2008	437
Jizi *et al.*	Journal of business ethics	"Corporate governance and corporate social responsibility disclosure: evidence from the US banking sector"	2014	428
Michelon and Parbonetti	Journal of management and governance	"The effect of corporate governance on sustainability disclosure"	2012	392
Cho *et al.*	Accounting organizations and society	"The language of US corporate environmental disclosure"	2010	389
Brammer and Pavelin	Journal of business finance and accounting	"Voluntary environmental disclosures by large UK companies"	2006	360
Said *et al.*	Social Responsibility Journal	"The relationship between corporate social responsibility disclosure and corporate governance characteristics in Malaysian public listed companies"	2009	348
Hussain *et al.*	Journal of Business Ethics	"Corporate Governance and Sustainability Performance: Analysis of Triple Bottom Line Performance"	2018	332
Dhaliwal *et al.*	Accounting Review	"Nonfinancial disclosure and analyst forecast accuracy: international evidence on corporate social responsibility disclosure"	2012	326
Prado-Lorenzo and Garcia-Sanchez	Journal of business ethics	"The role of the board of directors in disseminating relevant information on greenhouse gases"	2010	322
Holder-Webb *et al.*	Journal of business ethics	"The supply of corporate social responsibility disclosures among US firms"	2009	318
Ghazali	Corporate governance – the international journal of business in society	"Ownership structure and corporate social responsibility disclosure: some Malaysian evidence"	2007	297
Trotman and Bradley	Accounting, organizations, and society	"Associations between social responsibility disclosure and characteristics of companies"	1981	279
Platonova *et al.*	Journal of Business Ethics	"The impact of corporate social responsibility disclosure on financial performance evidence from the gcc Islamic banking SectorR"	2018	220
Frias *et al.*	Business Strategy and the Environment	"Explanatory factors of integrated sustainability and financial reporting"	2014	213
Magness	Accounting, Auditing, and Accountability Journal	"Strategic posture financial performance and environmental disclosure an empirical test of legitimacy theory"	2006	209

Figure 4 illustrates the areas with the highest density and their relationship to the fields of study, assisting in identifying the most significant clusters and areas with the most research. Additionally, Figure 4 highlights the topics that have received the least attention from researchers. After applying the filter for the keywords "Sustainability Disclosure," "Sustainability Report," "CSR Disclosure," "Social Responsibility Report," and "Social Responsibility Disclosure" in the Web of Science, the data was imported into the VOSviewer software using the "binary counting" method, including titles and summaries. Table 3 provides a detailed breakdown of the most cited clusters, identifying a total of seven clusters.

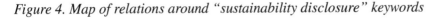

Figure 4. Map of relations around "sustainability disclosure" keywords

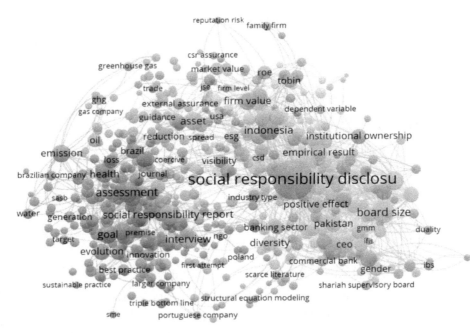

As depicted in Figure 4, there are several areas that have not been extensively researched, providing opportunities for future studies. For instance, "Corporate Transparency" and "Forecast Accuracy" may be viable subjects of study due to the inconsistent form and, in some cases, the omission of negative factors that can damage the image of an organization, as well as the weak performance of companies in terms of disclosure or result forecasts. Additionally, "Family Companies" may also be a worthwhile area of study due to their limited concern for this topic, as they are often subject to weak demand and poor control, and lack the resources to promote sustainability in their practices. Other areas that have been identified as opportunities for future research include "ESG Disclosure," "Women Directors," "SME," and "Biodiversity." Furthermore, Figure 5 also illustrates the most frequently cited authors in relation to the keyword "Sustainability Disclosure."

Figure 5. Most relevant authors

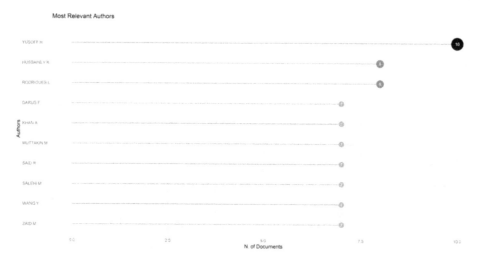

Figure 6 illustrates the countries that have produced the most publications on the topic of Sustainability Disclosure. The top seven countries, in descending order, are (1) Indonesia, (2) United Kingdom, (3) Malaysia, (4) China, (5) Australia, (6) Spain, (7) Italy, (8) India, (9) United States, and (10) Tunisia.

Figure 6. Country scientific production

Figure 7. Country production over time

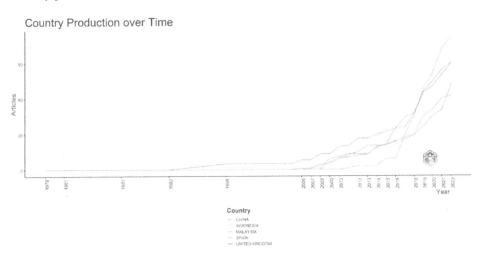

Figure 8. Country collaboration

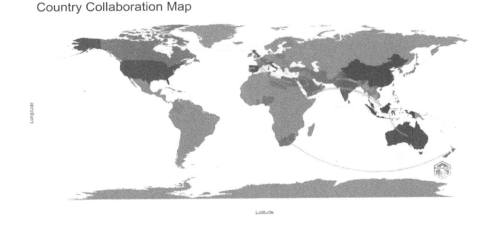

Figure 8 presents a graphical representation of the collaboration networks between countries and their publications, enabling identification of countries that have collaborated most frequently on the subjects under study.

Figure 9 displays the top 20 most cited journals for the terms analyzed. The journal "Social Responsibility Journal" is the most cited, with 34 articles published. Other notable journals include "Journal of Business Ethics," "Sustainability," and "Corporate Social Responsibility and Environmental Management." Furthermore, Figure 10 illustrates that "Journal of Business Ethics," "Social Responsibility Journal," and "Sustainability" are the journals that have experienced the most significant growth in recent years.

Figure 9. Country collaboration

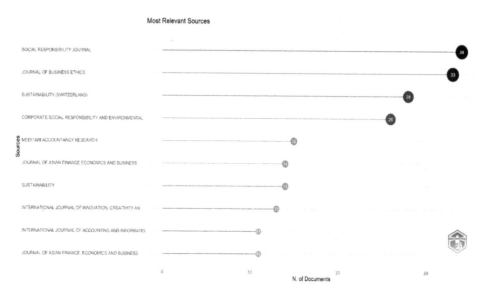

Figure 10. Source growth

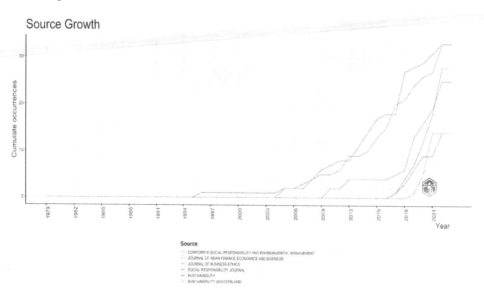

Based on H. Index the most important journal is "Journal of Business Ethics" with 26 impact factors. Follows the "Social Responsibility Journal" and "Corporate Social Responsibility and Environmental Management" with 19 and 16 impact factors, respectively.

Figure 11. Source growth

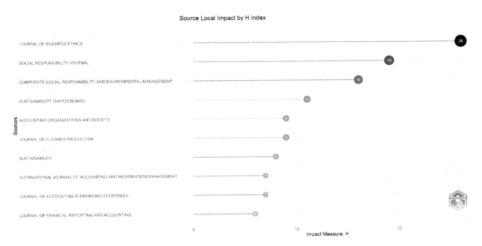

Source Local Impact by H index

To conclude the analysis of the results obtained, the clusters identified in Table 3 were characterized. It was observed that the first cluster comprises 25 items, the second cluster comprises 19 items, the third cluster comprises 9 items, the fourth cluster comprises 10 items, the fifth cluster comprises 12 items and the sixth cluster comprises 10 items.

Table 3. Top 20 most cited authors for "sustainability disclosure" keyword

Cluster 1	Cluster 2	Cluster 3	Cluster 4	Cluster 5	Cluster 6
25 Items	*19 Items*	*9 Items*	*10 Items*	*12 Items*	*10 Items*
Adherence	Analyst Forecast	Corporate image	Banking industry	Agency theory	Board characteristic
Assessment	accuracy	Corporate	Community involvement	Audit committee	Board diversity
Brazil	Asset	sustainability image	Csr disclosure level	Bursa Malaysia	Board Size
Competitive Advantage	Bangladesh	Corporate website	Csr disclosure practice	Companies annual report	Ceo
Corporate Sustainability	Banking sector	Csr communication	Disclosure score	Corporate governance	Ceo duality
Corporate Sustainability Index	Bloomberg	Large company	Esg	Character	Diversity
Economic performance	Carbon disclosure	Manufacturing company	Esg disclosure	Corporate governance mechanism	Empirical result
Emission	Project	Social responsibility information	Financial leverage	Csrd	Gender diversity
Energy	Content analysis	South Africa	Independent director	Duality	Panel data
Environmental impact	Technique	Visibility	Ownership	Earning management	Women director
Environmental sustainability	Equity			Institutional ownership	
Evaluation	Legislation			Islamic bank	
Evolution	Market participant			Social responsibility disclosure	
Goal	Market performance				
Gri guideline	Oil				
Health	Provider				
Innovation	Roa				
Performance indicator	Roe				
Recognition	Sensitive Industry				
Social issue	Tobin				
Sustainability indicator					
Sustainability practice					
Sustainability Strategy					
Water					
Waste					

From a general perspective, Table 3 identifies six clusters that can be considered at the intersection of literature and sustainability disclosure. Cluster 1 encompasses indices and practices that are crucial for assessing corporate performance. Cluster 2 emphasizes the importance of sustainability in financial performance. Cluster 3 highlights the importance of sustainability in enhancing corporate image and reputation. Cluster 4 emphasizes the importance of sustainable disclosure practices as a means of creating value for all stakeholders. Cluster 5 and 6 demonstrate the importance of theories and characteristics of organizational structures in the development of transparent and efficient sustainability reporting.

A more in-depth and individualized analysis of these clusters was conducted. In cluster 1, it is possible to observe factors that are directly related to sustainable indices and practices, such as "Corporate Sustainability Index," "Economic Performance," "Emission," "Environmental Aspect," "Environmental Impact," "Environmental Sustainability," "Evaluation," "Evolution," "Goal," "Performance Indicator," and "Sustainability Practices." The literature indicates that companies cannot operate in isolation from their environment. To demonstrate their value, it is not sufficient for companies to only present financial results at the end of the year as an indicator of organizational sustainability. Stakeholders are increasingly demanding, so companies must seek to capture value more fully through indicators of the different dimensions of the business, including environmental, social, and economic. A more comprehensive, informed, and transparent report will unequivocally demonstrate the value delivered by the organization, attracting investors and achieving the necessary social legitimacy to operate.

Cluster 2 illustrates the importance of sustainability for financial performance, using expressions such as "Analyst Forecast Accuracy," "Asset," "Carbon Disclosure," "Equity," "Market Performance," "ROA," "ROE," and "Tobin." The literature suggests that there is a strong relationship between sustainable practices and the financial performance of companies. Combining financial and non-financial aspects can serve as a powerful source for assessing the competencies and viability of a company (Oncioiu, et al., 2020). It is now imperative for companies to effectively and accurately link sustainability and their financial performance. A gap identified in the literature is the poor accuracy of the data provided, thus companies must strive to improve this disclosure.

Cluster 3 highlights the importance of sustainability for "Corporate Image" and "Corporate Sustainability Image" with words such as "Corporate Website," "CSR Communication," "Social Responsibility Information," and "Visibility" standing out. These reports also allow society to form an image of the company based on its practices, results, and disclosure. The reputation of a brand is one of the most valuable assets that companies must protect and cultivate. It enables them to convey their values and customs to stakeholders and demonstrate how they differ from their competitors. Furthermore, it serves as a source of attracting and retaining talent. Therefore, according to Petrescu et al. (2020), sustainability becomes essential for promoting the company and, on the other hand, strengthening its image before consumers, researchers, and potential stakeholders.

In Cluster 4, the importance of "CSR Disclosure Practice" and "CSR Disclosure Level" for value creation by companies for their stakeholders is evident. CSR Disclosure is considered a means of reconciling corporate objectives with ethical and social purposes (Riyadh et al., 2019). However, the quality of sustainability reporting is still low, and although the GRI guidelines are considered important to change this, they are not being implemented (Diouf and Boiral, 2017).

Cluster 5 examines research related to corporate governance, highlighting that academics are engaged with this subject, specifically through "Agency Theory" and "Institutional Ownership," as well as "Corporate Governance Character," "Corporate Governance Mechanism," and "Ownership Concentration." Literature has an added importance for companies. It helps to identify strategies and trends, and what researchers and academics advocate in their studies. With the theories developed, it allows managers to discuss and set their strategies based on a reliable, safe, and effective source. Hussain et al. (2018) defend the claims made by the theories, namely "Agency Theory" and "Stakeholder Theory," which argue that a more independent board and more frequent CSR committee meetings will provide results and control over environmental and social disclosures.

Finally, Cluster 6 is related to the characteristics/structures of the managers of organizations, specifically "Board Characteristics," "Board Diversity," "Board Size," "Decision-Making Process," "Gender Diversity," and "Women Directors." The characteristics of the executive and sustainability departments are crucial for improving sustainability reporting. When there is diversity in cultures, ages, experiences, and gender, the disclosure of business dimensions such as environmental, social, and economic will be more comprehensive, accurate, and transparent. As shown by literature, the inclusion and increased participation of women in decision-making positions has a positive impact on the quality of disclosure.

Trends and Future Investigation

In this study, an in-depth examination of articles published between 2018 and 2020 was conducted to gather current and accurate information on the gaps and opportunities in the literature. By analyzing the 20 most cited articles from this time period, two key aspects were identified: (1) gaps in the literature, where the authors identified areas in need of further research and provided new methodologies, insights, and conclusions to address these gaps; and (2) opportunities for further research that the authors acknowledged at the end of their articles.

The main gaps identified in this study pertain to the examination of independent variables that impact sustainability reports and their relationship to the company and market. Specifically, these gaps include:

1. An individual analysis of the three dimensions of corporate sustainability (Hussain et al., 2018);
2. The extension of this study to developing countries (Katmon et al., 2019);
3. The impact of corporate social responsibility (CSR) reporting on creating authority in the market (Michelon et al., 2019);
4. The influence of independent board characteristics on the quality of corporate disclosure (Fernandez-Gago et al., 2018);
5. The relationship between non-financial reporting and the value proposition for the firm (Taylor et al., 2018).

In contrast, when the authors discussed future research opportunities, four main areas were identified:

1. A study focusing on various characteristics of boards of directors to provide more detailed and precise conclusions (Cucari et al., 2018);
2. An expansion of the research to include a larger number of organizations and a longer time period (Pistoni et al., 2018);
3. An individual examination of the various dimensions that make up sustainability reports (Bae et al., 2018);
4. An analysis of the main business factors that impact sustainability reporting (Zhang et al., 2019).

Sustainability reporting remains a relevant topic with potential for further developments. The role of management in reporting is a significant research opportunity. Additionally, the areas covered by sustainability reporting warrant further investigation. Expanding the research to developing countries may provide insight into sustainability and sustainability disclosure in under-researched and under-developed regions.

Table 4. Top 20 most cited articles on sustainability disclosure and content analysis (2018-2020)

Author	Journal	Title	Gaps	Suggestions for Future research
Hussain *et al.*	Journal of business ethics	"Corporate governance and sustainability performance: analysis of triple bottom line performance"	Thorough analysis addressing the three dimensions of corporate sustainability	Study of other elements of corporate governance, such as the frequency of board meetings and social performance
Chen *et al.*	Journal of accounting and economics	"The effect of mandatory CSR disclosure on firm profitability and social externalities: evidence from China"	Comparison between mandatory CSR reporting and non-mandatory reporting	No recommendations for future research
Cucari *et al.*	Corporate social responsibility and environmental management	"Diversity of board of directors and environmental social governance: evidence from Italian listed companies"	Investigating government variables that affect corporate disclosure	Enclose more specific information, studying in detail the characteristics of the organizational structures
Platonova *et al.*	Journal of business ethics	"The impact of corporate social responsibility disclosure on financial performance: evidence from the GCC Islamic banking sector"	Relationship between CSR and financial performances of Islamic institutions	No recommendations for future research
Bae *et al.*	Sustainability	"A cross-country investigation of corporate governance and corporate sustainability disclosure: a signaling theory perspective"	Cross-cutting analysis of sustainable disclosure and its effect on corporate governance	Individual study and analysis of the social, environmental and economic aspects
Katmon *et al.*	Corporate social responsibility environment management	"Comprehensive board diversity and quality of corporate social responsibility disclosure: evidence from an emerging market"	Study with evidence for developing countries as well as emerging economies	Supplementary study for each of the characteristics of the board of directors
Pistoni *et al.*	Corporate social responsibility environment management	"Integrated reporting quality: an empirical analysis"	Assessment of the quality of reports issued by the companies	Increase in the number of companies studied, as well as the time interval in which they are carried out
Zhang *et al.*	Journal of cleaner production	"Drivers, motivations, and barriers to the implementation of corporate social responsibility practices by construction enterprises: a review"	Systematic research on CSR in order to identify the motivations of companies in disclosure	Study of the factors influencing corporate sustainability reporting
Mahmood *et al.*	Sustainability	"Does corporate governance affect sustainability disclosure? A mixed methods study"	Relationship between corporate management and corporate sustainability in Pakistan's context	Increase in the number of interviews in quantitative studies so that the results are more rigorous and real
Fernandez-gago *et al.*	Corporate social responsibility environment management	"Independent directors ´background and CSR disclosure"	The influence of independent boards on CSR disclosure	Analysis of other characteristics that explain the positive effect of independent boards on CSR disclosure
Mura *et al.*	International journal of management reviews	"The evolution of sustainability measurement research"	General literature review of sustainability measurement	Focus on the analysis of more specific and distinct activities in the reporting process, such as information gathering, analysis, and communication
Gong *et al.*	Journal of business ethics	"On the value of corporate social responsibility disclosure: an empirical investigation of corporate bond issues in China"	Analysis of the Relationship between the Quality of CSR Reporting and Bond Costs in China	No recommendations for future research
Taliento *et al.*	Sustainability	"Impact of environmental, social, and governance information on economic performance: evidence of a corporate ´sustainability advantage´ from Europe"	Analytical study of non-financial dimensions	More detailed analysis of different markets, periods and alternatives to ESG
Cabeza-Garcia *et al.*	European management review	"Do board gender diversity and director typology impact CSR reporting"	Quantitative and qualitative analysis of the influence of gender on CSR disclosures	Expansion of the analysis to an international level, as social, economic and political structures tend to vary from country to country

Continued on following page

Table 4. Continued

Author	Journal	Title	Gaps	Suggestions for Future research
Taylor *et al.*	Corporate social responsibility environment management	"Are corporate social responsibility (CSR) initiatives such as sustainable development and environmental policies value enhancing or window dressing?"	Research on voluntary disclosure of non-financial data and its value to the company	Enhancing the understanding of documentation, reporting, and interpretation of management in ESG practices
Wang *et al.*	Journal of business ethics	"Mandatory corporate social responsibility (CSR) reporting and financial reporting quality: evidence from a quasi-natural experimental	Impact of mandatory CSR reporting on the quality of financial reporting	Study of CSR reports in the different markets to complement the findings
Beck *et al.*	Australian Journal of management	"CSR disclosure and financial performance revisited: a cross-country analysis"	Relationship between CSR and financial performance	Extension of this study to other time periods, in view of providing guidelines to businesses
Hussain *et al.*	Corporate social responsibility environment management	"Does it pay to be sustainable? Looking inside the black box of the relationship between sustainability performance and financial performance"	Relationship between sustainable performance and disclosure in financial performances	Alternative research and different methods of data collection to obtain new data on the characteristics of boards of directors
Muttakin *et al.*	Journal of business ethics	"The effect of board capital and CEO power on corporate social responsibility disclosures"	Effect of the human variable on CSR disclosure	Alternative research and different methods for data collection, in order to obtain new data on the characteristics of administrative councils
Michelon *et al.*	European accounting review	"Creating legitimacy for sustainability assurance practices: evidence from sustainability restatements"	The role of sustainability reports in the creation of notoriety in the market	Study focus on countries where the reports have a broader scope and an understanding of the influence of the environment on different outlook

CONCLUSION

Discussion

This study aims to enhance existing research by providing valuable insights and identifying trends, gaps, and research opportunities through the collection and content analysis of recent and highly cited articles on sustainability disclosure (Garcia-Gonzalez and Ramirez-Montoya, 2019).

It has been established that societies play a crucial role in corporate strategies and subsequent disclosures, particularly in relation to financial information (Al-Shaer, 2020), environmental information (Alda, 2019), social information, and information about products and services.

As sustainability reports become increasingly important, companies are directing more efforts towards transparent and rigorous reporting (Xiao and Shailer, 2021). However, the literature recognizes a significant gap in the absence of a universal model for writing and structuring these reports (Garcia-Torea et al., 2020). Despite this, the accurate and consistent preparation of these reports brings benefits to organizations, such as supporting a long-term thriving strategy (Maria Garcia-Sanchez et al., 2019), enhancing the company's image and reputation (Ahsan and Qureshi, 2021), financial benefits, and reducing management risk (Ullah et al., 2021). It is clear that sustainability is essential for the success and survival of companies today (Jindřichovská et al., 2020). This study was important in providing an overall understanding of the main positive and negative points recognized in the literature on sustainability reporting.

In addition to identifying gaps and opportunities in the literature, this study also found several variables that impact the quality and transparency of different types of sustainability reports. These variables include the presence of women in management (Giron et al., 2020), the role and composition of boards of directors (Naciti, 2019), and the size of the company (Tyas and Khafid, 2020).

Other notable contributions of this study include the observation that the term "social responsibility disclosure" is the primary keyword used when referring to studies on sustainability disclosure. Additionally, the study highlights the significant increase in the number of articles published on the subject in recent years, with a 1,255% increase in the volume of publications from 2010 to 2020.

Furthermore, this study provides an analysis of the main journals, authors, institutions, and keywords in the literature on sustainability disclosure, revealing that: (1) the literature on sustainability disclosure has grown significantly over the years, (2) only three papers have more than 500 citations, (3) the USA and China are the countries with the highest number of citations, and (4) the "Sustainability" journal stands out from the rest in terms of the number of papers and citations.

Finally, the research provides an analysis of the most recent and relevant content present in the WoS database, exploring popular research areas and topics. The study also identifies gaps in the research field, which serve as a basis for future research, such as an individualized study of other characteristics that influence sustainability reporting (Hussain et al., 2018) and broader and deeper study in both numbers of companies and periods.

Contributions

With this approach, we have showed the significance of a literature review in identifying new areas of research within the scope of sustainability disclosure. Our study aims to emphasize this research area by achieving the following:

The approach adopted underscores the pivotal role of literature review in identifying emerging research areas within the realm of sustainability disclosure. Our study aims to contribute to the advancement of this research field by accomplishing the following:

1. Mapping Rapid Progress: By conducting an in-depth bibliometric analysis, we have effectively mapped the rapid progress and evolution of research in the investigated topic. This provides critical insights into the trajectory of sustainability disclosure research over time.

2. Identifying Relevant Themes and Research Gaps: Our analysis has identified the most relevant themes within the literature while also pinpointing gaps and offering suggestions for further research. This process not only sheds light on the current state of the field but also offers valuable opportunities and research priorities for the future. Specifically, our contributions include:

At the same time, we call for more detailed and individualized analyses of various characteristics of boards of directors in the context of sustainability disclosure. Therefore, we recommend expanding the scope of research by including a greater number of companies and extending the period of analysis, facilitating a more comprehensive understanding of sustainability reporting practices. Our findings suggest the need for individualized studies focusing on different components of sustainability reports, allowing for a nuanced examination of each element's impact. Furthermore, in response to the literature's emphasis on sustainability reporting in powerful and prominent countries, we advocate for research in regions beyond the conventional scope, exploring sustainability disclosure practices in countries that may have been overlooked.

Our study concludes by echoing the literature's call for the development of a standardized template for sustainability reporting. Such a template holds the promise of enhancing uniformity, precision, and transparency in the communication of sustainability-related information. Overall, our bibliometric analysis contributes to the field of sustainability disclosure by uncovering its evolution, identifying pertinent themes and research gaps, and emphasizing the need for future investigations to enhance precision and transparency in sustainability reporting practices.

Managerial Implications

This bibliometric analysis can highlight best practices and benchmarks in sustainability disclosure. Managers can use this information to compare their organization's practices with those of industry leaders and identify areas for improvement. At the same time, managers can gain insights into how their competitors are approaching sustainability disclosure through bibliometric analysis. This information can be valuable in developing strategies to gain a competitive advantage in this area. Therefore, understanding the research landscape in sustainability disclosure can inform strategic decision-making. For example, it can help in setting priorities, resource allocation, and long-term planning related to sustainability initiatives, as well as to identify potential risks and challenges associated with sustainability disclosure. Managers can use this information to proactively address issues and mitigate risks.

Furthermore, understanding the key topics and concerns in sustainability disclosure can aid in stakeholder engagement. Managers can tailor their communication and engagement strategies to align with the interests of various stakeholders, such as investors, customers, and regulatory bodies. At the same time, it can help finding opportunities for innovation, thought leadership, and potentially influencing the direction of future research in the field.Finally, a bibliometric analysis of sustainability disclosure can provide valuable insights for managerial decision-making, strategic planning, and staying competitive in an increasingly sustainability-focused business environment.

Limitations

The use of bibliometric analysis based on specific technical decisions, such as the selection of research fields, may result in the omission of important data and documents for the development of more comprehensive analysis. The exclusive use of the Web of Science platform is also acknowledged as a limitation. A multisource method, which compares different databases, may provide a more comprehensive overview of the research, including different perspectives and analyses present in the different databases. However, by considering only high-quality papers, other sources of information such as conferences, book chapters, or dissertations which could provide key information for future research trends are excluded. Additionally, it should be noted that a bibliometric analysis provides a purely descriptive analysis and may lack the depth and detail to produce more comprehensive, rigorous, and informative results and conclusions.

REFERENCES

Ahsan, T., & Qureshi, M. A. (2021). The nexus between policy uncertainty, sustainability disclosure and firm performance. *Applied Economics, 53*(4), 441–453. doi:10.1080/00036846.2020.1808178

Al-Amin, A. Q., Leal Filho, W., & Kabir, M. A. (2018). The Challenges of Sustainability in Business: How Governments May Ensure Sustainability for Offshore Firms. *Technological and Economic Development of Economy, 24*(1), 108–140. doi:10.3846/20294913.2015.1075442

Al-Shaer, H. (2020). Sustainability reporting quality and post-audit financial reporting quality: Empirical evidence from the UK. *Business Strategy and the Environment, 29*(6), 2355–2373. doi:10.1002/bse.2507

Albertini, E. (2019). Integrated reporting: An exploratory study of French companies. *The Journal of Management and Governance, 23*(2), 513–535. doi:10.100710997-018-9428-6

Alda, M. (2019). Corporate sustainability and institutional shareholders: The pressure of social responsible pension funds on environmental firm practices. *Business Strategy and the Environment, 28*(6), 1060–1071. doi:10.1002/bse.2301

Antonio, I., Simone, P., Lea, I., & Mario, T. (2020). Communicating the stakeholder engagement process: A cross- country analysis in the tourism sector. *Corporate Social Responsibility and Environmental Management, 27*(4), 1642–1652. doi:10.1002/csr.1913

Ates, S. (2020). Membership of sustainability index in an emerging market: Implications for sustainability. *Journal of Cleaner Production, 250*, 119465. Advance online publication. doi:10.1016/j.jclepro.2019.119465

Aureli, S., Gigli, S., Medei, R., & Supino, E. (2020). The value relevance of environmental, social, and governance disclosure: Evidence from Dow Jones Sustainability World Index listed companies. *Corporate Social Responsibility and Environmental Management, 27*(1), 43–52. doi:10.1002/csr.1772

Bae, S. M., Masud, M. A. K., & Kim, J. D. (2018). A Cross-Country Investigation of Corporate Governance and Corporate Sustainability Disclosure: A Signaling Theory Perspective. *Sustainability (Basel), 10*(8), 2611. Advance online publication. doi:10.3390u10082611

Bai, X., Coelho, A., & Lopes Cancela, B. (2023). The relationship between green supply chain and green innovation based on the push of green strategic alliances. *Corporate Social Responsibility and Environmental Management*, csr.2619. doi:10.1002/csr.2619

Baier, C., Goettsche, M., Hellmann, A., & Schiemann, F. (2021). Too Good To Be True: Influencing Credibility Perceptions with Signaling Reference Explicitness and Assurance Depth. *Journal of Business Ethics.*

Bastas, A., & Liyanage, K. (2019). Setting a framework for organisational sustainable development. *Sustainable Production and Consumption, 20*, 207–229. doi:10.1016/j.spc.2019.06.005

Beekaroo, D., Callychurn, D. S., & Hurreeram, D. K. (2019). Developing a sustainability index for Mauritian manufacturing companies. *Ecological Indicators, 96*, 250–257. doi:10.1016/j.ecolind.2018.09.003

Berne-Manero, C., & Marzo-Navarro, M. (2020). Exploring How Influencer and Relationship Marketing Serve Corporate Sustainability. *Sustainability (Basel)*, *12*(11), 4392. doi:10.3390u12114392

Birkle, C., Pendlebury, D. A., Schnell, J., & Adams, J. (2020). Web of Science as a data source for research on scientific and scholarly activity. *Quantitative Science Studies*, *1*(1), 363–376. doi:10.1162/qss_a_00018

Cancela, B. L., Coelho, A., & Duarte Neves, M. E. (2022). Greening the business: How ambidextrous companies succeed in green innovation through to sustainable development. *Business Strategy and the Environment*.

Channuntapipat, C. (2021). Can sustainability report assurance be a collaborative process and practice beyond the ritual of verification? *Business Strategy and the Environment*, *30*(2), 775–786. doi:10.1002/bse.2653

Chantziaras, A., Dedoulis, E., Grougiou, V., & Leventis, S. (2020). The impact of religiosity and corruption on CSR reporting: The case of U.S. banks. *Journal of Business Research*, *109*, 362–374. doi:10.1016/j.jbusres.2019.12.025

Chen, C., Yu, Y., Osei-Kyei, R., Chan, A. P. C., & Xu, J. (2019). Developing a project sustainability index for sustainable development in transnational public–private partnership projects. *Sustainable Development*, *27*(6), 1034–1048. . doi:10.1002/sd.1954

Cheng, S., Jianfu, S., Alrasheedi, M., Saeidi, P., Mishra, A. R., & Rani, P. (2021). A New Extended VIKOR Approach Using q-Rung Orthopair Fuzzy Sets for Sustainable Enterprise Risk Management Assessment in Manufacturing Small and Medium-Sized Enterprises. *International Journal of Fuzzy Systems*, *23*(5), 1347–1369. Advance online publication. doi:10.100740815-020-01024-3

Chiaramonte, L., Dreassi, A., Paltrinieri, A., & Piserà, S. (2020). Sustainability Practices and Stability in the Insurance Industry. *Sustainability (Basel)*, *12*(4), 5530. Advance online publication. doi:10.3390u12145530

Corciolani, M., Nieri, F., & Tuan, A. (2020). Does involvement in corporate social irresponsibility affect the linguistic features of corporate social responsibility reports? *Corporate Social Responsibility and Environmental Management*, *27*(2), 670–680. doi:10.1002/csr.1832

Cowan, K., & Guzman, F. (2020). How CSR reputation, sustainability signals, and country-of-origin sustainability reputation contribute to corporate brand performance: An exploratory study. *Journal of Business Research*, *117*, 683–693. doi:10.1016/j.jbusres.2018.11.017

Csomos, G., Vida, Z. V., & Lengyel, B. (2020). Exploring the changing geographical pattern of international scientific collaborations through the prism of cities. *PLoS One*, *15*(11), e0242468. Advance online publication. doi:10.1371/journal.pone.0242468 PMID:33196668

Cucari, N., De Falco, S. E., & Orlando, B. (2018). Diversity of Board of Directors and Environmental Social Governance: Evidence from Italian Listed Companies. *Corporate Social Responsibility and Environmental Management*, *25*(3), 250–266. doi:10.1002/csr.1452 de Villiers, C., & Sharma, U. (2020). A critical reflection on the future of financial, intellectual capital, sustainability and integrated reporting. *Critical Perspectives on Accounting, 70*, 101999. doi:10.1016/j.cpa.2017.05.003

Diouf, D., & Boiral, O. (2017). The quality of sustainability reports and impression management A stakeholder perspective. *Accounting, Auditing & Accountability Journal, 30*(3), 643–667. doi:10.1108/AAAJ-04-2015-2044

Domingues, A. R., Lozano, R., Ceulemans, K., & Ramos, T. B. (2017). Sustainability reporting in public sector organisations: Exploring the relation between the reporting process and organisational change management for sustainability. *Journal of Environmental Management, 192*, 292–301. doi:10.1016/j.jenvman.2017.01.074 PMID:28183029

Dwekat, A., Seguí-Mas, E., & Tormo-Carbó, G. (2020). The effect of the board on corporate social responsibility: Bibliometric and social network analysis. *Ekonomska Istrazivanja, 33*(1), 3580–3603. doi:10.1080/1331677X.2020.1776139

Elkington, J. (2020). *Green Swans: The Coming Boom in Regenerative Capitalism*. Academic Press.

Farooq, Q., Hao, Y., & Liu, X. (2019). Understanding corporate social responsibility with cross-cultural differences: A deeper look at religiosity. *Corporate Social Responsibility and Environmental Management, 26*(4), 965–971. doi:10.1002/csr.1736

Fernandez-Gago, R., Cabeza-Garcia, L., & Nieto, M. (2018). Independent directors' background and CSR disclosure. *Corporate Social Responsibility and Environmental Management, 25*(5), 991–1001. doi:10.1002/csr.1515

Fontoura, P., & Coelho, A. (2022). How to boost green innovation and performance through collaboration in the supply chain: Insights into a more sustainable economy. *Journal of Cleaner Production, 359*, 132005. doi:10.1016/j.jclepro.2022.132005

Freeman, R. E., Dmytriyev, S. D., & Phillips, R. A. (2021). Stakeholder Theory and the Resource-Based View of the Firm. *Journal of Management, 47*(7), 1757–1770. Advance online publication. doi:10.1177/0149206321993576

Gamerschlag, R., Moeller, K., & Verbeeten, F. (2011). Determinants of voluntary CSR disclosure: Empirical evidence from Germany. *Review of Managerial Science, 5*(2/3), 233–26. doi:10.100711846-010-0052-3

Garcia-Sanchez, I.-M., Hussain, N., Martinez-Ferrero, J., & Ruiz-Barbadillo, E. (2019). Impact of disclosure and assurance quality of corporate sustainability reports on access to finance. *Corporate Social Responsibility and Environmental Management, 26*(4), 832–848. doi:10.1002/csr.1724

Garcia-Torea, N., Fernandez-Feijoo, B., & De La Cuesta, M. (2020). CSR reporting communication: Defective reporting models or misapplication? *Corporate Social Responsibility and Environmental Management, 27*(2), 952–968. doi:10.1002/csr.1858

Gazzola, P., Amelio, S., Papagiannis, F., & Michaelides, Z. (2019). Sustainability reporting practices and their social impact to NGO funding in Italy. *Critical Perspectives on Accounting, 79*, 102085. Advance online publication. doi:10.1016/j.cpa.2019.04.006

Giron, A., Kazemikhasragh, A., Cicchiello, A. F., & Panetti, E. (2020). Sustainability Reporting and Firms' Economic Performance: Evidence from Asia and Africa. *Journal of the Knowledge Economy*, *12*(4), 1741–1759. doi:10.100713132-020-00693-7

Haney, A. B., Pope, J., & Arden, Z. (2020). Making It Personal: Developing Sustainability Leaders in Business. *Organization & Environment*, *33*(2), 155–174. doi:10.1177/1086026618806201

Hehenberger-Risse, D., Straub, J., Niechoj, D., & Lutzenberger, A. (2019). Sustainability Index to Assess the Environmental Impact of Heat Supply Systems. *Chemical Engineering & Technology*, *42*(9), 1923–1927. doi:10.1002/ceat.201800647

Hickman, L., & Akdere, M. (2019). Exploring information technology-business alignment through stakeholder theory: A review of literature. *Industrial and Commercial Training*, *51*(4), 228–243. doi:10.1108/ICT-11-2018-0098

Holt, T. V., Statler, M., Atz, U., Whelan, T., van Loggerenberg, M., & Cebulla, J. (2020). The cultural consensus of sustainability-driven innovation: Strategies for success. *Business Strategy and the Environment*, *29*(8), 3399–3409. doi:10.1002/bse.2584

Hussain, N., Rigoni, U., & Orij, R. P. (2018). Corporate Governance and Sustainability Performance: Analysis of Triple Bottom Line Performance. *Journal of Business Ethics*, *149*(2), 411–432. doi:10.100710551-016-3099-5

Jacobsen, S. S., Korsgaard, S., & Gunzel-Jensen, F. (2020). Towards a Typology of Sustainability Practices: A Study of the Potentials and Challenges of Sustainable Practices at the Firm Level. *Sustainability (Basel)*, *12*(12), 5166. doi:10.3390u12125166

Jindřichovská, I., Kubíčková, D., & Mocanu, M. (2020). Case Study Analysis of Sustainability Reporting of an Agri-Food Giant. *Sustainability (Basel)*, *12*(11), 4491. doi:10.3390u12114491

Jones, T. M., Harrison, J. S., & Felps, W. (2018). How Applying Instrumental Stakeholder Theory Can Provide Sustainable Competitive Advantage. *Academy of Management Review*, *43*(3), 371–391. doi:10.5465/amr.2016.0111

Karaman, A. S., Orazalin, N., Uyar, A., & Shahbaz, M. (2021). CSR achievement, reporting, and assurance in the energy sector: Does economic development matter? *Energy Policy*, *149*, 112007. doi:10.1016/j.enpol.2020.112007

Katmon, N., Mohamad, Z. Z., Norwani, N. M., & Al Farooque, O. (2019). Comprehensive Board Diversity and Quality of Corporate Social Responsibility Disclosure: Evidence from an Emerging Market. *Journal of Business Ethics*, *157*(2), 447–481. doi:10.100710551-017-3672-6

Khan, M., Lockhart, J., & Bathurst, R. (2020). A multi-level institutional perspective of corporate social responsibility reporting: A mixed-method study. *Journal of Cleaner Production*, *265*, 121739. doi:10.1016/j.jclepro.2020.121739

Kouaib, A., Mhiri, S., & Jarboui, A. (2020). Board of directors' effectiveness and sustainable performance: The triple bottom line. *The Journal of High Technology Management Research*, *31*(2), 100390. doi:10.1016/j.hitech.2020.100390

Lueg, K., Krastev, B., & Lueg, R. (2019). Bidirectional effects between organizational sustainability disclosure and risk. *Journal of Cleaner Production, 229*, 268–277. doi:10.1016/j.jclepro.2019.04.379

Luo, Z., Miao, F., Hu, M., & Wang, Y. (2020). Research Development on Horseshoe Crab: A 30-Year Bibliometric Analysis. *Frontiers in Marine Science, 7*(41), 41. Advance online publication. doi:10.3389/fmars.2020.00041

Manning, B., Braam, G., & Reimsbach, D. (2019). Corporate governance and sustainable business conduct—Effects of board monitoring effectiveness and stakeholder engagement on corporate sustainability performance and disclosure choices. *Corporate Social Responsibility and Environmental Management, 26*(2), 351–366. doi:10.1002/csr.1687

Maria Garcia-Sanchez, I., Gomez-Miranda, M.-E., David, F., & Rodriguez-Ariza, L. (2019). The explanatory effect of CSR committee and assurance services on the adoption of the IFC performance standards, as a means of enhancing corporate transparency. *Sustainability Accounting Management and Policy Journal, 10*(5), 773–797. doi:10.1108/SAMPJ-09-2018-0261

Martin-Miguel, J., Prado-Roman, C., Cachon-Rodriguez, G., & Avendaño-Miranda, L. L. (2020). Determinants of Reputation at Private Graduate Online Schools. *Sustainability (Basel), 12*(22), 9659. doi:10.3390u12229659

Meho, L. I., & Yang, K. (2007). Impact of data sources on citation counts and rankings of LIS faculty: Web of science versus scopus and google scholar. *Journal of the American Society for Information Science and Technology, 58*(13), 2105–2125. doi:10.1002/asi.20677

Merigó, J. M., & Yang, J.-B. (2017). A bibliometric analysis of operations research and management science. *Omega, 73*, 37–48. doi:10.1016/j.omega.2016.12.004

Michelon, G., Patten, D. M., & Romi, A. M. (2019). Creating Legitimacy for Sustainability Assurance Practices: Evidence from Sustainability Restatements. *European Accounting Review, 28*(2), 395–422. doi:10.1080/09638180.2018.1469424

Muslu, V., Mutlu, S., Radhakrishnan, S., & Tsang, A. (2019). Corporate Social Responsibility Report Narratives and Analyst Forecast Accuracy. *Journal of Business Ethics, 154*(4), 1119–1142. doi:10.100710551-016-3429-7

Naciti, V. (2019). Corporate governance and board of directors: The effect of a board composition on firm sustainability performance. *Journal of Cleaner Production, 237*, 117727. doi:10.1016/j.jclepro.2019.117727

Nazari, J. A., Hrazdil, K., & Mahmoudian, F. (2017). Assessing social and environmental performance through narrative complexity in CSR reports. *Journal of Contemporary Accounting & Economics, 13*(2), 166–178. doi:10.1016/j.jcae.2017.05.002

Oncioiu, I., Petrescu, A.-G., Bilcan, F.-R., Petrescu, M., Popescu, D.-M., & Anghel, E. (2020). Corporate Sustainability Reporting and Financial Performance. *Sustainability (Basel), 12*(10), 4297. doi:10.3390u12104297

Orazalin, N., & Mahmood, M. (2018). Economic, environmental, and social performance indicators of sustainability reporting: Evidence from the Russian oil and gas industry. *Energy Policy*, *121*, 70–79. doi:10.1016/j.enpol.2018.06.015

Paoloni, N., Mattei, G., Dello Strologo, A., & Celli, M. (2020). The present and future of intellectual capital in the healthcare sector A systematic literature review. *Journal of Intellectual Capital*, *21*(3), 357–379. doi:10.1108/JIC-10-2019-0237

Pham, H. S. T., & Tran, H. T. (2020). CSR disclosure and firm performance: The mediating role of corporate reputation and moderating role of CEO integrity. *Journal of Business Research*, *120*, 127–136. doi:10.1016/j.jbusres.2020.08.002

Pistoni, A., Songini, L., & Bavagnoli, F. (2018). Integrated Reporting Quality: An Empirical Analysis. *Corporate Social Responsibility and Environmental Management*, *25*(4), 489–507. doi:10.1002/csr.1474

Plieninger, T., Fagerholm, N., & Bieling, C. (2021). How to run a sustainability science research group sustainably? *Sustainability Science*, *16*(1), 321–328. doi:10.100711625-020-00857-z PMID:32863971

Qureshi, M. A., Kirkerud, S., Theresa, K., & Ahsan, T. (2020). The impact of sustainability (environmental, social, and governance) disclosure and board diversity on firm value: The moderating role of industry sensitivity. *Business Strategy and the Environment*, *29*(3), 1199–1214. doi:10.1002/bse.2427

Reverte, C. (2020). Do investors value the voluntary assurance of sustainability information? Evidence from the Spanish stock market. *Sustainable Development (Bradford)*, *29*(5), 793–809. Advance online publication. doi:10.1002d.2157

Riyadh, H. A., Sukoharsono, E. G., & Alfaiza, S. A. (2019). The impact of corporate social responsibility disclosure and board characteristics on corporate performance. *Cogent Business & Management*, *6*(1), 1647917. doi:10.1080/23311975.2019.1647917

Ruiz-Barbadillo, E., & Martinez-Ferrero, J. (2020). What impact do countries have on levels of sustainability assurance? A complementary-substitutive perspective. *Corporate Social Responsibility and Environmental Management*, *27*(5), 2329–2341. Advance online publication. doi:10.1002/csr.1967

Schiehll, E., & Kolahgar, S. (2021). Financial materiality in the informativeness of sustainability reporting. *Business Strategy and the Environment*, *30*(2), 840–855. doi:10.1002/bse.2657

Shang, H., Chen, R., & Li, Z. (2020). Dynamic sustainability capabilities and corporate sustainability performance: The mediating effect of resource management capabilities. *Sustainable Development (Bradford)*, *28*(4), 595–612. doi:10.1002d.2011

Slišăne, D., Gaumigs, G., Lauka, D., & Blumberga, D. (2020). Assessment of Energy Sustainability in Statistical Regions of Latvia using Energy Sustainability Index. *Environmental and Climate Technologies*, *24*(2), 160–169. doi:10.2478/rtuect-2020-0063

Taylor, J., Vithayathil, J., & Yim, D. (2018). Are corporate social responsibility (CSR) initiatives such as sustainable development and environmental policies value enhancing or window dressing? *Corporate Social Responsibility and Environmental Management*, *2*(5), 971–980. doi:10.1002/csr.1513

Teixeira, P., Coelho, A., Fontoura, P., Sá, J. C., Silva, F. J., Santos, G., & Ferreira, L. P. (2022). Combining lean and green practices to achieve a superior performance: The contribution for a sustainable development and competitiveness—An empirical study on the Portuguese context. *Corporate Social Responsibility and Environmental Management, 29*(4), 887–903. doi:10.1002/csr.2242

Torelli, R., Balluchi, F., & Furlotti, K. (2020). The materiality assessment and stakeholder engagement: A content analysis of sustainability reports. *Corporate Social Responsibility and Environmental Management, 27*(2), 470–484. doi:10.1002/csr.1813

Tran, M., & Beddewela, E. (2020). Does context matter for sustainability disclosure? Institutional factors in Southeast Asia. *Business Ethics (Oxford, England), 29*(2), 282–302. doi:10.1111/beer.12265

Traxler, A. A., Schrack, D., & Greiling, D. (2020). Sustainability reporting and management control – A systematic exploratory literature review. *Journal of Cleaner Production, 276*, 122725. Advance online publication. doi:10.1016/j.jclepro.2020.122725

Tsalis, T. A., Stylianou, M. S., & Nikolaou, I. E. (2018). Evaluating the quality of corporate social responsibility reports: The case of occupational health and safety disclosures. *Safety Science, 109*, 313–323. doi:10.1016/j.ssci.2018.06.015

Tyas, V. A., & Khafid, M. (2020). The Effect of Company Characteristics on Sustainability Report Disclosure with Corporate Governance as Moderating Variable. *Accounting Analysis Journal, 9*(3), 159–165. doi:10.15294/aaj.v9i3.41430

Ullah, F., Qayyum, S., Thaheem, M. J., Al-Turjman, F., & Sepasgozar, S. M. E. (2021). Risk management in sustainable smart cities governance: A TOE framework. *Technological Forecasting and Social Change, 167*, 120743. Advance online publication. doi:10.1016/j.techfore.2021.120743

Vieira, A. P., & Radonjič, G. (2020). Disclosure of eco-innovation activities in European large companies' sustainability reporting. *Corporate Social Responsibility and Environmental Management, 27*(5), 2240–2253. doi:10.1002/csr.1961

Waltman, L., van Eck, N. J., & Noyons, E. C. M. (2010). A unified approach to mapping and clustering of bibliometric networks. *Journal of Informetrics, 4*(4), 629–635. doi:10.1016/j.joi.2010.07.002

Wasara, T. M., & Ganda, F. (2019). The Relationship between Corporate Sustainability Disclosure and Firm Financial Performance in Johannesburg Stock Exchange (JSE) Listed Mining Companies. *Sustainability (Basel), 11*(16), 4496. Advance online publication. doi:10.3390u11164496

Wolff, S., Brönner, M., Held, M., & Lienkamp, M. (2020). Transforming automotive companies into sustainability leaders: A concept for managing current challenges. *Journal of Cleaner Production, 276*, 124179. Advance online publication. doi:10.1016/j.jclepro.2020.124179

Xiao, X., & Shailer, G. (2021). Stakeholders' perceptions of factors affecting the credibility of sustainability reports. *The British Accounting Review, 54*(1), 101002. Advance online publication. doi:10.1016/j.bar.2021.101002

Yáñez, S., Uruburu, Á., Moreno, A., & Lumbreras, J. (2019). The sustainability report as an essential tool for the holistic and strategic vision of higher education institutions. *Journal of Cleaner Production, 207*, 57–66. doi:10.1016/j.jclepro.2018.09.171

Zhang, Q., Oo, B. L., & Lim, B. T. H. (2019). Drivers, motivations, and barriers to the implementation of corporate social responsibility practices by construction enterprises: A review. *Journal of Cleaner Production*, *210*, 563–584. doi:10.1016/j.jclepro.2018.11.050

Chapter 8
Financial Information Transparency:
The European Banks' Evidence of the Tax Havens, Effective Tax Rates, Performance, and Productivity

Pedro Pinho
Porto Accounting and Business School, Polytechnic of Porto, Portugal

Catarina Libório Morais Cepêda
https://orcid.org/0000-0002-4942-079X
University of Trás-os-Montes and Alto Douro, Portugal & Porto Accounting and Business School, Polytechnic of Porto, Portugal

José Campos Amorim
Porto Accounting and Business School, CEOS, Polytechnic of Porto, Portugal

Albertina Paula Monteiro
Porto Accounting and Business School, CEOS, Polytechnic of Porto, Portugal

ABSTRACT

Over the years, companies have not been required to disclose information about their activities, profits, and the taxes that they pay in all the countries where they operate, which has allowed them to hide their presence in many low-tax jurisdictions. For this reason, country-by-country reporting (CbCR) has emerged as one of the measures to increase organizational transparency. With a sample of the 36 largest European banks, based in 11 EU countries, in more than 90 jurisdictions around the world, this study aims to analyze the relationship between European banks' presence in tax havens, effective tax rates, performance, and productivity. Based on 3587 observations, the results reveal a tendency for European banks to move their profits to tax havens, which allows them to pay less tax or none. In addition, the results show that banks with lower effective tax rates have better performance; however, they did not prove a significant relationship with productivity. This study highlights the importance of the CbCR in the fight against tax evasion and profit shifting.

DOI: 10.4018/978-1-6684-9076-1.ch008

INTRODUCTION

The trend for institutions to be subject to constant scrutiny is increasingly gaining momentum, giving rise to a global debate around transparency and how multinational organizations should be taxed. Transparency not only requires the managers and owners' involvement, but also raises questions regarding the organization's behavior towards stakeholders, including society (Hebb, 2006). Tax evasion has a significant social impact, and it is therefore important that institutions disclose information about the taxes paid in the countries where they operate.

Several academics and researchers argue that multinational organizations shift a substantial portion of their profits to low-tax countries, namely with tax havens and tax-privileged regimes, to avoid paying their fair share of tax in the highertax countries where they produce and sell most of their products (Fuest *et al.*, 2022). Given the necessity to prevent such abuses and improve transparency among organizations, Murphy (2019) debated and proposed the CbCR as an accounting information reporting standard. His proposal generated numerous debates among various international stakeholders (Murphy, 2019).

The CbCR is included in Action 13 of the Organization for Economic Cooperation and Development (OECD) BEPS (Base Erosion and Profit Shifting) and requires certain multinational organizations to report their aggregate income and economic activities by country (Hanlon, 2018). The first period for which the report was completed was for fiscal years beginning January 1, 2016 (Hanlon, 2018). With the CbCR introduction, the individuals, citizens, politicians, investors, and researchers can access information about the activity of certain institutions and the actual taxes paid in the countries where they operate (among other information).

The literature reveals that there is an understanding lack of the technical and structural deficiencies in accounting for the response, in a cross-border context, to this regulation (Murphy, Janský & Shah, 2019). According to these authors, the CbCR is destined to fail in achieving its regulatory objectives unless a reform to the regulations is undertaken. The corporate transparency required under this initiative is contingent on institutional powers.

Thus, based on institutional theory, this study focuses on the regulation contribution to corporate transparency at the national and international levels. Nevertheless, and according to the internalization theory of multinational firms, emerging market firms internalize the benefits of investing in tax havens and reduce their transaction costs, thus achieving unperceived regulatory or institutional arbitrage (e.g., Boisot and Meyer 2015; Buckley *et al.* 2015; Deng, Yan and Sun, 2020). Indeed, there is much to be done to overcome these remaining gaps.

The relevance of CbCR to ongoing debates in the social sciences goes beyond the literature on policy effectiveness and financial reporting (Hugger, 2019). This topicality broader issue is information governance underpinned by the globalization phenomenon (Wójcik, 2015).

The literature review has identified gaps in the literature, namely the scarcity of studies focused on the relevance and effects of information reporting within the CbCR scope. Thus, the aim of this study is to highlight the CbCR value for organizational transparency and to combat tax evasion and fraud, and to analyze the impact of tax havens on the taxation and performance of the largest European banks.

In section 2, a literature review is conducted on the tax havens topic and their connection with the operations conducted by the largest European banks. Then, the effects of effective tax rates will be analyzed, namely to what extent companies can transfer their profits to countries with low effective tax rates and finally, the CbCR contributions in the fight against tax evasion and fraud will be highlighted. The same section will also present the research hypotheses formulated in this study. The section 3 exposes the methodology followed in this investigation and section 4 shows the results and their discussion. Finally, section 5 presents the main conclusions.

LITERATURE REVIEW AND RESEARCH HYPOTHESES

The Tax Havens Problematic

The fight against tax fraud and evasion has been extensively discussed in literature (Amorim, Monteiro, Cepêda & Coelho, 2021). For a long time, companies artificially shifted their profits to countries with low effective tax rates, which is evidenced by companies reporting very low profits, or even losses, in countries with higher corporate tax rates (Aubry & Dauphin, 2017). Some companies have started moving to low-tax jurisdictions, including tax havens, to shift their profits to countries with reduced tax burdens (Fatica & Gregori, 2020).

Tax havens can be classified as countries and territories that provide foreign investors with relatively low-tax rates to attract investment and thereby stimulate economic activity (Hines, 2010; Menkhoff & Miethe, 2019). In turn, Dharmapala and Hines (2009) define tax havens as places with low-tax rates and other tax attributes designed to appeal to foreign investors. Tax havens are privileged tax regimes, where the lack of transparency, low or no taxation, bank secrecy, and no exchange of information stand out (Amorim *et al.*, 2021). They are territories averse to the application of international law standards and, in addition, they participate in the money laundering process, protecting the owner's identity of such capital by guaranteeing absolute banking secrecy (Amorim *et al.*, 2021).

The tax havens benefits are diverse. For instance, the Bouvatier *et al.* (2017) study, with a sample of 36 European banks and data from 2015, found that a country being considered a tax haven increases the presence of foreign subsidiaries by 168% and the respective tax savings of European Union (EU) banks is between 1 and 3.6 billion euros. Similarly, Fatica and Gregori (2020), whose study objective was to determine to what extent the largest European banks engage in profit shifting to reduce their tax burden, observed that low-tax jurisdictions, namely tax havens, attract disproportionately high profits.

According to Torslov *et al.* (2020), around 40% of multinational companies' profits are globally diverted to tax havens. Aliprandi *et al.* (2021) complement this by mentioning that the largest European banks divert about €20 billion annually to tax havens, which corresponds to 14% of their total profits. The study also highlights that these profits booked by banks in tax havens are quite high: €238.000 per employee, as opposed to about €65.000 in other countries.

In the same line, the study by Jansky (2020), concludes that some tax havens have higher percentage of profits than non tax haven jurisdictions, in contrast to the number of employees and even the turnover, which have lower percentages. These results thus represent a possible indicator of the profit shifting to tax haven occurrence.

Therefore, tax havens have been the subject of much controversy and criticism not only in the literature, but also among international organizations, politicians, and the media (Deng *et al.*,2020).

The Effects of Effective Tax Rates

The effective tax rate is a common measure used to compare tax burdens between companies over time and detect tax evasion. Essentially, the general idea behind the effective tax rate is to look at a company's effective tax contribution by dividing income tax by a measure of taxable income (Drake et al., 2020).

Using financial statement information from about 11.602 companies from 82 different countries over the period 1988 to 2009, Markle and Shackelford (2011) aimed to estimate and analyze effective tax rates. According to these authors, the effective multinationals' tax rate headquartered in high-tax countries is approximately twice that of low-tax countries, with companies headquartered in Japan having the highest effective tax rate, followed by the US, France, and Germany. On the other hand, multinationals based in tax havens have lower effective tax rates.

Recent studies corroborate the Markle and Shackelford (2011) results, showing that effective tax rates in tax havens are substantially lower than those in other countries, thus revealing the multinationals' tendency to transfer their profits to these countries (e.g., Brown et al., 2019; Procházka, 2020). Given that, it is concluded, despite advances as CbCR, there remains a great tendency for multinationals carrying out tax haven activities to aggregate, their geographic disclosure (Akamah et al., 2018).

The Country-by-Country Reporting

Country-by-Country Reporting represents a set of information regarding the multinational company's tax activity whose total consolidated income is equal to or greater than €750.000.000 in the last tax period (OECD, 2017). Through this declaration, these companies are required to publicly report their profits, taxes paid, and economic activity between the tax jurisdictions in which they operate.

The purpose of introducing this document was to allow stakeholders to better understand the structures of financial groups, their activities, and their geographic presence, as well as, to help understand whether taxes are being properly paid where the business activity is located (Murphy et al., 2019).

According to Kang and Gray (2019), these reports involve multinational organizations to disclose the operating activities and financial results in different countries. Dutt et al. (2018) state that this additional information can serve as a tool to better control tax avoidance activities by managers and limit their possibilities related to the extraction of private benefits, which supports agency theory.

The debate on this topic can also be seen in the global economic governance context being reconfigured in the global financial crisis wake (Hugger, 2019). Transparency systems and the global crisis are often addressed together. These two variables emerge in high-level policy debates driven by a new perception of the need for public action.

Previous studies suggest that investors view increased tax transparency as a key tool in combating tax evasion. Overesch and Wolff (2021) found that European multinational banks reduced their tax avoidance after the CbCR implementation. More specifically, the authors analyzed the effect that tax transparency had on European banks' tax evasion and concluded that European banks exposed to greater transparency by disclosing their activities in tax havens reacted positively to the mandatory CbCR submission. Additionally, Overesch and Wolff (2021) argue that the CbCR is making banks less likely to shift their profits to tax havens, proving to be an effective tool in reducing global corporate tax planning.

Similarly, Eberhartinger et al. (2020) observed that the tax havens' presence decreased significantly after the CbCR introduction for European banks, compared to the insurance sector which is not subject to this regulation.

Research Hypothesis

In this study, based on CbCR data, we intend to analyze the largest European bank's role of tax havens in the taxation and performance. To perform this analysis, the effective tax rate was used. In a first stage, we will analyze the sample effective tax rate to test if it is lower in tax havens than in non-tax havens. We also will test if higher performing banks are operating mainly in tax havens. In a second stage, we will study the effects of a low effective tax rate on the banks' performance.

According to the existing literature, multinational companies tend to transfer their profits to tax havens (Garcia-Bernardo *et al.*, 2021). One of the objectives of this research will be to analyze whether tax havens have lower effective tax rates compared to other countries. As in previous studies, in this study we expect that multinationals based in tax havens exhibit lower effective tax rates (e.g., Brown *et al.*, 2019; Dutt *et al.*, 2019; Markle and Shackelford, 2011 Procházka, 2020). Against this background, the first research hypothesis is formulated in this study.

H1: Multinational banks with a presence in tax havens have a lower effective tax rate.

Low-tax jurisdictions play a valuable role in the global economy. Economic studies indicate that so-called tax havens provide a tax-efficient platform for cross-border investments, help boost savings and investment, and hence global economic growth (Yilmaz, 2006).

According to Garcia-Bernardo *et al.* (2021), low effective tax rates are associated with higher levels of reported profits. In this context, it is intended to observe to what extent the effective tax rate can influence financial performance, more specifically it is intended to analyze whether reduced effective tax rates contribute to performance levels increase of European banks. Therefore, the second research hypothesis is formulated:

H2: A reduced effective tax rate contributes to European banks' higher financial performance.

According to Garcia-Bernardo *et al.* (2021) reduced effective tax rates are associated with higher levels of reported profits. In this context, it is intended to observe to what extent the effective tax rate can influence a firm's performance. Thus, this study expects that low effective tax rates will contribute positively to the European banks' performance. In view of the above, the third research hypothesis is presented:

H3: A lower effective tax rate contributes to increased productivity in the largest European banks.

Tax havens have boosted growth and job creation (Yilmaz, 2006). According to Prochazka (2020), labor is less mobile than capital, which better reflects changes in real economies. In this sense, it is aimed to verify whether reduced effective tax rates have a positive influence on productivity, that is, whether they have a positive economic impact on the profits per worker earned. Therefore, the following research hypothesis is formulated:

H4: The largest European banks' productivity is higher in those operating in tax havens.

Countries that belong to tax havens offer foreign investors lower tax rates and other tax benefits to attract investment and thus stimulate economic activity (Hines, 2005). Therefore, according to Aubry and Dauphin (2017), multinational banks artificially shift their profits from one country to a tax haven to reduce the amount of taxes paid. To do so, they operate as agents to facilitate tax evasion for their clients through the services they provide in tax havens. The financial transactions carried out in tax havens allow circumvention of regulatory and legal obligations. In this sense, we intend to analyze whether the multinational banks with the best financial performance levels are those with operations in tax havens. In this context, the fifth and last research hypothesis is formulated.

H5: Performance is higher in Largest European banks that operate in tax havens.

METHODOLOGY

Sample Selection

This work sample execution was selected from the EU Tax Observatory database. This database allows anyone to observe and analyze the financial data published by the largest European banks and provides greater transparency in the corporate tax landscape, since it allows the visualization of the tax amounts reported by banks in the countries where they operate. Thus, this database contains the CbCR data of the 36 largest and most important European banks, based in 11 EU countries, in more than 90 jurisdictions worldwide (table 1). These datasets cover the period 2014 to 2020 and include all items required by Directive 2013/36/EU.

Table 1. List of the 36 largest European banks by total assets (according to EU Tax Observatory)

Bank	Country	Bank	Country
ABN AMRO Group NV	Netherlands	ING Groep NV	Netherlands
Banca Monte dei Paschi di Siena SpA	Italy	Intesa Sanpaolo SpA	Italy
Banco de Sabadell SA	Spain	KBC Group NV	Bélgica
Banco Santander SA	Spain	Landesbank Baden-Wurttemberg	Germany
BFA Sociedad Tenedora de Acciones SAL	Spain	Landesbank Hessen-Thuringen Girozentrale	Germany
Barclays plc	United Kingdom	Lloyds Banking Group plc	United Kingdom
Bayerische Landesbank	Germany	Nationwide Building Society	United Kingdom
BBVA SA	Spain	Norddeutsche Landesbank Girozentrale	Germany
BNP Paribas SA	France	NatWest Group AG	United Kingdom
Commerzbank AG	Germany	Nordea Bank AB	Sweden
Crédit Agricole Group	France	Nykredit A/S	Denmark
Crédit Mutuel Group	France	Rabobank	Netherlands
Danske Bank A/S	Denmark	Skandinaviska Enskilda Banken	Sweden
Deutsche Bank AG	Germany	Sóciété Générale SA	France
DZ Bank A/S	Germany	Standard Chartered plc	United Kingdom
Erste Group Bank AG	Austria	Svenska Handelsbanken AB	Sweden
Group BPCE	France	Swedbank AB	Sweden
HSBC Holdings plc	United Kingdom	UniCredit SpA	Italy

For each reporting year, one observation is considered. We included in the sample banks with at least one subsidiary. Initially, our sample consisted of 6587 observations, being each observation a tax report of any given bank's subsidiary in a given jurisdiction. In a first stage, countries classified as "Other" were eliminated from the database. By consulting the individual banks' CRCs, it was possible to observe that some banks identify certain countries as "Other". This term encompasses smaller countries, i.e., countries with small amounts of revenues, but which the banks themselves choose not to disclose in their

CbCRs. However, this "Other" category, present in the data published by some banks, refutes the basic idea of the CbCR, i.e., that the information should be presented on a country-by-country basis and not by groups of countries, as it limits its usefulness. Therefore, they were excluded from the present study, resulting in a smaller sample of 6495 observations.

Following Fatica and Gregori's (2020) methodology, observations of whether turnover, pre-tax profit or loss, and taxes paid on profit or loss have negative values were also eliminated. According to the respective authors, the exclusion of these values is because incentives for profit transfers are greater among entities that show positive profitability. In this sense, a total sample of 4587 observations was used in this study; 927 observations refer to tax havens, which is equivalent to 20.20%, while the remaining 3660 observations refer to the remaining countries (79.80%). Table 2 presents the composition of the sample by tax havens and remaining countries.

Table 2. Final sample selection

	Frequency	Percentage	Valid Percentage	Cumulative Percentage
Remaining countries	3660	79.80%	79.80%	79.80%
Tax heavens	927	20.20%	20.20%	100.00%
Total	**4587**	**100.00%**	**100.00%**	

Research Variables

In order to calculate the effective tax rate, the traditional calculation method used by various authors was used. In this sense, and following Markle and Shackelford (2011), Procházka (2020) and Garcia-Bernardo *et al.* (2021), the effective tax rate was calculated based on the ratio between the amount of tax paid and the profit before tax. Essentially, the taxes paid were added up and divided by the sum of total profits over the period from 2014 to 2020.

It should also be noted that the effective tax rate can only be calculated if both indicators are positive. Otherwise, the resulting effective tax rate would be negative, which has no economic significance and, as such, could skew the results (Fatica & Gregori, 2020).

Therefore, since CbCRs provide information about pre-tax profits and the taxes paid on those profits, the effective tax rate can be calculated using this data. In this sense, the following formula was used to calculate the effective tax rates for banks in all the countries in which they operate:

Efective tax rate=(Tax paid on profits or losses))/(Profits or losses before taxes)

In this investigation, the study method used by several authors such as Brown *et al.* (2019), Fatica and Gregori (2020), Procházka (2020) and Fuest *et al.* (2022), to calculate the following variables: 'performance' and 'labor productivity'. These variables are fundamental to study, as they can be calculated using CbCR data, which is why they will be the subject of this investigation.

Performance was measured by the sales profitability ratio. This ratio is obtained by dividing net profits by the total value of sales (Lopes *et al.*, 2014).

However, since CbCR only provides data on pre-tax profits/losses, this will be the indicator used in the calculations and respective analysis. This time, and based on the authors mentioned above, the profitability of sales of international banks was calculated through the ratio between profits before tax and turnover, expressed as follows:

Sales Profitability=(Profit or loss before taxes)/Turnover

On the other hand, labor productivity can also be calculated through pre-tax profit or loss, as it indicates how much profit (or loss) is made per worker. In this way, we can determine this value by dividing the profit or loss before taxes by the number of workers, resulting in the following formula:

Labor productivity=(Profit or loss before taxes)/(Number of full-time workers)

For the purposes of our study, the list of tax havens popularized by Hines (2010) was used, consisting of 52 countries and territories.

Statistical Tests

The Mann Whitney test is a non-parametric test and is normally used to test whether two groups of independent samples, at the level of a dependent variable, have the same distribution or not (Yang & Fang, 2020). In this sense, the hypotheses considered in this investigation will be the following:
H0: The two independent samples have the same distribution.
H1: The two independent samples have different distributions.
In turn, the Spearman Correlation Coefficient is a non-parametric test, that is, without distribution, which measures the intensity and direction of the monotonous relationship between two or more ordinal variables (Xiao *et al.*, 2015), generating a value which varies between 1 and +1. Thus, if the value obtained is positive, the increase in one variable implies an increase in the other variable. On the other hand, if the value obtained is negative, it means that an increase in one variable causes a decrease in the other.
In this way, Spearman's Correlation Coefficient gives rise to the following hypotheses:
H0: There is no relationship between the variables in question.
H1: There is a relationship between the variables in question.
In order to carry out the aforementioned statistical tests, version 26 of the Statistical Package for the Social Sciences (SPSS) software was used.

RESULTS ANALYSIS AND DISCUSSION

From the results analysis, we can draw the following conclusions.
Regarding hypothesis 1, which aims to determine whether multinational banks in tax havens have a lower effective tax rate.

Table 3. Relationship between banks with presence in tax havens/other banks and effective tax rate

	Tax havens	Nº observations	Average position	Sum of Ratings
Effective tax rate	No	3660	2468,88	9036116,50
	Yes	927	1603,52	1486461,50
	Total	4587		
U de Mann-Whitney		1056333,500		
Wilcoxon W		1486461,500		
Z		-17,819		
Significance Sig. (bilateral)		0,000		

Given the probability value obtained (p-value=.000 < 0.001), we find a statistically significant variation, which means that there are significant differences between the groups under analysis, i.e., between tax havens and other countries in terms of the effective tax rate. Additionally, by consulting the column "Average position", we can observe, as expected, that the effective tax rate is lower in banks headquartered in tax havens (table 3).

This result is consistent with the findings of several authors (e.g. Brown *et al.,* 2019; Dutt *et al.,* 2019; Markle & Shackelford, 2011; Procházka, 2020), since they prove that banking institutions have economic and financial benefits operating in tax havens, thus being able to manage their results, decreasing the amount of taxes paid in these countries compared to the others. In view of such a result, multinational companies end up paying less taxes by locating their operations in tax havens, through the transfer of profits from high-tax countries to low-tax countries, thus exploiting possible differences between the tax rules of different countries (Rego, 2003).

Table 4. Relationship between the effective tax rate and banks performance

			Effective Tax Rate	Performance
Rô de Spearman	Effective tax rate	Correlation Coefficient Sig (2 extremities) Observations Nº	1.00 4587	-0.83** 0.000 4587
	Performance	Correlation Coefficient Sig (2 extremities) Observations Nº	-0.83** 0.000 4587	1.000 4587

Note: ** Correlation is significant at the 0.01 level (2 ends)

Based on the results obtained (table 4), we can see that there is a statistically significant relationship between the variables 'effective tax rate' and 'performance' of European banks. However, as we can see, the correlation coefficient value is negative (-0.083), which allows us to conclude that the lower the effective tax rate, the higher the profitability of sales, i.e., the higher European banks financial performance.

This result was expected, because multinational companies have incentives to transfer their profits from high-tax countries, where much of their economic activity occurs, to low-tax countries. Thus, less profitable economic operations subject to standard effective rates can become more profitable when applied at a reduced effective tax rate (Hines & Rice, 1994). Thus, reduced effective rates have the effect of reducing the taxes paid by firms, but on the other hand allow them to attract capital and profits from abroad (Torslov *et al.*, 2020).

In contrast, we find that European banks based in countries with high effective tax rates perform less well. Since high amounts of pre-tax profits are associated with higher corporate tax burdens (Rego, 2003), and given that generally large economies tax corporations more, this means that the amounts of taxes payable by these corporations are high, which in turn decreases the profitability of banking institutions.

In hypothesis 3, the question arises whether a lower effective tax rate contributes to an increase in multinational banks' productivity.

Table 5. Relationship between effective tax rate and banks labor productivity

			Effective Tax Rate	Labor Productivity
Rô de Spearman	Effective tax rate	Correlation Coefficient Sig (2 extremities) Observations N°	1.00 4587	-0.007 0.633 4587
	Labor productivity	Correlation Coefficient Sig (2 extremities) Observations N°	-0.007 0.633 4587	1.000 4587

As we can see from table 5, the correlation found between the 'effective tax rate' and 'labor productivity' is -0.007 with an associated probability of p = 0.633. Given the p-value obtained, we can conclude that, for a significance level of 5%, there is no statistically significant correlation (p-value = 0.633 > 0.05) for the variables in question. Thus, we can conclude that there is no relationship between the 'effective tax rate' and 'labor productivity'. In other words, we can conclude that a low effective tax rate does not contribute to an increase in productivity, that is, a low effective tax rate does not imply that profits per worker are high. These results are not consistent with the findings of Garcia-Bernardo *et al.* (2021) who found that low effective tax rates are associated with higher levels of reported profits.

In hypothesis 4, the question of whether the largest European banks' productivity varies according to whether or not they belong to tax havens is analyzed.

Table 6. Relation between banks operating in tax havens/other banks and labor productivity

	Tax Haven	Nº Observations	Average Position	Sum of Ratings
Labor Productivity	No	3660	2188.94	8011525,00
	Yes	927	2708.80	2511053,00
	Total	4587		
		Labor productivity		
	U de Mann-Whitney	1311895,000		
	Wilcoxon W	8011525,000		
	Z	-10.676		
	Significance Sig. (bilateral)	0,000		

Through Table 6, we can thus see that the most productive multinational banks are those with subsidiaries based in tax havens. This result is corroborative with the findings of Brown *et al.* (2019); Dutt *et al.* (2019) and Fatica and Gregori (2020) since these authors also observed that banks based in tax havens have higher labor productivity, i.e., European multinational banks earn high profits amounts per worker in these countries.

Since high productivity ratios indicate that the higher the pre-tax profits earned, the lower the number of full-time workers, and given that most tax havens are small countries with small populations, we can conclude that these countries are more likely to be used by firms as a means of avoiding taxation rather than having actual production activities in these countries. Complementing this information is the study by Aliprandi *et al.* (2021) where they showed that, on average, profit per worker is about € 283,000 per worker in tax havens, while in non tax havens profit per worker is, on average, about € 68,000 per worker, which once again demonstrates the discrepancy between productivity rates in tax havens and in non tax havens.

In hypothesis 5, we want to know whether financial performance is higher in multinational banks with economic activity in tax havens.

In Table 7, we can see that there is a statistically significant variation in the performance of multinational banks according to whether or not they are present in tax havens (p-value = 0.000 < 0.001).

Table 7. Relationship between banks operating in tax havens/other banks and performance

	Tax Haven	Nº Observations	Average Position	Sum of Ratings
Performance	No	3660	2230.69	8164341.50
	Yes	927	2543.94	2358236.50
	Total	4587		
U de Mann-Whitney		1464711.500		
Wilcoxon W		8164341.500		
Z		-6.433		
Significance Sig. (bilateral)		0,000		

We conclude that the largest European banks, with high performance indices, are those with economic activity in tax havens. These results are in line with the rationale of Hines (2005) and Aubry and Dauphin (2017) where it was found that economic activity is stimulated in companies that have economic activity in tax havens.

Once again, it was possible to observe that the results obtained are consistent with the other authors findings, in which we highlight the Brown *et al.* (2019), Procházka (2020) and Fuest *et al.* (2022) investigations.

Overall, these results once again illustrate the economic and financial benefits that European banks obtain through their activities in tax havens, thus indicating possible profit transfers to these countries.

CONCLUSION

In general, the present study aimed to observe the CbCR value in the fight against tax evasion and fraud, highlighting the role it provides for a greater transparency of the financial information disclosed by banks. More specifically, it was intended to determine, through this data, the tax havens' influence on the largest European banks and to what extent they engage in possible profit transfers to these countries.

Through the results obtained, it was possible to conclude that tax havens are the countries with the lowest effective tax rates. This result is corroborated by numerous authors, among which we can highlight Markle and Shackelford (2011), Brown *et al.* (2019) and Torslov *et al.* (2020) and confirms the company's tendency to transfer their profits to these countries, which allows them to pay lower taxes, or even none, thus benefiting from a more favorable tax regime.

Regarding the effective tax rates impact on firm performance, it was possible to conclude that the lower the effective tax rates, the higher the profitability of sales, i.e., the higher the multinational banks' performance, which is in line with the observations of Hines and Rice (1994), Pratama and Padjadjaran (2017), and Procházka (2020). Since firms pay lower tax, they can maximize their profits, attract greater investment from abroad, and thus achieve higher economic and financial performance. In turn, the results indicate that a lower effective tax rate does not contribute to an increase in productivity in multinational banks.

Still on productivity, the results also reveal that productivity varies depending on whether r or not they belong to tax havens, going against the findings of Brown *et al.* (2019); Dutt *et al.* (2019) and Fatica and Gregori (2020) who observed that banks based in tax havens have higher labor productivity, i.e., European multinational banks obtain high amounts of profits per worker in these countries.

Finally, the results illustrate that the most profitable banks are those with economic activity in tax havens, being in line with the findings of Brown *et al.* (2019), Procházka (2020) and Fuest *et al.* (2022).

This study allows us to extol the CbCR significance in combating tax evasion and profit shifting, and the role it provides for greater tax transparency. With the availability of the data to the public, researchers and governments now have access to detailed information, so they can analyze the countries that are affected by profit shifting and the EU banking institutions that use tax havens for their tax planning.

Throughout this research, it was possible to verify some limitations: first, it was possible to observe in the database that some banks tend to encompass in a category called "Other", values from countries whose amounts are small. This is problematic because it not only compromises the CbCR objective, that is, the disclosure of information on a country-by-country basis, but it may also call into question the results obtained, since this category may include tax havens that are not considered in the research.

Finally, the other limitation is that this data is not sufficient to draw further conclusions. As reinforced by Aliprandri *et al.* (2021), the CbCR does not require these firms to disclose their tangible assets, which may limit evidence of profit shifting. However, if they did, we could eventually calculate the return on assets ratio to understand whether these firms are more efficient in tax havens or in other countries, since it would allow measuring the ability of their tangible assets to generate results.

As suggestions for future research, we suggest analyzing the CbCR data from the next few years more extensively and with a larger number of banks, or possibly studying other types of existing initiatives that allow us to extract other types of fundamental information on this topic.

Conceptualization: Data curation Pinho, P; Amorim, J;Formal analysis Pinho, P; Amorim, Investigation Pinho, P; Amorim, J; Monteiro, A; Cepêda, C; Methodology Pinho, P; Amorim; Project administration Pinho, P; Amorim,; Resources Pinho, P; Amorim,; Software Pinho, P; Amorim,; Supervision Monteiro, A; Cepêda, C; Validation Pinho, P; Amorim, J; Monteiro, A; Cepêda, C; Visualization Pinho, P; Amorim, J; Monteiro, A; Cepêda, C; Roles/Writing - original draft Pinho, P; Amorim, J; Monteiro, A; Cepêda, C; Writing - review & editing Monteiro, A; Cepêda, C.

REFERENCES

Aliprandi, G., Barake, M., & Chouc, P.-E. (2021). Have European banks left tax havens? Evidence from country-by-country data. *EUTAX Observatory*, *2*, 1–60.

Amorim, J. C., Monteiro, A. P., Cepêda, C. L. M., & Coelho, G. R. T. F. (2021). Análise comparativa do regime fiscal das Zonas Francas na Europa. *e3-Revista de Economia, Empresas e Empreendedores na CPLP*, *7*(2), 31-55.

Aubry, M., & Dauphin, T. (2017). *Opening the Vaults: The use of tax havens by Europe's biggest banks*. Oxfam. https://oxfamilibrary.openrepository.com

Bouvatier, V., Capelle-Blancard, G., & Delatte, A.-L. (2017). *Banks in Tax Havens: First Evidence Based on Country-by-Country Reporting*. Discussion Paper (055). https://economy-finance.ec.europa.eu

Brown, R. J., Jorgensen, B. N., & Pope, P. F. (2019). The interplay between mandatory country-by-country reporting, geographic segment reporting, and tax havens: Evidence from the European Union. *Journal of Accounting and Public Policy*, *38*(2), 106–129. doi:10.1016/j.jaccpubpol.2019.02.001

Buckley, P. J., Sutherland, D., Voss, H., & El-Gohari, A. (2015). The economic geography of offshore incorporation in tax havens and offshore financial centers: The case of Chinese MNEs. *Journal of Economic Geography*, *15*(1), 103–128. doi:10.1093/jeg/lbt040

Deng, Z., Yan, J., & Sun, P. (2020). Political status and tax haven investment of emerging market firms: Evidence from China. *Journal of Business Ethics*, *165*(3), 469–488. doi:10.100710551-018-4090-0

Dharmapala, D., & Hines, J. R. Jr. (2009). Which countries become tax havens? *Journal of Public Economics*, *93*(9-10), 1058–1068. doi:10.1016/j.jpubeco.2009.07.005

Drake, K. D., Hamilton, R., & Lusch, S. J. (2020). Are declining effective tax rates indicative of tax avoidance? Insight from effective tax rate reconciliations. *Journal of Accounting and Economics*, *70*(1), 101317. doi:10.1016/j.jacceco.2020.101317

Dutt, V. K., Ludwig, C. A., Nicolay, K., Vay, H., & Voget, J. (2019). Increasing tax transparency: Investor reactions to the country-by-country reporting requirement for EU financial institutions. *International Tax and Public Finance*, *26*(6), 1259–1290. doi:10.100710797-019-09575-4

Eberhartinger, E., Speitmann, R., & Sureth-Sloane, C. (2020). *Real Effects of Public Country-by-Country Reporting and the Firm Structure of European Banks*. Arqus Discussion Paper, 255. Disponível em: https://econstor.eu

Fatica, S., & Gregori, W. D. (2020). How much profit shifting do European banks do? *Economic Modelling*, *90*, 536–551. doi:10.1016/j.econmod.2020.01.026

Fuest, C., Hugger, F., & Neumeier, F. (2022). Corporate profit shifting and the role of tax havens: Evidence from German country-by-country reporting data. *Journal of Economic Behavior & Organization*, *194*, 454–477. doi:10.1016/j.jebo.2021.11.016

Garcia-Bernardo, J., Janský, P., & Thorslov, T. (2021). Multinational corporations and tax havens: Evidence from country-by-country reporting. *International Tax and Public Finance*, *28*(6), 1519–1561. doi:10.100710797-020-09639-w

Hanlon, M. (2018). *Country-by-country reporting and the international allocation of taxing rights*. International Bureau of Fiscal Documentation (IBFD).

Hebb, T. (2006). The economic inefficiency of secrecy: Pension fund investors' corporate transparency concerns. *Journal of Business Ethics*, *63*(4), 385–405. doi:10.100710551-005-3968-9

Hines, J. R. Jr. (2010). Treasure islands. *The Journal of Economic Perspectives*, *24*(4), 103–126. doi:10.1257/jep.24.4.103

Hines, J. R., & Rice, E. M. (1994). Fiscal Paradise: Foreign Tax Havens and American Business. *The Quarterly Journal of Economics*, *109*(1), 149–182. doi:10.2307/2118431

Hugger, F. (2019). *The impact of country-by-country reporting on corporate tax avoidance* (No. 304). IFO Working Paper.

Janský, P. (2020). European banks and tax havens: Evidence from country-by-country reporting. *Applied Economics*, *52*(54), 5967–5985. doi:10.1080/00036846.2020.1781773

Kang, H., & Gray, S. J. (2019). Country-specific risks and geographic disclosure aggregation: Voluntary disclosure behaviour by British multinationals. *The British Accounting Review*, *51*(3), 259–276. doi:10.1016/j.bar.2019.02.001

Lopes, J. C., Nunes, A., & Garnacho, A. D. C. (2014). Indicadores e Rácios que Determinam a Rentabilidade dos Capitais Próprios. *XXIV Jornadas Luso Espanholas de Gestão Científica*. https://core.ac.uk/download/pdf/154409576.pdf

Markle, K. S., & Shackelford, D. A. (2011). Cross-country comparisons of the effects of leverage, intangible assets, and tax havens on corporate income taxes. *Tax L. Rev*, *65*, 415.

Menkhoff, L., & Miethe, J. (2019). Tax evasion in new disguise? Examining tax havens´ international bank deposits. *Journal of Public Economics*, *176*, 53–78. doi:10.1016/j.jpubeco.2019.06.003

Murphy, R. (2019). 'Corporate tax avoidance: is tax transparency the solution?': a practitioner view. *Accounting and Business Research*, *49*(5), 584–586. doi:10.1080/00014788.2019.1611728

Murphy, R., Shah, A., & Janský, P. (2019). BEPS Policy Failure — The Case of EU. *Nordic Tax Journal*, 1–24.

OECD. (2017). *Background Brief. Inclusive Framework on BEPS.* https://www.oecd.org/tax/beps/background-brief-inclusive-framework-on-beps.pdf

Overesch, M., & Wolff, H. (2021). Financial Transparency to the Rescue: Effects of Public Country-by-Country Reporting in the European Union Banking Sector on Tax Avoidance. *Contemporary Accounting Research*, *38*(3), 1616–1642. doi:10.1111/1911-3846.12669

Pratama, A., & Padjadjaran, U. (2017). Company Characteristics, Corporate Governance and Agressive Tax Avoidance Practice: A Study of Indonesian Companies. *Review of Integrative Business and Economics Research*, *6*(4), 70–81.

Procházka, P. (2020). Jurisdictions with lowest effective tax rates in the post-BEPS landscape: CbCR evidence and implications. *European Financial and Accounting Journal*, *15*(1), 33–52. doi:10.18267/j.efaj.231

Rego, S. O. (2003). Tax-Avoidance Activities of U.S. Multinational Corporations. *Contemporary Accounting Research*, *20*(4), 805–833. doi:10.1506/VANN-B7UB-GMFA-9E6W

Torslov, T. R., Wier, L. S., & Zucman, G. (2020). *The Missing Profits of Nations.* National Bureau of Economic Research Working Paper, 24071. https://www.nber.org/papers/w24071

Wójcik, D. (2015). Accounting for globalization: Evaluating the potential effectiveness of country-by-country reporting. *Environment and Planning. C, Government & Policy*, *33*(5), 1173–1189. doi:10.1177/0263774X15612338

Xiao, C., Ye, J., Esteves, R. M., & Rong, C. (2015). Using Spearman's correlation coefficient for exploratory data analysis on big dataset. *Concurrency and Computation*, *28*(14), 3866–3878. doi:10.1002/cpe.3745

Yang, C., & Fang, H. (2020). A New Nonlinear Model-Based Fault Detection Method Using Mann-Whitney Test. *IEEE Transactions on Industrial Electronics*, *67*(12), 10856–10864. doi:10.1109/TIE.2019.2958297

Yilmaz, Y. (2006). Tax havens, tax competition, and economic performance. *Tax Notes International*, *43*(7), 587.

Chapter 9
Online Environmental Disclosure Practice Among Big Polluters in Serbia

Aida Hanić
https://orcid.org/0000-0003-4378-7002
Institute of Economic Sciences, Belgrade, Serbia

Slavica Stevanović
https://orcid.org/0000-0002-8545-4540
Institute of Economic Sciences, Belgrade, Serbia

Petar Mitić
https://orcid.org/0000-0002-7998-9215
Institute of Economic Sciences, Belgrade, Serbia

ABSTRACT

This chapter aims to analyze the online environmental disclosure practice by big polluters in Serbia. The analysis was based on a sample of 69 companies, classified into five affiliation sectors, from the Pollutant Release and Transfer Register (PRTR). The results show that big Serbian polluters still use the traditional management approach since the level of disclosure is less than 30%. To quantify the level of disclosure, Environmental Disclosure Index was employed, containing 15 variables. Most of the analyzed companies on their websites disclosed their environmental certification, environmental policy, and waste management and reduction, while the less informed variable was pollutant types and emissions. Also, the results show that big polluters in Serbia are willing to disclose only positive environmental activities and results.

DOI: 10.4018/978-1-6684-9076-1.ch009

INTRODUCTION

The Industrial Revolution spurred economic growth worldwide but also caused a decline in environmental quality, leading to global warming and climate change concerns. It is further exacerbated by the substantial increase in CO_2 emissions from energy use in newly industrialized economies since the 1990s compared to already industrialized countries (Mitić et al., 2023a). Extreme climate changes resulted in increased environmental pollution and GHG emissions by all business subjects, which led to the need to accomplish optimal ecological, social, and economic performance (Bazhair et al., 2022). This is particularly important for big polluters since *"100 active fossil fuel producers account for 71% of global industrial GHG emissions since 1988 and 52% of all global industrial GHGs emitted since the start of the industrial revolution in 1751."* (CDP Carbon Majors Report 2017, pp. 5-8). Companies should reveal their environmental actions to present current activities and future commitments concerning reducing pollution and GHG emissions, as they both contribute to and solve these environmentally hazardous activities. But the question is, do they do that, and at which level?

Understanding and implementing the data disclosure concept requires considering two issues: why is disclosure necessary, and how much data should companies disclose? Mathews (1997) describes data disclosure as the voluntary disclosure of information, qualitative and quantitative, by an organization to inform or influence the public, whereby the published quantitative information can be financial or non-financial. Disclosure can be mandatory and voluntary. In the first case, there are legal requirements related to what to disclose where failure to do so may cause a penalty (Akhter et al., 2022), and in the second one, it depends on the company.

Hendriksen (1982) distinguishes three types of the disclosure: adequate (minimum degree of disclosure but sufficient so that the user of the report is not misled), fair (ethical goal of providing equal treatment to potential readers), and complete (presentation of all relevant information). According to Frooman (1997), disclosure is essential for enlightened self-interest where companies promote the interests of shareholders, while Smith (2003) notes it is not just good but also a smart thing to do because it reduces information asymmetry (Nobanee & Ellili, 2016). Also, disclosure can have a positive impact on financial performance (Carnini Pulino et al., 2022), which leads to growth and sustainability. But other authors, like Deegan et al. (2002), go in the other direction and relate it to the organization's survival. It gives a good foundation to conclude that, in general, disclosure is essential to increase transparency and ensure legitimacy. This is closely related to the legitimacy theory that refers to social expectations in the form of prevailing social ideologies, managers' attitudes toward what they consider legitimate social expectations, and business behavior. Barnett (2007) believes that legitimacy arises from the congruence between the company's activities and social expectations, stressing that the loss of legitimacy can occur when a company acts contrary to social expectations and as a result of changes in social expectations.

Regarding disclosure related to environmental issues, one of the conclusions of COP27 was that *"transparency and openness in sharing climate change data and carbon disclosure are essential "*(UNESCO, 2022). In other words, transparency enables accountability, and only a responsible business institution can lead the entire society's progress. In that aspect, environmental disclosure can be observed as a communication tool about the organization's impact on the environment (Chaklader & Gulati, 2015). In a wider aspect, environmental disclosure is reporting about a company's contribution, positive or negative (Ahmad, 2012) to the accomplishment of 3P - profit, people, and planet (Elkington, 1998). This triple-bottom-line concept was later used to develop the concept of sustainable development. Ikram et al. (2019) note that in the long run, environmental disclosure practice can be observed as a tool to achieve the sustainable development of enterprises. Based on this, in the literature, we can find many terms related to reporting about corporation environmental practices, such as Environmental, Social, and Governance (ESG) disclosure (Frost et al., 2023); sustainability reporting (Farisyi et al., 2022); Sustainability Performance Reporting (Osobajo et al., 2022) or Corporate sustainability reporting (European Commission, 2022).

Initially, environmental disclosure was voluntary and mainly depended on the company's decision or motivation to disclose non-financial information. But as time passed, this issue gained more attention, and many stakeholders (shareholders, Government, consumers, investors, researchers, scientists, etc.) started to be aware of the harmful effect the companies can have on the environment. Pan et al. (2022) research shows that the relationship between environmental disclosure and concern about environmental issues is inverted U-shaped. In other words, 1% increase in environmental disclosure, the public environmental concern can increase by 1.7%. In that aspect, the public started to request business subjects to be more transparent and take more initiative regarding environmental issues, which changed the nature of the regulatory framework (Baalouch et al., 2019). This increased mandatory and voluntary environmental disclosure in many countries where companies disclose their environmental activities in annual or separate sustainable reports (Farisyi et al., 2022) or by creating a specific environmental website (Thimm and Rasmussen, 2020).

According to Adams (2002), the reporting practice depends on several factors, such as a) the corporation characteristics (size, industry to which the corporation belongs, financial/economic performance, etc.); b) contextual factors (country of origin, social, political, cultural, and economic context), c) internal contextual factors (various aspects of corporate governance). Seo (2021) also includes peer factors in how group behavior influences individual group members' behavior. When it comes to the industry type and its effect on the disclosure, Lambrechts et al. (2019) note that priorities are different for different stakeholders and that industry effect is very important (Park & Jang, 2021), especially in the case of environmentally sensitive industries (Long et al., 2022; Garcia et al., 2017).

There is a big difference in disclosure practices among developed and developing countries regarding the country effect. Generally, a country's corporate governance and institutional infrastructure are very important for economic and financial development (Doidge et al., 2007). For instance, developed countries usually have well-established regulatory frameworks that mandate comprehensive disclosure requirements for companies and tend to have well-defined corporate governance practices that emphasize transparency, accountability, and shareholder rights. On the opposite, in developing countries regulatory and legal systems are weaker (Isukul & Chizea, 2017) and the overall transparency of business operations is not adequate (Hanić et al., 2021). In a study done by Acar et al. (2021) on a sample of 27,847 firms from 72 countries or financial districts in 2002-2017, firms with higher state ownership that operate in a developed country have higher environmental disclosure, opposite to firms that operate in developing countries. At the same time, firms with higher institutional ownership have a negative effect on environmental disclosure. This result is consistent with the research done by Orazalin and Mahmood (2019), who state that the difference between the disclosure practices of developed and developing countries is based on socio-economic and political factors. Besides this, Mateo-Márquez et al. (2020) note that countries' climate change-related institutional profile affects voluntary environmental disclosures and how much the country corresponds to the emitted levels of GHG. This notion is also mentioned by Kojić et al. (2022), who state that various levels of societal and economic development do not always correspond to GHG emission values.

In this regard, the objective of this study is to assess the practice of online disclosure among major polluting entities in Serbia. The selected companies are drawn from the national Pollutant Release and Transfer Register (PRTR), with 175 identified as polluting firms in the 2021 list. After excluding four types of companies, we focused on 69 big polluters from different industries. The focus is on online disclosure since, via the Internet, stakeholders can quickly analyze the company's websites and gather required information (Gajewski and Li, 2015; Rosa Portella and Borba, 2020) by transcending geographical boundaries. At the same time, a website can provide updated and more detailed information about environmental activities (Kiliç, 2016). Additionally, the adoption of online disclosure eliminates the necessity for printing and physically distributing documents, aligning with environmentally sustainable practices and contributing to cost efficiency.

Authors employed content analysis as a standard method of examining content (Adams et al., 1998; Sobhani et al., 2012).

Accordingly, there are several reasons for this research. First, Serbia faces pollution problems because it relies on lignite and coal-fuelled power stations, where around 75% of the energy comes from fossil fuels. Contrary to this, Serbia committed to decarbonizing its economy and fully implementing all obligations accepted by signed international carbon neutrality agreements. This means that environmental issues will be fundamental in the future. Second, the Serbian economic growth rate has been among the highest in the region, and there is evidence that it harmed the environment (Mitić et al., 2023b). Due to the low disclosure levels in Serbian legal and reporting practice, the public is unaware of how much big polluters contribute to overall GHG emissions. Third, there is not enough research on this topic, primarily focused on online environmental disclosure. Stevanović et al. (2014) concluded that many business entities in Serbia do not attach great importance to environmental disclosure.

Based on the previous, this paper focuses on three main points:

- Online analysis of the environmental disclosure practice of big polluters in Serbia
- What is the motivation for implementing the environmental disclosure, or what are the reasons why analyzed firms do not use online environmental reporting and,
- Legitimacy theory as the basis for implementing the environmental disclosure practice.

This paper comprises four parts, including the introduction and the conclusion. Environmental disclosure and legitimacy theory and Environmental disclosure in Serbia are presented in the second and third sections, respectively. The fourth section explains the Research Methodology used. The fifth section explains the data and results.

ENVIRONMENTAL DISCLOSURE AND LEGITIMACY THEORY LITERATURE REVIEW

In the literature, the 1970-1980 period can be observed as a starting point regarding reporting about the social aspect of the business (Mathews, 1997). For instance, Ramanathan (1976) related the organization's interaction with people, products, and the environment using the term social accounting, while Ullmann (1976) offered an early model dedicated exclusively to the environment, called the corporate environmental accounting system (CEAS). As mentioned above, Elkington (1998) made a very significant contribution with 3P since this principle is not a trade-off where the realization of one occurs at the expense of the other. Hence, companies started to realize that focusing only on financial results, in the long run, is not good for the company's survival. In general, characteristics of non-financial reporting during the period 1971–1980. means the use of various terms, such as "socio-economic accounting."

Period 1981-1990 Mathews (1997) marks as complex primarily due to the increased sophistication in social accounting, the transfer of the sphere of research to environmental accounting, and the increased interest in the educational aspects of this field. At the same time, in the '90s, the issue of environmental protection comes into focus through green accounting (Mathews, 1997).

Ugur and Erdogan (2007) note that in the period 1996-2006, there are two specific features: a) corporate practices related to environmental protection and social reporting, discussed from the theoretical framework of stakeholder theory, legitimacy theory, and political economy, and b) a difference in the disclosure degree depending on the country or region. One element that is very important regarding the disclosure practice is whether the company's report is based on certain internal guidelines or standardized reporting. In this context, on a global level, the Global Reporting Initiative (GRI) was formed in 1997 to standardize reports, especially the segment related to non-financial indicators and the context of sustainability. According to the KPMG Survey of Sustainability Reporting 2020 (2020), there are five major non-financial reporting organizations. This is presented in the following table. It is important to note that these standards, guidelines, and frameworks aim to turn reporting practices from abstract issues to understandable and concrete ones.

Table 1. Five major non-financial reporting organizations

	IIRC (International Integrated Reporting Council)	GRI (Global Reporting Initiative)	SASB (Sustainability Accounting Standards Board)	CDSB (Climate Disclosure Standards Board)	CDP (Climate Disclosure Project)
Type of Guidance	Framework	Standards	Standards	Framework	Framework
Application	Voluntary	Voluntary	Voluntary	Voluntary	Voluntary
Objective	Help organizations explain to providers of financial capital how they create value over time	Enable all organizations— regardless of size, sector, or location— to report the sustainability information that matters	Help public corporations disclose material sustainability information in mandatory SEC filings	Help organizations prepare and present environmental information in mainstream reports	Requests standardized climate change, water, and forest information through annual questionnaires sent on behalf of institutional investors.
Target Audience	Providers of financial capital	Multiple stakeholders	Investors	Investors	Investors, companies, cities, states, and regions

Source: IFC (2018). Beyond the Balance Sheet.

During the 2000s, heterogeneity was present in the understanding and definition of non-financial reporting (Stolowy and Paugam, 2018). At the same time, in this period, the motivation and the form of environmental disclosure changed. For example, companies started to disclose statements about their environmental policy, pollution control processes, and to which level the company complies with the regulation. Also, many companies began to disclose financial data regarding environmental costs, such as purchasing equipment to reduce pollution, paying taxes, training their employees about climate change risk, etc. In this aspect, Long et al. (2022) distinguish internal and external motivation factors, including corporate scale, growth, culture, governance, etc., and external regulatory policies, such as industry characteristics, market competitiveness, and others.

Besides this, since the 2000s, ESG disclosure has become mandatory in many countries. For instance, in a study done by Krueger et al. (2023), authors find that in the period 2002-2020, 22 countries implemented comprehensive mandatory ESG disclosure, which includes that all three (E, S, G) elements were introduced at once, while 13 countries introduced E, S, and G one by one.

At the same time, in the 2000s, many theories developed to explain the importance of reporting and not just to describe it. This relates primarily to the legitimacy theory, which has become widely accepted in social accounting and disclosure-based research. This theory emphasizes that a company has obligations toward society since the community is affected by the company's behavior. In other words, the company should strive to create a strong bond between the social values and behavior they represent and the societal norms since any dissidence creates a potential threat in the form of economic, legal, or other sanctions (Joshi et al., 2011).

According to Mahadeo et al. (2011), companies need to demonstrate that they have achieved moral legitimacy (their business activities will not harm society) and pragmatic legitimacy (companies consider how their decisions affect their stakeholders). Hence, legitimacy theory suggests that a company can survive if it operates in a socially acceptable manner (Panwar et al., 2012). Palazzo and Scherer (2006) believe that legitimacy can be understood as the confirmation of social norms, values, and expectations,. Nevertheless, the most frequently used and cited definition in the literature is the one given by Suchman (1995), who defines legitimacy as *"a generalized perception or assumption that the actions of an entity are desirable, proper, or appropriate within some socially constructed system of norms, values, beliefs, and definitions"* (Suchman, 1955, p. 574).

The same author divides legitimacy into two different approaches: strategic and institutional. The conclusion about a strategic element of legitimacy adopts a management perspective. It highlights how organizations instrumentally manipulate and deploy evocative symbols to garner social support. On the other hand, the institutional approach adopts a detached attitude. It emphasizes how the dynamics of sectoral structuring generate cultural pressures that go beyond the purpose of controlling each organization. That is why the issue of disclosure is significant because the disclosure represents what the public should see.

Deegan and Unerman (2011) note that legitimacy theory ensures that companies implement the boundaries and norms of the society in which they operate. The authors also point out that these norms do not have a fixed character but change over time. In this domain, Palazzo and Scherer (2006) point out that legitimacy as such is crucial for those companies that operate globally. For instance, Patten (1992) analyzed the reports of oil companies in South America after the environmental disaster caused by the Exxon Valdez oil spill. The author concluded that there was an increase in disclosed activities after the disaster and that companies used annual reports to legitimize current business activities.

The legitimacy theory is closely related to the social contract theory because, according to Holub (2003), the key to legitimacy is the concept of the social contract between organizations and society members. Based on this, society also allows business entities to operate to the extent that they work to benefit the community and to the extent that they are ready to respond to its needs. Environmental disclosures can significantly affect society as a part of legitimacy, so companies are reporting about their environmental performance using their annual reports, websites, and other forms of publications to mitigate legitimacy pressure (Gregory et al., 2016).

In general, regarding the disclosure practice worldwide, this issue was analyzed in detail in a study by KPMG called "The KPMG Survey of Sustainability Reporting 2020". The study consists of two components:

a. N 100, which refers to a worldwide sample of 5,200 companies. It comprises the top 100 companies by revenue in each of the 52 countries and jurisdictions;

b. G250, which refers to the 250 largest companies by revenue that make up the Global Fortune 500.

Results reveal that in 2020, 80% of N100 companies worldwide reported on sustainability; in 2017, that percentage was 78% (KPMG International Survey of Corporate, 2017). At the same time, since 2011, 90% or more of the G250 have reported on sustainability as presented in the Chart 1 (KPMG Survey of Sustainability Reporting, 2020). When it comes to regions, America is the leader, while in Europe, the sustainability reporting rate in 2020 was the same as in 2017 (77%), with a difference between Eastern and Western Europe in favor of Eastern Europe.

Figure 1. Sustainability reporting by N100 and G250 companies
Source: KPMG Survey of Sustainability Reporting (2020)

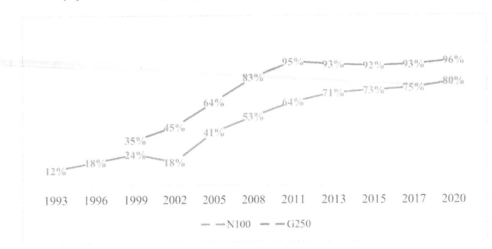

Some authors consider online disclosure a comprehensive information tool (Lipe, 2018) that started to be used more since annual reports couldn't reach all stakeholders (Cormier et al., 2009), especially for disclosing environmental activities. In practical terms, companies have several compelling reasons to reveal their operations, particularly those related to environmental concerns:

● Strengthening the company's dedication to sustainability is facilitated by disclosing information on carbon emissions, waste management practices, and environmental initiatives. This transparency enables stakeholders to assess the extent of the company's commitment to societal well-being.

- Providing investors with a clearer perspective on the company's risk mitigation is crucial. Proactive disclosure of environmental initiatives not only instills confidence in investors but also helps mitigate risks associated with evolving regulatory landscapes and changing consumer preferences.
- Fostering trust with stakeholders is a potent outcome of disclosure practices, especially concerning consumer awareness.
- Adhering to regulatory compliance becomes imperative for adapting to new legislations and requirements, as many governments deem disclosure mandatory.

Regarding the research, Thimm and Rasmussen (2020) collected data from 154 European production companies randomly selected. They categorized them into two groups: medium-sized and very large companies. The analyses revealed that corporate websites don't contain much information about environmental management and environmental compliance management. At the same time, the result showed that large companies disclose more than small companies. There were also significant differences among countries since only the Swedish companies publish more extensively than companies in other analyzed countries.

A comparable conclusion was made by authors Rosa Portella and Borba (2020). The authors wanted to explore the extent of their environmental disclosure by employing an environmental disclosure index (EDI) with ten categories and 40 subcategories. The result shows that organization size, the business sector, and the company's country of origin explain the extension of environmental disclosure where the US companies disclose more about environmental responsibility than the Brazilian.

Environmental Disclosure in Serbia

According to the Environmental Performance Index (EPI), which uses 40 performance indicators across 11 issue categories and ranks 180 countries in climate change performance, environmental health, and ecosystem vitality, in 2022, Serbia was ranked 79th country with a 43.90 EPI score. This is no surprise since around 75% of the energy in Serbia is obtained from fossil fuels. But, in 2015, the Republic of Serbia adopted the NDC (Nationally Determined Contribution) with the aim of reducing GHG emissions by 9.8% in 2030 compared to 1990. The updated NDC for the period 2021-2030 was adopted by the Republic of Serbia in 2020, in which it increased its ambitions to reduce greenhouse gas emissions by 33.3%, compared to 1990, until 2030. Likewise, in 2020, the Republic of Serbia signed the Sofia Declaration on the Green Agenda for the Western Balkans, assuming obligations to implement measures in five areas: I Climate, energy, mobility, II Circular economies, III Depollution, IV Sustainable agriculture and food production and V Biodiversity.

To reduce GHG emissions in a cost-effective and economically efficient manner, Serbia adopted the Law on Climate Change in 2021. As an EU candidate country, Serbia will need to harmonize its regulation with the EU standards, especially regarding the environment. It is important to emphasize that in 2022, European Council introduced The Corporate Sustainability Reporting Directive (CSRD) as an EU ESG standard. CSRD will apply to companies with:

- over 250 employees
- more than 40€ million in annual revenue
- more than 20€ million in total assets
- publicly-listed equities and have more than ten employees or 20€ million revenue

- international and non-EU companies with more than 150€ million annual revenue within the EU and which have at least one subsidiary or branch in the EU exceeding certain thresholds.

Regarding disclosure practice reporting in Serbia, relying on European comparative practice, non-financial reporting was introduced into domestic legislation with the adoption of amendments to the Accounting Act in October 2019. The law entered into force on January 1, 2020, with the delayed implementation of certain provisions due to the time required for adjustment. According to this Law, obligees of non-financial reporting are large legal entities that are companies of public interest and that, on the balance sheet date, exceed the criterion of an average number of 500 employees during the business year. According to Article 37 of this Law, the annual report includes a non-financial report that contains the information necessary for understanding the development, business results, and position of the legal entity, as well as the results of its activities related to environmental protection, social and personnel issues, respect for human rights, the fight against corruption and issues related to bribery.

The number of studies on environmental reporting practices in Serbia is limited in the scientific aspect. Stevanović et al. (2014) analyzed the environmental disclosure practice of polluting companies in Serbia by analyzing their financial reports. Results show that voluntary disclosure was not on an adequate level. In a similar research, Stevanović (2018) analyzed the environmental reporting practice of polluter companies located in Novi Sad, the second largest city in Serbia. Findings show that polluters disclosed data about their activities as a note to a financial report or as an integrated part of an annual report. Mijatović et al. (2015) found that the Serbian company's reports expressed philanthropy and humanitarian activities. This can be related to the fact that Serbian society is strongly influenced by collectivism (Videnović et al., 2021). Denčić-Mihajlov and Spasić (2016) investigated mandatory and voluntary disclosure practices of non-financial listed companies on the Belgrade Stock Exchange. The results show a low level of both mandatory and voluntary disclosures. This is consistent with Stojanović-Blab et al. (2017), who found that the level of the implementation of GRI Guidelines by Serbian companies is low and unsatisfactory.

Mijoković et al. (2020) researched a sample of 113 companies listed on the Belgrade Stock Exchange from different business and industry sectors. Their focus was on the period before the adoption of the new law on Accounting. They conclude that listed companies on the Serbian capital market can expect increased share prices as a reward for their socially responsible reporting. Hanić et al. (2021) researched environmental disclosure by Serbian banks, concluding that reports are not standardized and that the systemically important banks in Serbia do not have better disclosure practices.

Analyzing the eco-efficiency and profitability relationship of Serbian companies, Stevanović et al. (2023) point out that the largest polluters in Serbia must be profitable and environmentally responsible while trying to reduce and preclude the harmful impact of their business activities on the environment. Stevanović et al. (2019) investigate the relationship between liquidity, profitability, and pollution, suggesting that enhancing the liquid assets' and current liabilities' efficiency and employing green technologies could be significant profitability drivers of polluting medium-sized enterprises. To the best of our knowledge of online environmental disclosure in Serbia, there was no research on this topic.

RESEARCH METHODOLOGY

In the analysis of the disclosure practice, it is essential to note the measurement aspect since some authors, like Harrington (1987), point out that to understand, control, and improve something, it is necessary to measure it. To measure the environmental disclosure practice of big Serbian polluters, the authors used the content analysis method, the most common method in these types of research (Long et al., 2022). Content analysis is based on the principle of quantification (Neuendorf, 2002) and a qualitative approach (Unerman, 2003).

The content analysis method works on the principle of "counting" and determines whether the requested item is mentioned qualitatively or numerically. Using it, researchers can systematically process a large amount of data. In practice, it is a systematic technique based on replicability that translates many words into smaller meaningful categories, respecting explicit coding rules (Stemler, 2001). But the specificity of the content analysis method is that there has been a long debate about whether this method is quantitative or qualitative. Neuendorf (2002) points out that it is a systematic and objective method where quantification is key and where one does not go into the "depth" of the analysis. On the other hand, Unerman (2003) believes that qualitatively oriented approaches are more valid. In this paper, we used the Unerman (2003) approach since conclusions made on such an approach are more meaningful.

This approach aims to establish how transparent companies in Serbia are regarding their relationship with the environment, especially considering that they are major polluters. Also, it gives a closer look at whether Serbian companies accepted a modern management practice where a website is a valid tool that can be used to highlight their environmental responsibility. Hence, the content analysis is based on a binary coding system where 1 indicates that the unit of analysis is present, and 0 indicates the opposite. The methodology focuses on using the Environmental Disclosure Index (EDI). Since most of the companies in Serbia still do not use some of the most used standards, guidelines, and frameworks, we used a composite index based on the indexes of previous studies made by Hanić et al. (2021), Rosa Portella and Borba (2020), and Kiliç (2016).

Hanić et al. (2021) focused on environmental disclosure in the Serbian banking sector. Kiliç (2016) analyzed the extent to which 25 banks from the Republic of Türkiye report online about their CSR practices. In this research, we used only those elements applicable to any industry regarding environmental disclosure. Rosa Portella and Borba (2020) analyzed the corporate websites of 57 companies from Brazil and 60 from the USA. Ultimately, EDI employed in this research has 15 variables and is based on the characteristics of the Serbian reporting practice.

Environmental Disclosure Index (EDI) is calculated as follows:

$$EDI_{jt} = \frac{\sum_{i=1}^{n} X_{ijt}}{N};$$

Where EDI is the environmental disclosure index, N is the number of constructs or items disclosed by the company and in this case it is 15 so $N \leq 15$, and $X_{ij} = 1$ if the construct or item is disclosed, 0 if the construct or item is not disclosed, so that $0 <= i_j <= 1$.

The index is calculated based on 15 variables where the maximum value of the index is 1, which means 100% disclosure, while the minimum value is 0. EDI variables are presented in the following table.

Table 2. Environmental disclosure index variables

No.	Component
1.	Environmental policy
2.	Water, energy, and paper utilization efficiency
3.	Waste management and reduction
4.	Environmental management system
5.	Environmental protection measures and improvement
6.	Pollutant types and emissions
7.	Environmental awareness, training & education related disclosure
8.	Energy saving measures and results
9.	Environmental certification
10.	Environmental awards
11.	Cooperation with the local community to implement environmental protection projects
12.	Use of new technologies in the production process
13.	Environmental protection investment
14.	Equipping the company's headquarters or branches using eco-friendly materials
15.	Environmental protection costs - monetary value

Source: Hanić et al. (2021); Rosa Portella and Borba (2020); Kiliç (2016)

DATA AND RESULTS

The total sample has 175 companies included in the PRTR register of the Serbian Environmental Protection Agency in 2021 as a part of the National Register of Pollution Sources (SEPA, 2021). Their business activities cause emissions of pollutants in the environment (air and/or water pollutants and/or generated waste). The Pollutant Release and Transfer (PRTR) Register represents a special international treaty developed as a Protocol of the Aarhus Convention and is a new environmental agreement (SEPA, 2022). From the sample of 175 big polluters in Serbia in 2021, we included 69 from the PRTR register, classified into five affiliations sectors. The companies that were excluded from the sample were those who:

a) didn't have their website;
b) didn't disclose any environmental information on their website;
c) are companies that are public enterprises for communal works;
d) "mother companies" that don't have a website for a Serbian daughter company.

This classification is presented in chart 2.

Figure 2. Companies excluded from the sample
Source: Authors' calculation based on SEPA (2021) data

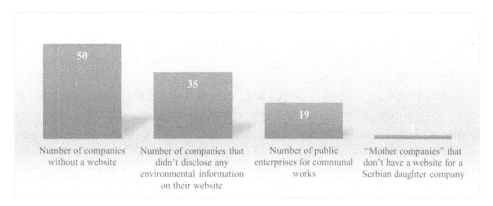

As seen from the chart, 50 polluters registered in the PTPR don't have a website, while 35 didn't disclose anything related to the environmental issue or practices. This leads to the conclusion that management practice in Serbia is mainly focused on the traditional approach, which aligns with Stojanović-Blab et al. (2017). We could also say that these companies don't consider their legitimacy as a resource.

The sample of 69 analyzed companies treats the environmental issue very differently on their websites. In general, there are three approaches to this aspect. The first one, which is mostly present, is that companies disclose their environmental strategy in the section "About us" or the section called "Environment". The second approach, mainly related to those companies whose mother companies are MNCs, has a separate section on their website called "Sustainable development". It is interesting to note that their CSR practice is separated on their websites, which means that the company is aware of its influence on the environment. The third approach includes that sampled companies have their environmental policy in the section "Social responsibility," where they consider environmental activities as an integrated CSR part.

In our analysis, we didn't focus only on one sector but included all sectors from the PRTR to see if there is a difference between sectors in Serbia regarding online environmental disclosure practice. Sample sector affiliation and the number of companies are presented in the following table.

Table 3. Sector affiliation of the sample companies

Sector Affiliation	Number of Companies
Agricultural, forestry, and fishing	6
Mining	5
Manufacturing	53
Water supply; sewerage, waste management and remediation activities	4
Administrative and service support activities	1

Source: Authors' calculation based on SEPA (2021) data

When it comes to the most disclosed variables of EDI, it is definitely environmental certification. Most companies have their certificate on the homepage of their website. The second mostly disclosed variable is environmental policy, while the third one is waste management and reduction. Regarding the variables that were less disclosed, just one of the 69 companies included in the sample disclosed their pollutant types and emissions in real-time. Also, very few companies disclosed the monetary value of environmental protection costs and the use of eco-friendly materials when equipping the company's headquarters or branches. Considering the disclosing included variables, it is evident that big Serbian polluters are not willing to disclose any negative information about their activities. This means that big Serbian polluting companies are aware of its legitimacy, but not on an adequate level.

Regarding the results of EDI, they are presented in the following table by the given sector affiliation.

Table 4. Average EDI value by sector affiliation

Sector Affiliation	Average EDI Score
Agricultural, forestry and fishing	0,11 (11%)
Mining	0,23 (23%)
Manufacturing	0,18 (18%)
Water supply; sewerage, waste management and remediation activities	0,085 (8,5%)
Administrative and service support activities	0,13 (13%)

When observing Table 4, our first impression is that all 69 sampled companies, classified in 5 sector affiliations, have a disclosure level of less than 30%, which is very low. At the same time, there are no big differences between industries, meaning that big polluters in Serbia treat environmental issues almost the same way. But it is important to note that we classified companies by sector affiliation, although not all companies have the same disclosure practice within one sector affiliation. Also, the sample is not balanced since not all sectors have the same or similar companies included. For instance, there are 53 companies from the manufacturing sector and only one from the administrative and service support activities. In that aspect, we wanted to explore the level of online environmental disclosure among companies included in the manufacturing sector, as the largest one. This is presented in the following table.

Table 5. EDI value among companies in the manufacturing sector

Industry	Number of Companies	EDI Value
Manufacture of food products	13	0,17 (17%)
Manufacture of beverages	3	0,27 (27%)
Manufacture of wood and of products of wood, cork, straw and plaiting materials, except furniture	1	0,07 (7%)
Manufacture of paper and paper products	3	0,24 (24%)
Printing and reproduction of recorded media	1	0.07 (7%)
Manufacture of coke and refined petroleum products	1	0.07 (7%)
Manufacture of chemicals and chemical products	9	0,19 (19%)
Manufacture of rubber and plastics products	1	0.47 (47%)
Manufacture of other non-metallic mineral products	10	0,19 (19%)
Manufacture of basic metals	7	0,16 (16%)
Manufacture of fabricated metal products, except machinery and equipment	2	0,1 (10%)
Manufacture of electrical equipment	1	0.13 (13%)
Manufacture of motor vehicles, trailers and semi-trailers	1	0.13 (13%)

As seen from Table 5, manufacturing rubber and plastics products has the highest disclosure, 47%. But we only have one company in this industry so we compared the manufacture of food, other non-metallic minerals, and other non-metallic mineral products as industries with almost the same number of companies included. The result shows that their online environmental disclosure is less than 20%.

Based on the above, we can conclude that all sampled companies are aware of their environmental effect, but the level of online environmental disclosure is very low, even in the manufacturing sector, the largest one. That means that stakeholders still don't have full access to all environmental activities by big Serbian polluters.

CONCLUSION

Climate changes and pollution have led to companies needing to be more responsible towards their stakeholders. This doesn't include only taking care of the company's profit but being more socially responsible, especially regarding the environment. In that aspect, environmental disclosure is a very good tool for the company to disclose its environmental activities, positive or negative, so that the public could be aware of its effect. Previously, environmental disclosure had a voluntary character, but in the last decade, it became mandatory in many countries. Companies in those countries must follow best practices regarding disclosure standards, guidelines, and frameworks. This is particularly the case in most developed countries. But in developing or transition countries, disclosure is still voluntary. In that aspect, our analysis focuses on the websites of 69 big Serbian polluters, classified into five affiliations sectors, to determine the level of online environmental disclosure since Serbia recently started implementing non-financial reporting in its legislation.

From the sample of 175 big polluters in Serbia in 2021, we included only 69 from the PRTR register, since 50 companies didn't have their website; 35 didn't disclose any environmental information on their website; 18 companies were public enterprises for communal works and 2 "mother companies" didn't have a website for a Serbian daughter company. Our focus is on online disclosure because, besides disclosing environmental activities by using integrated annual or sustainability reports, many companies can use their website that can reach more stakeholders and give updated information about the company's activities.

The results show that big Serbian polluters are still unaware of the importance of environmental disclosure in all affiliation sectors since the level of disclosure is less than 30%. At the same time, big Serbian polluters use three approaches to disclose their environmental activities on their websites. The mostly present include that companies disclose their environmental strategy in the section "About us" or the section called "Environment". The second approach gives special attention to sustainable development in terms that there is a special part of the site committed to sustainable activities. This practice is mainly related to those companies whose mother companies are MNCs. The third approach includes that sampled companies have their environmental policy in the section "Social responsibility," where they consider environmental activities as an integrated CSR part.

Regarding what big Serbian polluters disclose the most, it relates to environmental certification, environmental policy, and waste management and reduction, while the less informed variable relates to pollutant types and emissions. Only one company from the sample gave full disclosure on pollutants. Also, the results show that big polluters in Serbia are willing to disclose only positive environmental activities and results.

But just like every research, this one also has its limitations. Besides the website, we didn't analyze the company's annual and sustainable reports, which would undoubtedly affect the level of disclosure. Also, we focused only on 15 variables, while the index could include more or less.

ACKNOWLEDGMENT

This research was funded by the Ministry of Science, Technological Development and 408 Innovation of the Republic of Serbia under contract number 451-03-47/2023-01/200005.

REFERENCES

Acar, E., Tunca Çalıyurt, K., & Zengin-Karaibrahimoglu, Y. (2021). Does ownership type affect environmental disclosure? *International Journal of Climate Change Strategies and Management, 13*(2), 120–141. doi:10.1108/IJCCSM-02-2020-0016

Adams, C. A. (2002). Internal organisational factors influencing corporate social and ethical reporting: Beyond current theorising. *Accounting, Auditing & Accountability Journal, 15*(2), 223–250. doi:10.1108/09513570210418905

Adams, C. A., Hill, W., & Roberts, C. (1998). Corporate Social Reporting Practices in Western Europe: Legitimating Corporate Behaviour? *The British Accounting Review, 30*(1), 1–21. doi:10.1006/bare.1997.0060

Ahmad, A. (2012). Environmental Accounting and Reporting Practices: Significance and Issues: A Case from Bangladeshi Companies. *Global Journal of Management and Business Research, 12*(14).

Akhter, F., Hossain, M. M., Elrehail, H., Rehman, S. U., & Almansour, B. Y. (2022). Environmental disclosures and corporate attributes, from the lens of legitimacy theory: a longitudinal analysis on a developing country. *European Journal of Management and Business Economics*. doi:10.1108/EJMBE-01-2021-0008

Baalouch, F., Ayadi, S. D., & Hussainey, K. (2019). A study of the determinants of environmental disclosure quality: Evidence from French listed companies. *The Journal of Management and Governance, 23*(4), 939–971. doi:10.100710997-019-09474-0

Barnett, M. L. (2007). Tarred and untarred by the same brush: Exploring interdependence in the volatility of stock returns. *Corporate Reputation Review, 10*(1), 3–21. doi:10.1057/palgrave.crr.1550035

Bazhair, A. H., Khatib, S. F. A., & Al Amosh, H. (2022). Taking Stock of Carbon Disclosure Research While Looking to the Future: A Systematic Literature Review. *Sustainability (Basel), 14*(20), 13475. doi:10.3390u142013475

Carbon Majors Report, C. D. P. (2017). *Carbon Majors Report*. https://cdn.cdp.net/cdp-production/cms/reports/documents/000/002/327/original/Carbon-Majors-Report-2017.pdf?1501833772

Carnini Pulino, S., Ciaburri, M., Magnanelli, B. S., & Nasta, L. (2022). Does ESG Disclosure Influence Firm Performance? *Sustainability (Basel), 14*(13), 7595. doi:10.3390u14137595

Chaklader, B., & Gulati, P. A. (2015). A Study of Corporate Environmental Disclosure Practices of Companies Doing Business in India. *Global Business Review, 16*(2), 321–335. doi:10.1177/0972150914564430

Cormier, D., Ledoux, M. J., & Magnan, M. (2009). The use of Web sites as a disclosure platform for corporate performance. *International Journal of Accounting Information Systems, 10*(1), 1–24. doi:10.1016/j.accinf.2008.04.002

Deegan, C., Rankin, M., & Tobin, J. (2002). An examination of the corporate social and environmental disclosures of BHP from 1983–1997: A test of legitimacy theory. *Accounting, Auditing & Accountability Journal, 15*(3), 312–343. doi:10.1108/09513570210435861

Deegan, C., & Unerman, J. (2011). *Financial Accounting Theory*. McGraw-Hill Higher Education.

Doidge, C., Karolyi, G. A., & Stulz, R. M. (2007). Why do countries matter so much for corporate governance? *Journal of Financial Economics, 86*(1), 1–39. doi:10.1016/j.jfineco.2006.09.002

Elkington, J. (1998). Partnerships from Cannibals with Forks: The Triple Bottom Line of 21st- Century Business. *Environmental Quality Management, 8*(1), 37–51. doi:10.1002/tqem.3310080106

European Comission. (2022). *Corporate sustainability reporting*. https://finance.ec.europa.eu/capital-markets-union-and-financial-markets/company-reporting-and-auditing/company-reporting/corporate-sustainability-reporting_en

Farisyi, S., Musadieq, M. A., Utami, H. N., & Damayanti, C. R. (2022). A Systematic Literature Review: Determinants of Sustainability Reporting in Developing Countries. *Sustainability (Basel), 14*(16), 10222. doi:10.3390u141610222

Frooman, J. (1997). Socially Irresponsible and Illegal Behaviour and Shareholder Wealth: A Meta-Analysis of Event Studies. *Business & Society*, *36*, 221–249. doi:10.1177/000765039703600302

FrostT.TsangA.CaoH. (2022). Environmental, Social, and Governance (ESG) Disclosure: A Literature Review. *Social Science Research Network*. doi:10.2139/ssrn.4270942

Gajewski, J. F., & Li, L. (2015). Can Internet-based disclosure reduce information asymmetry? *Advances in Accounting*, *31*(1), 115–124. doi:10.1016/j.adiac.2015.03.013

Garcia, A. S., Mendes-Da-Silva, W., & Orsato, R. J. (2017). Sensitive industries produce better ESG performance: Evidence from emerging markets. *Journal of Cleaner Production*, *150*, 135–147. doi:10.1016/j.jclepro.2017.02.180

Gregory, A., Whittaker, J. M., & Yan, X. (2016). Corporate Social Performance, Competitive Advantage, Earnings Persistence and Firm Value. *Journal of Business Finance & Accounting*, *43*(1–2), 3–30. doi:10.1111/jbfa.12182

Hanić, A., Jovanović, O., & Stevanović, S. (2021). Environmental disclosure practice in the Serbian banking sector. *Management*, *26*(2), 115–144. doi:10.30924/mjcmi.26.2.7

Harrington, H. J. (1987). *The Improvement Process*. McGraw-Hill.

Hendriksen, E. S. (1982). *Accounting Theory*. Irwin International Accounting Standards.

Holub, J. M. (2003). Questioning Organizational Legitimacy: The Case of U.S. Expatriates. *Journal of Business Ethics*, *47*(3), 269–293. doi:10.1023/A:1026257229939

IFC. (2018). *Beyond the Balance Sheet*. https://www.ifc.org/wps/wcm/connect/d4bd76ad-ea04-4583-a54f-371b1a7e5cd0/Beyond_The_Balance_Sheet_IFC_Toolkit_for_Disclosure_Transparency.pdf?MOD=AJPERES&CVID=morp0vo

Ikram, M., Sroufe, R., Mohsin, M., Solangi, Y. A., Shah, S. Z. A., & Shahzad, F. (2019). Does CSR influence firm performance? A longitudinal study of SME sectors of Pakistan. *Journal of Global Responsibility*, *11*(1), 27–53. doi:10.1108/JGR-12-2018-0088

Isukul, A. C., & Chizea, J. J. (2017). Corporate Governance Disclosure in Developing Countries: A Comparative Analysis in Nigerian and South African Banks. *SAGE Open*, *7*(3), 215824401771911. doi:10.1177/2158244017719112

Joshi, P. L., Suwaidan, M. S., & Kumar, R. (2011). Determinants of environmental disclosures by Indian industrial listed companies: Empirical study. *International Journal of Accounting and Finance*, *3*(2), 109. doi:10.1504/IJAF.2011.043843

Kiliç, M. (2016). Online corporate social responsibility (CSR) disclosure in the banking industry. *International Journal of Bank Marketing*, *34*(4), 550–569. doi:10.1108/IJBM-04-2015-0060

Kojić, M., Schlüter, S., Mitić, P., & Hanić, A. (2022). Economy-environment nexus in developed European countries: Evidence from multifractal and wavelet analysis. *Chaos, Solitons, and Fractals*, *160*, 112189. doi:10.1016/j.chaos.2022.112189

KPMG. (2017). *KPMG International Survey of Corporate Responsibility*. KPMG.

KruegerP.SautnerZ.TangD. Y.ZhongR. (2021). The Effects of Mandatory ESG Disclosure around the World. *Social Science Research Network*. doi:10.2139/ssrn.3832745

Lambrechts, W., Son-Turan, S., Reis, L., & Semeijn, J. (2019). Lean, Green and Clean? Sustainability Reporting in the Logistics Sector. *Logistics*, *3*(1), 3. doi:10.3390/logistics3010003

Lipe, M. G. (2018). Unpacking the disclosure package: Using experiments to investigate investor reactions to narrative disclosures. *Accounting, Organizations and Society*, *68-69*, 15–20. doi:10.1016/j.aos.2018.05.001

Long, F., Chen, Q., Xu, L., Wang, J., & Vasa, L. (2022). Sustainable corporate environmental information disclosure: Evidence for green recovery from polluting firms of China. *Frontiers in Environmental Science*, *10*, 1019499. Advance online publication. doi:10.3389/fenvs.2022.1019499

Mahadeo, J. D., Oogarah-Hanuman, V., & Soobaroyen, T. (2011). Changes in social and environmental reporting practices in an emerging economy (2004–2007): Exploring the relevance of stakeholder and legitimacy theories. *Accounting Forum*, *35*(3), 158–175. doi:10.1016/j.accfor.2011.06.005

Mateo-Márquez, A. J., González-González, J. M., & Zamora-Ramírez, C. (2020b). The influence of countries' climate change-related institutional profile on voluntary environmental disclosures. *Business Strategy and the Environment*, *30*(2), 1357–1373. doi:10.1002/bse.2690

Mathews, M. (1997). Twenty-five years of social and environmental accounting research. *Accounting, Auditing & Accountability Journal*, *10*(4), 481–531. doi:10.1108/EUM0000000004417

Mijatović, I., Miladinović, S., & Stokić, D. (2015). Corporate Social Responsibility in Serbia:Between Corporate Philanthropy and Standards. In Corporate Social Responsibility in Finland: From Local Movements to Global Responsibility (pp. 333-350). Academic Press.

Mijoković, M., Knezevic, G., & Mizdraković, V. (2020). Analysing the link between csr reporting and financial performance variables of Belgrade stock exchange companies. *Teme*, *1369*, 1369. Advance online publication. doi:10.22190/TEME190513081M

Mitić, P., Fedajev, A., Radulescu, M., & Rehman, A. (2023a). The relationship between CO2 emissions, economic growth, available energy, and employment in SEE countries. *Environmental Science and Pollution Research International*, *30*(6), 16140–16155. doi:10.100711356-022-23356-3 PMID:36175729

Mitić, P., Hanić, A., Kojić, M., & Schlüter, S. (2023b). Environment and Economy Interactions in the Western Balkans: Current Situation and Prospects. In T. Tufek-Memišević, M. Arslanagić-Kalajdžić, & N. Ademović (Eds.), *Interdisciplinary Advances in Sustainable Development. ICSD 2022. Lecture Notes in Networks and Systems* (Vol. 529). Springer. doi:10.1007/978-3-031-17767-5_1

Neuendorf, K. A. (2002). The Content Analysis Guidebook. *Sage (Atlanta, Ga.)*.

Nobanee, H., & Ellili, N. (2016). Corporate sustainability disclosure in annual reports: Evidence from UAE banks: Islamic versus conventional. *Renewable & Sustainable Energy Reviews*, *55*, 1336–1341. doi:10.1016/j.rser.2015.07.084

Orazalin, N., & Mahmood, M. (2019). The financial crisis as a wake-up call: Corporate governance and bank performance in an emerging economy. *Corporate Governance (Bradford)*, *19*(1), 80–101. doi:10.1108/CG-02-2018-0080

Osobajo, O. A., Oke, A., Lawani, A., Omotayo, T. S., Ndubuka-McCallum, N., & Obi, L. (2022). Providing a Roadmap for Future Research Agenda: A Bibliometric Literature Review of Sustainability Performance Reporting (SPR). *Sustainability (Basel)*, *14*(14), 8523. doi:10.3390u14148523

Palazzo, G., & Scherer, A. G. (2006). Corporate Legitimacy as Deliberation: A Communicative Framework. *Journal of Business Ethics*, *66*(1), 71–88. doi:10.100710551-006-9044-2

Pan, D., Fan, W., & Kong, F. (2022). Dose environmental information disclosure raise public environmental concern? Generalized propensity score evidence from China. *Journal of Cleaner Production*, *379*, 134640. doi:10.1016/j.jclepro.2022.134640

Panwar, R., Paul, K., Nybakk, E., Hansen, E., & Thompson, D. P. (2014). The Legitimacy of CSR Actions of Publicly Traded Companies Versus Family-Owned Companies. *Journal of Business Ethics*, *125*(3), 481–496. doi:10.100710551-013-1933-6

Park, S. R., & Jang, J. Y. (2021). The Impact of ESG Management on Investment Decision: Institutional Investors' Perceptions of Country-Specific ESG Criteria. *International Journal of Financial Studies*, *9*(3). doi:10.1016/0361-3682(92)90042-Q

Patten, D. M. (1992). Intra-industry environmental disclosures in response to the Alaskan oil spill: A note on legitimacy theory. *Accounting, Organizations and Society*, *17*(5), 471–475. doi:10.1016/0361-3682(92)90042-Q

Ramanathan, K. V. (1976). Toward a theory of corporate social accounting. *The Accounting Review*, *51*(3), 516–528.

Rosa Portella, A., & Borba, J. A. (2020). Environmental disclosure in corporate websites: A study in Brazil and USA companies. *RAUSP Management Journal*, *55*(3), 309–324. doi:10.1108/RAUSP-07-2018-0053

Seo, H. (2021). Peer effects in corporate disclosure decisions. *Journal of Accounting and Economics*, *71*(1), 101364. doi:10.1016/j.jacceco.2020.101364

Smith, N. C. (2003). Corporate social responsibility: Whether or how? *California Management Review*, *45*(4), 52–76. doi:10.2307/41166188

Sobhani, F. A., Amran, A., & Zainuddin, Y. (2012). Sustainability disclosure in annual reports and websites: A study of the banking industry in Bangladesh. *Journal of Cleaner Production*, *23*(1), 75–85. doi:10.1016/j.jclepro.2011.09.023

Stemler, S. (2001). An Overview of Content Analysis. *Practical Assessment, Research & Evaluation*, *7*(17), 17. doi:10.7275/z6fm-2e34

Stevanović, S. (2018). Izveštavanje o zagađenju životne sredine: praksa velikih zagađivača i preduzeća u Novom Sadu. In *Pravni i ekonomski aspekti primene principa zagađivač plaća*. Institute of Economic Sciences.

Stevanović, S., Belopavlović, G., Lazarević-Moravčević, M. (2014). Obelodanjivanje informacija o zaštiti životne sredine: praksa u Srbiji. *Ecologica: nauka, privreda, iskustva, 21*(76), 679-683.

Stojanović-Blab, M., Blab, D., & Spasić, D. (2017). Sustainability reporting - a challenge for Serbian companies/Извештавање о одрживом пословању – изазов за српске компаније. *Teme, 1349*, 1349. Advance online publication. doi:10.22190/TEME1604349S

Stolowy, H., & Paugam, L. (2018). *The expansion of non-financial reporting: An exploratory study.* HEC Paris Research Paper No. ACC-2018-1262, 1-35.

Suchman, M. C. (1995). Managing Legitimacy: Strategic and Institutional Approaches. *Academy of Management Review, 20*(3), 571–610. doi:10.2307/258788

The KPMG. (2020). *Survey of Sustainability Reporting 2020.* https://kpmg.com/xx/en/home/insights/2020/11/the-time-has-come-survey-of-sustainability-reporting.html

Thimm, H., & Rasmussen, K. B. (2020). Website disclosure of environmental compliance management—The case of European production companies. *Journal of Environmental Studies and Sciences, 11*(4), 648–670. doi:10.100713412-020-00643-4

Ugur, K., & Erdogan, Y.H. (2007). *Remembering Thirty-five Years of Social Accounting: A Review of the Literature and the Practice.* MPRA Paper No. 3454.

Ullmann, A. E. (1976). The corporate environmental accounting system: A management tool for fighting environmental degradation. *Accounting, Organizations and Society, 1*(1), 71–79. doi:10.1016/0361-3682(76)90008-8

Unerman, J. (2003). Enhancing Organizational Global Hegemony with Narrative Accounting Disclosures: An Early Example. *Accounting Forum, 27*(4), 425–448. doi:10.1046/j.1467-6303.2003.t01-1-00113.x

UNESCO. (2022). *Disclosure, Digitalization, Decarbonization are the three important dimensions of carbon neutrality" asserted at the COP27 side-event.* https://www.unesco.org/en/articles/disclosure-digitalization-decarbonization-are-three-important-dimensions-carbon-neutrality-asserted

Videnović, S. D., Hanić, A., & Sućeska, A. (2021). Ethically relevant values and behavior of employees in Serbia during the Covid-19. *TM. Technisches Messen.* Advance online publication. doi:10.22190/teme200901023v

Warren, R. C. (2003). The evolution of business legitimacy. *European Business Review, 15*(3), 153–163. doi:10.1108/09555340310474659

Chapter 10

How a Smart, Green, Balanced Scorecard System Enhances Digital, Environmental, Social, and Governance Performance
Insight Into the Mediating Role of the Effectiveness of Sustainability Accounting Information Systems

Huy Quang Pham
https://orcid.org/0000-0002-5722-3462
University of Economics, Ho Chi Minh City, Vietnam

Phuc Kien Vu
https://orcid.org/0000-0002-5372-0517
University of Economics, Ho Chi Minh City, Vietnam

ABSTRACT

This research aims at exploring the interconnection between smart green balanced scorecard system (SGBSC) and digital environment, society, and governance performance (DESGP). Alternatively, it investigates how the effectiveness of sustainability accounting information system (ESAIS) induces a mediating impact on SGBSC and DESGP. The empirical portion of this study is based on statistical information gathered from a survey given to a cross-sectional sample of 883 SMEs in developing country. The findings from the structural equation modeling approach demonstrate that greater SGBSC implementation can result in higher DESGP. This interconnection is also partially mediated by ESAIS concurrently. The observations may provide practitioners and policymakers with fresher perspectives to develop focused strategies for SGBSC application and sustainability accounting information system implementation, which can ultimately result in beneficial outcomes in DESG establishment and operationalization.

DOI: 10.4018/978-1-6684-9076-1.ch010

1. INTRODUCTION

The "Brundtland Report" (Brundtland, 1987), which put forth the idea of sustainable development, was published by the United Nations Commission on Environment and Development in response to the rise of these problems. Since its release, the Brundtland report has engendered an enormous impact on sustainable development (Phillips, 2023). For the benefit of future generations, the Brundtland report emphasizes the importance of development options that satisfy current needs without endangering the environment (Brundtland, 1987). To put it more specifically, the report is successful in highlighting environmental issues as a key component of governmental initiatives (Gomes et al., 2023). In order to lessen the pressure society puts on the environment, businesses are stated to have a significant role in regulating the impact of population on ecosystems, resources, food security, and sustainable economies (Pazienza et al., 2022). Due to severe climate change, the depletion of natural resources, unfavorable working conditions, the escalating number of corporate scandals (Zhu & Huang, 2023), COVID-19, and global conflicts (Garel & Petit-Romec, 2021) the public's demand for businesses to be environmentally, socially, and ethically responsible has increased. Corporate social responsibility and sustainability are receiving more attention from customers and investors (Zhu & Huang, 2023). Businesses are likewise investigating better moral and environmentally friendly ways to conduct their business (Chen & Xie, 2022). Investors and fund companies increasingly take environmental, social, and governance (ESG) performance into account in addition to financial performance as part of a sustainable finance strategy (Friede et al., 2015). This implies that businesses in which investors participate are expected to be not only financially successful but also environmentally and socially conscious (Tsang et al., 2023). As a result, companies worldwide are aggressively implementing ESG management (Niu et al., 2022). Due to the advancement of economic, sociological, scientific, and technological knowledge, humans have achieved tremendous things (Eccles & Viviers, 2011). The COVID-19 pandemic, on the other hand, is accelerating the adoption of digital technologies in fields including the environment (Niu et al., 2022). Through the use of digital platforms, businesses may now execute and promote their good ESG practices (Puriwat & Tripopsakul, 2022). While the academic notes have reached the consensus on the significant and positive influence of digital transformation on ESG enhancement (Fu & Li, 2023; Lu et al., 2023; Wang & Esperança, 2023; Kwilinski et al., 2023; Su et al., 2023; Zhong et al., 2023) and Huang et al. (2023) advocate that digital innovation induces a substantial and positive effect on the performance of ESG, Fang et al. (2023) argue that digitization helps businesses improve goodwill and further boost social scores as well as lowering agency costs and raising governance scores. However, there is no evidence to support the claim that digitization raises businesses' environmental rankings. Against this backdrop, businesses need to proactively take these developments into account in order to adapt to the ongoing changes brought on by digitization and meet their obligations to a range of stakeholders (Khattak & Yousaf, 2021). Businesses today work to put digital projects into practice within the context of the corporate environment that has been digitalized and declare in their strategic planning their intentions towards the environment, society, and governance in relation to these varied digitalization agendas (Puriwat & Tripopsakul, 2022). In this way, a business uses digital technology to communicate with a variety of stakeholders and gives digital ESG top priority in its strategic planning (Puriwat & Tripopsakul, 2022).

According to Jassem et al. (2022), organizations need to implement strategic performance measuring methods if they wish to simultaneously improve their economy, environment, and society performance and therefore significantly advance sustainability. Scholars have so noted that there are many points of view in the presentation of reports as a result of the numerous definitions of sustainable performance that are feasible. In order to successfully assist corporate strategic decision-making and control procedures, they have suggested that the balanced scorecard (BSC) can be employed as a performance measuring technique, combining environmental and societal issues into major management systems (Groot & Selto, 2013). The sustainability BSC, according to Erokhina (2022), is a state-of-the-art management tool that companies use to successfully traverse the complex trends and requirements in the environment, society, and governance. While a huge body of literature has witnessed numerous academic works focused on BSC, the design and benefits of information technology (IT) BSC, the exploration on green IT BSC (i.e., Wati and Koo (2011); Maccani (2011)) and digital BSC (i.e., Fabac (2022)) has been still on the nascent stage. According to Perifanis and Kitsios (2023), integrating artificial intelligence (AI) into business and IT strategy can help firms create new business models and competitive advantages. Leading companies have recently begun investigating how AI might be incorporated into their BSC structure to enhance performance metrics and decision-making procedures. This is how AI might be introduced into each viewpoint to assist an organization better execute its strategy. In order to respond to the ongoing changes brought on by the digital revolution and meet their obligations to a range of stakeholders, businesses must proactively take into account the integration of AI into the green sustainability BSC. The smart green BSC (SGBSC) has been created in this way throughout time. Despite the BSC's continuous acceptance, there is conflicting empirical evidence regarding its efficacy, and it is unknown how much adopting the BSC will ultimately affect firm performance (Tawse & Tabesh, 2023) and digital ESG performance (DESGP).

More significantly, since the sustainable development goals call for corporate entities to implement environmental and social sustainability accounting practices in an effort to achieve sustainable development (Tauringana, 2020), many businesses regularly create and implement management and accounting strategies that are socially and environmentally responsible in order to further their sustainability goals (Soderstrom et al., 2017). Because it ensures business growth, sustainability, and greater prospects for participating in the global market, the effectiveness of sustainability accounting information system (ESAIS) is crucial. The BSC is one of the tools employed that has an impact on ESAIS. The results of ALmashkor (2020) reported a relationship between environmental management accounting and BSC methodologies.

In this inspiring venue, understanding SGBSC's position as an enabler in an organization's success in implementing digital ESG seems to constitute a significant theme for contributions. Another intriguing question is whether or not ESAIS or some other mediating component is required for the relationship between SGBSC architecture and DESGP. Starting with these ideas, a study of how SGBSC can improve DESGP through ESAIS serves as the primary driving force for this research and highlighted opportunities for theoretical and practical contributions. Intriguing research issues like the following are motivated by this theoretical gap.

RQ1. What is the impact of SGBSC on DESGP?

RQ2. Does ESAIS serve as a partial mediator on the interconnection between SGBSC and DESGP?

The current study provides contributions for the academic and practitioner communities by filling several gaps based on the examination of the overall findings and key insights. Although digital ESG has been considered as an advanced paradigm, startlingly, little has been known in the literature about the development of digital ESG (Puriwat & Tripopsakul, 2022). As such, the findings of this research thus contribute to the literature on ESG and digital transformation in SMEs. Additionally, the current research contributes to the field through providing fresh understandings on the interconnection between SGBSC and DESGP for pursuing this line of inquiry together with vigorous empirical evidence. In doing so, the current research also broadens the sparse literature on green IT BSC implementation in developing country. Remarkably, the current research is novel as it explicitly positioned to enrich the state-of-the-art research on the role of ESAIS in the interconnection between SGBSC and DESGP. Based on the proposal of Mathuva et al. (2017), in an emerging subject called sustainability accounting practices, data about an organization's environmental, social, and economic activities are identified, gathered, analyzed, and reported. Implementing sustainability accounting techniques aids in planning, managing, and making decisions related to an organization's sustainability efforts (Iredele, 2020).

Building on the suggestion of Puriwat and Tripopsakul (2022), businesses can change their emphasis to become more catastrophe-resistant by using the lessons acquired from the COVID-19 pandemic. By concentrating on solutions to social and environmental concerns rather than the typical firm operating outlook, forward-thinking organizations are creating a compass to better respond to upcoming crises and navigate through instability (dos Santos & Pereira, 2022). In the past few decades, stakeholder pressure has forced companies to make changes to lessen their impact on the environment, raise the value of their employees, diversify their partnerships, and maintain their profitability. Investors must find the right balance between an asset's risk and return before making a choice (Puriwat & Tripopsakul, 2022). As such, the managerial contribution of this manuscript is illustrated by the determination of potential prospects for managers interested in digital ESG implementation. The statistical study specifically highlights the urgent need for digital ESG implementation and the possible advantages associated with the adoption of SGBSC. As a result, the managers of small and medium enterprises (SMEs) will become more committed to ESG and increase their efforts to implement SGBSC, which will help them reach DESGP. The statistical analyses reveal that paying significantly more attention to sustainability accounting practices will give these managers a better chance of successfully boosting DESGP through SGBSC adoption.

In order to achieve the above-mentioned study objectives, the current manuscript is divided into the following sections. The pertinent literature review is presented in Section 2 and is divided into three sub-sections. Application of theoretical lenses is covered in the first sub-sections. The study's hypotheses are outlined in the third sub-sections after a brief examination of conceptual aspects in the second sub-sections. Section 3 describes the study methodologies and resources using these ideas as a framework. After that, Section 4 elaborates and analyzes the study analysis, and Section 5 highlights the implications for management before highlighting constraints and making recommendations for future research.

2. LITERATURE REVIEW

2.1. Theoretical Lenses Application

Contingency theory (CT). CT was developed by scholars at Ohio State University in 1950 (Nohria & Khurana, 2010), and because its concepts are deeply ingrained in organizational literature (Sauser et al., 2009), it has been employed in studies focusing on organizational challenges. According to Munyon et al. (2019), the organization's productivity strongly depended on how effectively the many sources of environmental volatility, technology, organizational scale, organizational structure quirks, and organizational information systems fitted together or matched. As technology was regarded to make a significant contribution to the variances in such organizational qualities (Woodward, 1958), formal structures were often conglomerated or well-accorded with the employment of various technologies according to the contingency aspect (Nohria & Khurana, 2010). CT has been utilized successfully to explain the contingency of "balanced" performance measures (such as BSC) and has been the inspiration for a considerable amount of empirical research on performance measurement (Lucianetti et al., 2018). Alternately, CT can be used to explain how the sustainability accounting information system was implemented (Dagiliene & Šutiene, 2019).

Stakeholder theory (ST). ST underwent a protracted development process thanks to the contributions of many scholars after it was first established by Freeman (1984). The achievement of stakeholder interests is specifically recommended as one of a firm's key aims, building on the viewpoints of ST (Freeman, 1999). Due to the ST's significant emphasis on business ethics and social responsibility (Chen & Xie, 2022), ESG performance obligations are therefore established (Belyaeva et al., 2020). According to Kim et al. (2022), ESG is viewed as a corporate strategy that strives to cultivate symbiotic connections with a number of stakeholders. This will aid enterprises in growing and maintaining their operations over the long run. In order to ensure that businesses have the resources they need to continue operating, it is crucial to manage stakeholder expectations, according to the ST. The employment of an internal management tool that emphasizes methods for non-financial purposes, such as trying to improve social welfare and the environment, is encouraged by the ST. Due to sound management techniques, such governance approaches that maximize value can also take into account shareholder values (Lee & Isa, 2023). As stakeholders pay more attention to corporate behavior during a crisis as they increase pressure on businesses to take more voluntary action in response to the demand for environmental and social activities, ST may thus offer a logical justification for findings by illuminating organizational responses to stakeholders' increasing concerns on sustainability (Al Amosh & Khatib, 2023).

2.2. Conceptual Respects

Digital environmental, social, and governance performance. ESG, which stands for "environment, social, and governance," is a measure of a company's non-financial performance (Galbreath, 2013). ESG values have their roots in the idea of socially responsible investing from the 1960s (Zhu & Huang, 2023). As a strategy for sustainable development, the United Nations launched ESG in 2004 (Hamzah et al., 2023) with the goal of further enhancing sustainability in the modern corporate environment. The ESG concept puts forth requirements for the strategic objectives of businesses in three areas, including corporate governance, social responsibility, and environmental responsibility. This concept has grown to be a crucial indicator that is generally accepted by all nations to measure the sustainable development of businesses under the green development model (Munoz-Torres et al., 2019; Wang & Sun, 2022). In academic circles, there is no agreement on the notion of digital transformation (Peng & Tao, 2022). The various traits of digital transformation are highlighted by these definitions (Vial, 2019). Digital transformation is the stage of an organization's journey toward digitalization that is the most prevalent (Melo et al., 2023). The definition of digital transformation used in this work is based on an idea from Verhoef et al. (2021). Consequently, digital transformation refers to the process through which a company uses digital technology to establish a new digital business model that enables the firm to generate and capture greater value (Verhoef et al., 2021). This definition clears up the ambiguity around the terms namely digital transformation, digitization, and digitalization in the literature and enables us to understand the phenomenon in a holistic context (Mergel et al. 2019). The adoption of digital technologies and their capacity to influence ESG goals are converging more and more as both seek to meet shifting stakeholder expectations as well as the effects of new business and operating models on society and the environment (Puriwat & Tripopsakul, 2022).

Effectiveness of sustainability accounting information system. According to Schaltegger and Buritt (2010), sustainability accounting is a broad concept that unifies the three pillars of the environment, society, and the economy. The sustainability accounting information system can be pondered a process for acquiring, analyzing, and communicating information about sustainability as well as methods for making decisions. (Dagiliene & Šutiene, 2019). According to Tran and Herzig (2023) sustainability accounting is connected to the linkages between accounting and sustainability, which refers to several dimensions (economy, environment, and society) and their dynamic relationships. The information gathered through sustainable accounting may be used for a variety of things. Companies can show external actors their status and level of maturity with relation to environmental and social values by gathering these data (Lee & Hutchison, 2005). Internal operational decisions can be adjusted based on sustainable accounting data to focus on sustainability goals such as maintenance, re-use, and remanufacturing as well as recycling goals such as lowering material consumption, reducing greenhouse gas emissions, and reducing waste (Burritt & Christ, 2016). A corporation can make decisions toward sustainable business models thanks to the data's significant input into its strategy process (Baines & Lightfoot, 2013; Kamp & Parry, 2017; Bressanelli et al., 2018). In this sense, the sustainability accounting information system can be deemed effective if its information quality, system quality, and cooperation quality are all deemed to be effective.

Smart green balanced scorecard. The BSC was first founded in 1992 and considered as a tool to help managers gain a better understanding of how well their organizations are performing (Tawse & Tabesh, 2023). Kaplan and Norton introduced the BSC as a multifunctional management tool that improved the efficiency of strategy execution and offered a more valuable, timely, and nuanced evaluation of business performance in two seminal articles published in 1996 (Kaplan & Norton, 1996a; 1996b). Since then, the BSC has been praised as a very effective management tool that is widely applied (Olson & Slater, 2002) and has been thoroughly investigated in a range of research and business contexts (Elbanna et al., 2022). Over half of the major firms in the United States, Europe, and Asia employ the balanced scorecard, making it one of the most important business concepts in the last 75 years. Since BSC was first introduced, the instrument has experienced a substantial evolution that has been influenced by a number of external influences, including the information technology (IT) environment (Cram, 2007). Some academics (i.e., Martinsons et al. (1999); Van Grembergen (2000)) have already studied the use of a BSC in IT functions and related procedures. Some IT scorecards, such those from Chand (2005), Rosemann and Wiese (1999), and Rosemann (2001), have used the IT BSC as their base. While a huge body of literature has witnessed numerous academic works focused on BSC, the design and benefits of IT BSC, the exploration on green IT BSC (i.e., Wati and Koo (2011); Maccani (2011)) and digital BSC (i.e., Fabac (2022)) has been still on the nascent stage. According to Borges et al. (2021), Johnson et al. (2022), Werle and Laumer (2022), there is a vast opportunity space for AI in disruptive firms at all levels, including operational and strategic levels that contribute to competitive advantage. In the current research, the SGBSC is formulated from fusing AI with green sustainability BSC.

2.3. Hypotheses Formulation

The BSC is a strategic management technique that enables an organization to keep all those measurements that indicate the essential factors for conducting business under control and linked. Additionally, it allows for the translation of organizational strategy through a set of action indicators that are consistent, which, when combined with other management tools, identifies intangible assets as a new key actor in the information age. As a result, BSC enables business units to be measured in a way that adds value to clients while also taking into account the potentialization of internal capacities, such as investments in people, systems, and processes that provide the foundation for improving the performance and long-term viability of business organizations (Vladimir et al., 2020). According to Quesado et al. (2018), the BSC acts as a forum for discussing strategic objectives as well as a data source for modifying and refining organizational plans. Nevertheless, the conventional BSC needs to be modified to account for the changing business environment because sustainability problems are not included in it (Jassem et al., 2022).

The sustainability BSC, a multi-dimensional performance evaluation and management control tool, is generating more study interest as it has the potential to be crucial for business sustainability (Hansen & Schaltegger, 2018). According to published research, the sustainability BSC may be a practical tool for meeting a variety of management requirements related to corporate sustainability issues, including helping businesses implement sustainable strategies, fostering sustainability management standards and decision-making, supporting regulatory data requirements, and satisfying stakeholders' information needs (Schaltegger & Wagner, 2006). Indeed, the sustainability BSC is a potential framework for fusing strategy with sustainability in firms (Hansen & Schaltegger, 2016).

The sustainability BSC, according to Erokhina (2022), is a state-of-the-art management tool that companies use to successfully traverse the complex trends and requirements in the ESG. While Wang et al. (2022) create the green sustainability BSC to investigate how businesses in Taiwan's LNG industry apply environmentally friendly practices to achieve green sustainability, in order to generate a competitive advantage, Wati and Koo (2011) developed the green IT BSC as a nomological management tool to systematically align IT strategy with business strategy from a perspective of environmental sustainability. In this regard, the objectives of the green IT BSC include evaluating technological performance while effectively integrating environmental factors, investigating both the tangible and intangible assets of green IT investments, coordinating IT performance and business performance, and turning the results into competitive advantage (Wati & Koo, 2011).

According to Borges et al. (2021), Johnson et al. (2022), Werle and Laumer (2022), there is a vast opportunity space for AI in disruptive firms at all levels, including operational and strategic levels that contribute to competitive advantage. By incorporating AI into green BSC, SGBSC will become a useful tool that includes the quantitative foundation for expectations of ESG goals and objectives, the comprehensiveness of planned activities, the prioritization of strategy and the detailed decomposition of strategy, a normative approach, a focus on barriers and success factors, guiding measures, agility, and all of the above. As such, the implementation of SGBSC can enable SMEs to control and address numerous environmental and social matters to reach ESG goals. In light of the analyses discussed above, the following was proposed as the first hypothesis for this study.

Hypothesis 1 (H1). *SGBSC has engendered an influence on DESGP in a significant and positive manner*

According to Tiwari and Khan (2020), sustainable accounting and reporting is a framework for identifying sustainability variables based on the triple bottom line model, defining and executing measurement procedures, and reporting the actual status of the variables in a company's public reports. The triple bottom line concept is incorporated into the framework for sustainability accounting and reporting. However, it has been challenging for the industries to build accurate and reliable measuring methodologies for these variables (Burritt & Christ, 2016; Stock & Seliger, 2016). Based on the perspectives of Burritt and Christ (2016), businesses could not have the technology necessary to gather accurate and timely data, which could damage the reputation of environmental efforts and leave room for charges of "greenwashing" (Hsu et al., 2013; Pei-yi Yu et al., 2020; Pimonenko et al., 2020). Additionally, businesses want more comprehensive information and better information technology (Burritt & Christ, 2016). In a similar line, sustainability accounting practices mandate the use of cutting-edge information technology to complement the organization's overall competitive strategy (Maelah et al., 2017).

AI has had a significant impact on the development of modern business (Haenlein & Kaplan, 2019) and the accounting profession (Johnson et al., 2021; Petkov, 2020; Warren et al., 2015). Companies increasingly acquire and store massive amounts and a wide variety of data due to improvements in data collection technology and a significant decrease in storage costs (Dai & Vasarhelyi, 2016). The need for technology like AI that can conduct efficient and effective analyses has been sparked by the growing availability of data. In order to do certain tasks, AI makes use of machines to analyze and learn from data (Kaplan & Haenlein, 2019). With the aid of AI, management accountants can perform complex analyses in order to enhance corporate performance measurement (Appelbaum et al., 2017), create efficient management control systems (Warren et al., 2015), and enhance the standard of managerial accounting (Chen et al., 2021).

As the results of ALmashkor (2020) reported a relationship between environmental management accounting and balanced scorecard methodologies, the integration of AI into green BSC will transform SGBSC into a useful tool for ESAIS enhancement. In light of the analyses discussed above, the following was proposed as the second hypothesis for this study.

Hypothesis 2 (H2). *SGBSC has engendered an influence on ESAIS in a significant and positive manner*

According to Mathuva et al. (2017), the discipline of sustainability accounting techniques promotes the identification, collecting, analysis, and reporting of data related to an organization's environmental, social, and economic activities. As appropriate information is provided by sustainability accounting methods, this aids organizations in achieving their sustainable goals (Cadez & Guilding, 2012; Oyewo et al., 2023). Alternatively, implementation of sustainability accounting facilitates planning, controlling, and decision-making with regard to an organization's sustainability endeavors (Iredele, 2020). Internal operational decisions can be adjusted based on sustainable accounting data to focus on sustainability goals such as maintenance, re-use, and remanufacturing as well as recycling goals such as lowering material consumption, reducing greenhouse gas emissions, and reducing waste (Burritt & Christ, 2016). A corporation can make decisions toward sustainable business models thanks to the data's significant input into its strategy process (Baines & Lightfoot, 2013; Kamp & Parry, 2017; Bressanelli et al., 2018). In this regard, ESAIS may help SMEs in this area by enhancing the management and operation of environmental departments, fostering the wise exploitation of natural resources, minimizing environmental harm, and assisting in the achievement of sustainable development. In light of the analyses discussed above, the following was proposed as the third hypothesis for this study.

Hypothesis 3 (H3). *ESAIS has engendered an influence on DESGP in a significant and positive manner*

The study model is shown in Figure 1 based on the conversation that has already taken place. It displays the suggested connections between SGBSC, DESGM, and ESAIS.

Figure 1. Hypothesized model

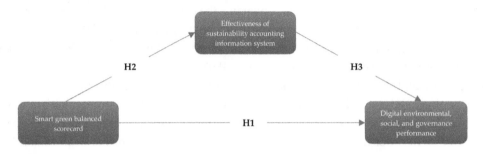

3. METHODOLOGY OVERVIEW AND JUSTIFICATION

3.1. Operationalization of Hypothesized Construct

In this study, self-administered closed-ended structured questionnaire is used to collect research data. The constructs in this research were quantified by pre-validated scales that had been examined for reliability and validity in the given context. Since the scales were developed from works of English literature, back translation was carried out to ensure conceptual equivalency (Cai et al., 2010). To put it more specifically, an expert later set up and translated the English version into Vietnamese. To check the accuracy of the translation, a back-translated English version was created by another expert and compared with the original English version.

In order to reduce unexpected complexity because the questionnaire for this study was established in many contexts, both culturally and environmentally, a pretest with eight experts was initially conducted. The constructs were changed to remove unclear measuring items based on the feedback of experts. A pilot study with 30 respondents with traits similar to those of the survey population was conducted to assess the questionnaire in order to maintain the inputs' corroboration. Subsequently, the questionnaire was altered and rewritten.

Digital environmental, social, and governance performance. The first construct of DESGP comprised of 3 components namely Digital environmental performance, Digital social performance and Digital governance performance stemmed from the contributions of Moisescu (2015); Maignan (2001); Salmones et al. (2005); Mohr and Webb (2005); Becker-Olsen et al. (2011); Wagner et al. (2008); Turker (2008); Öberseder et al. (2014); Pérez and Rodríguez del Bosque (2013); Mandhachitara and Poolthong (2011), Puriwat and Tripopsakul (2022) and were examined by small-scale pilot test.

Effectiveness of sustainability accounting information system. The first construct of ESAIS comprised of 3 components namely Collaboration quality, Information quality, System quality. More concretely, the measurement scale for Collaboration quality was stemmed from the contributions of Urbach et al. (2010) and were examined by small-scale pilot test. The measurement scale for Information quality and System quality was derived from the contributions of Ifinedo et al. (2010) and were examined by small-scale pilot test.

Smart green balanced scorecard. The first construct of SGBSC comprised of 4 ingredients namely Economic object, Societal object, Green operational object, Environmental object which was stemmed from the combination of the contributions of Wang et al (2022), Wati and Koo (2011) as well as the findings of Upadhyay et al. (2023), Perifanis and Kitsios (2023).

3.2. Sample Design and Data Collection

To represent the research population and gather the essential primary data, the production enterprise was chosen as the target. In the meanwhile, the participants were accountants in this type of company. The COVID-19 circumstance resulted in the selection of Vietnam as the geographic location for data collection. During COVID-19, the majority of SMEs in Vietnam began to take ESG into account, and the researcher took use of this development to create a research report.

The researchers requested permission from the senior management of those organizations to gather the contact information of employees before inviting them to take part in the study. After acquiring their informed consent from participants, the questionnaires were distributed in person to participants by the researchers. In doing so, researchers would have the chance to inform participants about the proper way to complete questionnaires, decrease the common method variance, and inform them about the anonymity and confidentiality of the study's findings. Participants are promised secrecy and anonymity and they can withdraw freely from the investigation at any time and for any reason.

The sample for this study was formulated via convenience and snowball sampling due to time and budget restrictions on the investigation. The sample size is thought to be 10 times the number of structural paths to the dependent variables and increasing the sample size is crucial for enhancing the model's dependability (Hair et al., 2021).

Data collecting started in the first week of June 2022 and continued through the second week of March 2023. The researcher takes every effort to protect the data. With an 80.23 percent response rate, 883 valid questionnaires were collected. Since the study's valid sample size of 883 exceeds the number specified by Hair et al. (2021), the sample size is sufficient for developing SEM, and larger sample sizes improve and increase the reliability and generalization of the results obtained (Iacobucci, 2010). A thorough summary of the demographic information gathered throughout the survey is provided in **Table 1**.

Table 1. Demographic characteristics of survey respondents

Item	Contents	Frequency	Valid (%)
Gender			
	Male	528	59.80
	Female	355	40.20
Age (years)			
	25 - Under 35	217	24.58
	35 - Under 45	437	49.49
	45 - Under 55	229	25.93
Education			
	Undergraduate	794	89.92
	Postgraduate	89	10.08
Experience (years)			
	Under 10	95	10.76
	10 - Under 20	559	63.31
	20- Under 30	229	25.93
Firm industry			
	Agrochemicals	25	2.83
	Clothes and accessories	32	3.62
	Electronic components	28	3.17
	Food and beverages	644	72.93
	Footwear	15	1.70
	Furniture	27	3.06
	Pharmaceuticals	12	1.36
	Rubber and plastics	26	2.94
	Stationery	35	3.96
	Textiles	21	2.38
	Watches and clocks	18	2.04

3.3. Data Analysis Techniques

Following several basic descriptive analyses with IBM SPSS Statistics 28, PLS-SEM with SmartPLS 4.0.8.5 was carried out. It was suited for the goals of this research because PLS-SEM is frequently linked to the investigation and advancement of theory. As such, the two-step technique, which involved evaluating the measurement model and the structural model, was used to evaluate and interpret the data (Hair et al., 2022).

4. RESULTS AND ELUCIDATION ANALYTICAL OBSERVATIONS

4.1. Measurement Model

Content validity. According to cross-loading, which was used to assess content validity, the questionnaire items' meanings were identical to those incorporated into specific concepts by Ur Rehman et al. (2019). In order to do this, a construct's value required to be greater than that of the other constructs in the same rows and columns (Hair et al., 2010). On the basis of the values for all assessed constructs shown in **Table 2**, it is possible to conclude that the measurement scale used in this study achieved complete content validity.

Table 2. Results summary for the content validity

	CQ	DEP	DGP	IQ	DSP	ENO	EO	GOO	SO	SQ
CQ1	0.856	0.128	0.085	0.268	0.073	-0.034	0.025	0.043	0.003	-0.023
CQ2	0.780	0.133	0.121	0.210	0.119	-0.048	0.088	0.051	-0.023	0.038
CQ3	0.912	0.165	0.085	0.286	0.115	-0.030	0.052	0.064	0.039	0.003
CQ4	0.849	0.164	0.089	0.285	0.142	-0.027	0.030	0.052	0.049	0.037
DEP1	0.185	0.846	0.132	0.109	0.094	0.089	0.121	0.060	0.072	0.097
DEP2	0.166	0.887	0.107	0.103	0.076	0.053	0.125	0.047	0.124	0.070
DEP3	0.107	0.880	0.186	0.052	0.072	0.008	0.045	0.062	0.053	0.034
DGP1	0.118	0.163	0.885	0.210	0.093	0.096	0.102	0.108	0.180	0.052
DGP2	0.083	0.160	0.894	0.120	0.067	0.051	0.082	0.077	0.181	0.075
DGP3	0.091	0.108	0.874	0.119	0.054	0.008	0.064	0.068	0.105	0.054
IQ1	0.191	0.040	0.124	0.767	0.081	0.001	0.055	0.057	0.147	0.050
IQ2	0.257	0.086	0.104	0.783	0.119	0.030	0.105	0.071	0.180	0.057
IQ3	0.274	0.099	0.168	0.893	0.115	0.024	0.138	0.094	0.161	0.082
IQ4	0.289	0.097	0.159	0.838	0.148	0.050	0.142	0.055	0.158	0.051
DSP1	0.131	0.073	0.101	0.117	0.848	0.124	0.110	0.043	0.145	0.199
DSP2	0.128	0.086	0.041	0.125	0.834	0.012	0.102	0.046	0.142	0.204
DSP3	0.076	0.076	0.063	0.120	0.862	0.033	0.063	0.068	0.101	0.157
ENO1	-0.053	0.055	0.051	0.023	0.070	0.873	0.069	-0.003	0.144	0.085
ENO2	-0.024	0.068	0.070	0.047	0.076	0.859	0.022	0.002	0.137	0.057
ENO3	-0.026	0.024	0.036	0.016	0.032	0.864	0.048	-0.011	0.149	0.115
EO1	0.040	0.081	0.096	0.110	0.068	0.075	0.808	0.082	0.037	0.087
EO2	0.053	0.123	0.084	0.146	0.095	0.033	0.753	0.095	0.019	0.065
EO3	0.036	0.049	0.054	0.064	0.080	0.061	0.803	0.069	0.031	0.073
EO4	0.047	0.095	0.057	0.108	0.098	-0.012	0.743	0.082	0.000	0.066
GOO1	0.061	0.065	0.067	0.084	0.043	-0.009	0.112	0.885	-0.006	0.112
GOO2	0.054	0.040	0.096	0.081	0.061	-0.010	0.083	0.913	0.003	0.106
GOO3	0.051	0.069	0.097	0.063	0.062	0.006	0.086	0.892	0.000	0.124
SO1	0.007	0.072	0.170	0.165	0.139	0.111	0.034	0.005	0.861	0.073
SO2	0.023	0.107	0.134	0.153	0.091	0.129	0.008	-0.005	0.862	0.066
SO3	0.026	0.070	0.158	0.192	0.165	0.187	0.032	-0.003	0.882	0.134
SQ1	-0.020	0.054	0.032	0.052	0.193	0.123	0.115	0.120	0.130	0.874
SQ2	0.018	0.045	0.047	0.044	0.201	0.093	0.064	0.100	0.085	0.859
SQ3	0.035	0.094	0.091	0.090	0.190	0.058	0.075	0.115	0.074	0.906

Convergent validity. Initially, the factor loading values need to be determined. According to Hair et al. (2022), every factor in this study had a loading value greater than 0.70. All factors in this study are loading higher than 0.70, which is in accordance with Hair et al. (2022).

The internal consistency reliability calculation is carried out in the second phase. In this regard, the two most popular techniques are Cronbach's alpha and composite reliability (CR) (Xue et al., 2011). Cronbach's alpha and CR are more reliable when the values are higher. Exploratory research is to be carried out between 0.70 and 0.95 on the significant credibility scale, according to Hair et al. (2022). In this research, Cronbach's alpha (α) values range from 0.782 to 0.878, which is a suitable range for reliability (Hair et al., 2022). Alternatively, all CR ranges from 0.859 to 0.925 are higher than 0.70, in accordance with Hair et al. (2022) and Henseler et al. (2016). Similarly, the rho_A (ρA) values are evaluated, the obtained values of the hypothesized constructs oscillate between 0.787 and 0.880, which is significantly above the cutoff point of 0.70 (Dijkstra & Henseler, 2015). The third stage is to calculate the AVE values. Accordingly, AVE value for the constructs in this study varies from 0.604 to 0.804, which are significantly higher than 0.50 (Hair et al., 2017). Taken together, the statistical output demonstrated in **Table 3** provides proof that the constructs used in this research are distinct in their composition.

Table 3. Results summary for convergent validity

Constructs and Operationalization	Convergent Validity		Construct Reliability			Discriminant Validity
	Factor Loadings	AVE	Cronbach's Alpha	Composite Reliability	PA	
Smart green balanced scorecard						
Economic object	0.743- 0.808	0.604	0.782	0.859	0.787	**Yes**
Societal object	0.861- 0.882	0.755	0.838	0.902	0.840	**Yes**
Green operational object	0.885- 0.913	0.804	0.878	0.925	0.878	**Yes**
Environmental object	0.859- 0.873	0.749	0.832	0.900	0.833	**Yes**
Effectiveness of sustainability accounting information system						
Collaboration quality	0.780- 0.912	0.724	0.872	0.913	0.877	**Yes**
Information quality	0.767- 0.893	0.675	0.838	0.892	0.846	**Yes**
System quality	0.859- 0.906	0.774	0.855	0.911	0.880	**Yes**
Digital environmental, social, and governance performance						
Digital environmental performance	0.846- 0.887	0.759	0.841	0.904	0.842	**Yes**
Digital governance performance	0.874- 0.894	0.782	0.861	0.915	0.863	**Yes**
Digital social performance	0.834- 0.862	0.719	0.805	0.885	0.806	**Yes**

Building on the suggestions of Fornell and Larcker (1981) as well as Henseler et al. (2015), the Fornell and Larcker criterion, Heterotrait-Monotrait Ratio (HTMT), and the cross-loading analysis are investigated with regard to the discriminant validity. Concerning to this, it is crucial to note that the Fornell and Larcker criterion denotes the amount of variance that a construct captures from its indicators, which must be greater than the variance that the construct shares with the rest. The creation of a diagonal with the greatest values recorded in the data run is shown in Table 4.

Table 4. Results summary for discriminant validity on Fornell–Larker criterion

	CQ	DEP	DGP	IQ	DSP	ENO	EO	GOO	SO	SQ
CQ	0.851									
DEP	0.174	0.871								
DGP	0.110	0.164	0.885							
IQ	0.310	0.100	0.171	0.822						
DSP	0.132	0.092	0.082	0.142	0.848					
ENO	-0.040	0.056	0.060	0.033	0.068	0.865				
EO	0.056	0.110	0.094	0.137	0.108	0.054	0.777			
GOO	0.062	0.065	0.096	0.085	0.062	-0.005	0.105	0.897		
SO	0.022	0.095	0.177	0.196	0.152	0.166	0.029	-0.001	0.869	
SQ	0.016	0.076	0.068	0.073	0.220	0.099	0.094	0.127	0.106	0.880

Note: Economic object = EO; Societal object = SO; Green operational object = GOO; Environmental object = ENO; Collaboration quality = CQ; Information quality = IQ; System quality = SQ; Digital environmental performance = DEP; Digital governance performance = DGP; Digital social performance = DSP

The Heterotrait-Monotrait Ratio (HTMT) was the second measurement tool utilized to evaluate the discriminant variance. In order to achieve a satisfactory result, previous researchers like Imran et al. (2017) advise values less than 0.90; in response, Hair et al. (2019) recommend values less than 0.85. In reality, Table 5 demonstrates that all values are suitable and acceptable because they are less than 0.85.

Table 5. Results summary for discriminant validity on Heterotrait–Monotrait ratio

	CQ	DEP	DGP	IQ	DSP	ENO	EO	GOO	SO	SQ
CQ										
DEP	0.204									
DGP	0.129	0.190								
IQ	0.359	0.118	0.198							
DSP	0.158	0.113	0.096	0.172						
ENO	0.047	0.081	0.070	0.040	0.084					
EO	0.073	0.139	0.113	0.168	0.138	0.072				
GOO	0.070	0.075	0.110	0.098	0.073	0.015	0.127			
SO	0.042	0.115	0.207	0.234	0.184	0.196	0.044	0.009		
SQ	0.041	0.087	0.075	0.083	0.267	0.122	0.117	0.146	0.127	

Note: Economic object = EO; Societal object = SO; Green operational object = GOO; Environmental object = ENO; Collaboration quality = CQ; Information quality = IQ; System quality = SQ; Digital environmental performance = DEP; Digital governance performance = DGP; Digital social performance = DSP

The last criterion of discriminant validity assessment in this study is completed by the cross-loadings criterion. The factorial cross-loadings of the indicators that include a latent variable must be compared to the loads of the indicators that include the other latent variables. As a result, the information in Table 2 demonstrates that none of the items has a greater load in a construct other than the one it measures.

At this stage of the investigation, it is deemed acceptable that the constructs included in the conceptual model for this study have a discriminant validity. Taken together, its measurement is distinct empirically.

4.2. Structural Model

According to Hair et al. (2022) and Sarstedt et al. (2022), the structural model assessment procedures involved four steps namely determining collinearity, evaluating the significance and relevance of the relationships within the model, evaluating the model's explanatory power, and evaluating the model's predictive power.

In the first step, all inner variance inflation factor (VIF) values are considerably below the critical threshold value of 3, indicating no serious collinearity problems (Hair et al., 2022). The second phase was using SmartPLS 4 to evaluate the magnitude and relevance of the structural model relationships. The bootstrapping method (percentile bootstrapping, two-tailed test, 0.05 significance level, with 10,000 resamples) was used to examine the significance of the path coefficients (Streukens & Leroi-Werelds, 2016).

According to the bootstrap results, SGBSC substantially and positively affects DESGP and ESAIS ($\beta = 0.233$; t-value = 5.348; p-value = 0.000 and $\beta = 0.184$; t-value = 3.665; p-value = 0.000, respectively). As anticipated by H3, the results reveal that ESAIS demonstrates a direct positive impact on DESGP ($\beta = 0.244$; t-value = 6.432; p-value = 0.000). In light of this, H1, H2, and H3 are supported. Additionally, the mediating impact of ESAIS was evaluated. First, the significance of SGBSC's indirect impact on DESGP through ESAIS was evaluated. Given that the direct effects of SGBSC on DESGP are also supported and that the indirect effects were significant (t-value = 3.081; p-value = 0.002), it was determined that ESAIS partially mediates the association between SGBSC and DESGP (Hair et al., 2022). As a result, the findings indicate partial mediation.

The third phase involved evaluating the model's explanatory capacity (Shmueli & Koppius, 2011) or in-sample predictive power (Rigdon, 2012; Sarstedt al., 2014) using the coefficient of determination R^2, which evaluates the variance in each endogenous construct. R^2 values of 0.75, 0.50, and 0.25, respectively, can be regarded as significant, moderate, and weak, according to conventional guidelines (Hensele et al., 2009; Hair et al., 2011). The R^2 was 0.135 for DESGP and 0.034 for ESAIS. The f^2 effect size (Hair et al., 2022) was also employed to evaluate the strength of the structural model relationships. This measure shows the relative influence of an exogenous construct on an endogenous construct in terms of R^2 changes (Sarstedt et al., 2022).

According to Cohen (1988), values above 0.02 and up to 0.15 are considered to indicate a small influence, values between 0.15 and 0.35 are considered to indicate a medium effect, and values 0.35 and higher are considered to suggest a strong effect. The analysis reveals that SGBSC and ESAIS had a small effect size on DESGP (0.061 and 0.067, respectively). In the same vein, SGBSC had a small effect size on ESAIS (0.035).

Out-of-sample prediction was carried out in the fourth phase to evaluate the model's capability to predict fresh or upcoming observations (Hair et al., 2022). The values of Q2 should be positive and higher than zero, hence the findings show a respectable prediction potential, according to Hair et al. (2019). The predictive power was verified by Stone-Geisser's Q2, so that the values for DESGP were 0.071 and 0.030 for ESAIS.

Table 6 and Figure 2 depict the structural model that was created during the execution of the PLS algorithm in SmartPLS 4.

Table 6. Results of hypotheses testing

Relevant Path	Path Coefficient	SE	95% Confidence interval	t-Value	p-Value	Result
Direct effect						
SGBSC → DESGP	0.233	0.044	[0.125- 0.296]	5.348	0.000	Supported
SGBSC → ESAIS	0.184	0.050	[0.063- 0.264]	3.665	0.000	Supported
ESAIS → DESGP	0.244	0.038	[0.171- 0.320]	6.432	0.000	Supported
Indirect effect						
SGBSC → ESAIS → DESGP	0.045	0.015	[0.015- 0.073]	3.081	0.002	Supported
R^2	$R^2_{DESGP} = 0.135$; $R^2_{ESAIS} = 0.034$					
f^2	$f^2_{SGBSC => DESGP} = 0.061$; $f^2_{SGBSC => ESAIS} = 0.035$; $f^2_{ESAIS => DESGP} = 0.067$					
Q^2	$Q^2_{DESGP} = 0.071$; $Q^2_{ESAIS} = 0.030$					

Figure 2. Structural model

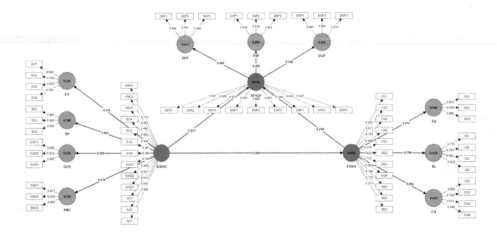

4.3. Discussion

The ESG concept has gained widespread popularity, which is reflected in a significant number of scientific papers (Leins, 2020; Gillan et al. 2021). This is because ESG practices could help businesses improve productivity (Shaikh, 2022), profitability (Kim & Li, 2021), reputation (Flammer & Bansal, 2017), and market value (Pedersen et al., 2021), as well as ease financing constraints (Christensen et al., 2021), reduce financial risk (Atif & Ali, 2021), and stock price volatility risk (Ashwin Kumar et al., 2016). The DESGP and its use in SMEs in developing nations have, however, received little conceptual or empirical study. Despite the BSC's continuous acceptance, there is conflicting empirical evidence regarding its efficacy, and it is unknown how much adopting the BSC will ultimately affect firm performance (Tawse & Tabesh, 2023) and DESGP. The main goal of the current research was to close this gap by formulating and building a model that would demonstrate the impact of SGBSC on DESGP in the setting of developing countries using a sample of accountants in SMEs. The investigation found that SGBSC and DESGP have a direct relationship, in addition to offering fresh perspectives on digital ESG, which is distinguished by the combination of digital transformation and ESG. This proof demonstrated that SGBSC is a comprehensive performance-oriented, performance-management tool that consists of effective measures linking the mission, core values, and future vision with initiatives, goals, and strategies aimed at enhancing digital ESG practices over time. In doing so, the current research enriches the understandings on IT BSC through the broadened the prevailing frontiers of findings of previous researcher (i.e., Wati and Koo (2011); Maccani (2011); Fabac (2022)).

More notably, the introduction of ESAIS in the current manuscript enhanced understanding of a potential mediator in the relationship between SGBSC and DESGP. These observations also shed light on the value of ESAIS. It seemed to be the appropriate as sustainability accounting is a developing field that supports the identification, gathering, analysis, and reporting of information pertaining to an organization's environmental, social, and economic actions (Mathuva et al., 2017). Based on the perspectives of Iredele (2020), planning, monitoring, and decision-making with regard to an organization's sustainability efforts are made easier by the sustainability accounting implementation. Businesses should concentrate on the ESAIS, particularly long-term performance and corporate sustainability as it is essential for better resource allocation, time management, environmental considerations, or even activity disclosure.

5. CONCLUDING THOUGHT AND FUTURE REFERRALS

Based on the current research's collected observations, several important implications and orientation for future research were deduced.

5.1. Practical Implications

The current research's empirical findings would be very helpful to practitioners and policymakers alike. More practically, the findings of this study were helpful for SMEs' leaders in recognizing and embracing the function of DESG. Therefore, it is advised that SMEs' leaders put more of an emphasis on DESG activities as one of their key organizational strategies. The results would allow for a prioritization of the practices, advising SMEs' leaders to focus more on SGBSC implementation in order to attain ESAIS, which would ultimately improve DESGP. Therefore, executives in SMEs should be aware of the benefits of contemporary information technology and look for practical, workable ways to make SGBSC adoption easier across all internal organizational activities. The leaders of SMEs were also urged to make every effort to evenly distribute the resources required for enhancing and strengthening the organization's information technology infrastructure and implementing sound human resource management procedures. The current paper shed interesting light on the function of ESAIS as a mediator between SGBSC and DESGP, and this finding could lead to a deeper understanding for individuals looking for fresh approaches to problems relating to DESGP.

The study's findings gave policymakers and other governmental influencers the potential to encourage the adoption of ESG implementation methodologies and sustainable accounting in SMEs. Additionally, it was anticipated that these results would aid in the creation of policies for the use of digital technologies by policymakers and other responsible organizations, hence fostering their wider adoption within SMEs.

5.2. Limitations and Orientation for Future Research

Because the study is focused on a particular area and is following a predetermined path, there are some limitations in relation to the research. These limitations, however, neither invalidate the research's contributions nor make its conclusions unreliable. Instead, noting the constraints can help readers spot any weaknesses in the work and support future researchers in strengthening it. Firstly, the current study's conclusions are based on an analysis of data that was gathered from accountants' contributions to SMEs in Vietnam. The sample size of businesses was limited since some respondents had access restrictions, making it challenging to extrapolate the results to other sectors and regions. To generalize the results found, future studies could test this model using larger random samples or respondents from different parts of the world. Second, as SGBSC and ESAIS were unable to fully explain the variance in DESGP, it may be necessary to look into additional predictors. It was also noted that ESAIS had a partially mediating impact on the connection between SGBSC and DESGP. Therefore, future research should concentrate on how other variables influence the relationship between SGBSC and DESGP. Thirdly, the conclusions are supported by such cross-sectional data, which introduces causality errors in the relationships between the constructs. In order to handle these flaws, it is advised that follow-up researchers do longitudinal investigations. Not to mention, as this was the first attempt to explain the idea of SGBSC based on the contributions of earlier academics, it would somehow fail to adequately depict the peculiarities of SGBSC. However, it seemed that it wouldn't be a constraint in the future when numerous arduous attempts were made for in-depth research on the primary quirks of SGBSC.

ACKNOWLEDGMENT

This research was funded by University of Economics Ho Chi Minh City (UEH) in Vietnam.

REFERENCES

Al Amosh, H., Khatib, S. F. A., & Ananzeh, H. (2023). Environmental, social and governance impact on financial performance: Evidence from the Levant countries. *Corporate Governance (Bradford)*, *23*(3), 493–513. doi:10.1108/CG-03-2022-0105

ALmashkor, I. A. S. (2020). Aligning Between the Balanced Scorecard and Environmental Management Accounting in Support of Sustainable Development. *Productivity Management, 1*, 402-418.

Appelbaum, D., Kogan, A., Vasarhelyi, M., & Yan, Z. (2017). Impact of business analytics and enterprise systems on managerial accounting. *International Journal of Accounting Information Systems*, *25*, 29–44. doi:10.1016/j.accinf.2017.03.003

Ashwin Kumar, N. C., Smith, C., Badis, L., Wang, N., Ambrosy, P., & Tavares, R. (2016). ESG factors and risk-adjusted performance: A new quantitative model. *Journal of Sustainable Finance & Investment*, *6*(4), 292–300. doi:10.1080/20430795.2016.1234909

Atif, M., & Ali, S. (2021). Environmental, social and governance disclosure and default risk. *Business Strategy and the Environment*, *30*(8), 3937–3959. doi:10.1002/bse.2850

Baines, T., & Lightfoot, H. W. (2013). Servitization of the manufacturing firm. *International Journal of Operations & Production Management*, *34*(1), 2–35. doi:10.1108/IJOPM-02-2012-0086

Becker-Olsen, K. L., Taylor, C. R., Hill, R. P., & Yalcinkaya, G. (2011). A Cross-Cultural Examination of Corporate Social Responsibility Marketing Communications in Mexico and the United States: Strategies for Global Brands. *Journal of International Marketing*, *19*(2), 30–44. doi:10.1509/jimk.19.2.30

Belyaeva, Z., Shams, S. M. R., Santoro, G., & Grandhi, B. (2020). Unpacking stakeholder relationship management in the public and private sectors: The comparative insights. *EuroMed Journal of Business*, *15*(3), 269–281. doi:10.1108/EMJB-06-2019-0085

Borges, A. F., Laurindo, F. J., Spínola, M. M., Gonçalves, R. F., & Mattos, C. A. (2021). The strategic use of artificial intelligence in the digital era: Systematic literature review and future research directions. *International Journal of Information Management*, *57*, 1–16. doi:10.1016/j.ijinfomgt.2020.102225

Bressanelli, G., Adrodegari, F., Perona, M., & Saccani, N. (2018). Exploring How Usage-Focused Business Models Enable Circular Economy through Digital Technologies. *Sustainability (Basel)*, *10*(3), 1–21. doi:10.3390u10030639

Brundtland, G. H. (1987). Our Common Future—Call for Action*. *Environmental Conservation*, *14*(4), 291–294. doi:10.1017/S0376892900016805

Burritt, R., & Christ, K. (2016). Industry 4.0 and environmental accounting: A new revolution? Asian. *Journal of Sustainability and Social Responsibility*, *1*(1), 23–38. doi:10.118641180-016-0007-y

Burritt, R. L., & Schaltegger, S. (2010). Sustainability accounting and reporting: Fad or trend? *Accounting, Auditing & Accountability Journal*, *23*(7), 829–846. doi:10.1108/09513571011080144

Cadez, S., & Guilding, C. (2012). Strategy, strategic management accounting and performance: A configurational analysis. *Industrial Management & Data Systems*, *112*(3), 484–501. doi:10.1108/02635571211210086

Cai, S., Jun, M., & Yang, Z. (2010). Implementing supply chain information integration in China: The role of institutional forces and trust. *Journal of Operations Management*, *28*(3), 257–268. doi:10.1016/j.jom.2009.11.005

Chand, D., Hachey, G., Hunton, J., Owhoso, V., & Vasudevan, S. (2005). A balanced scorecard based framework for assessing the strategic impacts of ERP systems. *Computers in Industry*, *56*(6), 558–572. doi:10.1016/j.compind.2005.02.011

Chen, C. X., Hudgins, R., & Wright, W. F. (2021). The Effect of Advice Valence on the Perceived Credibility of Data Analytics. *Journal of Management Accounting Research*, *34*(2), 97–116. doi:10.2308/JMAR-2020-015

Chen, Z., & Xie, G. (2022). ESG disclosure and financial performance: Moderating role of ESG investors. *International Review of Financial Analysis*, *83*, 1–16. doi:10.1016/j.irfa.2022.102291

Christensen, D. M., Serafeim, G., & Sikochi, A. (2021). Why is Corporate Virtue in the Eye of The Beholder? The Case of ESG Ratings. *The Accounting Review*, *97*(1), 147–175. doi:10.2308/TAR-2019-0506

Cram, A. (2007). The IT Balanced Scorecard Revisited. *Information System Control Journal, 3*, 1-5.

Dagiliene, L., & Šutiene, K. (2019). Corporate sustainability accounting information systems: A contingency-based approach. *Sustainability Accounting. Management and Policy Journal*, *10*(2), 260–289. doi:10.1108/SAMPJ-07-2018-0200

Dai, J., & Vasarhelyi, M. A. (2016). Imagineering Audit 4.0. *Journal of Emerging Technologies in Accounting*, *13*(1), 1–15. doi:10.2308/jeta-10494

Dijkstra, T. K., & Henseler, J. (2015). Consistent partial least squares path modeling. *Management Information Systems Quarterly*, *39*(2), 297–316. doi:10.25300/MISQ/2015/39.2.02

dos Santos, M. C., & Pereira, F. H. (2022). ESG performance scoring method to support responsible investments in port operations. *Case Studies on Transport Policy*, *10*(1), 664–673. doi:10.1016/j.cstp.2022.01.027

Eccles, N. S., & Viviers, S. (2011). The Origins and Meanings of Names Describing Investment Practices that Integrate a Consideration of ESG Issues in the Academic Literature. *Journal of Business Ethics*, *104*(3), 389–402. doi:10.100710551-011-0917-7

Erokhina, A. V. (2022) Implementing an ESG strategy using the Sustainability Balanced Scorecard. *Ekonomika: vchera, segodnya, zavtra, 12*(9A), 404-413. 10.34670/AR.2022.33.65.024

Fabac, R. (2022). Digital Balanced Scorecard System as a Supporting Strategy for Digital Transformation. *Sustainability (Basel)*, *14*(15), 1–26. doi:10.3390u14159690

Fang, M., Nie, H., & Shen, X. (2023). Can enterprise digitization improve ESG performance? *Economic Modelling*, *118*, 1–15. doi:10.1016/j.econmod.2022.106101

Flammer, C., & Bansal, P. (2017). Does a Long-Term Orientation Create Value? Evidence from a Regression Discontinuity. *Academy of Management Annual Meeting Proceedings, 38*, 1827–1847.

Fornell, C., & Larcker, D. F. (1981). Evaluating Structural Equation Models with Unobservable Variables and Measurement Error. *JMR, Journal of Marketing Research*, *18*(1), 39–50. doi:10.1177/002224378101800104

Freeman, R. E. (1984). *Strategic management: A stakeholder approach*. Pitman.

Freeman, R. E. (1999). Divergent stakeholder theory. *Academy of Management Review*, *24*(2), 233–236. doi:10.5465/amr.1999.1893932

Friede, G., Busch, T., & Bassen, A. (2015). ESG and financial performance: Aggregated evidence from more than 2000 empirical studies. *Journal of Sustainable Finance & Investment*, *5*(4), 210–233. doi:10.1080/20430795.2015.1118917

Fu, T., & Li, J. (2023). An empirical analysis of the impact of ESG on financial performance: The moderating role of digital transformation. *Frontiers in Environmental Science*, *11*, 1–12. doi:10.3389/fenvs.2023.1256052

Galbreath, J. (2013). ESG in Focus: The Australian Evidence. *Journal of Business Ethics*, *118*(3), 529–541. doi:10.100710551-012-1607-9

Garel, A., & Petit-Romec, A. (2021). Investor rewards to environmental responsibility: Evidence from the COVID-19 crisis. *Journal of Corporate Finance*, *68*, 1–20. doi:10.1016/j.jcorpfin.2021.101948

Gillan, S. L., Koch, A., & Starks, L. T. (2021). Firms and social responsibility: A review of ESG and CSR research in corporate finance. *Journal of Corporate Finance*, *66*, 1–16. doi:10.1016/j.jcorpfin.2021.101889

Gomes, D. R., Ribeiro, N., & Santos, M. J. (2023). "Searching for Gold" with Sustainable Human Resources Management and Internal Communication: Evaluating the Mediating Role of Employer Attractiveness for Explaining Turnover Intention and Performance. *Administrative Sciences*, *13*(24), 1–15. doi:10.3390/admsci13010024

Groot, T. L. C. M., & Selto, F. (2013). Integrated financial and non-financial measures. In T. L. C. M. Groot & F. Selto (Eds.), *Advanced Management Accounting*. Pearson Education.

Haenlein, M., & Kaplan, A. (2019). A Brief History of Artificial Intelligence: On the Past, Present, and Future of Artificial Intelligence. *California Management Review*, *61*(4), 5–14. doi:10.1177/0008125619864925

Hair, J. F. Jr, Anderson, R. E., Tatham, R. L., & Black, W. C. (2010). *Multivariate Data Analysis* (7th ed.). Pearson.

Hair, J. F., Astrachan, C. B., Moisescu, O. I., Radomir, L., Sarstedt, M., Vaithilingam, S., & Ringle, C. M. (2021). Executing and interpreting applications of PLS-SEM: Updates for family business researchers. *Journal of Family Business Strategy*, *12*(3), 1–8. doi:10.1016/j.jfbs.2020.100392

Hair, J. F., Hult, G. T. M., Ringle, C. M., & Sarstedt, M. (2022). *A Primer on Partial Least Squares Structural Equation Modeling (PLS-SEM)*. Sage.

Hair, J. F. Jr, Matthews, L. M., Matthews, R. L., & Sarstedt, M. (2017). PLS-SEM or CB-SEM: Updated guidelines on which method to use. *International Journal of Multivariate Data Analysis*, *1*(2), 107–123. doi:10.1504/IJMDA.2017.087624

Hair, J. F., Ringle, C. M., & Sarstedt, M. (2011). PLS-SEM: Indeed a Silver Bullet. *Journal of Marketing Theory and Practice*, *19*(2), 139–152. doi:10.2753/MTP1069-6679190202

Hair, J. F., Risher, J. J., Sarstedt, M., & Ringle, C. M. (2019). When to use and how to report the results of PLS-SEM. *European Business Review*, *31*(1), 2–24. doi:10.1108/EBR-11-2018-0203

Hamzah, S., Pangemanan, D., & Aprianti, E. (2023). The environmental and sustainable factors on the special economic zones development. *Civil Engineering Journal*, *9*(2), 334–342. doi:10.28991/CEJ-2023-09-02-06

Hansen, E. G., & Schaltegger, S. (2014). The Sustainability Balanced Scorecard: A Systematic Review of Architectures. *Journal of Business Ethics*, *133*(2), 193–221. doi:10.100710551-014-2340-3

Hansen, E. G., & Schaltegger, S. (2018). Sustainability Balanced Scorecards and their Architectures: Irrelevant or Misunderstood? *Journal of Business Ethics*, *150*(4), 937–952. doi:10.100710551-017-3531-5

Henseler, J., Hubona, G., & Ray, P. A. (2016). Using PLS path modeling in new technology research: Updated guidelines. *Industrial Management & Data Systems*, *116*(1), 2–20. doi:10.1108/IMDS-09-2015-0382

Henseler, J., Ringle, C. M., & Sarstedt, M. (2015). A new criterion for assessing discriminant validity in variance-based structural equation modeling. *Journal of the Academy of Marketing Science*, *43*(1), 115–135. doi:10.100711747-014-0403-8

Henseler, J., Ringle, C. M., & Sinkovics, R. R. (2009). The use of partial least squares path modeling in international marketing. In R. R. Sinkovics & P. N. Ghauri (Eds.), *New Challenges to International Marketing* (pp. 277–319). Emerald Group Publishing. doi:10.1108/S1474-7979(2009)0000020014

Hsu, C.-W., Lee, W.-H., & Chao, W.-C. (2013). Materiality analysis model in sustainability reporting: A case study at Lite-On Technology Corporation. *Journal of Cleaner Production*, *57*, 142–151. doi:10.1016/j.jclepro.2013.05.040

Huang, Q., Fang, J., Xue, X., & Gao, H. (2023). Does digital innovation cause better ESG performance? an empirical test of a-listed firms in China. *Research in International Business and Finance*, *66*, 1–20. doi:10.1016/j.ribaf.2023.102049

Iacobucci, D. (2010). Structural equations modeling: Fit Indices, sample size, and advanced topics. *Journal of Consumer Psychology*, *20*(1), 90–98. doi:10.1016/j.jcps.2009.09.003

Ifinedo, P. (2011). Examining the influences of external expertise and in-house computer/IT knowledge on ERP system success. *Journal of Systems and Software*, *84*(12), 2065–2078. doi:10.1016/j.jss.2011.05.017

Imran, M., Aziz, A., & Abdul Hamid, S. N. (2017). Determinants of SME export performance. *International Journal of Data and Network Science*, 39–58. . doi:10.5267/j.ijdns.2017.1.007

Iredele, O. O. (2020). Measuring performance in corporate environmental reporting in Nigeria. *Measuring Business Excellence*, *24*(2), 183–195. doi:10.1108/MBE-05-2019-0040

Jassem, S., Zakaria, Z., & Che Azmi, A. (2022). Sustainability balanced scorecard architecture and environmental performance outcomes: A systematic review. *International Journal of Productivity and Performance Management*, *71*(5), 1728–1760. doi:10.1108/IJPPM-12-2019-0582

Johnson, E., Petersen, M., Sloan, J., & Valencia, A. (2021). The Interest, Knowledge, and Usage of Artificial Intelligence in Accounting: Evidence from Accounting Professionals. *Accounting & Taxation*, *13*(1), 45–58.

Johnson, M., Albizri, A., Harfouche, A., & Fosso-Wamba, S. (2022). Integrating human knowledge into artificial intelligence for complex and ill-structured problems: Informed artificial intelligence. *International Journal of Information Management*, *64*, 1–15. doi:10.1016/j.ijinfomgt.2022.102479

Kamp, B., & Parry, G. (2017). Servitization and advanced business services as levers for competitiveness. *Industrial Marketing Management*, *60*, 11–16. doi:10.1016/j.indmarman.2016.12.008

Kaplan, A., & Haenlein, M. (2019). Siri, Siri, in my hand: Who's the fairest in the land? On the interpretations, illustrations, and implications of artificial intelligence. *Business Horizons*, *62*(1), 15–25. doi:10.1016/j.bushor.2018.08.004

Kaplan, R. S., & Norton, D. P. (1996a). Using the balanced scorecard as a strategic management system. *Harvard Business Review*, *74*(1), 75–85.

Kaplan, R. S., & Norton, D. P. (1996b). Linking the balanced scorecard to strategy. *California Management Review*, *39*(1), 53–79. doi:10.2307/41165876

Khattak, A., & Yousaf, Z. (2021). Digital Social Responsibility towards Corporate Social Responsibility and Strategic Performance of Hi-Tech SMEs: Customer Engagement as a Mediator. *Sustainability (Basel)*, *14*(1), 1–16. doi:10.3390u14010131

Kim, B.-J., Jung, J.-Y., & Cho, S.-W. (2022). Can ESG mitigate the diversification discount in cross-border M&A? *Borsa Istanbul Review*, *22*(3), 607–615. doi:10.1016/j.bir.2021.09.002

Kim, S., & Li, Z. (2021). Understanding the Impact of ESG Practices in Corporate Finance. *Sustainability (Basel)*, *13*(7), 1–15. doi:10.3390u13073746

Kwilinski, A., Lyulyov, O., & Pimonenko, T. (2023). Unlocking Sustainable Value through Digital Transformation: An Examination of ESG Performance. *Information (Basel)*, *14*(444), 1–18. doi:10.3390/info14080444

Lee, S.-P., & Isa, M. (2023). Environmental, social and governance (ESG) practices and financial performance of Shariah-compliant companies in Malaysia. *Journal of Islamic Accounting and Business Research*, *14*(2), 295–314. doi:10.1108/JIABR-06-2020-0183

Lee, T. M., & Hutchison, P. D. (2005). The Decision to Disclose Environmental Information: A Research Review and Agenda. *Advances in Accounting*, *21*, 83–111. doi:10.1016/S0882-6110(05)21004-0

Leins, S. (2020). "Responsible investment": ESG and the post-crisis ethical order. *Economy and Society*, *49*(1), 1–21. doi:10.1080/03085147.2020.1702414

Lu, Y., Xu, C., Zhu, B., & Sun, Y. (2023). Digitalization transformation and ESG performance: Evidence from China. *Business Strategy and the Environment*, 1–23. doi:10.1002/bse.3494

Lucianetti, L., Chiappetta Jabbour, C. J., Gunasekaran, A., & Latan, H. (2018). Contingency factors and complementary effects of adopting advanced manufacturing tools and managerial practices: Effects on organizational measurement systems and firms' performance. *International Journal of Production Economics*, *200*, 318–328. doi:10.1016/j.ijpe.2018.04.005

Maccani, G. (2011). *Green IT Balanced Scorecard* [Master Thesis]. Politecnico di Milano.

Maelah, R., Auzair, S., Amir, A., & Ahmad, A. (2017). Implementation process and lessons learned in the determination of educational cost using modified activity-based costing (ABC). *Social and Management Research Journal*, *14*(1), 1–32. doi:10.24191mrj.v14i1.5277

Maignan, I. (2001). Consumers' Perceptions of Corporate Social Responsibilities: A Cross-Cultural Comparison. *Journal of Business Ethics*, *30*(1), 57–72. doi:10.1023/A:1006433928640

Mandhachitara, R., & Poolthong, Y. (2011). A model of customer loyalty and corporate social responsibility. *Journal of Services Marketing, 25*(2), 122–133. doi:10.1108/08876041111119840

Martinsons, M., Davison, R., & Tse, D. (1999). The balanced scorecard: A foundation for the strategic management of information systems. *Decision Support Systems, 25*(1), 71–88. doi:10.1016/S0167-9236(98)00086-4

Mathuva, D., Barako, D., & Wachira, M. (2017). The Economic Consequences of Environmental, Social and Governance Disclosures by Firms Quoted on the Nairobi Securities Exchange. *African Accounting and Finance Journal, 1*(1), 5–28.

Melo, I. C., Queiroz, G. A., Junior, P. N. A., de Sousa, T. B., Yushimito, W. F., & Pereira, J. (2023). Sustainable digital transformation in small and medium enterprises (SMEs): A review on performance. *Heliyon, 9*(3), 1–21. doi:10.1016/j.heliyon.2023.e13908 PMID:36915489

Mergel, I., Edelmann, N., & Haug, N. (2019). Defining digital transformation: Results from expert interviews. *Government Information Quarterly, 36*(4), 1–16. doi:10.1016/j.giq.2019.06.002

Mohr, L. A., & Webb, D. J. (2005). The effects of corporate social responsibility and price on consumer responses. *The Journal of Consumer Affairs, 39*(1), 121–147. doi:10.1111/j.1745-6606.2005.00006.x

Moisescu, O. I. (2015). Development and Validation of a Measurement Scale for Customers' perceptions of Corporate Social Responsibility. *Management and Marketing Journal, 13*, 311–332.

Muñoz-Torres, M. J., Fernández-Izquierdo, M. Á., Rivera-Lirio, J. M., & Escrig-Olmedo, E. (2019). Can environmental, social, and governance rating agencies favor business models that promote a more sustainable development? *Corporate Social Responsibility and Environmental Management, 26*(2), 439–452. doi:10.1002/csr.1695

Munyon, T. P., Madden, L. T., Madden, T. M., & Vigoda-Gadot, E. (2019). (Dys)functional attachments?: How community embeddedness impacts workers during and after long-term unemployment. *Journal of Vocational Behavior, 112*, 35–50. doi:10.1016/j.jvb.2019.01.005

Niu, S., Park, B. I., & Jung, J. S. (2022). The Effects of Digital Leadership and ESG Management on Organizational Innovation and Sustainability. *Sustainability (Basel), 14*(23), 1–20. doi:10.3390u142315639

Nohria, N., & Khurana, R. (2010). *Handbook of Leadership Theory and Practice.* Harvard Business School Press.

Öberseder, M., Schlegelmilch, B. B., Murphy, P. E., & Gruber, V. (2014). Consumers' Perceptions of Corporate Social Responsibility: Scale Development and Validation. *Journal of Business Ethics, 124*(1), 101–115. doi:10.100710551-013-1787-y

Olson, E. M., & Slater, S. F. (2002). The balanced scorecard, competitive strategy, and performance. *Business Horizons, 45*(3), 11–16. doi:10.1016/S0007-6813(02)00198-2

Oyewo, B., Tawiah, V., & Hussain, S. T. (2023). Drivers of environmental and social sustainability accounting practices in Nigeria: A corporate governance perspective. *Corporate Governance (Bradford), 23*(2), 397–421. doi:10.1108/CG-09-2021-0336

Pazienza, M., de Jong, M., & Schoenmaker, D. (2022). Clarifying the Concept of Corporate Sustainability and Providing Convergence for Its Definition. *Sustainability (Basel)*, *14*(7838), 1–21. doi:10.3390u14137838

Pedersen, L. H., Fitzgibbons, S., & Pomorski, L. (2021). Responsible investing: The ESG-efficient frontier. *Journal of Financial Economics*, *142*(2), 572–597. doi:10.1016/j.jfineco.2020.11.001

Peng, Y. Z., & Tao, C. Q. (2022). Can digital transformation promote enterprise performance?-From the perspective of public policy and innovation. *Journal of Innovation & Knowledge*, *7*(3), 1–8. doi:10.1016/j.jik.2022.100198

Pérez, A., & Rodríguez del Bosque, I. (2013). Measuring CSR Image: Three Studies to Develop and to Validate a Reliable Measurement Tool. *Journal of Business Ethics*, *118*(2), 265–286. doi:10.100710551-012-1588-8

Perifanis, N.-A., & Kitsios, F. (2023). Investigating the Influence of Artificial Intelligence on Business Value in the Digital Era of Strategy: A Literature Review. *Information (Basel)*, *14*(2), 1–42. doi:10.3390/info14020085

Petkov, R. (2020). Artificial intelligence (AI) and the accounting function—A revisit and a new perspective for developing framework. *Journal of Emerging Technologies in Accounting*, *17*(1), 99–105. doi:10.2308/jeta-52648

Phillips, J. (2023). Quantifying the levels, nature, and dynamics of sustainability for the UK 2000–2018 from a Brundtland perspective. *Environment, Development and Sustainability*, 1–22. doi:10.100710668-023-03370-2

Pimonenko, T., Bilan, Y., Horák, J., Starchenko, L., & Gajda, W. (2020). Green Brand of Companies and Greenwashing under Sustainable Development Goals. *Sustainability (Basel)*, *12*(4), 1–15. doi:10.3390u12041679

Puriwat, W., & Tripopsakul, S. (2022). From ESG to DESG: The Impact of DESG (Digital Environmental, Social, and Governance) on Customer Attitudes and Brand Equity. *Sustainability (Basel)*, *14*(17), 1–15. doi:10.3390u141710480

Quesado, P., Aibar Guzmán, B., & Lima Rodrígues, L. (2018). Advantages and contributions in the balanced scorecard implementation. *Intangible Capital*, *14*(1), 186–201. doi:10.3926/ic.1110

Rigdon, E. E. (2012). Rethinking Partial Least Squares Path Modeling: In Praise of Simple Methods. *Long Range Planning*, *45*(5-6), 341–358. doi:10.1016/j.lrp.2012.09.010

Rosemann, M. (2001). Evaluating the Management of Enterprise Systems with the Balanced Scorecard. In W. Van Grembergen (Ed.), *Information Technology Evaluation Methods and Management* (pp. 171–184). Idea Group Publishing. doi:10.4018/978-1-878289-90-2.ch011

Rosemann, M., & Wiese, J. (1999). Measuring the performance of ERP software-a balanced scorecard approach. *Proceedings of 10th Australasian Conference on Information Systems*, 773-784.

Salmones, M. del M. G., Crespo, A. H., & Bosque, I. R. (2005). Influence of Corporate Social Responsibility on Loyalty and Valuation of Services. *Journal of Business Ethics*, *61*(4), 369–385. doi:10.100710551-005-5841-2

Sarstedt, M., Hair, J. F., Pick, M., Liengaard, B. D., Radomir, L., & Ringle, C. M. (2022). Progress in partial least squares structural equation modeling use in marketing research in the last decade. *Psychology and Marketing*, *39*(5), 1035–1064. doi:10.1002/mar.21640

Sarstedt, M., Ringle, C. M., Henseler, J., & Hair, J. F. (2014). On the Emancipation of PLS-SEM: A Commentary on Rigdon (2012). *Long Range Planning*, *47*(3), 154–160. doi:10.1016/j.lrp.2014.02.007

Saunders, M., Lewis, P., & Thornhill, A. (2009). *Research Methods for Business Students*. Pearson.

Schaltegger, S., & Wagner, M. (2006). Integrative management of sustainability performance, measurement and reporting. *International Journal of Accounting, Auditing and Performance Evaluation*, *3*(1), 1–19. doi:10.1504/IJAAPE.2006.010098

Shaikh, I. (2022). Environmental, social, and governance (ESG) practice and firm performance: An international evidence. *Journal of Business Economics and Management*, *23*(1), 218–237. doi:10.3846/jbem.2022.16202

Shmueli, G., & Koppius, O. R. (2011). Predictive analytics in information systems research. *Management Information Systems Quarterly*, *35*(3), 553–572. doi:10.2307/23042796

Soderstrom, K. M., Soderstrom, N. S., & Stewart, C. R. (2017). Sustainability/CSR Research in Management Accounting: A Review of the Literature. In Advances in Management Accounting (Vol. 28, pp. 59-85). Emerald Publishing Limited. doi:10.1108/S1474-787120170000028003

Stock, T., & Seliger, G. (2016). Opportunities of Sustainable Manufacturing in Industry 4.0. *Procedia CIRP*, *40*, 536–541. doi:10.1016/j.procir.2016.01.129

Streukens, S., & Leroi-Werelds, S. (2016). Bootstrapping and PLS-SEM: A step-by-step guide to get more out of your bootstrap results. *European Management Journal*, *34*(6), 618–632. doi:10.1016/j.emj.2016.06.003

Su, X., Wang, S., & Li, F. (2023). The Impact of Digital Transformation on ESG Performance Based on the Mediating Effect of Dynamic Capabilities. *Sustainability (Basel)*, *15*(13506), 1–22. doi:10.3390u151813506

Tauringana, V. (2020). Sustainability reporting adoption in developing countries: Managerial perception-based determinants evidence from Uganda. *Journal of Accounting in Emerging Economies*, *11*(2), 149–175. doi:10.1108/JAEE-07-2020-0184

Tawse, A., & Tabesh, P. (2023). Thirty years with the balanced scorecard: What we have learned. *Business Horizons*, *66*(1), 123–132. doi:10.1016/j.bushor.2022.03.005

Tiwari, K., & Khan, M. S. (2020). Sustainability Accounting and Reporting in the Industry 4.0. *Journal of Cleaner Production*, *258*, 1–14. doi:10.1016/j.jclepro.2020.120783

Tran, T. T., & Herzig, C. (2023). Blended case-based learning in a sustainability accounting course: An analysis of student perspectives. *Journal of Accounting Education*, *63*, 1–17. doi:10.1016/j.jaccedu.2023.100842

Tsang, Y. P., Fan, Y., & Feng, Z. P. (2023). Bridging the gap: Building environmental, social and governance capabilities in small and medium logistics companies. *Journal of Environmental Management*, *338*, 1–10. doi:10.1016/j.jenvman.2023.117758 PMID:36996566

Turker, D. (2008). Measuring Corporate Social Responsibility: A Scale Development Study. *Journal of Business Ethics*, *85*(4), 411–427. doi:10.100710551-008-9780-6

Upadhyay, N., Upadhyay, S., Al-Debei, M. M., Baabdullah, A. M., & Dwivedi, Y. K. (2023). The influence of digital entrepreneurship and entrepreneurial orientation on intention of family businesses to adopt artificial intelligence: Examining the mediating role of business innovativeness. *International Journal of Entrepreneurial Behaviour & Research*, *29*(1), 80–115. doi:10.1108/IJEBR-02-2022-0154

Ur Rehman, S., Bhatti, A., & Chaudhry, N. I. (2019). Mediating effect of innovative culture and organizational learning between leadership styles at third-order and organizational performance in Malaysian SMEs. *Journal of Global Entrepreneurship Research*, *9*(1), 1–24. doi:10.118640497-019-0159-1

Urbach, N., Smolnik, S., & Riempp, G. (2010). An empirical investigation of employee portal success. *The Journal of Strategic Information Systems*, *19*(3), 184–206. doi:10.1016/j.jsis.2010.06.002

Van Grembergen, W. (2000). The balanced scorecard and IT governance. *Information Systems Control Journal*, *2*, 1-3.

Verhoef, P. C., Broekhuizen, T., Bart, Y., Bhattacharya, A., Qi Dong, J., Fabian, N., & Haenlein, M. (2019). Digital transformation: A multidisciplinary reflection and research agenda. *Journal of Business Research*, *122*, 889–901. doi:10.1016/j.jbusres.2019.09.022

Vial, G. (2019). Understanding digital transformation: A review and a research agenda. *The Journal of Strategic Information Systems*, *28*(2), 118–144. doi:10.1016/j.jsis.2019.01.003

Vladimir, V. F., Mercedes, N. C., Francisca, C. M. M., & José, M. V. D. (2020). Balanced Scorecard: Key Tool for Strategic Learning and Strengthening in Business Organizations. *Academic Journal of Interdisciplinary Studies*, *9*(3), 1–11. doi:10.36941/ajis-2020-0036

Wagner, T., Bicen, P., & Hall, Z. R. (2008). The dark side of retailing: Towards a scale of corporate social irresponsibility. *International Journal of Retail & Distribution Management*, *36*(2), 124–142. doi:10.1108/09590550810853075

Wang, F., & Sun, Z. (2022). Does the environmental regulation intensity and ESG performance have a substitution effect on the impact of enterprise green innovation: Evidence from China. *International Journal of Environmental Research and Public Health*, *19*(14), 1–24. doi:10.3390/ijerph19148558 PMID:35886408

Wang, J.-S., Liu, C.-H., & Chen, Y.-T. (2022). Green sustainability balanced scorecard—Evidence from the Taiwan liquefied natural gas industry. *Environmental Technology & Innovation*, *28*, 1–18. doi:10.1016/j.eti.2022.102862

Wang, S., & Esperança, J. P. (2023). Can digital transformation improve market and ESG performance? Evidence from Chinese SMEs. *Journal of Cleaner Production, 419*, 1–12. doi:10.1016/j.jclepro.2023.137980

Warren, J. D. Jr, Moffitt, K. C., & Byrnes, P. (2015). How Big Data will change accounting. *Accounting Horizons, 29*(2), 397–407. doi:10.2308/acch-51069

Wati, Y., & Koo, C. (2011). An Introduction to the Green IT Balanced Scorecard as a Strategic IT Management System. *Proceedings of the 44th Hawaii International Conference on System Sciences*, 1-10. 10.1109/HICSS.2011.59

Werle, M., & Laumer, S. (2022). Competitor identification: A review of use cases, data sources, and algorithms. *International Journal of Information Management, 65*, 1–15. doi:10.1016/j.ijinfomgt.2022.102507

Woodward, J. (1958). *Management and technology*. HM Stationery Office.

Xue, S., Tang, Y.-Y., & Posner, M. I. (2011). Short-term meditation increases network efficiency of the anterior cingulate cortex. *Neuroreport, 22*(12), 570–574. doi:10.1097/WNR.0b013e328348c750 PMID:21691234

Yu, P., Luu, B. V., & Chen, C. H. (2020). Greenwashing in environmental, social and governance disclosures. *Research in International Business and Finance, 52*, 1–23. doi:10.1016/j.ribaf.2020.101192

Zhong, Y., Zhao, H., & Yin, T. (2023). Resource Bundling: How Does Enterprise Digital Transformation Affect Enterprise ESG Development? *Sustainability (Basel), 15*(1319), 1–18. doi:10.3390u15021319

Zhu, J., & Huang, F. (2023). Transformational Leadership, Organizational Innovation, and ESG Performance: Evidence from SMEs in China. *Sustainability (Basel), 15*(7), 1–23. doi:10.3390u15075756

Chapter 11
The Role of ESG Ratings in Investment Portfolio Choices

Massimiliano Kaucic

iD https://orcid.org/0000-0002-6565-0771

DEAMS, University of Trieste, Italy

Filippo Piccotto

DEAMS, University of Trieste, Italy

Paola Rossi

DEAMS, University of Trieste, Italy

Gabriele Sbaiz

DEAMS, University of Trieste, Italy

Giorgio Valentinuz

iD https://orcid.org/0000-0003-0266-4196

DEAMS, University of Trieste, Italy

ABSTRACT

The chapter presents a general model for constructing portfolios in which environmental, social, and governance (ESG) rating (or score) assessments are added alongside traditional risk and return objectives. The design of portfolios involves ESG scores as an additional objective. Then multiobjective optimisation models are employed to construct the corresponding efficient frontiers. Moreover, the authors introduce a technique for selecting the optimal portfolio according to the investor's preferences toward the three objectives. Six investor profiles that would position themselves in their optimal portfolio, using variance and conditional value at risk (CVaR) as risk measures, are identified for experimental analysis. Starting with Refinitiv's ESG ratings for 538 companies that are part of the STOXX Europe 600 Index from January 2016 to December 2021, the effectiveness of the proposed methodology is finally confirmed ex-post.

DOI: 10.4018/978-1-6684-9076-1.ch011

1. INTRODUCTION

The issue of socially responsible investment (SRI), born in a relatively circumscribed context and based on ethical or religious beliefs, has seen growing importance over time, assuming different and more widely shared connotations. In particular, SRIs were selected primarily for non-financial reasons, as opposed to traditional financial theory, which assumes that investors seek the best combination of risk and return. For example, Renneboog et al. (2008) emphasise that investors derive non-financial utility from investing in SRI practices.

To identify investments made into companies and funds that produce a positive social and environmental impact while producing financial returns, the Rockefeller Foundation, in 2007, formally used for the first time the term "Impact investing" (Bugg-Levine and Emerson, 2011). However, in a traditional view, the company that pursues objectives other than maximising shareholder value - for example, for the benefit of stakeholders not necessarily related to the company - risks destroying value and generating costly agency relationships. However, over time, the environmental issue and the consequent effects of global warming started to have an increasing weight on the agendas of international political authorities.

The Paris Agreement on climate change and, among others, the UN Principles for Responsible Investment (PRI), launched in 2006, and the UN 2030 Agenda for Sustainable Development are the necessary premises for a different way of tackling economic development, questioning the models which had hitherto been dominant. Thanks to the large amount of resources they can mobilise, the institutional investors and financial intermediates have been seen as possible "agents of change" towards a more sustainable path for both the planet and the economic system, with inclusive growth. The European Commission, with the Action Plan in 2018, has attributed specific concerns to financial intermediaries to drive flows toward sustainable investment, explicitly requiring portfolio managers to integrate factors relating to sustainability into their process. The need to urgently allocate capital deriving from the financial services sector (alongside those made available by public policies) is identified in the preamble of Regulation (EU) 2019/2088 on sustainability-related disclosure in the financial services sector (SFDR). Through this new regulation, the European Union (EU) tries to change behaviour patterns in the financial industry, discouraging greenwashing and promoting responsible and sustainable investments.

Albeit with significant differences, in an international context which shows a growing interest in sustainability issues, the EU is particularly active in transforming principles into behaviour, with the introduction of directives and regulations, both towards the world of investors and businesses. The EU has introduced some rules and initiatives to improve corporate disclosure and align it with the EU's priority objective of sustainable transition (reinforced with the adoption of the "Next Generation EU") and raise transparency and comparability of sustainability-related information for investors (e.g., the Non-Financial Reporting Directive, the already mentioned Sustainable Finance Disclosure Regulation, and the new Corporate Sustainability Reporting Directive). Some ad hoc directives (the Markets in Financial Instruments Directive and the Insurance Distribution Directive) require asset management firms and insurance companies to offer suitable products to meet their customers' needs and desires and to inform them of the sustainability of the financial instruments.

As part of impact investments, it is possible to identify green, social, and sustainability bonds. In particular, a green bond can be defined as "any type of bond instrument where the proceeds will be exclusively applied to finance or re-finance, in part or in full, new or/and existing eligible green projects" (ICMA, 2018), whereas social and sustainability bonds follow socially responsible goals. The difference between the yield on a conventional bond and a green bond with similar characteristics is defined as 'greenium' (or green premium) (Agliardi and Agliardi, 2019). More precisely, investors are disposed to accept a lower yield on a green asset compared to the traditional one, mainly on the secondary markets, putting in evidence strong investor demand in pro-environmental projects. This conclusion seems to be confirmed by most of the literature analysed by MacAskill et al. (2021) on green bonds. From their analysis, referring to the primary market, the 'greenium' seems not to be recorded by all the analysed papers, with 44% of the studies that do not account for a premium on green bonds (MacAskill et al., 2021).

While Corporate Social Responsibility (CSR), SRI, and ESG concepts differ, they are often used interchangeably. SRIs arise from excluding certain types of investments (and issuers) from the construction of portfolios, particularly those that do not respond to ethical considerations or do not follow socially responsible behaviour. CSR can instead be defined as a general framework of sustainability and responsible cultural influence of a company towards its shareholders. ESG is a measurable sustainability assessment. The ESG rating purpose is to measure compliance with the objectives and principles of sustainability broadly and - consequently - the greater or lesser consistency of an investment with the idea of impact investing. Liang and Renneboog (2020) link the concepts of CSR and ESG, referring corporate social responsibility to the incorporation of environmental, social and governance considerations into corporate management, financial decision-making and investor portfolio decisions. Nowadays, attention to ESG factors is relevant worldwide: Global Sustainable Investment Alliance (GSIA, 2020) recently reported that 36% of total professionally managed assets (around 35,3 trillion dollars) incorporate ESG factors. Furthermore, the volumes and percentages are snowballing.

Many investors use ESG scores (usually defined as ratings) to understand a firm's sustainability and – consequently – guide the allocation of their investments. These scores can be considered a framework used to evaluate a company's performance on specific environmental, social, and governance issues and transform the non-financial disclosure required, particularly by the EU rules, in numerical terms. So, the importance of ESG ratings is evident; but the lack of commonly unified standards for ESG measurement has led to considerable differences in how ESG is measured and evaluated by different data vendors (Zumente and Lāce, 2021). Berg et al. (2022), using a dataset of ESG ratings from six providers, identified that the correlations between the ratings are 0.54 on average, ranging from 0.38 to 0.71. As one of the consequences caused by this divergence in valuations, the authors suggest that the prices of stocks and bonds are less likely to reflect ESG performance, as investors do not have unique information. Depending on the rating agencies' preferences, weights of the constituting factors, and rating methodology, these rating inconsistencies represent a problem for the past and a challenge for future research (Liang and Renneboog, 2020). A consequence of such a broad and growing interest in ESG investments is the threat of a possible overvaluation of ESG products (Bofinger et al., 2022), which could be amplified by the effect of a growing investment demand - driven both by the context regulatory and by the request of the new generation of investors - towards potentially overvalued firms (Becker et al., 2022).

Different studies have been conducted to prove the relationship between impact investment and the rate of return for bonds and stocks (or mutual funds investing in green assets). In particular, the researchers often are interested in examining whether green or socially responsible focused products outperform their benchmarks or the 'traditional' investment. Literature reviews have been conducted on the link between ESG indicators and financial performance or market trends. A considerable number of papers have highlighted either a positive relationship (Clark et al., 2015; Verheyden et al., 2016) or at least a non-negative association (Friede et al., 2015) between ESG measures and performance. The analysed geographical area may impact the relationship's intensity (Auer and Schuhmach, 2016).

If yield is one of the most studied aspects in the various analyses, risk represents an equally important element in portfolio strategies. In the study by Fooladi and Hebb (2022), it is highlighted that the discussion of whether SRI in the portfolios of CSR firms can provide better risk-adjusted returns for investors is controversial (even if these firms are all profitable).

In this chapter, the authors propose a tri-objective framework, which extends the mean-risk analysis by including an objective of sustainability. They exploit the ESG ratings of the assets in the investable universe to define the sustainable grade of a given portfolio as the weighted value of the ESG scores of portfolio assets. The proposed methodology identifies portfolios that maximize both the expected return and the ESG assessment, and – in the meantime – minimize the risk profile. A tridimensional surface represents the resulting set of efficient alternatives in the risk-ESG-mean space. In addition, the authors introduce a method to guide the investor in the selection of the more suitable portfolio on this surface according to the attitudes toward the three objectives.

The upcoming sections are organized as follows. The next one provides a concise review of the existing body of knowledge about ESG integration in portfolio optimization. Section 3 is the Chapter's core, detailing the theoretical framework behind the developed approach for asset allocation based on ESG information. The fourth section showcases the results of an empirical experiment using data from the STOXX Europe 600 Index, pointing out the practical significance of the proposed multi-objective methodology concerning financial-only formulations for investors who consider ESG principles within the context of the European normative guidelines. Conclusions and future research directions are given in Section 5.

2. ESG IN PORTFOLIO OPTIMIZATION MODELS

Several methods have been proposed in the literature to incorporate ESG information into the portfolio optimisation process. The first approach for responsible investments involved a priori exclusion of assets and companies that did not align with sustainable and ethical practices. With the introduction of a more formal definition of environmental, social, and governance principles, and the development of a standardised metric that assesses the extent to which a company aligns with the ESG objectives, investors can now incorporate ESG considerations directly into their stock-picking strategies. For example, Liagkouras et al. (2022) have adopted a screening procedure to identify a subset of ESG-compliant stocks as constituents of a Mean-Variance (M-V) portfolio. Similarly, Pacelli et al. (2022) integrated a clustering procedure in the Mean-CVaR portfolio optimisation framework and showed the advantages of focusing on a preselection of assets with high ESG scores. Kaucic et al. (2023b) studied several ESG-based preselection techniques in a prospect theory-based portfolio model. Further, they assessed the profitability of the proposed asset allocation strategies using an investment pool from the STOXX Europe 600 index, showing that ESG-based stock-picking procedures improve the investments' financial performance.

Defining portfolio ESG score as the weighted average of its constituents' ESG scores, an investor can impose in the optimisation problem a constraint for the minimum acceptable level of portfolio ESG. De Spiegeleer et al. (2021) extended the M-V model following this approach; their analysis pointed out the impact of the choice of the rating agency as well as the specific market universe and investment period on the risk-return results. In the same framework, Morelli (2022), exploiting only the environmental scores of the components of the Euro Stoxx 50, incorporated a constraint on the selected parameter in the Mean-CVaR model. The ex-post analysis reveals that strategies prioritising the companies' environmental commitment in the portfolio obtain the best financial performance. Instead of setting a minimum threshold for the portfolio ESG score, Schmidt (2022) modified the minimising objective function of the M-V model so that portfolio weights are simultaneously optimised in terms of return, risk, and ESG value. This formulation includes two parameters, namely the well-known risk aversion parameter, which controls the risk-return trade-off, and the so-called ESG strength parameter, which is related to the investors' preferences for the portfolio ESG value. Higher values of the second parameter represent a greater interest in the ESG criterion.

Garcia-Bernabeu et al. (2019) extended the classical bi-criteria M-V framework by directly including sustainability as a third criterion. They first formalised the preference relation of an ESG-aware M-V investor and introduced a multiobjective genetic algorithm to identify the surface of optimal portfolios. Then, they analysed the range of values attainable and the trade-off between return, risk, and sustainability for a set of institutional SRI open-end funds from Morningstar using the level diagrams tool by Blasco et al. (2008). Similarly, Hilario-Caballero et al. (2020) used a multiobjective approach to include in the bi-criteria M-V optimisation problem the investor's preferences toward the carbon risk exposure of the portfolio. Moreover, they proposed an a-posteriori technique that extends the original level diagrams tool by including information on carbon risk and risk aversion-related preferences. Xidonas and Essner (2022) proposed a multiobjective minimax-based optimisation model to build optimal ESG portfolios, maximising at the same time the risk performance of the three ESG pillars. Cesarone et al. (2022) adapted the standard ε-constrained method from mathematical programming (Ehrgott, 2005) to solve the tri-objective M-V-ESG optimisation problem. They also investigated the possible effects of SRI regulatory developments and ESG rating on the portfolio selection process over the past 15 years using data from five real-world datasets involving major equity markets.

Lindquist et al. (2022) first combined ESG scores with financial returns to generate an ESG-valued return and applied this mixed measure in a general mean-risk optimisation framework. Then, they consider an application to the optimisation of Real Estate Investment Trust (REIT) portfolios, employing variance and CVaR to quantify the investment risk.

3. DESCRIPTION OF THE PROPOSED MODEL

In the optimal wealth allocation process among a finite number of risky assets, investors have to recognise the sources of risk and then quantify and control them. In this section, the authors first introduce the general mean-variance portfolio selection model (Markowitz, 1952). Then, they exhibit a generalisation of this approach that considers alternative proxies for estimating portfolio risk. Due to the increasing importance of the ESG information in the investment process for financial and ethical motives (Amel-Zadeh and Serafeim, 2018), in Section 3.3 the authors propose a novel portfolio selection approach that extends the mean-risk framework by introducing a third dimension linked to sustainability.

3.1 The Mean-Variance Asset Allocation Framework

A simple and effective way to measure risk is to consider the deviations of the observations of a random variable from a reference point. Thus, agents can measure portfolio uncertainty using mean deviations and quantify the risk with the standard deviation. Formally, given a random variable , its standard deviation is defined as the square root of the variance:

$$\tilde{A}(Z) = \sqrt{E\left(\left(Z - E(Z)\right)^2\right)}.$$

This quantity measures the uncertainty associated with Z. Moreover, the standard deviation respects the properties given in the following axiomatic definition (Rockafellar et al., 2006):

i. $\sigma(Z) = \sigma(Z+c)$, for all Z *and* $c \geq 0$ (sh*ift invariance*)
ii. $\sigma(0) = 0$, $\sigma(\lambda Z) = \lambda \sigma(Z)$, *for* all Z and $\lambda > 0$ (positive *homogeneity*)
iii. $\sigma(Z) \geq 0$ for all Z, with $\sigma(Z) > 0$ if Z is nonconstant (positivi*ty*)
iv. $\sigma(Z+Y) \leq \sigma(Z) + \sigma(Y)$ *for* all Z and Y (s*u*baddi*t*ivity).

*Subadd*itivity ensures that the standard deviation of a portfolio composed of two positions is not higher than the two components' volatility taken separately. Thus, it means that diversification does not increase uncertainty. For this reason, the standard deviation has been used to denote the diversification of a portfolio. The use of $\sigma(Z)$ in solving minimisation problems is not popular since the presence of the square root can lead to complex expressions when differentiated. However, if the square of the standard deviation, called variance, is minimised, the resulting quadratic minimisation problem is more easily solvable. Furthermore, minimising the standard deviation is equivalent to minimising the variance. For this reason, the choice of variance as a proxy for risk is more prevalent in asset allocation practice. In this framework, Markowitz (1952) developed the so-called M-V analysis, which represents the cornerstone of modern portfolio theory. This theory suggests that portfolio choice should be based on the information given by two quantities: the expected portfolio rate of return and the portfolio variance. The main principle behind this paradigm can be formulated in two ways.

1.   Among all portfolios with a given lower bound on the expected rate of return, find the ones with the lower variance.
2.   Among all portfolios with the same upper bound on volatility, find the ones with the highest expected rate of return.

Suppose that agents act on their investment decisions over a one-period horizon and assume that the investment universe consists of n risky assets, with their rates of return expressed by the random variables R1,...,Rn. The *r*andom variable $R_p(x) = \sum_{i=1}^{n} x_i R_i$ represents the rate of return of the portfolio x= (x1,...,xn$_{)}$T, w$_h$e^{r}e T is t^{h}e transpose operator. The portfolio expected rate of return is denoted by $\mu_p(x) = \sum_{i=1}^{n} x_i \mu_i$, where $\mu = (\mu 1,...,\mu n)_\top$ is t$_h$e vector of assets' expected rates of return. Finally, $\sigma_p^2(x) = \sum_{j=1}^{n} \sum_{i=1}^{n} x_i x_j \sigma_{i,j}$ expresses portfolio variance, where $\sigma i,j$ is t$_{he}$ covariance between assets i and j. Note *t*hat, given the n×n cova*r*iance matrix $\sum$, portfolio variance can also be expressed compactly as $\sigma_p^2(x) = x^\top \sum x$. In this work, the authors introduce the no short-selling constraint and the so-called budget constraint, which states that all the available wealth has to be invested in the portfolio since portfolio managers usually face these limitations in determining whether a portfolio is feasible. Thus, the feasible set can be expressed as follows:

$$\Delta = \left\{ x \in \mathbb{R}^n : x_i \geq 0, i = 1,...,n, \sum_{i=1}^{n} x_i = 1 \right\} \quad (1)$$

Hence, the M-V optimisation problem behind the first paradigm formulation is the following quadratic programming problem:

$$\min_{x \in \Delta} \ x^\top \sum x$$
$$s.t. \ x^\top \mu \geq \mu_*, \tag{2}$$

where μ^* is the lower bound on the portfolio's expected rate of return. Further, the optimisation problem behind the second formulation of the M-V principle can be expressed as a maximisation problem:

$$\max_{x \in \Delta} \ x^\top \mu$$
$$s.t. \ x^\top \sum x \leq \sigma^*, \tag{3}$$

where σ^* denotes the upper bound on the portfolio volatility.

A portfolio that solves Problem (2) or Problem (3) is called efficient. By varying μ^* in (2) or σ^* in (3), one can obtain the so-called efficient frontier in the variance-mean plane. By analysing the shape of the efficient frontier, investors can assess the trade-off between the portfolio's expected rate of return and its variance to select a portfolio aligned with their risk tolerance and investment objectives.

3.1.1 Criticism of Mean-Variance Optimization

The standard Markowitz's formulation uses the variance as a proxy for the portfolio risk. Even if considered a milestone in the field, the M-V approach presents two well-known drawbacks.

- Variance is not a good choice for a risk measure since it penalises both the negative and the positive deviation from the mean symmetrically. Hence, it does not account for the asymmetric nature of risk, which concerns losses only. When asset returns are heavily skewed, or portfolio returns distribution presents fat tails, risks could be underestimated, and the M-V approach could lead to sub-optimal portfolio choices.
- The M-V framework often identifies efficient portfolios concentrated in a small subset of the investable universe. This feature is particularly evident when there is a large number of assets. In particular, during times of financial crisis, a concentrated and unbalanced portfolio could lead to substantial losses.

A solution is to replace the variance with an alternative measure to estimate the uncertainty of a random variable, the downside semi-variance (Markowitz, 1959). Given a random variable Z, this measure only accounts for the negative deviations from the mean, and it is defined as follows:

$$\sigma^+(Z) = \sqrt{E\left(\left(Z - E(Z)\right)_+^2\right)},$$

where $(Z–E(Z))_+ = \max(Z–E(Z),0)$. The use of this measure in the asset allocation practice has been studied extensively, and the interested reader may refer to the works of Konno et al. (2002) and Markowitz et al. (1993).

Box constraints can also be introduced when specifying the feasible set in (1) to enhance portfolio diversification and tackle the second issue. These constraints introduce an upper and a lower bound on the wealth that can be allocated to a single asset. However, in this study, the problem of diversification is not investigated by the authors.

3.2 Extending the M-V Model: The Mean-Risk Approach

The mean-variance analysis can be significantly extended by replacing the variance with a suitable risk measure to evaluate portfolio risk. In other words, a risk measure quantifies the risk by associating a real number with a random payoff's loss distribution. Artzner et al. (1999) introduced the axiomatic definition of coherent risk measure, considering $\mathcal{R}(Z)$ which assigns a real value to a random variable Z that should satisfy the following properties:

i. $\mathcal{R}(Y) \leq \mathcal{R}(Z)$ if $Y \geq Z$ almost surely (*monotonicity*)
ii. $\mathcal{R}(0) = 0; \mathcal{R}(\lambda Z) = \lambda \mathcal{R}(Z)$, for all Z and $\lambda > 0$ (*positive homogeneity*)
iii. $\mathcal{R}(Z + Y) \leq \mathcal{R}(Z) + \mathcal{R}(Y)$, for all Z and Y (*subadditivity*)
iv. $\mathcal{R}(Z + c) = \mathcal{R}(Z) - c$, for all Z and $c \geq 0$ (*invariance*).

In this context, the M-V principle can be generalised using another risk measure instead of variance. This approach is called mean-risk (M-R) analysis. Now, the choice paradigm can be stated in the following two ways.

1. Among all portfolios with a given lower bound on the expected return, find the ones that minimise the risk.
2. Among all portfolios with a given upper limit on the risk, find the ones with the highest expected performance.

With abuse of notation, the authors will indicate the risk measure of the portfolio rate of return $R_p(x)$ by using $\mathcal{R}_p(x)$. This notation evidences the dependence from the vector of the portfolio weights x and simplifies the treatment. Hence, the M-R optimisation problems can be formulated as follows:

$$\min_{x \in \Delta} \ \mathcal{R}_p(x)$$
$$s.t. \ x^\top \mu \geq \mu_* \tag{4}$$

where μ^* is the lower bound on the expected performance. An equivalent formulation is the following:

$$\max_{x \in \Delta} \quad x^\top \mu$$
$$s.t. \quad \mathcal{R}_p(x) \leq \mathcal{R}^*, \tag{5}$$

where $\mathcal{R}^*$ is the upper bound on portfolio risk. Similarly to what is described above, a representation of the mean-risk efficient frontier can be obtained by solving Problems (4) and (5) with different lower and upper bounds μ^* and $\mathcal{R}^*$.

3.2.1 Quantile-Based Risk Measures

In the latest years, quantifying significant losses and dealing with tail events has become a priority in banking and insurance due to the importance of the recently introduced regulations for solvency capital requirement. For this reason, a class of risk measures called quantile-based risk measures occupies a leading position in the risk management sector. Measures such as value-at-risk (VaR) and conditional value-at-risk (CVaR) have become very popular in portfolio optimisation problems. If one considers a random variable Z that expresses a random payoff, and given the significance level α, with $\alpha \in [0,1]$, VaR can be defined as the threshold below which the payoff value falls with probability α (the so-called tail probability):

$$\text{VaR}_\alpha(Z) = -\inf_z \{ z : P(Z \leq z) \geq \alpha \}. \tag{6}$$

Although VaR is easy to use and intuitive, it presents some critical pitfalls. First, it does not account for losses that exceed the VaR threshold. Second, it does not respect subadditivity property, which is essential to guarantee that diversification does not enhance the risk. To deal with these shortcomings, the conditional value-at-risk (CVaR) has been introduced by Rockafellar et al. (2000). The CVaR of a random variable Z at significance level α is (Mausser and Romanko, 2018):

$$\text{CVaR}_\alpha(Z) = -E(Z \mid Z \leq -\text{VaR}_\alpha(Z)) \delta_\alpha - \text{VaR}_\alpha(Z)(1 - \delta_\alpha), \tag{7}$$

where $\delta_\alpha = \dfrac{P(Z \leq -\text{VaR}_\alpha(Z))}{\alpha}$. Note that if Z has a continuous and strictly increasing distribution function, then $\text{CVaR}_\alpha(Z) = -E(Z \mid Z \leq -\text{VaR}_\alpha(Z))$. In this case, the CVaR is a conditional expectation, namely the average of all losses greater or equal to VaR_α. Note that the CVaR risk measure satisfies all the above-presented axioms and is thus a coherent risk measure. For this reason, it has become popular in practical applications.

3.2.2 CVaR-Based Portfolio Optimisation

The mean-CVaR portfolio selection problem is a specification of the M-R model where an agent seeks to maximise return while minimising CVaR. Conceptually, the minimum CVaR portfolio with significance level α is formulated as follows:

$$\min_{x \in \Delta} \ \mathrm{CVaR}_\alpha \left(x \right)$$

$$s.t. \ x^\top \mu \geq \mu_*. \tag{8}$$

Notice that the authors have indicated the conditional value-at-risk of the portfolio returns distribution $R_p(x)$ with $\mathrm{CVaR}_\alpha(x)$ to underline the dependence of this measure on the portfolio weights and to simplify the treatment.

3.3 Inclusion of ESG Issues in the Mean-Risk Framework

The models introduced in the previous sections focus solely on financial features and do not account for the increasing sensibility of political institutions, portfolio managers, and investors toward socially responsible investing. However, the intrinsically multifaceted and context-dependent nature of ESG data and the lack of a theoretical foundation hamper the direct implementation of ESG strategies for most investors (Young In et al., 2019). Moreover, there are various ways to characterize the sustainability of a company. Widely used metrics are, for instance, the ESG rating provided by a given agency, the greenhouse gas emissions intensity (De Spiegeleer et al., 2021), and the carbon risk exposure (Hilario-Caballero et al., 2020). In this chapter, the authors consider the numerical scores associated with firms' ESG rating to guide the investment choices. The sustainable grade of a given portfolio is then defined as the weighted value of portfolio constituents' ESG scores. More formally, it can be calculated as:

$$ESG_p \left(x \right) = \sum_{i=1}^{n} x_i ESG_i \tag{9}$$

where ESG_i is the value of the ESG score for the i-th asset. Thus, $ESG_p(x)$ represents the sustainability propensity of portfolio x expressed in terms of ESG score. The preference relation of the M-R principle can be extended through the following formulation.

Definition 1. According to the mean-risk-ESG (M-R-ESG) portfolio selection model, a portfolio x is preferred to a portfolio y if and only if $\mu_p \left(x \right) \geq \mu_p \left(y \right), \mathcal{R}_p \left(x \right) \leq \mathcal{R}_p \left(y \right)$ and $ESG_p(x) \geq ESG_p(y)$, with at least one strict inequality.

In this manner, the ESG issues directly enter into the decision-making process. The proposed model maximises both the expected return and the ESG assessment and - in the meantime - minimises the risk profile.

It follows that the efficient frontier of the proposed mean-risk-ESG portfolio selection model can be obtained by solving the following tri-objective optimisation problem:

$$\min_{x \in \Delta} \left(-\mu_p \left(x \right), \mathcal{R}_p \left(x \right), -ESG_p \left(x \right) \right). \tag{10}$$

The choice of an appropriate portfolio risk measure $\mathcal{R}_p \left(x \right)$ in the model specification is crucial since different measures may capture completely different characteristics of the portfolio return distribution. For instance, the asset allocation problem when the standard deviation is considered as a proxy for portfolio risk declines as follows:

$$\min_{x \in \Delta} \left(-\mu_p \left(x \right), \sigma_p^2 \left(x \right), -ESG_p \left(x \right) \right), \tag{11}$$

while the respective model that minimises $CVaR_\alpha(x)$ is

$$\min_{x \in \Delta} \left(-\mu_p \left(x \right), CVaR_\alpha \left(x \right), -ESG_p \left(x \right) \right). \tag{12}$$

3.4 Computing M-R-ESG Efficient Frontiers

In this section, the authors will show how to practically find the efficient surface of the mean-variance-ESG and mean-CVaR-ESG models. First, the standard ε-constrained method (Ehrgott, 2005) is applied to reformulate Problem (10) into a single-objective optimisation problem. Let η and λ be the required target levels of the portfolio expected return and sustainability indicator, respectively. The resulting optimisation problem is the following:

$$\begin{aligned} &\min_{x \in \Delta} \ \mathcal{R}_p \left(x \right) \\ &s.t. \ x^\top \mu \geq \eta \\ &ESG_p \left(x \right) \geq \lambda. \end{aligned} \tag{13}$$

This single-objective asset allocation model minimises the risk measure with parametric lower bounds on the portfolio return and ESG. Computing the solutions of Problem (13) by appropriately varying η and λ leads to determining the mean-risk-ESG optimal portfolios. Following a procedure similar to Cesarone et al. (2022) and Lindquist et al. (2022), with this approach, the authors can obtain the M-R-ESG efficient portfolios and represent them in the risk-expected rate of return for several fixed levels of expected ESG thresholds.

First, a suitable interval $[\lambda min, \lambda max]$ for λ is set, where $\lambda_{\min} = ESG_p \left(x_{\min \mathcal{R}} \right)$, and $\lambda max =_{ES} Gp(xm_a x E_{SG).M}$ore specifically, λmin is the sustainability level of the portfolio that minimises the risk, $x_{\min \mathcal{R}} = \arg \min_{x \in \Delta} \mathcal{R}_p \left(x \right)$, and λmax is the maximum level of ESG obtainable from constructing a portfolio with the n available assets, namely $x_{\max ESG} = \arg \max_{x \in \Delta} ESG_p \left(x \right)$. Then, given a fixed ESG level λ, an appropriate interval $[\eta min(\lambda), \eta max(\lambda)]$ is determined. Notice that this interval depends on the choice of the threshold λ. On the one hand, $\eta_{\min} \left(\lambda \right) = \mu_p \left(x_{\min \mathcal{R}} \left(\lambda \right) \right)$ is the rate of return of the portfolio that minimises the risk with a given sustainability requirement, namely the optimal solution of the following problem:

$$\begin{aligned} &\min_{x \in \Delta} \ \mathcal{R}_p \left(x \right) \\ &s.t. \ ESG_p \left(x \right) \geq \lambda. \end{aligned} \tag{14}$$

On the other hand, $\eta max(\lambda) =_{\mu p(} xmax \mu(\lambda_)$ is the rate of return of the portfolio that maximises the performance with a lower bound on the ESG score, which is the solution of:

$$\begin{aligned} &\max_{x \in \Delta} \ \mu_p \left(x \right) \\ &s.t. \ ESG_p \left(x \right) \geq \lambda. \end{aligned} \tag{15}$$

Note that by solving Problem (13) with $\lambda \in [\lambda\min, \lambda\max]$ and with $\eta = \eta\min(\lambda)$, one can obtain the ESG-risk efficient frontier. More precisely, setting $\eta = \eta\min$ and $\lambda = \lambda\min$, the optimal solution is the global minimum risk portfolio. Furthermore, setting $\lambda = \lambda\max$, the frontier collapses in a single portfolio composed of the asset with the highest ESG value. Finally, solving Problem (13) with $\lambda \in [\lambda\min, \lambda\max]$ and with $\eta = \eta_{\max}(\lambda)$, the optimal solutions form the mean-ESG frontier.

3.5 Scenario-Based Framework for Portfolio Optimisation

Let h indicate the investment horizon for the considered asset allocation problem on a daily basis. In this work, the authors use a scenario-based generation technique to obtain simulations for the random h-step ahead portfolio return Rp(x) to estimate the values of the quantities involved in Problems (11) and (12). To this end, the authors consider the historical daily rates of return of the n risky assets observed during the time window [0,T].

The scenario-based generation technique works as follows. A set of *h* consecutive joint realizations of the rates of return for the *n* assets in a given time horizon represents a scenario. The authors use the so-called block bootstrap procedure to replicate the correlation structure of the financial time series, resampling blocks of data (instead of individual values). When historical observations are good proxies for future rates of return, block bootstrapping techniques have shown to be promising alternatives to econometric models in forecasting financial time series and preserving cross-sectional correlations (Guastaroba et al., 2009). It is worth noting that no distributional assumption is needed to implement these procedures. However, they can fail to adequately predict changes in the financial market since bootstrap methods do not contain more information about the time series than what is given in the original sample. Thus, the authors adopt the so-called stationary bootstrap technique (Politis and Romano, 1994). This procedure considers a random block size, a set of consecutive scenarios with variable length, to bring some robustness with respect to the standard block bootstrap, which uses a fixed block size. The procedure works as follows. First, an optimal average block size B* is selected following the technique introduced by Politis and White (2004). Then, a block of B* consecutive daily observations is extracted randomly from the observed data frame. Finally, the authors repeat this exercise until the extracted sample reaches the desired size h, adjusting the last block length if the procedure exceeds the desired number of periods. Through this technique, for each asset i there is a bootstrap sample $\widehat{R}_{i,k}$ of h rates of return, with i=1,...,n and k=1,...,h. Then, the bootstrap-simulated h step ahead rate of return of the i-th asset is calculated as $\widehat{R}_i = \prod_{k=1}^{h} \left(1 + \widehat{R}_{i,k}\right)$. Given a portfolio x, its h-step ahead rate of return is computed as $\widehat{R}_p(x) = \sum_{i=1}^{n} x_i \widehat{R}_i$. To obtain an estimation of the empirical distribution of Rp(x), this bootstrap procedure is repeated S times. Let $\widehat{R}_p^s(x)$ be the s-th simulation of the portfolio return Rp(x). Then, concerning Problem (11), the bootstrap estimators for μp(x) and $\sigma_p^2(x)$ are:

$$\widehat{\mu}_p(x) = \frac{1}{S} \sum_{s=1}^{S} \widehat{R}_p^s(x)$$

and

$$\widehat{\sigma}^2_{\,p}(x) = \sqrt{\frac{1}{S} \sum_{s=1}^{S} \left(\widehat{R}_p^s(x) - \widehat{\mu}_p(x)\right)^2}.$$

Regarding Problem (12), the CVaR expression in (7) can be estimated as an arithmetic mean, following the procedure suggested by Kaucic et al. (2019) and Rachev et al. (2008). Let $\widehat{R}_p^{(1)}(x) \leq \widehat{R}_p^{(2)}(x) \leq \ldots \leq \widehat{R}_p^{(S)}(x)$ be the sorted sequence of the bootstrap simulations. Thus, the value-at-risk at confidence level α can be defined as follows:

$$\widehat{VaR_\alpha}(x) = -\widehat{R}_p^{(\lfloor \alpha S \rfloor)}(x),$$

where $\lfloor \cdot \rfloor$ denotes the floor operator. Then, the bootstrap simulated conditional value-at-risk is:

$$\widehat{CVaR}_\alpha(x) = -\frac{1}{\alpha S}\left(\sum_{s=1}^{\alpha S}\widehat{R}_p^s(x) + (\alpha S - \alpha S)\widehat{R}_p^{(\lfloor \alpha S \rfloor)}(x)\right). \qquad (15)$$

3.6 Portfolio Selection Based on Agent's Preferences

The authors will denote the efficient frontier by $\mathcal{P}$, and choose on $\mathcal{P}$ the portfolio more compatible with the investor's attitude toward reward, risk, and sustainability as follows. First, the objective functions for each efficient portfolio $x \in \mathcal{P}$ are normalised using the formulas:

$$\tilde{\mu}_p(x) = \frac{\mu_p(x) - \mu_p^{\min}}{\mu_p^{\max} - \mu_p^{\min}},$$

$$\tilde{\mathcal{R}}_p(x) = \frac{\mathcal{R}_p^{max} - \mathcal{R}_p(x)}{\mathcal{R}_p^{max} - \mathcal{R}_p^{min}},$$

and

$$\widetilde{ESG}_p(x) = \frac{ESG_p(x) - ESG_p^{min}}{ESG_p^{max} - ESG_p^{min}}.$$

Note that, in the previous formulas,

$$\mu_p^{\max} = \max_{x \in \mathcal{P}} \mu_p(x) \text{ and } \mu_p^{\min} = \min_{x \in \mathcal{P}} \mu_p(x);$$

$$\mathcal{R}_p^{max} = max_{x \in \mathcal{P}}\mathcal{R}_p(x) \text{ and } \mathcal{R}_p^{min} = min_{x \in \mathcal{P}}\mathcal{R}_p(x);$$

$$ESG_p^{\max} = \max_{x \in \mathcal{P}} ESG_p(x) \text{ and } ESG_p^{\min} = \min_{x \in \mathcal{P}} ESG_p(x).$$

Next, the authors introduce a vector that expresses the agent's preferences $w_{pref} = (w_\mu, w_\mathcal{R}, w_{ESG})$ $\in [0,1]^3$ such that $w_\mu + w_\mathcal{R} + w_{ESG} = 1$. Finally, the efficient portfolio tailored to the investor's financial reward/risk/ESG profile w_{pref} can be obtained by solving the following single-objective problem that maximises the weighted sum of the normalised objective functions:

$$\max_{x \in \mathcal{P}} \left\{ w_\mu \tilde{\mu}_p\left(x\right) + w_\mathcal{R} \tilde{\mathcal{R}}_p\left(x\right) + w_{ESG} \widetilde{ESG}_p\left(x\right) \right\}.$$

4. EXPERIMENTAL PART

The experimental analysis focuses on the European market because the European Union, through Directive 2014/95/EU, has imposed the disclosure of companies' non-financial information from 2015. In this context, the investable universe consists of a subset of the STOXX Europe 600 Index constituents. The authors select a pool of stocks for which an ESG score from the same provider is available during the whole period. Among all the possible providers available in the market, the authors have decided to utilise Refinitiv's ESG scores since they are applied widely in the financial industry. These scores are based on a company's performance on over 400 ESG indicators across ten categories: climate change, emissions, environmental product innovation, water resources, human rights, labour practices, community development, supply chain, corporate governance, and anti-corruption. The score provider uses company-reported data and third-party data sources to assess ESG performance (including ESG controversies impacting the firms). Each indicator's weighting is determined through expert judgment, data analysis, and consultation with industry experts and stakeholders. Refinitiv's ESG scores are a percentile ranking, with 100 indicating the highest score and 0 indicating the lowest. The scores are based on the relative performance of ESG factors within the company's sector (for environmental and social) and country of incorporation (for governance) and are updated monthly. As a result, the dataset consists of the monthly rates of return and the monthly ESG ratings from 01/01/2016 to 31/12/2021 for 538 firms, downloaded from Refinitiv Datastream.

The empirical analysis consists of two stages. First, the authors investigate the relation among reward, risk, and ESG scores for instances (11) and (12) of the tri-objective optimisation problem (10). To achieve this goal, they consider a dotted representation of the efficient frontiers for each ex-post month, employing the procedure detailed in Section 3.4 with 10 values for parameter λ and, for each value of λ, 10 suitable levels of $\eta(\lambda)$, for a total of 100 portfolios. Then, the authors analyse the ex-post performance of a set of portfolios selected on the efficient frontiers based on six typical attitudes toward the reward, risk, and ESG criteria.

4.1 Mean-Risk-ESG Efficient Frontiers

The authors consider an investment plan with a one-month horizon and employ a rolling window scheme with 72 end-of-month investments from 29/01/2016 to 31/12/2021. For each choice of the risk measure in Problem (13) and for each month, the authors exploit an in-sample window of 1000 days to set up the financial parameters, which are μp, σ_p^2 and CVaRα. Then, they calculate the portfolio ESG score in (9) using the stocks' ESG scores at the beginning of the corresponding ex-post month.

4.1.1 Case 1: Mean-Variance-ESG Model

Regardless of the selected month, the authors note that, from a qualitative perspective, the relationships between expected return, variance, and ESG score remain consistent over time. Consequently, they discuss and provide a detailed commentary on the findings pertaining to a particular month. Specifically, the 100 optimal portfolios on December 31, 2021, are displayed in Figure 1 on the left in the mean-variance-ESG tridimensional space.

On the one hand, this dotted representation reveals a clear trade-off between portfolio reward, measured by the expected rate of return, and the portfolio's sustainability attitude, indicated by the ESG score. The graph illustrates that portfolios with higher rates of return tend to exhibit lower ESG scores, implying that pursuing greater financial gains may involve compromising sustainability considerations within the portfolio.

On the other hand, one can observe the relation between portfolio rate of return and portfolio variance. Indeed, portfolios with higher rates of return are typically associated with higher risks, in line with the modern portfolio theory. This is because the demand for higher financial rewards may involve investing in riskier assets that prioritise financial gains, which could be more sensitive to market fluctuations. To better relate these findings to the sustainability principles, Figure 1 on the right reports the projection of the 3D efficient frontier on the variance-mean plane for increasing levels of the ESG threshold. It can be noted that, at the same level of variance, increasing the ESG threshold leads to a reduction in portfolio profitability.

Figure 1. Dotted representation at 31/12/2021 of the mean-variance-ESG efficient frontier on the left, and corresponding projection on the variance-mean plane on the right for different values of the ESG threshold λ. The blue dotted line represents the mean-ESG frontier, while the red one is the ESG-variance frontier.

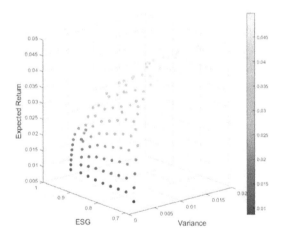 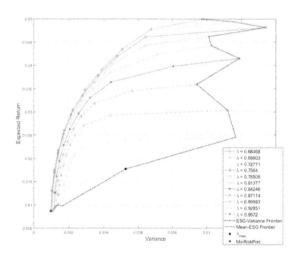

4.1.2 Case 2: Mean-CVaR-ESG Model

To analyse the robustness of the results in terms of increasing tail-risk severity, the authors consider two different tail levels, $\alpha=0.05$ and $\alpha=0.01$. The first choice is the most commonly used in practice, and it is also the suggested value by the solvency regulation, while the second choice represents a more prudential approach. Building upon the methodology employed in Case 1, the authors investigate the interplay among portfolio rate of return, CVaR, and ESG criteria during the final ex-post month. These findings can be extended to the other months involved in the analysis, suggesting consistent conclusions. More specifically, Figure 2 and Figure 3 report on the left the dotted approximations of the mean-CVaRα-$_{ES}$G frontiers with $\alpha=0.05$ and $\alpha=0.01$, respectively, and on the right, the corresponding projections on the CVaRα-mea$_n$ plane for increasing ESG thresholds. A first comparison reveals that the tail risk's severity does not significantly affect the frontier shape. As presented in Case 1, increasing the ESG threshold for fixed levels of CVaRα, lea$_{ds}$ to a decrease in the portfolio's expected rate of return. These results align with the existing literature, confirming that a higher sustainability demand within the portfolio entails a trade-off in terms of financial reward.

Figure 2. Dotted representation at 31/12/2021 of the mean-CVaR$_{0.05}$-ESG efficient frontier on the left, and corresponding projection on the CVaR$_{0.05}$-mean plane on the right for different values of the ESG threshold λ. The blue dotted line represents the mean-ESG frontier, while the red one is the ESG-CVaR$_{0.05}$ frontier.

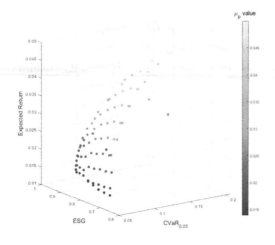 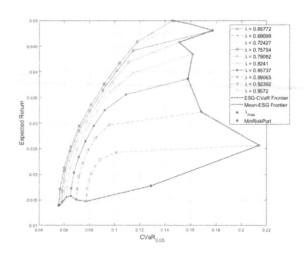

Figure 3. Dotted representation at 31/12/2021 of the mean-CVaR$_{0.01}$-ESG efficient frontier on the left, and corresponding projection on the CVaR$_{0.01}$-mean plane on the right for different values of the ESG threshold λ. The blue dotted line represents the mean-ESG frontier, while the red one is the ESG-CVaR$_{0.01}$ frontier.

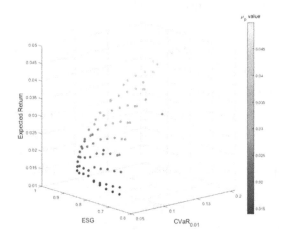 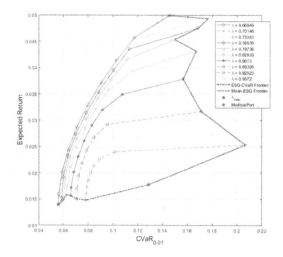

4.2 Ex-Post Investment Analysis

In this section, the authors focus on the profitability of portfolios selected from the proposed mean-risk-ESG efficient frontiers for different types of investors. Each agent described in Table 1 exhibits a specific attitude toward the three criteria. In particular, these preferences are encoded as a vector of non-negative weights that sum up to one, namely $w_{pref} = \left(w_\mu, w_\mathcal{R}, w_{ESG} \right)$. Higher values for a weight mean higher interest toward the corresponding criterion.

The first three agents strongly prefer one criterion while equally weighting the other two. The fourth preference combination represents an investor who allocates equal weights to the three objectives. The fifth agent makes decisions based on the M-R principle with little interest in sustainable criteria. Finally, Agent 6 pays great attention to both risk control and sustainability, with a marginal focus on financial reward.

Table 1. Types of agents considered in the ex-post analysis based on different attitudes toward the expected rate of return (w_μ, the risk measure ($w_\mathcal{R}$), and the ESG score (w_{ESG})

Agent	w_μ	$w_\mathcal{R}$	w_{ESG}
1	0.25	0.25	0.50
2	0.25	0.50	0.25
3	0.50	0.25	0.25
4	0.33	0.33	0.33
5	0.45	0.45	0.10
6	0.10	0.45	0.45

4.2.1 Ex-Post Performance Metrics

The authors evaluate the attractiveness of the investment opportunities from different points of view. In general terms, the random variable expressing the ex-post portfolio rate of return is denoted by r_p^{out}. Let $r_{p,t}^{out}$, $t=1,\ldots,72$ indicate the realised portfolio rates of return for each strategy in the ex-post (also called out-of-sample) window from 29/01/2016 to 31/12/2021. The STOXX Europe 600 Index from the European stock market is employed as a benchmark, and its rate of return in the out-of-sample period is indicated with r_b^{out}. Similarly, the realised ex-post benchmark returns are specified as $r_{b,t}^{out}$, $t=1,\ldots,7$.

At first, to measure the profitability of the analysed strategies, the authors consider the annualised mean return (AMR) during the ex-post window. Then, the authors examine the strategies' performance with respect to the benchmark by assessing the annualised excess mean return (AMER). Further, they conducted a *t*-test on the differences between observed portfolio and benchmark returns within the ex-post window.

To evaluate the compensation earned per unit of portfolio variance during the investment period, the authors consider the so-called Sharpe ratio (Sharpe, 1966). This measure is defined as the ratio between the average of the realised rates of return, $\mu o^{ut,}$ and their standard deviation, $\sigma o u^{t:}$

$$\text{SR} = \frac{\mu^{out}}{\sigma^{out}}.$$

Moreover, the authors account for a performance measure which is constructed based on conditional value-at-risk, the so-called Rachev ratio (Rachev, 2008). It considers the extra rates of return of the portfolio on the ex-post window, and it is defined as follows:

$$\text{RaR}_{\pm_1,\pm_2}^{out} = \frac{\text{CVaR}_{\alpha_1}\left(r_b^{out} - r_p^{out}\right)}{\text{CVaR}_{\alpha_2}\left(r_p^{out} - r_b^{out}\right)}.$$

This ratio is computed by dividing the conditional value-at-risk at level $\alpha1$ of the ex-post portfolio returns' distribution on the right tail by the conditional value-at-risk at level $\alpha1$ on the left tail. These quantities are estimated using the formula (15) with $\widehat{R}_p^s(x) = r_{p,t}^{out} - r_{b,t}^{out}$, and s=t. The Rachev ratio represents the reward potential for positive returns compared to the risk potential for negative returns at a quantile level defined by the user. In this analysis, the authors set $\alpha1 = _\alpha2 = 0.05$ and indicate the corresponding performance ratio with $\text{RaR}_{0.05}^{out}$.

Then, the diversification level of the optimal portfolios is measured using the normalised diversification index (DI), given by:

$$\text{DI} = \frac{1}{72}\sum_{t=1}^{72} \frac{1 - \sum_{i=1}^n \left(x_{i,t}\right)^2}{1 - \frac{1}{n}},$$

where $x_{i,t}$ is the weight of asset i at time t. This quantity equals 0 when all the capital is concentrated in one single asset and is 1 for the equally-weighted portfolio. Thus, more diversified portfolios present a higher DI value.

Moreover, to get an impression of the transaction costs involved, the authors calculate the average turnover over the out-of-sample period:

$$\text{TR} = \frac{1}{72}\sum_{t=1}^{72}\sum_{i=1}^{n}\left|x_{i,t} - x_{i,t-}\right|,$$

where $x_{i,t-}$ is the weight of asset i at ex-post time t immediately before the rebalancing phase. A greater value of TR indicates a more expensive investment strategy.

Finally, the authors analyse the risk exposure for the three proposed models (11) and (12) with $\alpha=0.01$ and $\alpha=0.05$ and the six considered agents using three measures: the ex-post standard deviation σ_{out} the conditional value-at-risk at the alpha level 0.05, $\text{CVaR}_{0.05}^{out}$, and the skewness of the out-of-sample returns distribution, Skew_{out}.

4.2.2 Analysis of the Best Investment Models

Table 2 and Table 3 present the results of the ex-post performance measures described in Section 4.2.1 for the three considered models and for the agents whose preferences are described in Table 1. The following points summarise the main findings for the ex-post analysis of the considered investment strategies.

1. Strategies employing conditional value-at-risk yield superior ex-post performance results in absolute terms (AMR) as well as in relative terms (AMER). For almost all the considered agents, the ex-post portfolio rates of return of the CVaR models exhibit statistically significant positive deviations from the benchmark. The only instance where the mean-variance-ESG model slightly outperforms in terms of AMR and AMER is for agent 5. In addition, all the considered strategies are superior to the benchmark in terms of ex-post Sharpe ratio, with values at least three times higher, meaning a better capability in terms of return-risk trade-off.

2. The authors analyse the relationships between the three objectives without introducing additional portfolio restrictions, such as diversification and turnover constraints, that could somehow affect the ex-post statistics. However, strategies that adopt CVaR as a risk measure show superior diversification levels while ensuring lower turnover. Additionally, regarding skewness, it is noteworthy to observe that only the realised rates of return of Agent 6 (the most conservative profile regarding risk-return-sustainability preferences) exhibit ex-post skewness of the same sign as the benchmark. In all other cases, the proposed strategies have positive skewness, suggesting a right-skewed distribution which implies potential profits in the right tails.

3. Incorporating ESG criteria into the standard mean-risk framework could lead to a reduction in tail-risk compared to the benchmark. As depicted in Table 3, all the studied asset allocation models exhibit a lower realised conditional value-at-risk than the benchmark. However, contrasting results emerge when examining portfolio standard deviation. Agents 3 and 5, representing profiles more inclined towards financial performance in addition to risk-ESG considerations, display higher exposure to standard deviation compared to both the benchmark and the other strategies considered.

Table 2. Ex-post performance measures for the three instances of Problem (10), corresponding to each preference vector outlined in Table 1. The third column represents the average rate of return, while the fourth column indicates the average excess rate of return over the STOXX Europe 600 Index. The fifth column reports the p-value of the t-test assessing the differences between ex-post portfolio returns and the benchmark. A single asterisk (*) denotes rejection of the null hypothesis of mean equality at a 5% significance level, while two asterisks (**) signify rejection at a 1% significance level. Lastly, the sixth and seventh columns display the ex-post Sharpe and Rachev ratios.

Agent	Risk	AMR	AMER	p-Value	SR	$RaR_{0.05}^{out}$
1	$\sigma 2$	0.1530	0.1035	0.1086	0.3228	1.8570
	$CVaR_{0.05}$	**0.1854**	**0.1360**	0.0431*	**0.4322**	1.9627
	$CVaR_{0.01}$	0.1798	0.1304	0.0479*	0.4252	**1.9656**
2	$\sigma 2$	0.1737	0.1243	0.0493	0.4616	1.9376
	$CVaR_{0.05}$	**0.2045**	**0.1550**	0.0251*	**0.5009**	**2.0755**
	$CVaR_{0.01}$	0.2009	0.1514	0.0271*	0.4959	2.0640
3	$\sigma 2$	0.3416	0.2922	0.0011**	**0.5983**	2.8373
	$CVaR_{0.05}$	**0.4416**	**0.3922**	0.0003**	0.5935	2.7423
	$CVaR_{0.01}$	0.4049	0.3555	0.0008**	0.5583	**2.9789**
4	$\sigma 2$	0.2061	0.1567	0.0204*	0.5192	**2.2592**
	$CVaR_{0.05}$	**0.2803**	**0.2309**	0.0022*	0.6064	2.1930
	$CVaR_{0.01}$	0.2777	0.2283	0.0021*	**0.6155**	2.1657
5	$\sigma 2$	**0.3521**	**0.3027**	0.0006**	**0.6205**	**3.0140**
	$CVaR_{0.05}$	0.3425	0.2931	0.0009**	0.5798	3.0260
	$CVaR_{0.01}$	0.3495	0.3001	0.0006**	0.6044	2.8550
6	$\sigma 2$	0.1114	0.0620	0.2231	0.2552	**1.8384**
	$CVaR_{0.05}$	**0.1312**	**0.0818**	0.1393	**0.3371**	1.6957
	$CVaR_{0.01}$	0.1305	0.0811	0.1432	0.3316	1.6997
Benchmark		0.0494	-	-	0.1040	-

4. Agents 3 and 5 exhibit the best ex-post performance in absolute and relative terms. Additionally, they demonstrate superior results in terms of the Rachev ratio. This fact implies that an investor with a profile more inclined towards return rather than risk and sustainability considerations has the potential to achieve higher profits than others. However, as highlighted in the previous point, they also display higher ex-post standard deviations, being potentially more vulnerable to sudden market fluctuations.

5. A highly promising investment profile that demonstrates excellent performance across all considered measures is represented by Agent 4. This configuration consistently exhibits the lowest ex-post standard deviation and ex-post CVaR values, regardless of the chosen risk measure in the multi-objective optimisation model. Additionally, it evidences good outcomes regarding diversification (ranked second-best strategy) and turnover (in line with the other agents but worse than Agent 6). The ability to contain variability and tail risk enables this configuration to achieve outstanding

results in the Sharpe ratio while maintaining a Rachev ratio comparable to that of Agents 3 and 5, albeit with slightly lower average rates of return.

In conclusion, these findings highlight the superiority of a well-balanced strategy (represented by Agent 4), which displays equal preferences for the three portfolio objectives. Moreover, while incorporating ESG criteria is crucial to reduce tail risk, relying solely on them (as for configurations 2 and 6) leads to mediocre outcomes. Optimal financial results are achieved by Agents 3 and 5, who approach the standard mean-variance framework, confirming the strength of the M-V model in investment decision-making.

Table 3. Ex-post performance measures for the three instances of Problem (10), corresponding to each preference vector outlined in Table 1. The third and fourth columns provide the average ex-post diversification index and the mean portfolio turnover. Then, the ex-post standard deviation is displayed in column 5, while the sixth column focuses on the conditional value-at-risk of the distribution of ex-post rates of return at the 0.05 significance level. In the end, the last column presents the skewness of the portfolio returns' distribution during the out-of-sample window.

Agent	Risk	DI	TR	σo^{ut}	$CVaR^{out}_{0.05}$	$Skew^{out}$
1	$\sigma 2$	0.7041	0.3564	0.0395	0.0626	**0.1852**
	$CVaR_{0.05}$	**0.7500**	0.2410	0.0358	**0.0542**	0.0903
	$CVaR_{0.01}$	0.7429	**0.2177**	**0.0352**	0.0545	0.1347
2	$\sigma 2$	0.8413	0.3255	**0.0313**	**0.0504**	-0.2293
	$CVaR_{0.05}$	**0.8780**	0.2920	0.0340	0.0526	**0.1736**
	$CVaR_{0.01}$	0.8728	0.3069	0.0337	0.0536	0.1381
3	$\sigma 2$	**0.6576**	0.6767	**0.0476**	**0.0501**	0.7494
	$CVaR_{0.05}$	0.6388	**0.5440**	0.0620	0.0748	0.7326
	$CVaR_{0.01}$	0.6352	0.5518	0.0604	0.0694	**0.8596**
4	$\sigma 2$	0.7975	0.4400	**0.0331**	0.0485	0.0483
	$CVaR_{0.05}$	**0.8223**	**0.3195**	0.0385	**0.0482**	**0.2787**
	$CVaR_{0.01}$	0.8203	0.3526	0.0376	0.0476	0.2748
5	$\sigma 2$	0.8397	0.3952	**0.0473**	**0.0544**	0.3290
	$CVaR_{0.05}$	**0.8522**	0.3331	0.0492	0.0553	**0.4494**
	$CVaR_{0.01}$	0.8481	0.3368	0.0482	0.0566	0.3862
6	$\sigma 2$	0.7849	0.1092	0.0364	0.0646	**-0.0597**
	$CVaR_{0.05}$	**0.8228**	**0.0970**	**0.0324**	0.0591	-0.4122
	$CVaR_{0.01}$	0.8191	0.0984	0.0328	**0.0598**	-0.4056
Benchmark		-	-	0.0396	0.0927	-0.5204

4.2.3 Ex-Post Net Wealth Evolution

To conclude this section, the authors assess the profitability of the different portfolio allocation strategies for each preference configuration. To achieve this goal, they consider an initial wealth allocation W_0=1,000,000€. Then, the authors explicitly evaluate the magnitude of the tradings through a transaction costs structure where the applied commissions depend on the range of traded monetary amount, as in Beraldi et al. (2021) and Kaucic et al. (2023a). More precisely, the transaction cost structure is characterised by decreasing cost rates as the traded value increases.

Figure 4 highlights the behaviour of the six investment strategies in terms of the produced net wealth for the two proposed investment models. The top graph displays the net wealth evolution of the six considered preference behaviours for the mean-variance-ESG model. The bottom left graph corresponds to the mean-CVaR$_{0.05}$-ESG model, while the bottom right graph shows the ex-post performance of the six agents using the CVaR$_{0.01}$ as a risk measure. As previously noted, configurations 3 and 5 demonstrate superior financial performance than the other ones. Concerning the mean-variance-ESG model, Agents 3 and 5 show a similar net wealth evolution. However, when employing the CVaR-based risk measure and specifically in the case of CVaR$_{0.01}$, Agent 3 exhibits a substantial outperformance, attaining within a span of just five years a final wealth that is eleven times greater than the initial investment. Moreover, the three plots confirm that, as described formerly, CVaR-based models yield superior ex-post results.

Figure 4. Ex-post net wealth evolution for the three models proposed and the six agents' configurations. Top figure shows the results for the mean-variance-ESG model. The figure on the bottom left displays the net wealth evolution for the mean-CVaR$_{0.05}$-ESG strategy. Finally, the on the bottom right shows results for the mean-CVaR$_{0.01}$-ESG model. The initial wealth investment is set equal to 1,000,000 €, and the transaction costs structure considered is characterized by decreasing cost rates as the traded amount increases.

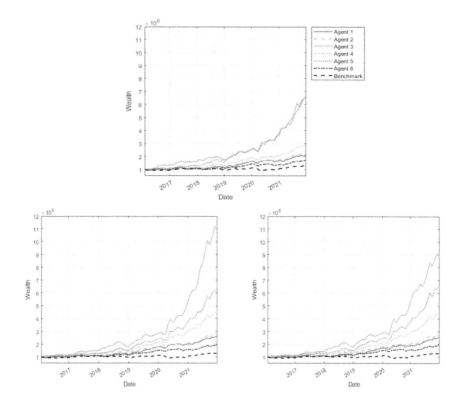

Overall, the proposed asset allocation models outperform the STOXX Europe 600 Index and show a remarkable trade-off between reward and risk. In particular, the authors highlight that configuration 3, which represents a balanced profile among risk, return, and sustainability, exhibits excellent results in terms of net wealth; thereby, it could be considered a viable investment option.

5. CONCLUSION

The risk measures employed in the proposed tri-objective portfolio selection model show a reduction in the profit opportunities but simultaneously a higher control on the risk, following the literature (see, for instance, Friede et al. (2015) and Cesarone et al. (2022)). Consequently, the results show that ESG scoring can be used for better risk control, especially during periods of high volatility. This is in line with Olofsson et al. (2021), who identify ethical investments as a hedging asset for portfolios during extreme market conditions, and with Yousaf et al. (2022), who show that green investments offer a significant risk reduction potential as well as improved risk-adjusted returns, particularly during turbulent market periods.

This finding supports the broad debate among scholars and practitioners about ESG relevance and disclosure in investment decisions. The discussion leads organisations to disclose information about their efforts to promote sustainability concerning the environment, society, and the economy. As noticed before, based on the increase in voluntary corporate non-financial disclosure, the European Commission (EC) has decided to implement mandatory disclosure across European countries. Introducing the European Union Directive 2014/95/EU, the EC requires organisations to disclose non-financial and diversity information. The Directive aims to increase transparency regarding social and environmental issues and ensure consistent and relevant information across companies. It requires large undertakings, public interest entities (PIEs), and organisations with over 500 employees to report information on environmental, social, employee, human rights, diversity, anti-corruption, and bribery matters.

Some studies (Clementino and Perkins, 2020; Mervelskemper and Streit, 2017; Santamaria et al., 2021) showed the importance of assessing the combinations of quality and quantity disclosures for ESG score, demonstrating the effectiveness of disclosure measurements on ESG score. However, these studies are based on different disclosure frameworks used by companies that could influence the ESG rating developed by various agencies. Indeed, the critical characteristic of the Directive is the lack of a specific standard/guideline to prepare non-financial information. The Directive neither suggests the content nor the reporting method for measuring, monitoring and managing undertakings' performance and their impact on society. Empirical studies (i.e. Cordazzo et al, 2020; Agostini et al, 2022) recognise the failure of companies to include crucial information that investors and other stakeholders consider essential under the new mandatory regime. Cordazzo et al. (2020), examining 231 Italian companies in the pre and post-implementation of the non-financial Directive, analysed the impact of ESG disclosure on the share price. They documented a moderate increase in non-financial information after the non-financial Directive, while the information on environment, employee, and society showed the highest increase. However, the transition from voluntary to mandatory non-financial disclosure had no effect on market shares. Authors explained their findings by the fact that the non-financial Directive only requires companies to disclose a minimum amount of information. Recently, Agostini et al. (2022) analysed the social and environmental disclosure of a sample of 20 Italian listed two years prior (2015–2016) and two years after (2017–2018) the Directive's application and their impact on corporate performance. Their results found that the Directive affected the quantity of non-financial information, but not the quality, and that the companies converted simply voluntary reporting into mandatory one by re-labeling similar reporting. Moreover, the mandatory non-financial information quality following the Directive does not show a significant relationship with corporate financial performance. Faced with this empirical evidence, the European Commission revised the non-financial Directive, issuing in December 2022 the new Corporate Social Responsibility Directive (CSRD), and in July 2023, the delegate acts about sustainability reporting standards proposed by EFRAG (ESRS). The architecture of these standards is composed of two cross-cutting standards (General Requirements and General Disclosures) and three topical standards (Environment, Social, and Governance). The aim of this detailed sustainability reporting - required by standards - is to improve the scope and quality of reports, promoting sustainable development through transparency. On the one hand, the ESRSs require companies to provide specific KPIs for each topical standard, adopting an electronic reporting format for sustainability data. On the other hand, the ESRSs are also subject to an external audit requirement, increasing the reliability of firms' provided information. The authors expect that the characteristics of the ESRS standards described above could reduce the differences between the ESG scores due to the detailed standard and reduce the risk of greenwashing, impacting the portfolio allocation strategies.

As seen previously, several studies have highlighted a limited correlation between the ESG rating opinions (on the same companies) issued by different providers. A possible development of the research could be to verify whether using other rating providers could lead to similar conclusions regarding the link between return, risk, and ESG evaluation, and - consequently - in terms of investment portfolio allocations. Furthermore, following the European regulatory evolution, aimed at giving rules for the homogenization of ESG rating assessments, using in the analysis specified and "standardized" drivers, and at increasing the companies involved in non-financial reporting, it would be fascinating to propose similar research again, in a different reference context, to understand if and how these efforts at homogenization and transparency could influence investment strategies and the consequent results.

ACKNOWLEDGMENT

The Authors thank Fabrizio Barbini and Beatrice Corso for the insights into the problem formulation.

REFERENCES

Agliardi, E., & Agliardi, R. (2019). Financing environmentally-sustainable projects with green bonds. *Environment and Development Economics*, *24*(6), 608–623. doi:10.1017/S1355770X19000020

Agostini, M., Costa, E., & Korca, B. (2022). Non-financial disclosure and corporate financial performance under directive 2014/95/EU: Evidence from Italian listed companies. *Accounting in Europe*, *19*(1), 78–109. doi:10.1080/17449480.2021.1979610

Amel-Zadeh, A., & Serafeim, G. (2018). Why and how investors use ESG information: Evidence from a global survey. *Financial Analysts Journal*, *74*(3), 87–103. doi:10.2469/faj.v74.n3.2

Artzner, P., Delbaen, F., Eber, M., & Heath, D. (1999). Coherent Measures of Risk. *Mathematical Finance*, *9*(3), 203–228. doi:10.1111/1467-9965.00068

Auer, B. R., & Schuhmach, F. (2016). Do socially (ir)responsible investments pay? New evidence from international ESG data. *The Quarterly Review of Economics and Finance*, *59*, 51–62. doi:10.1016/j.qref.2015.07.002

Becker, M. G., Martin, F., & Walter, A. (2022). The power of ESG transparency: The effect of the new SFDR sustainability labels on mutual funds and individual investors. *Finance Research Letters*, *47*, 102708. doi:10.1016/j.frl.2022.102708

Beraldi, P., Violi, A., Ferrara, M., Ciancio, C., & Pansera, B. A. (2021). Dealing with complex transaction costs in portfolio management. *Annals of Operations Research*, *299*(1-2), 7–22. doi:10.100710479-019-03210-5

Berg, F., Koelbel, J. F., & Rigobon, R. (2022). Aggregate confusion: The divergence of ESG ratings. *Review of Finance*, *26*(6), 1315–1344. doi:10.1093/rof/rfac033

Blasco, X., Herrero, J. M., Sanchis, J., & Martínez, M. (2008). A new graphical visualisation of n-dimensional Pareto front for decision-making in multiobjective optimisation. *Information Sciences*, *178*(20), 3908–3924. doi:10.1016/j.ins.2008.06.010

Bofinger, Y., Heyden, K. J., & Rock, B. (2022). Corporate social responsibility and market efficiency: Evidence from ESG and misvaluation measures. *Journal of Banking & Finance*, *134*, 106322. Advance online publication. doi:10.1016/j.jbankfin.2021.106322

Bugg-Levine, A., & Emerson, J. (2011). *Impact investing: Transforming how we make money while making a difference.* John Wiley & Sons.

Cesarone, F., Martino, M. L., & Carleo, A. (2022). Does ESG Impact Really Enhance Portfolio Profitability? *Sustainability (Basel)*, *14*(4), 2050. doi:10.3390u14042050

Clark, G., Feiner, A., & Viehs, M. (2015). *From the stockholder to the stakeholder: How sustainability can drive financial outperformance.* Oxford University & Arabesque Partners.

Clementino, E., & Perkins, R. (2021). How Do Companies Respond to Environmental, Social and Governance (ESG) ratings? Evidence from Italy. *Journal of Business Ethics*, *171*(2), 379–397. doi:10.100710551-020-04441-4

Cordazzo, M., Bini, L., & Marzo, G. (2020). Does the EU Directive on non-financial information influence the value relevance of ESG disclosure? Italian evidence. *Business Strategy and the Environment*, *29*(8), 3470–3483. doi:10.1002/bse.2589

De Spiegeleer, J., Höcht, S., Jakubowski, D., Reyners, S., & Schoutens, W. (2021). ESG: A new dimension in portfolio allocation. *Journal of Sustainable Finance & Investment*, 1–41. doi:10.1080/20430795.2021.1923336

Ehrgott, M. (2005). *Multicriteria Optimization.* Springer Science & Business Media.

Fooladi, I. J., & Hebb, G. (2022). Drivers of differences in performance of ESG-focused funds relative to their underlying benchmarks. *Global Finance Journal*, *100745*. Advance online publication. doi:10.1016/j.gfj.2022.100745

Friede, G., Busch, T., & Bassen, A. (2015). ESG and financial performance: Aggregated evidence from more than 2,000 empirical studies. *Journal of Sustainable Finance & Investment*, *5*(4), 210–233. doi:10.1080/20430795.2015.1118917

Garcia-Bernabeu, A., Salcedo, J. V., Hilario, A., Pla-Santamaria, D., & Herrero, J. M. (2019). Computing the mean-variance-sustainability nondominated surface by Ev-MOGA. *Complexity*, *2019*, 1–12. doi:10.1155/2019/6095712

GSIA. (2020). *Global Sustainable Investment Review.* https://www.gsi-alliance.org/wp-content/uploads/2021/08/GSIR-20201.pdf

Guastaroba, G., Mansini, R., & Speranza, M. G. (2009). On the effectiveness of scenario generation techniques in single-period portfolio optimisation. *European Journal of Operational Research*, *192*(2), 500–511. doi:10.1016/j.ejor.2007.09.042

Hilario-Caballero, A., Garcia-Bernabeu, A., Salcedo, J. V., & Vercher, M. (2020). Tri-Criterion Model for Constructing Low-Carbon Mutual Fund Portfolios: A Preference-Based Multiobjective Genetic Algorithm Approach. *International Journal of Environmental Research and Public Health*, *17*(17), 6324. doi:10.3390/ijerph17176324 PMID:32878037

ICMA. (2018). *Green Bond Principles 2018: Voluntary Process Guidelines for Issuing Green Bonds.* https://www.icmagroup.org/assets/documents/Regulatory/Green-Bonds/Green-Bonds-Principles-June-2018-270520.pdf

Kaucic, M., Moradi, M., & Mirzazadeh, M. (2019). Portfolio optimisation by improved NSGA-II and SPEA 2 based on different risk measures. *Financial Innovation*, *5*(26), 1–28. doi:10.118640854-019-0140-6

Kaucic, M., Piccotto, F., Sbaiz, G., & Valentinuz, G. (2023a). A hybrid level-based learning swarm algorithm with mutation operator for solving large-scale cardinality-constrained portfolio optimisation problems. *Information Sciences*, *634*, 321–339. doi:10.1016/j.ins.2023.03.115

Kaucic, M., Piccotto, F., Sbaiz, G., & Valentinuz, G. (2023b). Optimal Portfolio with Sustainable Attitudes under Cumulative Prospect Theory. *Journal of Applied Finance & Banking*. Advance online publication. doi:10.47260/jafb/1344

Konno, H., Waki, H., & Yuuki, A. (2002). Portfolio Optimisation under Lower Partial Risk Measures. *Asia-Pacific Financial Markets*, *9*(2), 127–140. doi:10.1023/A:1022238119491

Liagkouras, K., Metaxiotis, K., & Tsihrintzis, G. (2022). Incorporating environmental and social considerations into the portfolio optimisation process. *Annals of Operations Research*, *316*(2), 1493–1518. doi:10.100710479-020-03554-3

Liang, H., & Renneboog, L. (2020). Corporate social responsibility and sustainable finance: A review of the literature. *European Corporate Governance Institute–Finance Working Paper*, (701). www.ecgi.global/sites/default/files/working_papers/documents/liangrenneboogfinal.pdf.

Lindquist, W. B., Rachev, S. T., Hu, Y., & Shirvani, A. (2022). *Advanced REIT Portfolio Optimization.* Springer. doi:10.1007/978-3-031-15286-3

MacAskill, S., Roca, E., Liu, B., Stewart, R. A., & Sahin, O. (2021). Is there a green premium in the green bond market? Systematic literature review revealing premium determinants. *Journal of Cleaner Production*, *280*, 124491. doi:10.1016/j.jclepro.2020.124491

Markowitz, H., Todd, P., Xu, G., & Yamane, Y. (1993). Computation of mean-semivariance efficient sets by the Critical Line Algorithm. *Annals of Operations Research*, *45*(1), 307–317. doi:10.1007/BF02282055

Markowitz, H. M. (1952). Portfolio Selection. *The Journal of Finance*, *7*(1), 77–91. doi:10.2307/2975974

Markowitz, H. M. (1959). *Portfolio Selection: Efficient Diversification of Investments.* Yale University Press.

Mausser, H., & Romanko, O. (2018). Long-only equal risk contribution portfolios for CVaR under discrete distributions. *Quantitative Finance*, *18*(11), 1927–1945. doi:10.1080/14697688.2018.1434317

Mervelskemper, L., & Streit, D. (2017). Enhancing market valuation of ESG performance: Is integrated reporting keeping its promise? *Business Strategy and the Environment, 26*(4), 536–549. doi:10.1002/bse.1935

Morelli, G. (2023). Responsible investing and portfolio selection: A shapley-CVaR approach. *Annals of Operations Research*, 1–29. doi:10.100710479-022-05144-x

Olofsson, P., Raholm, A., Salah Uddin, G., Troster, V., & Hoon Kang, S. (2021). Ethical and unethical investments under extreme market conditions. *International Review of Financial Analysis, 78*, 101952. doi:10.1016/j.irfa.2021.101952

Pacelli, V., Pampurini, F., & Quaranta, A. G. (2023). Environmental, Social and Governance Investing: Does rating matter? *Business Strategy and the Environment, 32*(1), 30–41. doi:10.1002/bse.3116

Politis, D., & Romano, J. P. (1994). The Stationary Bootstrap. *Journal of the American Statistical Association, 89*(428), 1303–1313. doi:10.1080/01621459.1994.10476870

Politis, D., & White, H. (2004). Automatic block-length selection for the dependent bootstrap. *Econometric Reviews, 23*(1), 53–70. doi:10.1081/ETC-120028836

Rachev, S. T., Stoyanov, S. V., & Fabozzi, F. J. (2008). *Advanced stochastic models, risk assessment, and portfolio optimisation: The ideal risk, uncertainty, and performance measures.* Wiley.

Renneboog, L., Ter Horst, J., & Zhang, C. (2008). Socially responsible investments: Institutional aspects, performance, and investor behavior. *Journal of Banking & Finance, 32*(9), 1723–1742. doi:10.1016/j.jbankfin.2007.12.039

Rockafellar, R. T., Uryasev, S., & Zabarankin, M. (2002). Optimisation of conditional value-at-risk. *The Journal of Risk, 2*(3), 21–41. doi:10.21314/JOR.2000.038

Rockafellar, R. T., Uryasev, S., & Zabarankin, M. (2006). Generalised deviations in risk analysis. *Finance and Stochastics, 10*(1), 51–74. doi:10.100700780-005-0165-8

Santamaria, R., Paolone, F., Cucari, N., & Dezi, L. (2021). Non-financial strategy disclosure and environmental, social and governance score: Insight from a configurational approach. *Business Strategy and the Environment, 30*(4), 1993–2007. doi:10.1002/bse.2728

Schmidt, A. B. (2022). Optimal ESG portfolios: An example for the Dow Jones Index. *Journal of Sustainable Finance & Investment, 12*(2), 529–535. doi:10.1080/20430795.2020.1783180

Sharpe, W. F. (1966). Mutual fund performance. *The Journal of Business, 39*(S1), 119–138. doi:10.1086/294846

Verheyden, T., Eccles, R. G., & Feiner, A. (2016). ESG for all? The impact of ESG screening on return, risk, and diversification. *Journal of Applied Corporate Finance, 28*(2), 47–56. . doi:10.1111/jacf.12174

Xidonas, P., & Essner, E. (2022). On ESG Portfolio Construction: A Multiobjective Optimisation Approach. *Computational Economics*, 1–25. doi:10.100710614-022-10327-6 PMID:36268180

Young In, S., Rook, D., & Monk, A. (2019). Integrating alternative data (also known as ESG data) in investment decision making. *Global Economic Review, 48*(3), 237–260. doi:10.1080/1226508X.2019.1643059

Yousaf, I., Suleman, M. T., & Demirer, R. (2022). Green investments: A luxury good or a financial necessity? *Energy Economics*, *105*, 105745. doi:10.1016/j.eneco.2021.105745

Zumente, I., & Lāce, N. (2021). ESG Rating: Necessity for the Investor or the Company? *Sustainability (Basel)*, *13*(16), 8940. doi:10.3390u13168940

Compilation of References

Abdelhalim, K., & Eldin, A. G. (2019). Can CSR help achieve sustainable development? Applying a new assessment model to CSR cases from Egypt. *The International Journal of Sociology and Social Policy*, *39*(9/10), 773–795. doi:10.1108/IJSSP-06-2019-0120

Abdelsalam, O., Fethi, M. D., Matallín, J. C., & Tortosa-Ausina, E. (2014). On the comparative performance of socially responsible and Islamic mutual funds. *Journal of Economic Behavior & Organization*, *103*, 108–128. doi:10.1016/j.jebo.2013.06.011

ABNT – Associação Brasileira de Normas Técnicas. (2014). *Associação Brasileira de Normas Técnicas*. http://www.abnt.org.br/m2.asp?cod_pagina=963

Acar, E., Tunca Çalıyurt, K., & Zengin-Karaibrahimoglu, Y. (2021). Does ownership type affect environmental disclosure? *International Journal of Climate Change Strategies and Management*, *13*(2), 120–141. doi:10.1108/IJCCSM-02-2020-0016

Ackerman, R. W. (1973). How companies respond to social demands. *Harvard Business Review*, *51*(4), 88–98.

Adams, C. A. (2017). *The Sustainable Development Goals, integrated thinking and the integrated report*. International Integrated Reporting Council & ICAS. http://integratedreporting.org/resource/sdgs-integrated-thinking-and-the-integrated-report/

Adams, C. A. (2002). Internal organisational factors influencing corporate social and ethical reporting: Beyond current theorising. *Accounting, Auditing & Accountability Journal*, *15*(2), 223–250. doi:10.1108/09513570210418905

Adams, C. A., Hill, W., & Roberts, C. (1998). Corporate Social Reporting Practices in Western Europe: Legitimating Corporate Behaviour? *The British Accounting Review*, *30*(1), 1–21. doi:10.1006/bare.1997.0060

Adler, R., Mansi, M., & Pandey, R. (2018). Biodiversity and threatened species reporting by the top Fortune Global companies. *Accounting, Auditing & Accountability Journal*, *31*(3), 787–825. doi:10.1108/AAAJ-03-2016-2490

Adler, R., Mansi, M., Pandey, R., & Stringer, C. (2017). United Nations Decade on Biodiversity: A study of the reporting practices of the Australian mining industry. *Accounting, Auditing & Accountability Journal*, *30*(8), 1711–1745. doi:10.1108/AAAJ-04-2015-2028

Agliardi, E., & Agliardi, R. (2019). Financing environmentally-sustainable projects with green bonds. *Environment and Development Economics*, *24*(6), 608–623. doi:10.1017/S1355770X19000020

Agostini, M., Costa, E., & Korca, B. (2022). Non-financial disclosure and corporate financial performance under directive 2014/95/EU: Evidence from Italian listed companies. *Accounting in Europe*, *19*(1), 78–109. doi:10.1080/17449480.2021.1979610

Ahmad, A. (2012). Environmental Accounting and Reporting Practices: Significance and Issues: A Case from Bangladeshi Companies. *Global Journal of Management and Business Research, 12*(14).

Ahsan, M. J., & Ahmed, R. (2023). Green-Lean Practices and Production Performance: Evidence From SMEs of an Emerging Economy. In Emerging Trends in Sustainable Supply Chain Management and Green Logistics (pp. 75-97). IGI Global.

Ahsan, M. J. (2023). The role of emotional intelligence in effective corporate social responsibility leadership. *The International Journal of Organizational Analysis, 31*(8), 75–91. doi:10.1108/IJOA-02-2023-3615

Ahsan, M. J., & Khalid, M. H. (2023). Laissez-Faire Leadership. In *Leadership Approaches in Global Hospitality and Tourism* (pp. 61–72). IGI Global. doi:10.4018/978-1-6684-6713-8.ch004

Ahsan, T., & Qureshi, M. A. (2021). The nexus between policy uncertainty, sustainability disclosure and firm performance. *Applied Economics, 53*(4), 441–453. doi:10.1080/00036846.2020.1808178

Akhter, F., Hossain, M. M., Elrehail, H., Rehman, S. U., & Almansour, B. Y. (2022). Environmental disclosures and corporate attributes, from the lens of legitimacy theory: a longitudinal analysis on a developing country. *European Journal of Management and Business Economics*. doi:10.1108/EJMBE-01-2021-0008

Aktan, C. C., & Börü, D. (2007). Kurumsal sosyal sorumluluk. Kurumsal sosyal sorumluluk. *İşletmeler ve sosyal sorumluluk*, 11-36.

Al Amosh, H., Khatib, S. F. A., & Ananzeh, H. (2023). Environmental, social and governance impact on financial performance: Evidence from the Levant countries. *Corporate Governance (Bradford), 23*(3), 493–513. doi:10.1108/CG-03-2022-0105

Al-Amin, A. Q., Leal Filho, W., & Kabir, M. A. (2018). The Challenges of Sustainability in Business: How Governments May Ensure Sustainability for Offshore Firms. *Technological and Economic Development of Economy, 24*(1), 108–140. doi:10.3846/20294913.2015.1075442

Albertini, E. (2019). Integrated reporting: An exploratory study of French companies. *The Journal of Management and Governance, 23*(2), 513–535. doi:10.100710997-018-9428-6

Alda, M. (2019). Corporate sustainability and institutional shareholders: The pressure of social responsible pension funds on environmental firm practices. *Business Strategy and the Environment, 28*(6), 1060–1071. doi:10.1002/bse.2301

Aliprandi, G., Barake, M., & Chouc, P.-E. (2021). Have European banks left tax havens? Evidence from country-by-country data. *EUTAX Observatory, 2*, 1–60.

ALmashkor, I. A. S. (2020). Aligning Between the Balanced Scorecard and Environmental Management Accounting in Support of Sustainable Development. *Productivity Management, 1*, 402-418.

Alparslan, A. G. A., & Aygün, M. (2013). Kurumsal Sosyal Sorumluluk ve Firma Performansı. *Süleyman Demirel Üniversitesi İktisadi ve İdari Bilimler Fakültesi Dergisi, 18*(1), 435–448.

Alptekin, N. (2009). Performance evaluation of Turkish type a mutual funds and pension stock funds by using TOPSIS method. *International Journal of Economics and Finance Studies, 1*(2), 11–22.

Al-Shaer, H. (2020). Sustainability reporting quality and post-audit financial reporting quality: Empirical evidence from the UK. *Business Strategy and the Environment, 29*(6), 2355–2373. doi:10.1002/bse.2507

Amankwah-Amoah, J., Adomako, S., & Danso, A. (2018). Entrepreneurial orientation, environmental sustainability and new venture performance: Does stakeholder integration matter? *Business Strategy and the Environment, 28*(1), 79–87. doi:10.1002/bse.2191

Amazonas, S. (2018). Gestão ambiental hoteleira: Tecnologias e práticas sustentáveis e práticas sustentáveis aplicadas a hotéis. *Ambiente & Sociedade, 21*, 1–20.

Amel-Zadeh, A., & Serafeim, G. (2018). Why and how investors use ESG information: Evidence from a global survey. *Financial Analysts Journal, 74*(3), 87–103. doi:10.2469/faj.v74.n3.2

Amey, M., & Whooley, N. (2018). Corporate Reporting on the SDGs: Mapping a Sustainable Future. *Advisor Perspectives,* 1–7.

Amorim, J. C., Monteiro, A. P., Cepêda, C. L. M., & Coelho, G. R. T. F. (2021). Análise comparativa do regime fiscal das Zonas Francas na Europa. *e3-Revista de Economia, Empresas e Empreendedores na CPLP, 7*(2), 31-55.

Amran, A., Lee, S. P., & Devi, S. S. (2014). The influence of governance structure and strategic corporate social responsibility toward sustainability reporting quality. *Business Strategy and the Environment, 23*(4), 217–235. doi:10.1002/bse.1767

Antal, A. B., Dierkes, M., MacMillan, K., & Marz, L. (2002). Corporate social reporting revisited. *Journal of General Management, 28*(2), 22–42. doi:10.1177/030630700202800202

Antonio, I., Simone, P., Lea, I., & Mario, T. (2020). Communicating the stakeholder engagement process: A cross- country analysis in the tourism sector. *Corporate Social Responsibility and Environmental Management, 27*(4), 1642–1652. doi:10.1002/csr.1913

Appelbaum, D., Kogan, A., Vasarhelyi, M., & Yan, Z. (2017). Impact of business analytics and enterprise systems on managerial accounting. *International Journal of Accounting Information Systems, 25*, 29–44. doi:10.1016/j.accinf.2017.03.003

Artzner, P., Delbaen, F., Eber, M., & Heath, D. (1999). Coherent Measures of Risk. *Mathematical Finance, 9*(3), 203–228. doi:10.1111/1467-9965.00068

Ashwin Kumar, N. C., Smith, C., Badis, L., Wang, N., Ambrosy, P., & Tavares, R. (2016). ESG factors and risk-adjusted performance: A new quantitative model. *Journal of Sustainable Finance & Investment, 6*(4), 292–300. doi:10.1080/20 430795.2016.1234909

Ateş, M. H., Çakan, C. D., & Koç, İ. Ö. (2022). Türkiye'de sürdürülebilir temalı fonların geleneksel fonlarla karşılaştırmalı performans analizi. *Ekonomi Politika & Finans Araştırmaları Dergisi, 7*, 123-139. doi:10.30784/epfad.1148841

Ates, S. (2020). Membership of sustainability index in an emerging market: Implications for sustainability. *Journal of Cleaner Production, 250*, 119465. Advance online publication. doi:10.1016/j.jclepro.2019.119465

Atif, M., & Ali, S. (2021). Environmental, social and governance disclosure and default risk. *Business Strategy and the Environment, 30*(8), 3937–3959. doi:10.1002/bse.2850

Atkins, J., Barone, E., Maroun, W., & Atkins, B. (2016). Bee accounting and accountability in the UK. In J. Atkins & B. Atkins (Eds.), *The Business of Bees: An Integrated Approach to Bee Decline and Corporate Responsibility* (pp. 198–211). Greenleaf Publishers. doi:10.9774/GLEAF.9781783534340_12

Atkins, J., & Maroun, W. (2018). Integrated extinction accounting and accountability: Building an ark. *Accounting, Auditing & Accountability Journal, 31*(3), 750–786. doi:10.1108/AAAJ-06-2017-2957

Atkins, J., Maroun, W., Atkins, B. C., & Barone, E. (2018). From the Big Five to the Big Four? Exploring extinction accounting for the rhinoceros. *Accounting, Auditing & Accountability Journal, 31*(2), 674–702. doi:10.1108/AAAJ-12-2015-2320

Aubry, M., & Dauphin, T. (2017). *Opening the Vaults: The use of tax havens by Europe's biggest banks*. Oxfam. https://oxfamilibrary.openrepository.com

Auer, B. R., & Schuhmach, F. (2016). Do socially (ir)responsible investments pay? New evidence from international ESG data. *The Quarterly Review of Economics and Finance, 59*, 51–62. doi:10.1016/j.qref.2015.07.002

Aureli, S., Gigli, S., Medei, R., & Supino, E. (2020). The value relevance of environmental, social, and governance disclosure: Evidence from Dow Jones Sustainability World Index listed companies. *Corporate Social Responsibility and Environmental Management, 27*(1), 43–52. doi:10.1002/csr.1772

Awan, U., Khattak, A., & Kraslawski, A. (2019). Corporate social responsibility (CSR) priorities in the small and medium enterprises (SMEs) of the industrial sector of Sialkot, Pakistan. *Corporate social responsibility in the manufacturing and services sectors*, 267-278.

Ayçin, E. (2019). *Çok kriterli karar verme: Bilgisayar uygulamalı çözümler*. Nobel Akademik Yayıncılık.

Baalouch, F., Ayadi, S. D., & Hussainey, K. (2019). A study of the determinants of environmental disclosure quality: Evidence from French listed companies. *The Journal of Management and Governance, 23*(4), 939–971. doi:10.100710997-019-09474-0

Babiak, K., & Trendafilova, S. (2011). CSR and environmental responsibility: Motives and pressures to adopt green management practices. *Corporate Social Responsibility and Environmental Management, 18*(1), 11–24. doi:10.1002/csr.229

Bae, S. M., Masud, M. A. K., & Kim, J. D. (2018). A Cross-Country Investigation of Corporate Governance and Corporate Sustainability Disclosure: A Signaling Theory Perspective. *Sustainability (Basel), 10*(8), 2611. Advance online publication. doi:10.3390u10082611

Bahta, D., Yun, J., Islam, M. R., & Bikanyi, K. J. (2021). How does CSR enhance the financial performance of SMEs? The mediating role of firm reputation. *Ekonomska Istrazivanja, 34*(1), 1428–1451. doi:10.1080/1331677X.2020.1828130

Baier, C., Goettsche, M., Hellmann, A., & Schiemann, F. (2021). Too Good To Be True: Influencing Credibility Perceptions with Signaling Reference Explicitness and Assurance Depth. *Journal of Business Ethics*.

Baillie, J., Hilton-Taylor, C., & Stuart, S. N. (2004). *2004 IUCN Red List of Threatened Species: A Global Species Assessment*. IUCN Publications., doi:10.2305/IUCN.CH.2005.3

Baines, T., & Lightfoot, H. W. (2013). Servitization of the manufacturing firm. *International Journal of Operations & Production Management, 34*(1), 2–35. doi:10.1108/IJOPM-02-2012-0086

Bai, X., Coelho, A., & Lopes Cancela, B. (2023). The relationship between green supply chain and green innovation based on the push of green strategic alliances. *Corporate Social Responsibility and Environmental Management*, csr.2619. doi:10.1002/csr.2619

Barbosa, M., Castañeda-Ayarza, J. A., & Ferreira, D. H. L. (2020). Sustainable strategic management (GES): Sustainability in small business. *Journal of Cleaner Production, 258*, 120880. doi:10.1016/j.jclepro.2020.120880

Barnett, M. L. (2007). Tarred and untarred by the same brush: Exploring interdependence in the volatility of stock returns. *Corporate Reputation Review, 10*(1), 3–21. doi:10.1057/palgrave.crr.1550035

Barnosky, A. D., Matzke, N., Tomiya, S., Wogan, G. O., Swartz, B., Quental, T. B., Marshall, C., McGuire, J. L., Lindsey, E. L., Maguire, K. C., Mersey, B., & Ferrer, E. A. (2011). Has the Earth's sixth mass extinction already arrived? *Nature*, *471*(7336), 51–57. doi:10.1038/nature09678 PMID:21368823

Bastas, A., & Liyanage, K. (2019). Setting a framework for organisational sustainable development. *Sustainable Production and Consumption*, *20*, 207–229. doi:10.1016/j.spc.2019.06.005

Battisti, E., Nirino, N., Leonidou, E., & Thrassou, A. (2022). Corporate venture capital and CSR performance: An extended resource based view's perspective. *Journal of Business Research*, *139*, 1058–1066. doi:10.1016/j.jbusres.2021.10.054

Bauer, R., Koedijk, K., & Otten, R. (2005). International evidence on ethical mutual fund performance and investment style. *Journal of Banking & Finance*, *29*(7), 1751–1767. doi:10.1016/j.jbankfin.2004.06.035

Bazhair, A. H., Khatib, S. F. A., & Al Amosh, H. (2022). Taking Stock of Carbon Disclosure Research While Looking to the Future: A Systematic Literature Review. *Sustainability (Basel)*, *14*(20), 13475. doi:10.3390u142013475

Bebbington, J., & Unerman, J. (2018). Sustainable development: a review of the international development, business and accounting literature. *Accounting, Auditing, & Accountability*, *31*(1), 2 – 24. . doi:10.1108/AAAJ-05-2017-2929

Becchetti, L., Ciciretti, R., Dalò, A., & Herzel, S. (2015). Socially responsible and conventional investment funds: Performance comparison and the global financial crisis. *Applied Economics*, *47*(25), 2541–2562. doi:10.1080/00036846.2014.1000517

Beck, C., Dumay, J., & Frost, G. (2017). In pursuit of a 'single source of truth': From threatened legitimacy to integrated reporting. *Journal of Business Ethics*, *141*(1), 191–205. doi:10.100710551-014-2423-1

Becker, M. G., Martin, F., & Walter, A. (2022). The power of ESG transparency: The effect of the new SFDR sustainability labels on mutual funds and individual investors. *Finance Research Letters*, *47*, 102708. doi:10.1016/j.frl.2022.102708

Becker-Olsen, K. L., Taylor, C. R., Hill, R. P., & Yalcinkaya, G. (2011). A Cross-Cultural Examination of Corporate Social Responsibility Marketing Communications in Mexico and the United States: Strategies for Global Brands. *Journal of International Marketing*, *19*(2), 30–44. doi:10.1509/jimk.19.2.30

Bedenik, N. O., & Barišić, P. (2019). Nonfinancial Reporting: Theoretical and Empirical Evidence. *Sustainable Management Practices*. https://doi.org/http://dx.doi.org/10.5772/intechopen.87159

Beekaroo, D., Callychurn, D. S., & Hurreeram, D. K. (2019). Developing a sustainability index for Mauritian manufacturing companies. *Ecological Indicators*, *96*, 250–257. doi:10.1016/j.ecolind.2018.09.003

Bello, Z. Y. (2005). Socially responsible investing and portfolio diversification. *Journal of Financial Research*, *28*(1), 41–57. doi:10.1111/j.1475-6803.2005.00113.x

Belyaeva, Z., Shams, S. M. R., Santoro, G., & Grandhi, B. (2020). Unpacking stakeholder relationship management in the public and private sectors: The comparative insights. *EuroMed Journal of Business*, *15*(3), 269–281. doi:10.1108/EMJB-06-2019-0085

Beraldi, P., Violi, A., Ferrara, M., Ciancio, C., & Pansera, B. A. (2021). Dealing with complex transaction costs in portfolio management. *Annals of Operations Research*, *299*(1-2), 7–22. doi:10.100710479-019-03210-5

Berg, F., Koelbel, J. F., & Rigobon, R. (2022). Aggregate confusion: The divergence of ESG ratings. *Review of Finance*, *26*(6), 1315–1344. doi:10.1093/rof/rfac033

Berne-Manero, C., & Marzo-Navarro, M. (2020). Exploring How Influencer and Relationship Marketing Serve Corporate Sustainability. *Sustainability (Basel)*, *12*(11), 4392. doi:10.3390u12114392

Beuren, I. M., & Fiorentin, M. (2014). Influência de fatores contingenciais nos atributos do Sistema de Contabilidade Gerencial: Um estudo em empresas têxteis do Estado do Rio Grande do Sul. *Revista de Ciências da Administração, 16*(38), 195–212. doi:10.5007/2175-8077.2014v16n38p195

Bhimani, A., & Langfield-Smith, K. (2007). Structure, formality and the importance of financial and non-financial information in strategy development and implementation. *Management Accounting Research, 18*(1), 3–31. doi:10.1016/j. mar.2006.06.005

Birkle, C., Pendlebury, D. A., Schnell, J., & Adams, J. (2020). Web of Science as a data source for research on scientific and scholarly activity. *Quantitative Science Studies, 1*(1), 363–376. doi:10.1162/qss_a_00018

Blake, D. H., Frederick, W. C., & Myers, M. S. (1976). *Social auditing: evaluating the impact of corporate programs.* Greenwood.

Blasco, X., Herrero, J. M., Sanchis, J., & Martínez, M. (2008). A new graphical visualisation of n-dimensional Pareto front for decision-making in multiobjective optimisation. *Information Sciences, 178*(20), 3908–3924. doi:10.1016/j. ins.2008.06.010

Blomstrom, R., & Davis, K. (1975). *Business and society: Environment and responsibility.* McGraw-Hill.

Boakye, D. J., TIngbani, I., Ahinful, G., Damoah, I., & Tauringana, V. (2020). Sustainable environmental practices and financial performance: Evidence from listed small and medium-sized enterprise in the United Kingdom. *Business Strategy and the Environment, 29*(6), 2583–2602. doi:10.1002/bse.2522

Bofinger, Y., Heyden, K. J., & Rock, B. (2022). Corporate social responsibility and market efficiency: Evidence from ESG and misvaluation measures. *Journal of Banking & Finance, 134*, 106322. Advance online publication. doi:10.1016/j. jbankfin.2021.106322

Borges, A. F., Laurindo, F. J., Spínola, M. M., Gonçalves, R. F., & Mattos, C. A. (2021). The strategic use of artificial intelligence in the digital era: Systematic literature review and future research directions. *International Journal of Information Management, 57*, 1–16. doi:10.1016/j.ijinfomgt.2020.102225

Bouten, L., Everaert, P., Van Liedekerke, L., De Moor, L., & Christiaens, J. (2011). *Corporate social responsibility reporting: A comprehensive picture?* Paper presented at the Accounting forum. 10.1016/j.accfor.2011.06.007

Bouvatier, V., Capelle-Blancard, G., & Delatte, A.-L. (2017). *Banks in Tax Havens: First Evidence Based on Country-by-Country Reporting.* Discussion Paper (055). https://economy-finance.ec.europa.eu

Bowen, H. R. (1953). Graduate education in economics. *The American Economic Review, 43*(4), iv-223.

Brasil. (1976). *Lei 6.404, de 15 de dezembro de 1976. Dispõe sobre as sociedades por ações. Diário Oficial [da] República Federativa do Brasil, Brasília, DF.* http://www.planalto.gov.br

Brasil. (2007). *Lei 11.638, de 28 de dezembro de 2007. Diário Oficial [da] República Federativa do Brasil, Brasília, DF, 28 de dez. 2007.* http://www.planalto.gov.br

Bressanelli, G., Adrodegari, F., Perona, M., & Saccani, N. (2018). Exploring How Usage-Focused Business Models Enable Circular Economy through Digital Technologies. *Sustainability (Basel), 10*(3), 1–21. doi:10.3390u10030639

Brown, J. A., & Forster, W. R. (2013). CSR and stakeholder theory: A tale of Adam Smith. *Journal of Business Ethics, 112*(2), 301–312. doi:10.100710551-012-1251-4

Brown, N., & Deegan, C. (1998). The public disclosure of environmental performance information—A dual test of media agenda setting theory and legitimacy theory. *Accounting and Business Research*, 29(1), 21–41. doi:10.1080/00014788.1998.9729564

Brown, R. J., Jorgensen, B. N., & Pope, P. F. (2019). The interplay between mandatory country-by-country reporting, geographic segment reporting, and tax havens: Evidence from the European Union. *Journal of Accounting and Public Policy*, 38(2), 106–129. doi:10.1016/j.jaccpubpol.2019.02.001

Brundtland, G. H. (1987). Our Common Future—Call for Action*. *Environmental Conservation*, 14(4), 291–294. doi:10.1017/S0376892900016805

Buckley, P. J., Sutherland, D., Voss, H., & El-Gohari, A. (2015). The economic geography of offshore incorporation in tax havens and offshore financial centers: The case of Chinese MNEs. *Journal of Economic Geography*, 15(1), 103–128. doi:10.1093/jeg/lbt040

Bugg-Levine, A., & Emerson, J. (2011). *Impact investing: Transforming how we make money while making a difference*. John Wiley & Sons.

Burritt, R. L., & Schaltegger, S. (2010). Sustainability accounting and reporting: Fad or trend? *Accounting, Auditing & Accountability Journal*, 23(7), 829–846. doi:10.1108/09513571011080144

Burritt, R., & Christ, K. (2016). Industry 4.0 and environmental accounting: A new revolution? Asian. *Journal of Sustainability and Social Responsibility*, 1(1), 23–38. doi:10.118641180-016-0007-y

Cadez, S., & Guilding, C. (2012). Strategy, strategic management accounting and performance: A configurational analysis. *Industrial Management & Data Systems*, 112(3), 484–501. doi:10.1108/02635571211210086

Cai, S., Jun, M., & Yang, Z. (2010). Implementing supply chain information integration in China: The role of institutional forces and trust. *Journal of Operations Management*, 28(3), 257–268. doi:10.1016/j.jom.2009.11.005

Campbell, J. (2007). Why Would Corporations Behave in Socially Responsible Ways? An Institutional Theory of Corporate Social Responsibility. *Academy of Management Review*, 32(3), 946–967. doi:10.5465/amr.2007.25275684

Cancela, B. L., Coelho, A., & Duarte Neves, M. E. (2022). Greening the business: How ambidextrous companies succeed in green innovation through to sustainable development. *Business Strategy and the Environment*.

Cantele, S., & Cassia, F. (2020). Sustainability implementation in restaurants: A comprehensive model of drivers, barriers, and competitiveness-mediated effects on firm performance. *International Journal of Hospitality Management*, 87, 102510. doi:10.1016/j.ijhm.2020.102510

Carbon Majors Report, C. D. P. (2017). *Carbon Majors Report*. https://cdn.cdp.net/cdp-production/cms/reports/documents/000/002/327/original/Carbon-Majors-Report-2017.pdf?1501833772

Carnini Pulino, S., Ciaburri, M., Magnanelli, B. S., & Nasta, L. (2022). Does ESG Disclosure Influence Firm Performance? *Sustainability (Basel)*, 14(13), 7595. doi:10.3390u14137595

Carroll, A. B. (2008). A history of corporate social responsibility: Concepts and practices. The Oxford handbook of corporate social responsibility.

Carroll, A. B. (2021). Corporate social responsibility (CSR) and the COVID-19 pandemic: Organizational and managerial implications. *Journal of Strategy and Management*.

Carroll, A. B. (1979). A three-dimensional conceptual model of corporate performance. *Academy of Management Review*, 4(4), 497–505. doi:10.2307/257850

Carroll, A. B. (1991). The pyramid of corporate social responsibility: Toward the moral management of organizational stakeholders. *Business Horizons, 34*(4), 39–48. doi:10.1016/0007-6813(91)90005-G

Carvalho, F., Domingues, P., & Sampaio, P. (2019). *Communication of commitment towards sustainable development of certified Portuguese organisations Quality, environment and occupational health and safety.* International Journal of Quality & Reliability Management. doi:10.1108/IJQRM-04-2018-0099

Carvalho, F., Santos, G., & Gonçalves, J. (2018). The disclosure of information on Sustainable Development on the corporate website of the certified portuguese organizations. *International Journal of Qualitative Research, 12*(1), 253–276. doi:10.18421/IJQR12.01-14

Carvalho, F., Santos, G., & Gonçalves, J. (2019). Critical analysis of information about integrated management systems and environmental policy on the Portuguese firms' website, towards sustainable development. *Corporate Social Responsibility and Environmental Management, 27*(2), 1069–1088. doi:10.1002/csr.1866

Ceballos, G., Ehrlich, P. R., Barnosky, A. D., García, A., Pringle, R. M., & Palmer, T. M. (2015). Accelerated modern human–induced species losses: Entering the sixth mass extinction. *Science Advances, 1*(5), e1400253. doi:10.1126ciadv.1400253 PMID:26601195

Ceballos, G., Ehrlich, P. R., & Dirzo, R. (2017). Biological annihilation via the ongoing sixth mass extinction signaled by vertebrate population losses and declines. *Proceedings of the National Academy of Sciences of the United States of America, 114*(30), E6089–E6096. doi:10.1073/pnas.1704949114 PMID:28696295

Cecato, V. M. (2015). *A contribuição do processo de comunicação para a construção da cultura da sustentabilidade: um estudo de micro, pequenas e médias empresas brasileiras* [Dissertação de Mestrado]. Escola de Comunicações e Artes, Universidade de São Paulo, São Paulo. doi:10.11606/D.27.2016.tde-01022016-153822

Çelik, A. (2007). Şirketlerin Sosyal Sorumluluklari. Kurumsal sosyal sorumluluk. *İşletmeler ve sosyal sorumluluk*, 43-58.

Cesarone, F., Martino, M. L., & Carleo, A. (2022). Does ESG Impact Really Enhance Portfolio Profitability? *Sustainability (Basel), 14*(4), 2050. doi:10.3390u14042050

Chaffee, E. C. (2017). The origins of corporate social responsibility. *University of Cincinnati Law Review, 85*, 347–373.

Chaklader, B., & Gulati, P. A. (2015). A Study of Corporate Environmental Disclosure Practices of Companies Doing Business in India. *Global Business Review, 16*(2), 321–335. doi:10.1177/0972150914564430

Chand, D., Hachey, G., Hunton, J., Owhoso, V., & Vasudevan, S. (2005). A balanced scorecard based framework for assessing the strategic impacts of ERP systems. *Computers in Industry, 56*(6), 558–572. doi:10.1016/j.compind.2005.02.011

Chandler, D. (2016). *Strategic corporate social responsibility: Sustainable value creation.* SAGE Publications.

Chandler, D., & Werther, W. B. Jr. (2013). *Strategic corporate social responsibility: Stakeholders, globalization, and sustainable value creation.* Sage Publications.

Chang, C. E., & Witte, H. D. (2010). Performance evaluation of U.S. socially responsible mutual funds: Revisiting doing good and doing well. *American Journal of Business, 25*(1), 9–24. doi:10.1108/19355181201000001

Chang, C. H., Lin, J. J., Lin, J. H., & Chiang, M. C. (2010). Domestic open-end equity mutual fund performance evaluation using extended TOPSIS method with different distance approaches. *Expert Systems with Applications, 37*(6), 4642–4649. doi:10.1016/j.eswa.2009.12.044

Channuntapipat, C. (2021). Can sustainability report assurance be a collaborative process and practice beyond the ritual of verification? *Business Strategy and the Environment, 30*(2), 775–786. doi:10.1002/bse.2653

Chantziaras, A., Dedoulis, E., Grougiou, V., & Leventis, S. (2020). The impact of religiosity and corruption on CSR reporting: The case of U.S. banks. *Journal of Business Research*, *109*, 362–374. doi:10.1016/j.jbusres.2019.12.025

Chen, C., Yu, Y., Osei-Kyei, R., Chan, A. P. C., & Xu, J. (2019). Developing a project sustainability index for sustainable development in transnational public–private partnership projects. *Sustainable Development*, *27*(6), 1034–1048. . doi:10.1002/sd.1954

Chen, C. X., Hudgins, R., & Wright, W. F. (2021). The Effect of Advice Valence on the Perceived Credibility of Data Analytics. *Journal of Management Accounting Research*, *34*(2), 97–116. doi:10.2308/JMAR-2020-015

Cheng, S., Jianfu, S., Alrasheedi, M., Saeidi, P., Mishra, A. R., & Rani, P. (2021). A New Extended VIKOR Approach Using q-Rung Orthopair Fuzzy Sets for Sustainable Enterprise Risk Management Assessment in Manufacturing Small and Medium-Sized Enterprises. *International Journal of Fuzzy Systems*, *23*(5), 1347–1369. Advance online publication. doi:10.100740815-020-01024-3

Chenhall, R. H. (2003). Management control systems design within its organizational context: Findings from contingency-based research and directions for the future. *Accounting, Organizations and Society*, *28*(2–3), 127–168. doi:10.1016/S0361-3682(01)00027-7

Chen, Z., & Xie, G. (2022). ESG disclosure and financial performance: Moderating role of ESG investors. *International Review of Financial Analysis*, *83*, 1–16. doi:10.1016/j.irfa.2022.102291

Chiaramonte, L., Dreassi, A., Paltrinieri, A., & Piserà, S. (2020). Sustainability Practices and Stability in the Insurance Industry. *Sustainability (Basel)*, *12*(4), 5530. Advance online publication. doi:10.3390u12145530

Christensen, D. M., Serafeim, G., & Sikochi, A. (2021). Why is Corporate Virtue in the Eye of The Beholder? The Case of ESG Ratings. *The Accounting Review*, *97*(1), 147–175. doi:10.2308/TAR-2019-0506

Clark, G., Feiner, A., & Viehs, M. (2015). *From the stockholder to the stakeholder: How sustainability can drive financial outperformance*. Oxford University & Arabesque Partners.

Clarkson, P. M., Li, Y., Richardson, G. D., & Vasvari, F. P. (2008). Revisiting the relation between environmental performance and environmental disclosure: An empirical analysis. *Accounting, Organizations and Society*, *33*(4-5), 303–327. doi:10.1016/j.aos.2007.05.003

Clementino, E., & Perkins, R. (2021). How Do Companies Respond to Environmental, Social and Governance (ESG) ratings? Evidence from Italy. *Journal of Business Ethics*, *171*(2), 379–397. doi:10.100710551-020-04441-4

Corciolani, M., Nieri, F., & Tuan, A. (2020). Does involvement in corporate social irresponsibility affect the linguistic features of corporate social responsibility reports? *Corporate Social Responsibility and Environmental Management*, *27*(2), 670–680. doi:10.1002/csr.1832

Cordazzo, M., Bini, L., & Marzo, G. (2020). Does the EU Directive on non-financial information influence the value relevance of ESG disclosure? Italian evidence. *Business Strategy and the Environment*, *29*(8), 3470–3483. doi:10.1002/bse.2589

Cormier, D., Ledoux, M. J., & Magnan, M. (2009). The use of Web sites as a disclosure platform for corporate performance. *International Journal of Accounting Information Systems*, *10*(1), 1–24. doi:10.1016/j.accinf.2008.04.002

Corporate Finance Institute. (2023). *Ethical Investing*. https://corporatefinanceinstitute.com/resources/knowledge/trading-investing/ethical-investing/

Cortez, M. C., Silva, F., & Areal, N. (2009). The performance of European socially responsible funds. *Journal of Business Ethics*, *87*(4), 573–588. doi:10.100710551-008-9959-x

Cowan, K., & Guzman, F. (2020). How CSR reputation, sustainability signals, and country-of-origin sustainability reputation contribute to corporate brand performance: An exploratory study. *Journal of Business Research, 117*, 683–693. doi:10.1016/j.jbusres.2018.11.017

CPC 26 (R1) (2019). *Apresentação das demonstrações contábeis.* Brasília. https://www.cpc.org.br/CPC/Documentos-Emitidos/Pronunciamentos/Pronunciamento?Id=57

Cram, A. (2007). The IT Balanced Scorecard Revisited. *Information System Control Journal, 3*, 1-5.

Crowther, D., & Aras, G. (2008). *Corporate social responsibility.* Bookboon.

Crozatti, J. (1998). Modelo de gestão e cultura organizacional: conceitos e interações. *Caderno de estudos*, (18), 01-20. https://doi.org/ doi:10.1590/S1413-92511998000200004

Csomos, G., Vida, Z. V., & Lengyel, B. (2020). Exploring the changing geographical pattern of international scientific collaborations through the prism of cities. *PLoS One, 15*(11), e0242468. Advance online publication. doi:10.1371/journal.pone.0242468 PMID:33196668

Cucari, N., De Falco, S. E., & Orlando, B. (2018). Diversity of Board of Directors and Environmental Social Governance: Evidence from Italian Listed Companies. *Corporate Social Responsibility and Environmental Management, 25*(3), 250–266. doi:10.1002/csr.1452

Cuckston, T. (2018). Making extinction calculable. *Accounting, Auditing & Accountability Journal, 31*(3), 849–874. doi:10.1108/AAAJ-10-2015-2264

Cummings, L. S. (2000). The financial performance of ethical investment trusts: An Australian perspective. *Journal of Business Ethics, 25*(1), 79–92. doi:10.1023/A:1006102802904

Curtó-Pagès, F., Ortega-Rivera, E., Castellón-Durán, M., & Jané-Llopis, E. (2021). Coming in from the cold: A longitudinal analysis of SDG reporting practices by Spanish listed companies since the approval of the 2030 agenda. *Sustainability (Basel), 13*(3), 1–27. doi:10.3390u13031178

Dagiliene, L., & Šutiene, K. (2019). Corporate sustainability accounting information systems: A contingency-based approach. *Sustainability Accounting. Management and Policy Journal, 10*(2), 260–289. doi:10.1108/SAMPJ-07-2018-0200

Dai, J., & Vasarhelyi, M. A. (2016). Imagineering Audit 4.0. *Journal of Emerging Technologies in Accounting, 13*(1), 1–15. doi:10.2308/jeta-10494

Dallabona, L., Silva, D. & Lavarda, C. (2019). Contingent Variables, leadership styles and organizational slack predominant in a Santa Catarina textile industry. *Revista Capital Científico – Eletrônica, 17*(1). . doi:10.5935/2177-4153.20190002

Danso, A., Adomako, S., Owusu-Agyei, S., & Konadu, R. (2019). Environmental sustainability orientation, competitive strategy and financial performance. *Business Strategy and the Environment, 28*(5), 885–895. doi:10.1002/bse.2291

Das, L. (2022). Evaluation of mutual funds using TOPSIS method, *REST Journal on Banking. Accounting and Business, 1*(2), 34–43. doi:10.46632/jbab/1/2/6

Datta, S., & Goyal, S. (2022). Determinants of SDG Reporting by Businesses: A Literature Analysis and Conceptual Model. *Vision (Basel).* Advance online publication. doi:10.1177/09722629221096047

Davis, G. F., & Cobb, J. A. (2010). Resource dependence theory: Past and future. *Stanford's organization theory renaissance, 1970–2000.*

Davis, K. (1960). Can business afford to ignore social responsibilities? *California Management Review, 2*(3), 70–76. doi:10.2307/41166246

Davis, K. (1975). Five propositions for social responsibility. *Business Horizons, 18*(3), 19–24. doi:10.1016/0007-6813(75)90048-8

De Boer, Y., & Van Bergen, B. (2012). *Expect the unexpected: building business value in a changing world.* KPMG International.

De Carvalho, S. S., da Silva Pimentel, M. A., & de Lima, A. M. M. (2019). Desafios da área de proteção ambiental em território insular: Proposição de planejamento para gestão de recursos hídricos sob a perspectiva dos moradores da ilha do Combu, Belém, Pará. *Brazilian Journal of Environmental Sciences, 51*(51), 62–78. doi:10.5327/Z2176-947820190446

De Spiegeleer, J., Höcht, S., Jakubowski, D., Reyners, S., & Schoutens, W. (2021). ESG: A new dimension in portfolio allocation. *Journal of Sustainable Finance & Investment,* 1–41. doi:10.1080/20430795.2021.1923336

de Villiers, C., & Sharma, U. (2020). A critical reflection on the future of financial, intellectual capital, sustainability and integrated reporting. *Critical Perspectives on Accounting, 70,* 101999. doi:10.1016/j.cpa.2017.05.003

Deegan, C. (2006). Legitimacy theory. In *Methodological issues in accounting research: theories, methods and issues* (pp. 161–181). Spiramus Press Ltd.

Deegan, C., Rankin, M., & Tobin, J. (2002). An examination of the corporate social and environmental disclosures of BHP from 1983–1997: A test of legitimacy theory. *Accounting, Auditing & Accountability Journal, 15*(3), 312–343. doi:10.1108/09513570210435861

Deegan, C., & Unerman, J. (2011). *Financial Accounting Theory.* McGraw-Hill Higher Education.

Deliberal, J. P., Tondolo, V. A. G., Camargo, M. E., & Tondolo, R. R. P. (2016). Gestão Ambiental como uma Capacidade Estratégica: Um Estudo no Cluster Fabricação de Móveis no Sul do Brasil. *Brazilian Business Review, 13*(4), 124–147. doi:10.15728/bbr.2016.13.4.6

Deng, Z., Yan, J., & Sun, P. (2020). Political status and tax haven investment of emerging market firms: Evidence from China. *Journal of Business Ethics, 165*(3), 469–488. doi:10.100710551-018-4090-0

Derwall, J., Guenster, N., Bauer, R., & Koedijk, K. (2005). The eco-efficiency premium puzzle. *Financial Analysts Journal, 61*(2), 51–63. doi:10.2469/faj.v61.n2.2716

Dharmapala, D., & Hines, J. R. Jr. (2009). Which countries become tax havens? *Journal of Public Economics, 93*(9-10), 1058–1068. doi:10.1016/j.jpubeco.2009.07.005

Di Vaio, A., Varriale, L., Di Gregorio, A., & Adomako, S. (2022). Corporate social performance and non-financial reporting in the cruise industry: Paving the way towards UN Agenda 2030. *Corporate Social Responsibility and Environmental Management, 29*(6), 1931–1953. doi:10.1002/csr.2292

Diamond, J. M. (1989). Quaternary megafaunal extinctions: Variations on a theme by Paganini. *Journal of Archaeological Science, 16*(2), 167–175. doi:10.1016/0305-4403(89)90064-2

Diaz-Sarachaga, J. M. (2021). Shortcomings in reporting contributions towards the sustainable development goals. *Corporate Social Responsibility and Environmental Management, 28*(4), 1299–1312. doi:10.1002/csr.2129

Dijkstra, T. K., & Henseler, J. (2015). Consistent partial least squares path modeling. *Management Information Systems Quarterly, 39*(2), 297–316. doi:10.25300/MISQ/2015/39.2.02

Diltz, J. D. (1995). Does social screening affect portfolio performance? *Journal of Investing, 4*(1), 64–69. doi:10.3905/joi.4.1.64

Diouf, D., & Boiral, O. (2017). The quality of sustainability reports and impression management A stakeholder perspective. *Accounting, Auditing & Accountability Journal*, *30*(3), 643–667. doi:10.1108/AAAJ-04-2015-2044

Doidge, C., Karolyi, G. A., & Stulz, R. M. (2007). Why do countries matter so much for corporate governance? *Journal of Financial Economics*, *86*(1), 1–39. doi:10.1016/j.jfineco.2006.09.002

Domingues, A. R., Lozano, R., Ceulemans, K., & Ramos, T. B. (2017). Sustainability reporting in public sector organisations: Exploring the relation between the reporting process and organisational change management for sustainability. *Journal of Environmental Management*, *192*, 292–301. doi:10.1016/j.jenvman.2017.01.074 PMID:28183029

Domini, A. L., & Kinder, P. D. (1986). *Ethical investing, how to make profitable investments without sacrificing your principles* (1st ed.). Addison Wesley.

Donaldson, T., & Preston, L. E. (1995). The stakeholder theory of the corporation: Concepts, evidence, and implications. *Academy of Management Review*, *20*(1), 65–91. doi:10.2307/258887

dos Santos, M. C., & Pereira, F. H. (2022). ESG performance scoring method to support responsible investments in port operations. *Case Studies on Transport Policy*, *10*(1), 664–673. doi:10.1016/j.cstp.2022.01.027

Drake, K. D., Hamilton, R., & Lusch, S. J. (2020). Are declining effective tax rates indicative of tax avoidance? Insight from effective tax rate reconciliations. *Journal of Accounting and Economics*, *70*(1), 101317. doi:10.1016/j.jacceco.2020.101317

Dumay, J., Bernardi, C., Guthrie, J., & Demartini, P. (2016). Integrated reporting: A structured literature review. *Accounting Forum*, *40*(3), 166–185. doi:10.1016/j.accfor.2016.06.001

Du, S., Bhattacharya, C. B., & Sen, S. (2010). Maximizing business returns to corporate social responsibility (CSR): The role of CSR communication. *International Journal of Management Reviews*, *12*(1), 8–19. doi:10.1111/j.1468-2370.2009.00276.x

Du, S., & Xie, C. (2021). Paradoxes of artificial intelligence in consumer markets: Ethical challenges and opportunities. *Journal of Business Research*, *129*, 961–974. doi:10.1016/j.jbusres.2020.08.024

Dutt, V. K., Ludwig, C. A., Nicolay, K., Vay, H., & Voget, J. (2019). Increasing tax transparency: Investor reactions to the country-by-country reporting requirement for EU financial institutions. *International Tax and Public Finance*, *26*(6), 1259–1290. doi:10.100710797-019-09575-4

Dwekat, A., Seguí-Mas, E., & Tormo-Carbó, G. (2020). The effect of the board on corporate social responsibility: Bibliometric and social network analysis. *Ekonomska Istrazivanja*, *33*(1), 3580–3603. doi:10.1080/1331677X.2020.1776139

Dwivedi, Y. K., Hughes, L., Baabdullah, A. M., Ribeiro-Navarrete, S., Giannakis, M., Al-Debei, M. M., ... Cheung, C. M. (2022). Metaverse beyond the hype: Multidisciplinary perspectives on emerging challenges, opportunities, and agenda for research, practice and policy. *International Journal of Information Management*, *66*, 102542. doi:10.1016/j.ijinfomgt.2022.102542

Eberhartinger, E., Speitmann, R., & Sureth-Sloane, C. (2020). *Real Effects of Public Country-by-Country Reporting and the Firm Structure of European Banks*. Arqus Discussion Paper, 255. Disponível em: https://econstor.eu

Eccles, R. G., & Krzus, M. P. (2010). One report: Integrated reporting for a sustainable strategy. John Wiley & Sons.

Eccles, R. G., & Serafeim, G. (2017). Corporate and integrated reporting: A functional perspective. *Corporate Stewardship: Achieving Sustainable Effectiveness*, 156–171. doi:10.9774/GLEAF.9781783532605_10

Eccles, N. S., & Viviers, S. (2011). The Origins and Meanings of Names Describing Investment Practices that Integrate a Consideration of ESG Issues in the Academic Literature. *Journal of Business Ethics, 104*(3), 389–402. doi:10.100710551-011-0917-7

Eccles, R. G., Saltzman, D., Muniandy, B., Ali, M. J., Today, A., Team, E., ... Déclaration, L. (2011). Achieving Sustainability Through Integrated Reporting. *Stanford Social Innovation Review*. Advance online publication. doi:10.1016/j.sbspro.2013.08.672

Effatpanah, S. K., Ahmadi, M. H., Aungkulanon, P., Maleki, A., Sadeghzadeh, M., Sharifpur, M., & Chen, L. (2022). Comparative analysis of five widely-used multi-criteria decision-making methods to evaluate clean energy technologies: A case study. *Sustainability (Basel), 14*(3), 1403. Advance online publication. doi:10.3390u14031403

Ehrgott, M. (2005). *Multicriteria Optimization*. Springer Science & Business Media.

Eilbirt, H., & Parket, I. R. (1973). The practice of business: The current status of corporate social responsibility. *Business Horizons, 16*(4), 5–14. doi:10.1016/0007-6813(73)90043-8

Eizaguirre, A., García-Feijoo, M., & Laka, J. P. (2019). Defining sustainability core competencies in business and management studies based on multinational stakeholders' perceptions. *Sustainability (Basel), 11*(8), 2303. doi:10.3390u11082303

Elalfy, A., Weber, O., & Geobey, S. (2021). The Sustainable Development Goals (SDGs): a rising tide lifts all boats? Global reporting implications in a post SDGs world. *Journal of Applied Accounting Research*. . doi:10.1108/JAAR-06-2020-0116

Elkington, J. (2020). *Green Swans: The Coming Boom in Regenerative Capitalism*. Academic Press.

Elkington, J. (1998). Partnerships from Cannibals with Forks: The Triple Bottom Line of 21st- Century Business. *Environmental Quality Management, 8*(1), 37–51. doi:10.1002/tqem.3310080106

Elkington, J. (2004). Enter the triple bottom line. In *The Triple Bottom Line* (pp. 1–16). Routledge.

Erokhina, A. V. (2022) Implementing an ESG strategy using the Sustainability Balanced Scorecard. *Ekonomika: vchera, segodnya, zavtra, 12*(9A), 404-413. doi:10.34670/AR.2022.33.65.024

Espejo, M. M. S. B. (2008). Perfil dos Atributos do Sistema Orçamentário sob a Perspectiva Contingencial: uma Abordagem Multivariada. Tese Doutoramento em Ciências Contábeis, Programa de Pós-Graduação em Ciências Contábeis, Faculdade de Economia, Administração e Contabilidade da Universidade de São Paulo.

European Comission. (2022). *Corporate sustainability reporting*. https://finance.ec.europa.eu/capital-markets-union-and-financial-markets/company-reporting-and-auditing/company-reporting/corporate-sustainability-reporting_en

Fabac, R. (2022). Digital Balanced Scorecard System as a Supporting Strategy for Digital Transformation. *Sustainability (Basel), 14*(15), 1–26. doi:10.3390u14159690

Fagundes, J. A., Petri, M., Lavarda, R. B., Rodrigues, M. R., Lavarda, C. E. F., & Soller, C. C. (2010). Estrutura Organizacional E Gestão Sob A Ótica Da Teoria Da Contingência. *Gestão & Regionalidade, 26*(78). Advance online publication. doi:10.13037/gr.vol26n78

Fang, M., Nie, H., & Shen, X. (2023). Can enterprise digitization improve ESG performance? *Economic Modelling, 118*, 1–15. doi:10.1016/j.econmod.2022.106101

Farisyi, S., Musadieq, M. A., Utami, H. N., & Damayanti, C. R. (2022). A Systematic Literature Review: Determinants of Sustainability Reporting in Developing Countries. *Sustainability (Basel), 14*(16), 10222. doi:10.3390u141610222

Farooq, Q., Hao, Y., & Liu, X. (2019). Understanding corporate social responsibility with cross-cultural differences: A deeper look at religiosity. *Corporate Social Responsibility and Environmental Management, 26*(4), 965–971. doi:10.1002/csr.1736

Fatica, S., & Gregori, W. D. (2020). How much profit shifting do European banks do? *Economic Modelling, 90,* 536–551. doi:10.1016/j.econmod.2020.01.026

Fernandes, C. C., Mazzola, B. G., Esteves, K., & Oliveira, M. M. (2016). Práticas e indicadores de sustentabilidade em incubadoras de empresa: um estudo no Estado de São Paulo. *Revista de administração, contabilidade e economia da FUNDACE, 7*(3), 34-50.

Fernandez-Gago, R., Cabeza-Garcia, L., & Nieto, M. (2018). Independent directors' background and CSR disclosure. *Corporate Social Responsibility and Environmental Management, 25*(5), 991–1001. doi:10.1002/csr.1515

Fernandez-Izquierdo, A., & Matallin-Saez, J. C. (2008). Performance of ethical mutual funds in Spain: Sacrifice or premium? *Journal of Business Ethics, 81*(2), 247–260. doi:10.100710551-007-9492-3

Ferreira, A. O. (2016). Gestão de micro e pequenas empresas na perspectiva da teoria da contingência: um estudo em restaurantes da Região Metropolitana de Campinas – RMC [Tese de mestrado]. Faculdade Campo Limpo Paulista, Campo Limpo Paulista, SP, Brasil.

Flammer, C., & Bansal, P. (2017). Does a Long-Term Orientation Create Value? Evidence from a Regression Discontinuity. *Academy of Management Annual Meeting Proceedings, 38,* 1827–1847.

Flower, J. (2015). The international integrated reporting council: A story of failure. *Critical Perspectives on Accounting, 27,* 1–17. doi:10.1016/j.cpa.2014.07.002

Fonseca, L., & Carvalho, F. (2019). The Reporting of SDGs by Quality, Environmental, and Occupational Health and The Reporting of SDGs by Quality, Environmental, and Occupational Health and Safety-Certified Organizations. *Sustainability (Basel), 11*(20), 5797. doi:10.3390u11205797

Fonseca, S. A., & Martins, P. S. (2010). Gestão ambiental: uma súplica do planeta, um desafio para políticas públicas, incubadoras e pequenas empresas. Production, 20(4). https://doi.org/ doi:10.1590/S0103-65132010005000056

Fontoura, P., & Coelho, A. (2022). How to boost green innovation and performance through collaboration in the supply chain: Insights into a more sustainable economy. *Journal of Cleaner Production, 359,* 132005. doi:10.1016/j.jclepro.2022.132005

Fooladi, I. J., & Hebb, G. (2022). Drivers of differences in performance of ESG-focused funds relative to their underlying benchmarks. *Global Finance Journal, 100745.* Advance online publication. doi:10.1016/j.gfj.2022.100745

Fornell, C., & Larcker, D. F. (1981). Evaluating Structural Equation Models with Unobservable Variables and Measurement Error. *JMR, Journal of Marketing Research, 18*(1), 39–50. doi:10.1177/002224378101800104

Forray, J. M., & Leigh, J. S. (2012). A primer on the principles of responsible management education: Intellectual roots and waves of change. *Journal of Management Education, 36*(3), 295–309. doi:10.1177/1052562911433031

Fowler, S. J., & Hope, C. (2007). A critical review of sustainable business indices and their impact. *Journal of Business Ethics, 76*(3), 243–252. doi:10.100710551-007-9590-2

Freeman, R. E., & Dmytriyev, S. (2017). Corporate Social Responsibility and Stakeholder Theory: Learning From Each Other. *Symphonya. Emerging Issues in Management,* 7-15. https://doi.org/. doi:10.4468/2017.1.02

Freeman, R. E., & Velamuri, S. R. (2021). A New Approach to CSR: Company Stakeholder Responsibility 1. In The Routledge Companion to Corporate Social Responsibility (pp. 203-213). Routledge.

Freeman, R. E., Harrison, J. S., Wicks, A. C., Parmar, B. L., & De Colle, S. (2010). *Stakeholder theory: The state of the art*. Academic Press.

Freeman, R. E. (1984). Strategic Management: A Stakeholder Approach, Boston, Pitman. In L. Janina (Ed.), *Ethik als Standard in der Beschaffung. Werte und Normen als Gestaltungsausgangspunkt von Nicht-Regierungs-Organisationen*. Springer Gabler.

Freeman, R. E. (1994). The politics of stakeholder theory: Some future directions. *Business Ethics Quarterly*, *4*(4), 409–421. doi:10.2307/3857340

Freeman, R. E. (1999). Divergent stakeholder theory. *Academy of Management Review*, *24*(2), 233–236. doi:10.5465/amr.1999.1893932

Freeman, R. E. (2010). *Strategic management: A stakeholder approach*. Cambridge university press. doi:10.1017/CBO9781139192675

Freeman, R. E., Dmytriyev, S. D., & Phillips, R. A. (2021). Stakeholder Theory and the Resource-Based View of the Firm. *Journal of Management*, *47*(7), 1757–1770. Advance online publication. doi:10.1177/0149206321993576

Freire, J. C. S. (2002). *Juventude Ribeirinha: Identidade e Cotidiano* [Dissertação de Mestrado em Planejamento do Desenvolvimento – PLADES]. Núcleo de Altos Estudos Amazônicos, Universidade Federal do Pará, Belém, Brasil.

Freudenreich, B., Lüdeke-Freund, F., & Schaltegger, S. A. (2020). Stakeholder Theory Perspective on Business Models: Value Creation for Sustainability. *Journal of Business Ethics*, *166*(1), 3–18. doi:10.100710551-019-04112-z

Friede, G., Busch, T., & Bassen, A. (2015). ESG and financial performance: Aggregated evidence from more than 2000 empirical studies. *Journal of Sustainable Finance & Investment*, *5*(4), 210–233. doi:10.1080/20430795.2015.1118917

Friedman, A. L., & Miles, S. (2001). Socially responsible investment and corporate social and environmental reporting in the UK: An exploratory study. *The British Accounting Review*, *33*(4), 523–548. doi:10.1006/bare.2001.0172

Friedman, A. L., & Miles, S. (2002). Developing stakeholder theory. *Journal of Management Studies*, *39*(1), 1–21. doi:10.1111/1467-6486.00280

Frooman, J. (1997). Socially Irresponsible and Illegal Behaviour and Shareholder Wealth: A Meta-Analysis of Event Studies. *Business & Society*, *36*, 221–249. doi:10.1177/000765039703600302

FrostT.TsangA.CaoH. (2022). Environmental, Social, and Governance (ESG) Disclosure: A Literature Review. *Social Science Research Network*. doi:10.2139/ssrn.4270942

Fuest, C., Hugger, F., & Neumeier, F. (2022). Corporate profit shifting and the role of tax havens: Evidence from German country-by-country reporting data. *Journal of Economic Behavior & Organization*, *194*, 454–477. doi:10.1016/j.jebo.2021.11.016

Fu, T., & Li, J. (2023). An empirical analysis of the impact of ESG on financial performance: The moderating role of digital transformation. *Frontiers in Environmental Science*, *11*, 1–12. doi:10.3389/fenvs.2023.1256052

Gaia, S., & Jones, M. J. (2017). UK local councils reporting of biodiversity values: A stakeholder perspective. *Accounting, Auditing & Accountability Journal*, *30*(7), 1614–1638. doi:10.1108/AAAJ-12-2015-2367

Gajewski, J. F., & Li, L. (2015). Can Internet-based disclosure reduce information asymmetry? *Advances in Accounting*, *31*(1), 115–124. doi:10.1016/j.adiac.2015.03.013

Galbreath, J. (2013). ESG in Focus: The Australian Evidence. *Journal of Business Ethics*, *118*(3), 529–541. doi:10.100710551-012-1607-9

Gamerschlag, R., Moeller, K., & Verbeeten, F. (2011). Determinants of voluntary CSR disclosure: Empirical evidence from Germany. *Review of Managerial Science*, *5*(2/3), 233–26. doi:10.100711846-010-0052-3

Garcia, A. S., Mendes-Da-Silva, W., & Orsato, R. J. (2017). Sensitive industries produce better ESG performance: Evidence from emerging markets. *Journal of Cleaner Production*, *150*, 135–147. doi:10.1016/j.jclepro.2017.02.180

Garcia-Bernabeu, A., Salcedo, J. V., Hilario, A., Pla-Santamaria, D., & Herrero, J. M. (2019). Computing the mean-variance-sustainability nondominated surface by Ev-MOGA. *Complexity*, *2019*, 1–12. doi:10.1155/2019/6095712

Garcia-Bernardo, J., Janský, P., & Thorslov, T. (2021). Multinational corporations and tax havens: Evidence from country-by-country reporting. *International Tax and Public Finance*, *28*(6), 1519–1561. doi:10.100710797-020-09639-w

García-Sánchez, I. M., Gómez-Miranda, M. E., David, F., & Rodríguez-Ariza, L. (2019). Board independence and GRI-IFC performance standards: The mediating effect of the CSR committee. *Journal of Cleaner Production*, *225*, 554–562. doi:10.1016/j.jclepro.2019.03.337

Garcia-Sanchez, I.-M., Hussain, N., Martinez-Ferrero, J., & Ruiz-Barbadillo, E. (2019). Impact of disclosure and assurance quality of corporate sustainability reports on access to finance. *Corporate Social Responsibility and Environmental Management*, *26*(4), 832–848. doi:10.1002/csr.1724

Garcia-Torea, N., Fernandez-Feijoo, B., & De La Cuesta, M. (2020). CSR reporting communication: Defective reporting models or misapplication? *Corporate Social Responsibility and Environmental Management*, *27*(2), 952–968. doi:10.1002/csr.1858

Garel, A., & Petit-Romec, A. (2021). Investor rewards to environmental responsibility: Evidence from the COVID-19 crisis. *Journal of Corporate Finance*, *68*, 1–20. doi:10.1016/j.jcorpfin.2021.101948

Gatti, L., Vishwanath, B., Seele, P., & Cottier, B. (2019). Are we moving beyond voluntary CSR? Exploring theoretical and managerial implications of mandatory CSR resulting from the new Indian companies act. *Journal of Business Ethics*, *160*(4), 961–972. doi:10.100710551-018-3783-8

Gazzola, P., Amelio, S., Papagiannis, F., & Michaelides, Z. (2019). Sustainability reporting practices and their social impact to NGO funding in Italy. *Critical Perspectives on Accounting*, *79*, 102085. Advance online publication. doi:10.1016/j.cpa.2019.04.006

Gazzola, P., Pezzetti, R., Amelio, S., & Grechi, D. (2020). Non-financial information disclosure in Italian public interest companies: A sustainability reporting perspective. *Sustainability (Basel)*, *12*(15), 1–16. doi:10.3390u12156063

Getzner, M., & Grabner-Krauter, S. (2004). Consumer preferences and marketing strategies for 'green shares': Specifics of the Austrian market. *International Journal of Bank Marketing*, *22*(4), 260–278. doi:10.1108/02652320410542545

Gibassier, D. (2015). Six Capitals–The Revolution Capitalism Has to Have–Or Can Accountants Save the Planet? *Social and Environmental Accountability Journal*, *35*(3), 204–205. doi:10.1080/0969160X.2015.1093782

Gil-Bazo, J., Ruiz-Verdú, P., & Santos, A. A. P. (2010). The performance of socially responsible mutual funds: The role of fees and management companies. *Journal of Business Ethics*, *94*(2), 243–263. doi:10.100710551-009-0260-4

Gillan, S. L., Koch, A., & Starks, L. T. (2021). Firms and social responsibility: A review of ESG and CSR research in corporate finance. *Journal of Corporate Finance*, *66*, 1–16. doi:10.1016/j.jcorpfin.2021.101889

Giron, A., Kazemikhasragh, A., Cicchiello, A. F., & Panetti, E. (2020). Sustainability Reporting and Firms' Economic Performance: Evidence from Asia and Africa. *Journal of the Knowledge Economy, 12*(4), 1741–1759. doi:10.100713132-020-00693-7

Global Sustainable Investment Alliance. (2018). *Global Sustainable Investmet Review*. https://www.google.com/url?sa=t&rct=j&q=&esrc=s&source=web&cd=&cad=rja&uact=8&ved=2ahUKEwiH7OWh_uHwAhUYgf0HHdgnBxgQFjABegQIBhAD&url=http%3A%2F%2Fwww.gsi-alliance.org%2Fwpcontent%2Fuploads%2F2019%2F03%2FGSIR_Review2018.3.28.pdf&usg=AOvVaw3A7tZh80HJW6ZAqMQ_zGe7

Godfrey, J., Hodgson, A., Tarca, A., Hamilton, J., & Holmen, S. (2010). *Accounting*. John Wiley & Sons, Inc.

Gök, İ. Y., & Özdemír, O. (2017). Borsa İstanbul Sürdürülebilirlik Endeksinin performans karakteristiği. *Sosyoekonomi, 25*(34), 87–105.

Gold, A., Heilmann, M., Pott, C., & Rematzki, J. (2020). Do key audit matters impact financial reporting behavior? *International Journal of Auditing, 24*(2), 232–244. doi:10.1111/ijau.12190

Goldreyer, E. F., Ahmed, P., & Diltz, J. D. (1999). The performance of socially responsible mutual funds: Incorporating sociopolitical information in portfolio selection. *Managerial Finance, 25*(1), 23–36. doi:10.1108/03074359910765830

Gomes, D. R., Ribeiro, N., & Santos, M. J. (2023). "Searching for Gold" with Sustainable Human Resources Management and Internal Communication: Evaluating the Mediating Role of Employer Attractiveness for Explaining Turnover Intention and Performance. *Administrative Sciences, 13*(24), 1–15. doi:10.3390/admsci13010024

Gomes, S. F., Eugénio, T. C. P., & Branco, M. C. (2015). Sustainability reporting and assurance in Portugal. *Corporate Governance (Bradford), 15*(3), 281–292. doi:10.1108/CG-07-2013-0097

Goyal, L. (2022). Stakeholder theory: Revisiting the origins. *Journal of Public Affairs, 22*(3), e2559. doi:10.1002/pa.2559

Gray, R. (2010). Is accounting for sustainability actually accounting for sustainability… and how would we know? An exploration of narratives of organisations and the planet. *Accounting, Organizations and Society, 35*(1), 47–62. doi:10.1016/j.aos.2009.04.006

Gray, R., & Milne, M. J. (2018). Perhaps the Dodo should have accounted for human beings? Accounts of humanity and (its) extinction. *Accounting, Auditing & Accountability Journal, 31*(3), 826–848. doi:10.1108/AAAJ-03-2016-2483

Gregory, A., Whittaker, J. M., & Yan, X. (2016). Corporate Social Performance, Competitive Advantage, Earnings Persistence and Firm Value. *Journal of Business Finance & Accounting, 43*(1–2), 3–30. doi:10.1111/jbfa.12182

GRI. (2022). *State of progress: business contributions to the SDGs. A 2020-2021 study in support of the Sustainable Development Goals*. https://globescan.com/wp-content/up

Groot, T. L. C. M., & Selto, F. (2013). Integrated financial and non-financial measures. In T. L. C. M. Groot & F. Selto (Eds.), *Advanced Management Accounting*. Pearson Education.

GSIA. (2020). *Global Sustainable Investment Review*. https://www.gsi-alliance.org/wp-content/uploads/2021/08/GSIR-20201.pdf

Guastaroba, G., Mansini, R., & Speranza, M. G. (2009). On the effectiveness of scenario generation techniques in single-period portfolio optimisation. *European Journal of Operational Research, 192*(2), 500–511. doi:10.1016/j.ejor.2007.09.042

Gupta, H., Nishi, M., & Gasparatos, A. (2022). Community-based responses for tackling environmental and socio-economic change and impacts in mountain social–ecological systems. *Ambio, 51*(5), 1123–1142. doi:10.100713280-021-01651-6 PMID:34784008

Hack, L., Kenyon, A. J., & Wood, E. H. (2014). A critical corporate social responsibility (CSR) timeline: How should it be understood now. *International Journal of Management Cases, 16*(4), 46–55.

Haenlein, M., & Kaplan, A. (2019). A Brief History of Artificial Intelligence: On the Past, Present, and Future of Artificial Intelligence. *California Management Review, 61*(4), 5–14. doi:10.1177/0008125619864925

Haigh, M., & Hazelton, J. (2004). Financial markets: A tool for social responsibility? *Journal of Business Ethics, 52*(1), 59–71. doi:10.1023/B:BUSI.0000033107.22587.0b

Hair, J. F., Astrachan, C. B., Moisescu, O. I., Radomir, L., Sarstedt, M., Vaithilingam, S., & Ringle, C. M. (2021). Executing and interpreting applications of PLS-SEM: Updates for family business researchers. *Journal of Family Business Strategy, 12*(3), 1–8. doi:10.1016/j.jfbs.2020.100392

Hair, J. F., Hult, G. T. M., Ringle, C. M., & Sarstedt, M. (2022). *A Primer on Partial Least Squares Structural Equation Modeling (PLS-SEM)*. Sage.

Hair, J. F. Jr, Anderson, R. E., Tatham, R. L., & Black, W. C. (2010). *Multivariate Data Analysis* (7th ed.). Pearson.

Hair, J. F. Jr, Matthews, L. M., Matthews, R. L., & Sarstedt, M. (2017). PLS-SEM or CB-SEM: Updated guidelines on which method to use. *International Journal of Multivariate Data Analysis, 1*(2), 107–123. doi:10.1504/IJMDA.2017.087624

Hair, J. F., Ringle, C. M., & Sarstedt, M. (2011). PLS-SEM: Indeed a Silver Bullet. *Journal of Marketing Theory and Practice, 19*(2), 139–152. doi:10.2753/MTP1069-6679190202

Hair, J. F., Risher, J. J., Sarstedt, M., & Ringle, C. M. (2019). When to use and how to report the results of PLS-SEM. *European Business Review, 31*(1), 2–24. doi:10.1108/EBR-11-2018-0203

Hamilton, S., Jo, H., & Statman, M. (1993). Doing well while doing good? The investment performance of socially responsible mutual funds. *Financial Analysts Journal, 49*(6), 62–66. doi:10.2469/faj.v49.n6.62

Hamzah, S., Pangemanan, D., & Aprianti, E. (2023). The environmental and sustainable factors on the special economic zones development. *Civil Engineering Journal, 9*(2), 334–342. doi:10.28991/CEJ-2023-09-02-06

Haney, A. B., Pope, J., & Arden, Z. (2020). Making It Personal: Developing Sustainability Leaders in Business. *Organization & Environment, 33*(2), 155–174. doi:10.1177/1086026618806201

Hanić, A., Jovanović, O., & Stevanović, S. (2021). Environmental disclosure practice in the Serbian banking sector. *Management, 26*(2), 115–144. doi:10.30924/mjcmi.26.2.7

Hanlon, M. (2018). *Country-by-country reporting and the international allocation of taxing rights*. International Bureau of Fiscal Documentation (IBFD).

Hansen, E. G., & Schaltegger, S. (2014). The Sustainability Balanced Scorecard: A Systematic Review of Architectures. *Journal of Business Ethics, 133*(2), 193–221. doi:10.100710551-014-2340-3

Hansen, E. G., & Schaltegger, S. (2018). Sustainability Balanced Scorecards and their Architectures: Irrelevant or Misunderstood? *Journal of Business Ethics, 150*(4), 937–952. doi:10.100710551-017-3531-5

Harrington, H. J. (1987). *The Improvement Process*. McGraw-Hill.

Hassan, A. M., Roberts, L., & Atkins, J. (2020). Exploring factors relating to extinction disclosures: What motivates companies to report on biodiversity and species protection? *Business Strategy and the Environment, 29*(3), 1419–1436. doi:10.1002/bse.2442

Haydon, S., Jung, T., & Russell, S. (2021). 'You've been framed': A critical review of academic discourse on philanthrocapitalism. *International Journal of Management Reviews*, *23*(3), 353–375. doi:10.1111/ijmr.12255

Haywood, L. K., & Boihang, M. (2021). Business and the SDGs: Examining the early disclosure of the SDGs in annual reports. *Development Southern Africa*, *38*(2), 175–188. doi:10.1080/0376835X.2020.1818548

Heald, M. (1957). Management's responsibility to society: The growth of an idea. *Business History Review*, *31*(4), 375–384. doi:10.2307/3111413

Hebb, T. (2006). The economic inefficiency of secrecy: Pension fund investors' corporate transparency concerns. *Journal of Business Ethics*, *63*(4), 385–405. doi:10.100710551-005-3968-9

He, H., & Harris, L. (2020). The impact of Covid-19 pandemic on corporate social responsibility and marketing philosophy. *Journal of Business Research*, *116*, 176–182. doi:10.1016/j.jbusres.2020.05.030 PMID:32457556

Hehenberger-Risse, D., Straub, J., Niechoj, D., & Lutzenberger, A. (2019). Sustainability Index to Assess the Environmental Impact of Heat Supply Systems. *Chemical Engineering & Technology*, *42*(9), 1923–1927. doi:10.1002/ceat.201800647

Heinkel, R., Kraus, A., & Zechner, J. (2001). The effect of green investment on corporate behavior. *Journal of Financial and Quantitative Analysis*, *36*(4), 431–449. doi:10.2307/2676219

Hellsten, S., & Mallin, C. (2006). Are "ethical" or "socially responsible" investments socially responsible? *Journal of Business Ethics*, *66*(4), 393–406. doi:10.100710551-006-0001-x

Hendriksen, E. S. (1982). *Accounting Theory*. Irwin International Accounting Standards.

Henseler, J., Hubona, G., & Ray, P. A. (2016). Using PLS path modeling in new technology research: Updated guidelines. *Industrial Management & Data Systems*, *116*(1), 2–20. doi:10.1108/IMDS-09-2015-0382

Henseler, J., Ringle, C. M., & Sarstedt, M. (2015). A new criterion for assessing discriminant validity in variance-based structural equation modeling. *Journal of the Academy of Marketing Science*, *43*(1), 115–135. doi:10.100711747-014-0403-8

Henseler, J., Ringle, C. M., & Sinkovics, R. R. (2009). The use of partial least squares path modeling in international marketing. In R. R. Sinkovics & P. N. Ghauri (Eds.), *New Challenges to International Marketing* (pp. 277–319). Emerald Group Publishing. doi:10.1108/S1474-7979(2009)0000020014

Heras-Saizarbitoria, I., Urbieta, L., & Boiral, O. (2022). Organizations' engagement with sustainable development goals: From cherry-picking to SDG-washing? *Corporate Social Responsibility and Environmental Management*, *29*(2), 316–328. doi:10.1002/csr.2202

Hess, D. (2008). The three pillars of corporate social reporting as new governance regulation: Disclosure, dialogue, and development. *Business Ethics Quarterly*, *18*(4), 447–482. doi:10.5840/beq200818434

Hickman, L., & Akdere, M. (2019). Exploring information technology-business alignment through stakeholder theory: A review of literature. *Industrial and Commercial Training*, *51*(4), 228–243. doi:10.1108/ICT-11-2018-0098

Hilario-Caballero, A., Garcia-Bernabeu, A., Salcedo, J. V., & Vercher, M. (2020). Tri-Criterion Model for Constructing Low-Carbon Mutual Fund Portfolios: A Preference-Based Multiobjective Genetic Algorithm Approach. *International Journal of Environmental Research and Public Health*, *17*(17), 6324. doi:10.3390/ijerph17176324 PMID:32878037

Hillman, A. J., Withers, M. C., & Collins, B. J. (2009). Resource dependence theory: A review. *Journal of Management*, *35*(6), 1404–1427. doi:10.1177/0149206309343469

Hines, J. R. Jr. (2010). Treasure islands. *The Journal of Economic Perspectives*, *24*(4), 103–126. doi:10.1257/jep.24.4.103

Hines, J. R., & Rice, E. M. (1994). Fiscal Paradise: Foreign Tax Havens and American Business. *The Quarterly Journal of Economics*, *109*(1), 149–182. doi:10.2307/2118431

Holt, T. V., Statler, M., Atz, U., Whelan, T., van Loggerenberg, M., & Cebulla, J. (2020). The cultural consensus of sustainability-driven innovation: Strategies for success. *Business Strategy and the Environment*, *29*(8), 3399–3409. doi:10.1002/bse.2584

Holub, J. M. (2003). Questioning Organizational Legitimacy: The Case of U.S. Expatriates. *Journal of Business Ethics*, *47*(3), 269–293. doi:10.1023/A:1026257229939

Hooghiemstra, R. (2000). Corporate communication and impression management–new perspectives why companies engage in corporate social reporting. *Journal of Business Ethics*, *27*(1), 55–68. doi:10.1023/A:1006400707757

Hsu, C.-W., Lee, W.-H., & Chao, W.-C. (2013). Materiality analysis model in sustainability reporting: A case study at Lite-On Technology Corporation. *Journal of Cleaner Production*, *57*, 142–151. doi:10.1016/j.jclepro.2013.05.040

Huang, Q., Fang, J., Xue, X., & Gao, H. (2023). Does digital innovation cause better ESG performance? an empirical test of a-listed firms in China. *Research in International Business and Finance*, *66*, 1–20. doi:10.1016/j.ribaf.2023.102049

Hugger, F. (2019). *The impact of country-by-country reporting on corporate tax avoidance* (No. 304). IFO Working Paper.

Hu, H. H., Parsa, H. G., & Self, J. (2010). The dynamics of green restaurant patronage. *Cornell Hospitality Quarterly*, *51*(3), 344–362. doi:10.1177/1938965510370564

Hummel, K., & Szekely, M. (2021). Disclosure on the Sustainable Development Goals–Evidence from Europe. *Accounting in Europe*, *19*(1), 152-189. . doi:10.1080/17449480.2021.1894347

Hussain, N., Rigoni, U., & Orij, R. P. (2018). Corporate Governance and Sustainability Performance: Analysis of Triple Bottom Line Performance. *Journal of Business Ethics*, *149*(2), 411–432. doi:10.100710551-016-3099-5

Hussein, K., & Omran, M. (2005). Ethical investment revisited: Evidence from Dow Jones Islamic indexes. *Journal of Investing*, *14*(3), 105–126. doi:10.3905/joi.2005.580557

Hwang, C. L., & Yoon, K. P. (1981). *Multiple attribute decision making: Methods and applications* (Vol. 186). Springer-Verlag., doi:10.1007/978-3-642-48318-9

Hwang, K., & Lee, B. (2019). Pride, mindfulness, public self-awareness, affective satisfaction, and customer citizenship behaviour among green restaurant customers. *International Journal of Hospitality Management*, *83*, 169–179. doi:10.1016/j.ijhm.2019.05.009

Iacobucci, D. (2010). Structural equations modeling: Fit Indices, sample size, and advanced topics. *Journal of Consumer Psychology*, *20*(1), 90–98. doi:10.1016/j.jcps.2009.09.003

ICMA. (2018). *Green Bond Principles 2018: Voluntary Process Guidelines for Issuing Green Bonds*. https://www.icmagroup.org/assets/documents/Regulatory/Green-Bonds/Green-Bonds-Principles-June-2018-270520.pdf

IFC. (2018). *Beyond the Balance Sheet*. https://www.ifc.org/wps/wcm/connect/d4bd76ad-ea04-4583-a54f-371b1a7e5cd0/Beyond_The_Balance_Sheet_IFC_Toolkit_for_Disclosure_Transparency.pdf?MOD=AJPERES&CVID=morp0vo

Ifinedo, P. (2011). Examining the influences of external expertise and in-house computer/IT knowledge on ERP system success. *Journal of Systems and Software*, *84*(12), 2065–2078. doi:10.1016/j.jss.2011.05.017

IIRC - International Integrated Reporting Council (2013). *The International Framework Integrated Reporting*. Author.

Ikram, M., Sroufe, R., Mohsin, M., Solangi, Y. A., Shah, S. Z. A., & Shahzad, F. (2019). Does CSR influence firm performance? A longitudinal study of SME sectors of Pakistan. *Journal of Global Responsibility*, *11*(1), 27–53. doi:10.1108/JGR-12-2018-0088

Imran, M., Aziz, A., & Abdul Hamid, S. N. (2017). Determinants of SME export performance. *International Journal of Data and Network Science*, 39–58. . doi:10.5267/j.ijdns.2017.1.007

IOD. (2016). *King IV report on corporate governance in South Africa Johannesburg*. Lexis Nexus South Africa.

Iredele, O. O. (2020). Measuring performance in corporate environmental reporting in Nigeria. *Measuring Business Excellence*, *24*(2), 183–195. doi:10.1108/MBE-05-2019-0040

Isukul, A. C., & Chizea, J. J. (2017). Corporate Governance Disclosure in Developing Countries: A Comparative Analysis in Nigerian and South African Banks. *SAGE Open*, *7*(3), 215824401771911. doi:10.1177/2158244017719112

Izzo, M. F., Ciaburri, M., & Tiscini, R. (2020). The challenge of sustainable development goal reporting: The first evidence from italian listed companies. *Sustainability (Basel)*, *12*(8), 3494. Advance online publication. doi:10.3390u12083494

Izzo, M. F., Dello Strologo, A., & Graná, F. (2020). Learning from the Best : New Challenges and Trends in IR Reporters' Disclosure and the Role of SDGs. *Sustainability (Basel)*, *12*(5545), 1–22. doi:10.3390u12145545

Jacobsen, S. S., Korsgaard, S., & Gunzel-Jensen, F. (2020). Towards a Typology of Sustainability Practices: A Study of the Potentials and Challenges of Sustainable Practices at the Firm Level. *Sustainability (Basel)*, *12*(12), 5166. doi:10.3390u12125166

Jamali, D., Zanhour, M., & Keshishian, T. (2009). Peculiar strengths and relational attributes of SMEs in the context of CSR. *Journal of Business Ethics*, *87*(3), 355–377. doi:10.100710551-008-9925-7

Jan, A., Marimuthu, M., & Bin, P. M. (2019, August 10). The nexus of sustainability practices and financial performance: From the perspective of Islamic banking. *Journal of Cleaner Production*, *228*, 703–717. doi:10.1016/j.jclepro.2019.04.208

Janský, P. (2020). European banks and tax havens: Evidence from country-by-country reporting. *Applied Economics*, *52*(54), 5967–5985. doi:10.1080/00036846.2020.1781773

Jassem, S., Zakaria, Z., & Che Azmi, A. (2022). Sustainability balanced scorecard architecture and environmental performance outcomes: A systematic review. *International Journal of Productivity and Performance Management*, *71*(5), 1728–1760. doi:10.1108/IJPPM-12-2019-0582

Jindřichovská, I., Kubíčková, D., & Mocanu, M. (2020). Case Study Analysis of Sustainability Reporting of an Agri-Food Giant. *Sustainability (Basel)*, *12*(11), 4491. doi:10.3390u12114491

Jin, J., & Han, L. (2018). Assessment of Chinese green funds: Performance and industry allocation. *Journal of Cleaner Production*, *171*, 1084–1093. doi:10.1016/j.jclepro.2017.09.211

Johnson, E., Petersen, M., Sloan, J., & Valencia, A. (2021). The Interest, Knowledge, and Usage of Artificial Intelligence in Accounting: Evidence from Accounting Professionals. *Accounting & Taxation*, *13*(1), 45–58.

Johnson, M., Albizri, A., Harfouche, A., & Fosso-Wamba, S. (2022). Integrating human knowledge into artificial intelligence for complex and ill-structured problems: Informed artificial intelligence. *International Journal of Information Management*, *64*, 1–15. doi:10.1016/j.ijinfomgt.2022.102479

Jones, G. J., Edwards, M. B., Bocarro, J. N., Svensson, P. G., & Misener, K. (2020). A community capacity building approach to sport-based youth development. *Sport Management Review*, *23*(4), 563–575. doi:10.1016/j.smr.2019.09.001

Jones, M. (2014). Ecosystem and natural inventory biodiversity frameworks. In M. Jones (Ed.), *Accounting for biodiversity* (pp. 39–61). Routledge. doi:10.4324/9780203097472-13

Jones, M. J. (1996). Accounting for biodiversity: A pilot study. *The British Accounting Review*, *28*(4), 281–303. doi:10.1006/bare.1996.0019

Jones, M. J. (2010). Accounting for the environment: Towards a theoretical perspective for environmental accounting and reporting. *Accounting Forum*, *34*(2), 123–138. doi:10.1016/j.accfor.2010.03.001

Jones, M. J., & Solomon, J. F. (2013). Problematising accounting for biodiversity. *Accounting, Auditing & Accountability Journal*, *26*(5), 668–687. doi:10.1108/AAAJ-03-2013-1255

Jones, S., Van der Laan, S., Frost, G., & Loftus, J. (2008). The investment performance of socially responsible investment funds in Australia. *Journal of Business Ethics*, *80*(2), 181–203. doi:10.100710551-007-9412-6

Jones, T. M. (1980). Corporate social responsibility revisited, redefined. *California Management Review*, *22*(3), 59–67. doi:10.2307/41164877

Jones, T. M., Harrison, J. S., & Felps, W. (2018). How Applying Instrumental Stakeholder Theory Can Provide Sustainable Competitive Advantage. *Academy of Management Review*, *43*(3), 371–391. doi:10.5465/amr.2016.0111

Joshi, P. L., Suwaidan, M. S., & Kumar, R. (2011). Determinants of environmental disclosures by Indian industrial listed companies: Empirical study. *International Journal of Accounting and Finance*, *3*(2), 109. doi:10.1504/IJAF.2011.043843

Julong, D. (1989). Introduction to grey system theory. *Journal of Grey System*, *1*(1), 1–24.

Kamp, B., & Parry, G. (2017). Servitization and advanced business services as levers for competitiveness. *Industrial Marketing Management*, *60*, 11–16. doi:10.1016/j.indmarman.2016.12.008

Kang, H., & Gray, S. J. (2019). Country-specific risks and geographic disclosure aggregation: Voluntary disclosure behaviour by British multinationals. *The British Accounting Review*, *51*(3), 259–276. doi:10.1016/j.bar.2019.02.001

Kanji, R., & Agrawal, R. (2016). Models of Corporate Social Responsibility: Comparison, Evolution and Convergence. *IIM Kozhikode Society & Management Review*, *5*(2), 141–155. doi:10.1177/2277975216634478

KAP Public Disclosure Platform. (2021). *Yatırım Fonları*. https://www.kap.org.tr/tr/YatirimFonlari/YF

Kaplan, A., & Haenlein, M. (2019). Siri, Siri, in my hand: Who's the fairest in the land? On the interpretations, illustrations, and implications of artificial intelligence. *Business Horizons*, *62*(1), 15–25. doi:10.1016/j.bushor.2018.08.004

Kaplan, R. S., & Norton, D. P. (1996a). Using the balanced scorecard as a strategic management system. *Harvard Business Review*, *74*(1), 75–85.

Kaplan, R. S., & Norton, D. P. (1996b). Linking the balanced scorecard to strategy. *California Management Review*, *39*(1), 53–79. doi:10.2307/41165876

Karaatlı, M., Ömürbek, N., Budak, İ., & Dağ, O. (2015). Çok kriterli karar verme yöntemleri ile yaşanabilir illerin sıralanması. *Selçuk Üniversitesi Sosyal Bilimler Enstitüsü Dergisi*, *33*, 215–228.

Karaman, A. S., Orazalin, N., Uyar, A., & Shahbaz, M. (2021). CSR achievement, reporting, and assurance in the energy sector: Does economic development matter? *Energy Policy*, *149*, 112007. doi:10.1016/j.enpol.2020.112007

Karmakar, P., Paromita, D., & Biswas, S. (2018). Assessment of mutual fund performance using distance based multi-criteria decision making techniques: An Indian perspective. *Research Bulletin (International Commission for the Northwest Atlantic Fisheries)*, *44*(1), 17–38. doi:10.33516/rb.v44i1.17-38p

Katmon, N., Mohamad, Z. Z., Norwani, N. M., & Al Farooque, O. (2019). Comprehensive Board Diversity and Quality of Corporate Social Responsibility Disclosure: Evidence from an Emerging Market. *Journal of Business Ethics*, *157*(2), 447–481. doi:10.100710551-017-3672-6

Kaucic, M., Moradi, M., & Mirzazadeh, M. (2019). Portfolio optimisation by improved NSGA-II and SPEA 2 based on different risk measures. *Financial Innovation*, *5*(26), 1–28. doi:10.118640854-019-0140-6

Kaucic, M., Piccotto, F., Sbaiz, G., & Valentinuz, G. (2023a). A hybrid level-based learning swarm algorithm with mutation operator for solving large-scale cardinality-constrained portfolio optimisation problems. *Information Sciences*, *634*, 321–339. doi:10.1016/j.ins.2023.03.115

Kaucic, M., Piccotto, F., Sbaiz, G., & Valentinuz, G. (2023b). Optimal Portfolio with Sustainable Attitudes under Cumulative Prospect Theory. *Journal of Applied Finance & Banking*. Advance online publication. doi:10.47260/jafb/1344

Khaled, R., Ali, H., & Mohamed, E. K. (2021). The Sustainable Development Goals and corporate sustainability performance: Mapping, extent and determinants. *Journal of Cleaner Production*, *311*, 127599. doi:10.1016/j.jclepro.2021.127599

Khan, M., Lockhart, J., & Bathurst, R. (2020). A multi-level institutional perspective of corporate social responsibility reporting: A mixed-method study. *Journal of Cleaner Production*, *265*, 121739. doi:10.1016/j.jclepro.2020.121739

Khattak, A., & Yousaf, Z. (2021). Digital Social Responsibility towards Corporate Social Responsibility and Strategic Performance of Hi-Tech SMEs: Customer Engagement as a Mediator. *Sustainability (Basel)*, *14*(1), 1–16. doi:10.3390u14010131

Kiliç, M. (2016). Online corporate social responsibility (CSR) disclosure in the banking industry. *International Journal of Bank Marketing*, *34*(4), 550–569. doi:10.1108/IJBM-04-2015-0060

Kim, B.-J., Jung, J.-Y., & Cho, S.-W. (2022). Can ESG mitigate the diversification discount in cross-border M&A? *Borsa Istanbul Review*, *22*(3), 607–615. doi:10.1016/j.bir.2021.09.002

Kim, M. J., & Hall, C. M. (2020). Can sustainable restaurant practices enhance customer loyalty? The roles of value theory and environmental concerns. *Journal of Hospitality and Tourism Management*, *43*, 127–138. doi:10.1016/j.jhtm.2020.03.004

Kim, S., & Li, Z. (2021). Understanding the Impact of ESG Practices in Corporate Finance. *Sustainability (Basel)*, *13*(7), 1–15. doi:10.3390u13073746

Kojić, M., Schlüter, S., Mitić, P., & Hanić, A. (2022). Economy-environment nexus in developed European countries: Evidence from multifractal and wavelet analysis. *Chaos, Solitons, and Fractals*, *160*, 112189. doi:10.1016/j.chaos.2022.112189

Kolbert, E. (2014). *The Sixth Extinction. An Unnatural History*. Henry Holt and Company.

Kolk, A. (2003). Trends in sustainability reporting by the Fortune Global 250. *Business Strategy and the Environment*, *12*(5), 279–291. doi:10.1002/bse.370

Kolk, A. (2004). A decade of sustainability reporting: Developments and significance. *International Journal of Environment and Sustainable Development*, *3*(1), 51–64. doi:10.1504/IJESD.2004.004688

Konno, H., Waki, H., & Yuuki, A. (2002). Portfolio Optimisation under Lower Partial Risk Measures. *Asia-Pacific Financial Markets*, *9*(2), 127–140. doi:10.1023/A:1022238119491

Kouaib, A., Mhiri, S., & Jarboui, A. (2020). Board of directors' effectiveness and sustainable performance: The triple bottom line. *The Journal of High Technology Management Research*, *31*(2), 100390. doi:10.1016/j.hitech.2020.100390

KPMG. (2017). *KPMG International Survey of Corporate Responsibility*. KPMG.

KPMG. (2017). The road ahead. In *Operators for Similarity Search. SpringerBriefs in Computer Science.* Springer. doi:10.1007/978-3-319-21257-9_7

KPMG. (2020). *The Time Has Come: The KPMG Survey of Sustainability Reporting 2020.* KPMG.

Krause, R. W., & Bahls, Á. A. (2013). Orientações gerais para uma gastronomia sustentável. *Turismo: visão e ação, 15*(3), 434-450. . doi:10.14210/rtva.v15n3.p434-450

Kreander, N., Gray, R. H., Power, D. M., & Sinclair, C. D. (2005). Evaluating the performance of ethical and non-ethical funds: A matched pair analysis. *Journal of Business Finance & Accounting, 32*(7-8), 1465–1493. doi:10.1111/j.0306-686X.2005.00636.x

KruegerP.SautnerZ.TangD. Y.ZhongR. (2021). The Effects of Mandatory ESG Disclosure around the World. *Social Science Research Network.* doi:10.2139/ssrn.3832745

Kurtz, L. (1997). No effect, or no net effect? Studies on socially responsible investing. *Journal of Investing, 6*(4), 37–49. doi:10.3905/joi.1997.37

Kurucz, E. C., Colbert, B. A., & Wheeler, D. (2008). The business case for corporate social responsibility. In The Oxford handbook of corporate social responsibility (pp. 83-112). doi:10.1093/oxfordhb/9780199211593.003.0004

Kuzma, E. L., Doliveira, S. L. D., Gonzaga, C. A. M., & Novak, M. A. L. (2016). A Inserção da Sustentabilidade na Formação de Administradores. *Revista de Gestão Ambiental e Sustentabilidade, 5*(2), 146–165. doi:10.5585/geas.v5i2.430

Kuzmina, J., Atstaja, D., Purvins, M., Baakashvili, G., & Chkareuli, V. (2023). In search of sustainability and financial returns: The case of ESG energy funds. *Sustainability (Basel), 15*(3), 1–16. doi:10.3390u15032716

Kwilinski, A., Lyulyov, O., & Pimonenko, T. (2023). Unlocking Sustainable Value through Digital Transformation: An Examination of ESG Performance. *Information (Basel), 14*(444), 1–18. doi:10.3390/info14080444

La Torre, M., Sabelfeld, S., Blomkvist, M., & Dumay, J. (2020). Rebuilding trust: Sustainability and non-financial reporting and the European Union regulation. *Meditari Accountancy Research, 28*(5), 701–725. doi:10.1108/MEDAR-06-2020-0914

Lambrechts, W., Son-Turan, S., Reis, L., & Semeijn, J. (2019). Lean, Green and Clean? Sustainability Reporting in the Logistics Sector. *Logistics, 3*(1), 3. doi:10.3390/logistics3010003

Latapí Agudelo, M. A., Jóhannsdóttir, L., & Davídsdóttir, B. (2019). A literature review of the history and evolution of corporate social responsibility. *International Journal of Corporate Social Responsibility, 4*(1), 1–23. doi:10.118640991-018-0039-y

Latif, B., Mahmood, Z., San, O. T., Mohd, S. R., & Bakhsh, A. (2020). Coercive, Normative and Mimetic Pressures as Drivers of Environmental Management Accounting Adoption. *Sustainability (Basel), 12*(11), 4506. doi:10.3390u12114506

Laufer, W. S. (2003). Social accountability and corporate greenwashing. *Journal of Business Ethics, 43*(3), 253–261. doi:10.1023/A:1022962719299

Lean, H. H., Ang, W. R., & Smyth, R. (2015). Performance and performance persistence of socially responsible investment funds in Europe and North America. *The North American Journal of Economics and Finance, 34*, 254–266. doi:10.1016/j.najef.2015.09.011

Lee, S.-P., & Isa, M. (2023). Environmental, social and governance (ESG) practices and financial performance of Shariah-compliant companies in Malaysia. *Journal of Islamic Accounting and Business Research, 14*(2), 295–314. doi:10.1108/JIABR-06-2020-0183

Lee, T. M., & Hutchison, P. D. (2005). The Decision to Disclose Environmental Information: A Research Review and Agenda. *Advances in Accounting*, *21*, 83–111. doi:10.1016/S0882-6110(05)21004-0

Leins, S. (2020). "Responsible investment": ESG and the post-crisis ethical order. *Economy and Society*, *49*(1), 1–21. doi:10.1080/03085147.2020.1702414

Leone, N. M. C. P. G. (1999). As especificidades das pequenas e médias empresas. *RAUSP Management Journal*, *34*(2), 91-94. http://www.spell.org.br/documentos/ver/18123/as-especificidades-das-pequenas-e-medias-empresas/i/pt-br

Liagkouras, K., Metaxiotis, K., & Tsihrintzis, G. (2022). Incorporating environmental and social considerations into the portfolio optimisation process. *Annals of Operations Research*, *316*(2), 1493–1518. doi:10.100710479-020-03554-3

Liang, H., & Renneboog, L. (2020). Corporate social responsibility and sustainable finance: A review of the literature. *European Corporate Governance Institute–Finance Working Paper*, (701). www.ecgi.global/sites/default/files/working_papers/documents/liangrenneboogfinal.pdf.

Lindblom, B. (1983). Economy of speech gestures. In *The production of speech* (pp. 217–245). Springer. doi:10.1007/978-1-4613-8202-7_10

Lindquist, W. B., Rachev, S. T., Hu, Y., & Shirvani, A. (2022). *Advanced REIT Portfolio Optimization*. Springer. doi:10.1007/978-3-031-15286-3

Lin, J. J., Chiang, M. C., & Chang, C. H. (2007). A comparison of usual indices and extended TOPSIS methods in mutual funds' performance evaluation. *Journal of Statistics and Management Systems*, *10*(6), 869–883. doi:10.1080/09720510.2007.10701289

Lipe, M. G. (2018). Unpacking the disclosure package: Using experiments to investigate investor reactions to narrative disclosures. *Accounting, Organizations and Society*, *68-69*, 15–20. doi:10.1016/j.aos.2018.05.001

Long, F., Chen, Q., Xu, L., Wang, J., & Vasa, L. (2022). Sustainable corporate environmental information disclosure: Evidence for green recovery from polluting firms of China. *Frontiers in Environmental Science*, *10*, 1019499. Advance online publication. doi:10.3389/fenvs.2022.1019499

Lopes, J. C., Nunes, A., & Garnacho, A. D. C. (2014). Indicadores e Rácios que Determinam a Rentabilidade dos Capitais Próprios. *XXIV Jornadas Luso Espanholas de Gestão Científica*. https://core.ac.uk/download/pdf/154409576.pdf

Louche, C., & Lydenberg, S. (2006). Socially responsible investment: Differences between Europe and the United States. *Vlerick Leuven Gent Working Paper Series*, 2006/22.

Lozano, J. M., Albareda, L., & Balaguer, M. R. (2006). Socially responsible investment in the Spanish financial market. *Journal of Business Ethics*, *69*(3), 305–316. doi:10.100710551-006-9092-7

Lucianetti, L., Chiappetta Jabbour, C. J., Gunasekaran, A., & Latan, H. (2018). Contingency factors and complementary effects of adopting advanced manufacturing tools and managerial practices: Effects on organizational measurement systems and firms' performance. *International Journal of Production Economics*, *200*, 318–328. doi:10.1016/j.ijpe.2018.04.005

Lueg, K., Krastev, B., & Lueg, R. (2019). Bidirectional effects between organizational sustainability disclosure and risk. *Journal of Cleaner Production*, *229*, 268–277. doi:10.1016/j.jclepro.2019.04.379

Lu, J., Liang, M., Zhang, C., Rong, D., Guan, H., Mazeikaite, K., & Streimikis, J. (2021). Assessment of corporate social responsibility by addressing sustainable development goals. *Corporate Social Responsibility and Environmental Management*, *28*(2), 686–703. doi:10.1002/csr.2081

Luo, Z., Miao, F., Hu, M., & Wang, Y. (2020). Research Development on Horseshoe Crab: A 30-Year Bibliometric Analysis. *Frontiers in Marine Science*, *7*(41), 41. Advance online publication. doi:10.3389/fmars.2020.00041

Luther, R. G., Matatko, J., & Corner, D. C. (1992). The investment performance of U.K. "ethical" unit trusts. *Accounting, Auditing & Accountability Journal*, *5*(4), 57–70. doi:10.1108/09513579210019521

Lu, Y., Xu, C., Zhu, B., & Sun, Y. (2023). Digitalization transformation and ESG performance: Evidence from China. *Business Strategy and the Environment*, 1–23. doi:10.1002/bse.3494

MacAskill, S., Roca, E., Liu, B., Stewart, R. A., & Sahin, O. (2021). Is there a green premium in the green bond market? Systematic literature review revealing premium determinants. *Journal of Cleaner Production*, *280*, 124491. doi:10.1016/j.jclepro.2020.124491

Maccani, G. (2011). *Green IT Balanced Scorecard* [Master Thesis]. Politecnico di Milano.

Madhani, P. M. (2008). Role of voluntary disclosure and transparency in financial reporting. In D. Alagiri & K. Mallela (Eds.), *Corporate financial reporting - changing scenario* (pp. 75–81). ICFAI University Press.

Maelah, R., Auzair, S., Amir, A., & Ahmad, A. (2017). Implementation process and lessons learned in the determination of educational cost using modified activity-based costing (ABC). *Social and Management Research Journal*, *14*(1), 1–32. doi:10.24191mrj.v14i1.5277

Mahadeo, J. D., Oogarah-Hanuman, V., & Soobaroyen, T. (2011). Changes in social and environmental reporting practices in an emerging economy (2004–2007): Exploring the relevance of stakeholder and legitimacy theories. *Accounting Forum*, *35*(3), 158–175. doi:10.1016/j.accfor.2011.06.005

Maignan, I. (2001). Consumers' Perceptions of Corporate Social Responsibilities: A Cross-Cultural Comparison. *Journal of Business Ethics*, *30*(1), 57–72. doi:10.1023/A:1006433928640

Maletič, M., Maletič, D., & Gomišček, B. (2017). The role of contingency factors on the relationship between sustainability practices and organizational performance. *Journal of Cleaner Production*, *171*(10), 423–433. Advance online publication. doi:10.1016/j.jclepro.2017.09.172

Mallin, C. A., Saadouni, B., & Briston, R. J. (1995). The financial performance of ethical investment funds. *Journal of Business Finance & Accounting*, *22*(4), 483–496. doi:10.1111/j.1468-5957.1995.tb00373.x

Mandhachitara, R., & Poolthong, Y. (2011). A model of customer loyalty and corporate social responsibility. *Journal of Services Marketing*, *25*(2), 122–133. doi:10.1108/08876041111119840

Manning, B., Braam, G., & Reimsbach, D. (2019). Corporate governance and sustainable business conduct—Effects of board monitoring effectiveness and stakeholder engagement on corporate sustainability performance and disclosure choices. *Corporate Social Responsibility and Environmental Management*, *26*(2), 351–366. doi:10.1002/csr.1687

Mansoor, H., & Maroun, W. (2016). An initial review of biodiversity reporting by South African corporates: The case of the food and mining sectors. *Suid-Afrikaanse Tydskrif vir Ekonomiese en Bestuurswetenskappe*, *19*(4), 592–614. doi:10.4102ajems.v19i4.1477

Maria Garcia-Sanchez, I., Gomez-Miranda, M.-E., David, F., & Rodriguez-Ariza, L. (2019). The explanatory effect of CSR committee and assurance services on the adoption of the IFC performance standards, as a means of enhancing corporate transparency. *Sustainability Accounting Management and Policy Journal*, *10*(5), 773–797. doi:10.1108/SAMPJ-09-2018-0261

Markle, K. S., & Shackelford, D. A. (2011). Cross-country comparisons of the effects of leverage, intangible assets, and tax havens on corporate income taxes. *Tax L. Rev*, *65*, 415.

Markowitz, H. M. (1952). Portfolio Selection. *The Journal of Finance, 7*(1), 77–91. doi:10.2307/2975974

Markowitz, H. M. (1959). *Portfolio Selection: Efficient Diversification of Investments.* Yale University Press.

Markowitz, H., Todd, P., Xu, G., & Yamane, Y. (1993). Computation of mean-semivariance efficient sets by the Critical Line Algorithm. *Annals of Operations Research, 45*(1), 307–317. doi:10.1007/BF02282055

Maroun, W., & Atkins, J. (2018). The emancipatory potential of extinction accounting: Exploring current practice in integrated reports. *Accounting Forum, 42*(1) 102-118. doi:10.1016/j.accfor.2017.12.001

Martínez-Ferrero, J., Garcia-Sanchez, I. M., & Cuadrado-Ballesteros, B. (2015). Effect of financial reporting quality on sustainability information disclosure. *Corporate Social Responsibility and Environmental Management, 22*(1), 45–64. doi:10.1002/csr.1330

Martin-Miguel, J., Prado-Roman, C., Cachon-Rodriguez, G., & Avendaño-Miranda, L. L. (2020). Determinants of Reputation at Private Graduate Online Schools. *Sustainability (Basel), 12*(22), 9659. doi:10.3390u12229659

Martins, M. A. M. D. M., Costa, K. C., Martins, S. D. M., Formigoni, A., & Rossini, A. M. (2017). Crimes ambientais e sustentabilidade: discussão sobre a responsabilidade penal dos gestores e administradores de empresas. *Revista Metropolitana de Sustentabilidade, 7*(3), 143-158. http://revistaseletronicas.fmu.br/index.php/rms/article/view/1575

Martinsons, M., Davison, R., & Tse, D. (1999). The balanced scorecard: A foundation for the strategic management of information systems. *Decision Support Systems, 25*(1), 71–88. doi:10.1016/S0167-9236(98)00086-4

Mateo-Márquez, A. J., González-González, J. M., & Zamora-Ramírez, C. (2020b). The influence of countries' climate change-related institutional profile on voluntary environmental disclosures. *Business Strategy and the Environment, 30*(2), 1357–1373. doi:10.1002/bse.2690

Mathews, M. (1997). Twenty-five years of social and environmental accounting research. *Accounting, Auditing & Accountability Journal, 10*(4), 481–531. doi:10.1108/EUM0000000004417

Mathews, M. R. (1984). A suggested classification for social accounting research. *Journal of Accounting and Public Policy, 3*(3), 199–221. doi:10.1016/0278-4254(84)90017-6

Mathuva, D., Barako, D., & Wachira, M. (2017). The Economic Consequences of Environmental, Social and Governance Disclosures by Firms Quoted on the Nairobi Securities Exchange. *African Accounting and Finance Journal, 1*(1), 5–28.

Matten, D., & Moon, J. (2020). Reflections on the 2018 decade award: The meaning and dynamics of corporate social responsibility. *Academy of Management Review, 45*(1), 7–28. doi:10.5465/amr.2019.0348

Mausser, H., & Romanko, O. (2018). Long-only equal risk contribution portfolios for CVaR under discrete distributions. *Quantitative Finance, 18*(11), 1927–1945. doi:10.1080/14697688.2018.1434317

McElhaney, K. (2009). A strategic approach to corporate social responsibility. *Leader to Leader, 52*(1), 30–36. doi:10.1002/ltl.327

McWilliams, A., & Siegel, D. (2001). Corporate social responsibility: A theory of the firm perspective. *Academy of Management Review, 26*(1), 117–127. doi:10.2307/259398

Meho, L. I., & Yang, K. (2007). Impact of data sources on citation counts and rankings of LIS faculty: Web of science versus scopus and google scholar. *Journal of the American Society for Information Science and Technology, 58*(13), 2105–2125. doi:10.1002/asi.20677

Melo, I. C., Queiroz, G. A., Junior, P. N. A., de Sousa, T. B., Yushimito, W. F., & Pereira, J. (2023). Sustainable digital transformation in small and medium enterprises (SMEs): A review on performance. *Heliyon, 9*(3), 1–21. doi:10.1016/j. heliyon.2023.e13908 PMID:36915489

Melo, T., & Garrido-Morgado, A. (2012). Corporate reputation: A combination of social responsibility and industry. *Corporate Social Responsibility and Environmental Management, 19*(1), 11–31. doi:10.1002/csr.260

Menghwar, P. S., & Daood, A. (2021). Creating shared value: A systematic review, synthesis and integrative perspective. *International Journal of Management Reviews, 23*(4), 466–485. doi:10.1111/ijmr.12252

Menkhoff, L., & Miethe, J. (2019). Tax evasion in new disguise? Examining tax havens´ international bank deposits. *Journal of Public Economics, 176*, 53–78. doi:10.1016/j.jpubeco.2019.06.003

Mergel, I., Edelmann, N., & Haug, N. (2019). Defining digital transformation: Results from expert interviews. *Government Information Quarterly, 36*(4), 1–16. doi:10.1016/j.giq.2019.06.002

Merigó, J. M., & Yang, J.-B. (2017). A bibliometric analysis of operations research and management science. *Omega, 73*, 37–48. doi:10.1016/j.omega.2016.12.004

Mervelskemper, L., & Streit, D. (2017). Enhancing market valuation of ESG performance: Is integrated reporting keeping its promise? *Business Strategy and the Environment, 26*(4), 536–549. doi:10.1002/bse.1935

Meyer, J. P., & Allen, N. J. (1997). *Commitment in the workplace: Theory, research, and application.* Sage Publications. doi:10.4135/9781452231556

Michelon, G., Patten, D. M., & Romi, A. M. (2019). Creating Legitimacy for Sustainability Assurance Practices: Evidence from Sustainability Restatements. *European Accounting Review, 28*(2), 395–422. doi:10.1080/09638180.2018.1469424

Mijatović, I., Miladinović, S., & Stokić, D. (2015). Corporate Social Responsibility in Serbia:Between Corporate Philanthropy and Standards. In Corporate Social Responsibility in Finland: From Local Movements to Global Responsibility (pp. 333-350). Academic Press.

Mijoković, M., Knezevic, G., & Mizdraković, V. (2020). Analysing the link between csr reporting and financial performance variables of Belgrade stock exchange companies. *Teme, 1369*, 1369. Advance online publication. doi:10.22190/TEME190513081M

Miles, R. E., & Snow, C. C. (1984). Fit, failure and the hall of fame. *California Management Review, 26*(3), 10–28. doi:10.2307/41165078

Milonas, N., Rompotis, G., & Moutzouris, C. (2022). The Performance of ESG Funds vis-à-vis Non-ESG Funds. *The Journal of Impact and ESG Investing, 2*(4), 96–115. doi:10.3905/jesg.2022.1.041

Minasse, M. H. (2015). *Eu como cultura? Notas sobre políticas de valorização da gastronomia no Brasil.* Seminário Nacional de Pesquisa e Pós-Graduação em Turismo, Universidade Federal do Rio Grande do Norte.

Ministério do Meio Ambiente. (2014). *Portaria 444.* http://www.icmbio.gov.br/portal/images/stories/docs-plano-de-acao/00-saiba-mais/04_PORTARIA_MMA_N%C2%BA_444_DE_17_DE_DEZ_DE_2014.pdf

Ministério do Meio Ambiente. (2014a). *Portaria 445.* http://www.icmbio.gov.br/cepsul/images/stories/legislacao/Portaria/2014/p_mma_445_2014_lista_peixes_amea%C3%A7ados_extin%C3%A7%C3%A3o.pdf

Ministério do Meio Ambiente. (2019). *Biodiversidade – Fauna.* http://www.mma.gov.br/mma-em-numeros/biodiversidade

Mitić, P., Fedajev, A., Radulescu, M., & Rehman, A. (2023a). The relationship between CO2 emissions, economic growth, available energy, and employment in SEE countries. *Environmental Science and Pollution Research International, 30*(6), 16140–16155. doi:10.100711356-022-23356-3 PMID:36175729

Mitić, P., Hanić, A., Kojić, M., & Schlüter, S. (2023b). Environment and Economy Interactions in the Western Balkans: Current Situation and Prospects. In T. Tufek-Memišević, M. Arslanagić-Kalajdžić, & N. Ademović (Eds.), *Interdisciplinary Advances in Sustainable Development. ICSD 2022. Lecture Notes in Networks and Systems* (Vol. 529). Springer. doi:10.1007/978-3-031-17767-5_1

Mohr, L. A., & Webb, D. J. (2005). The effects of corporate social responsibility and price on consumer responses. *The Journal of Consumer Affairs, 39*(1), 121–147. doi:10.1111/j.1745-6606.2005.00006.x

Moisescu, O. I. (2015). Development and Validation of a Measurement Scale for Customers' perceptions of Corporate Social Responsibility. *Management and Marketing Journal, 13*, 311–332.

Monteiro, S., Ribeiro, V., & Lemos, K. (2022). Linking Corporate Social Responsibility Reporting with the UN Sustainable Development Goals: Evidence from the Portuguese Stock Market. In I. Management Association (Ed.), Research Anthology on Measuring and Achieving Sustainable Development Goals (pp. 250-268). IGI Global.

Monteiro, S., Ribeiro, V., & Lemos, K. (2020). Linking Corporate Social Responsibility Reporting With the UN Sustainable Development Goals: Evidence from the Portuguese Stock Market. In S. Monteiro, V. Ribeiro, & K. Lemos (Eds.), *Conceptual and Theoretical Approaches to Corporate Social Responsibility, Entrepreneurial Orientation, and Financial Performance* (pp. 134–151). IGI Global. doi:10.4018/978-1-7998-2128-1.ch007

Moon, J. (2007). The contribution of corporate social responsibility to sustainable development. *Sustainable Development (Bradford), 15*(5), 296–306. doi:10.1002d.346

Morais, D. O. C., da Silva Oliveira, N. Q., & de Souza, E. M. (2014). As práticas de sustentabilidade ambiental e suas influências na nova formatação institucional das organizações. *Revista de Gestão Ambiental e Sustentabilidade, 3*(3), 90-106. http://www.spell.org.br/documentos/ver/39221/as-praticas-de-sustentabilidade-ambiental-e-suas-influencias-na-nova-formatacao-institucional-das-organizacoes/i/pt-br

Morelli, G. (2023). Responsible investing and portfolio selection: A shapley-CVaR approach. *Annals of Operations Research*, 1–29. doi:10.100710479-022-05144-x

Morgan Stanley. (2019a). *Sustainability Reality: Analyzing Risks and Returns of Sustainable Funds*. https://www.morganstanley.com/content/dam/msdotcom/ideas/sustainable-investing-offers-financial-performance-loweredrisk/Sustainable_Reality_Analyzing_Risk_and_Returns_of_Sustainable_Funds.pdf

Morgan Stanley. (2019b). *Sustainable Signals: Growth and Opportunity in Asset Management*. https://www.morganstanley.com/assets/pdfs/2415532_Sustainable_Signals_Asset_Mgmt_L.pdf

Morgan, S. (2018). *Sustainable Signals: New Data from the Individual Investor*. https://www.morganstanley.com/pub/content/dam/msdotcom/ideas/sustainablesignals/pdf/Sustainabl_Signals_Whitepaper.pdf

Motta, S. D., Bianchi, R. C., Zonatto, P. A. F., Silva, A. C. C. J., & Boligon, J. A. R. (2019). Análise Das Práticas Sustentáveis. In *Microempresas Do Setor Industrial Da Região Central Do Estado Do Rio Grande Do Sul* (pp. 1127–1144). Revista de Administração da UFSM. doi:10.5902/1983465939047

Muldoon, R. (2016). *Social contract theory for a diverse world: Beyond tolerance*. Routledge. doi:10.4324/9781315545882

Muñoz-Torres, M. J., Fernández-Izquierdo, M. Á., Rivera-Lirio, J. M., & Escrig-Olmedo, E. (2019). Can environmental, social, and governance rating agencies favor business models that promote a more sustainable development? *Corporate Social Responsibility and Environmental Management*, *26*(2), 439–452. doi:10.1002/csr.1695

Munyon, T. P., Madden, L. T., Madden, T. M., & Vigoda-Gadot, E. (2019). (Dys)functional attachments?: How community embeddedness impacts workers during and after long-term unemployment. *Journal of Vocational Behavior*, *112*, 35–50. doi:10.1016/j.jvb.2019.01.005

Murphy, R., Shah, A., & Janský, P. (2019). BEPS Policy Failure — The Case of EU. *Nordic Tax Journal*, 1–24.

Murphy, R. (2019). 'Corporate tax avoidance: is tax transparency the solution?': a practitioner view. *Accounting and Business Research*, *49*(5), 584–586. doi:10.1080/00014788.2019.1611728

Murray, K. B., & Montanari, J. B. (1986). Strategic management of the socially responsible firm: Integrating management and marketing theory. *Academy of Management Review*, *11*(4), 815–827. doi:10.2307/258399

Musbah, H., Ali, G., Aly, H. H., & Little, T. A. (2022). Energy management using multi-criteria decision making and machine learning classification algorithms for intelligent system. *Electric Power Systems Research*, *203*, 107645. Advance online publication. doi:10.1016/j.epsr.2021.107645

Muslu, V., Mutlu, S., Radhakrishnan, S., & Tsang, A. (2019). Corporate Social Responsibility Report Narratives and Analyst Forecast Accuracy. *Journal of Business Ethics*, *154*(4), 1119–1142. doi:10.100710551-016-3429-7

Naciti, V. (2019). Corporate governance and board of directors: The effect of a board composition on firm sustainability performance. *Journal of Cleaner Production*, *237*, 117727. doi:10.1016/j.jclepro.2019.117727

Narayanan, S., & Das, J. R. (2022). Can the marketing innovation of purpose branding make brands meaningful and relevant? *International Journal of Innovation Science*, *14*(3/4), 519–536. doi:10.1108/IJIS-11-2020-0272

Nascimento, N. S., Farias, M. S., de Lima, N. G., & Miranda, R. S. (2010). *Um estudo dos problemas ambientais da área de proteção ambiental da ilha do Combú Belém-PA*. https://www.ibeas.org.br/congresso/Trabalhos2010/V-002.pdf

Nave, A., & Ferreira, J. (2019). Corporate social responsibility strategies: Past research and future challenges. *Corporate Social Responsibility and Environmental Management*, *26*(4), 885–901. doi:10.1002/csr.1729

Nazari, J. A., Hrazdil, K., & Mahmoudian, F. (2017). Assessing social and environmental performance through narrative complexity in CSR reports. *Journal of Contemporary Accounting & Economics*, *13*(2), 166–178. doi:10.1016/j.jcae.2017.05.002

Neuendorf, K. A. (2002). The Content Analysis Guidebook. *Sage (Atlanta, Ga.)*.

Nguyen, A. T., Parker, L., Brennan, L., & Lockrey, S. (2020). A consumer definition of eco-friendly packaging. *Journal of Cleaner Production*, *252*, 119792. doi:10.1016/j.jclepro.2019.119792

Nichita, E.-M., Nechita, E., Manea, C.-L., Manea, D., & Irimescu, A.-M. (2020). Reporting on Sustainable Development Goals. A score-based approach with company-level evidence from Central-Eastern Europe economies. *Journal of Accounting and Management Information Systems*, *19*(3), 502–542. doi:10.24818/jamis.2020.03004

Nicolò, G., Zanellato, G., Tiron-Tudor, A., & Tartaglia Polcini, P. (2023). Revealing the corporate contribution to sustainable development goals through integrated reporting: A worldwide perspective. *Social Responsibility Journal*, *19*(5), 829–857. doi:10.1108/SRJ-09-2021-0373

Niu, S., Park, B. I., & Jung, J. S. (2022). The Effects of Digital Leadership and ESG Management on Organizational Innovation and Sustainability. *Sustainability (Basel)*, *14*(23), 1–20. doi:10.3390u142315639

Nobanee, H., & Ellili, N. (2016). Corporate sustainability disclosure in annual reports: Evidence from UAE banks: Islamic versus conventional. *Renewable & Sustainable Energy Reviews*, *55*, 1336–1341. doi:10.1016/j.rser.2015.07.084

Nohria, N., & Khurana, R. (2010). *Handbook of Leadership Theory and Practice*. Harvard Business School Press.

Nor-Aishah, H., Ahmad, N. H., & Ramayah, T. (2020). Entrepreneurial Leadership and Sustainable Performance of Manufacturing SMEs in Malaysia: The Contingent Role of Entrepreneurial Bricolage. *Sustainability (Basel)*, *12*(8), 3100. doi:10.3390u12083100

Öberseder, M., Schlegelmilch, B. B., Murphy, P. E., & Gruber, V. (2014). Consumers' Perceptions of Corporate Social Responsibility: Scale Development and Validation. *Journal of Business Ethics*, *124*(1), 101–115. doi:10.100710551-013-1787-y

OECD. (2001). *Corporate Social Responsibility: Partners for Progress*. OECD.

OECD. (2017). *Background Brief. Inclusive Framework on BEPS*. https://www.oecd.org/tax/beps/background-brief-inclusive-framework-on-beps.pdf

Oliveira, A. S. de, & Callado, A. A. C. (2018).Fatores contigenciais e o controle gerencial: uma avaliação em organizações não governamentais (ONGS) brasileiras. *Advances in Scientific and Applied Accounting*, *11*(1), 92–109.

Oliver, R. L. (2010). *Satisfaction: A behavioral perspective on the consumer*. ME Sharpe. Inc.

Olofsson, P., Raholm, A., Salah Uddin, G., Troster, V., & Hoon Kang, S. (2021). Ethical and unethical investments under extreme market conditions. *International Review of Financial Analysis*, *78*, 101952. doi:10.1016/j.irfa.2021.101952

Olson, E. M., & Slater, S. F. (2002). The balanced scorecard, competitive strategy, and performance. *Business Horizons*, *45*(3), 11–16. doi:10.1016/S0007-6813(02)00198-2

Oncioiu, I., Petrescu, A.-G., Bilcan, F.-R., Petrescu, M., Popescu, D.-M., & Anghel, E. (2020). Corporate Sustainability Reporting and Financial Performance. *Sustainability (Basel)*, *12*(10), 4297. doi:10.3390u12104297

Orazalin, N., & Mahmood, M. (2018). Economic, environmental, and social performance indicators of sustainability reporting: Evidence from the Russian oil and gas industry. *Energy Policy*, *121*, 70–79. doi:10.1016/j.enpol.2018.06.015

Orazalin, N., & Mahmood, M. (2019). The financial crisis as a wake-up call: Corporate governance and bank performance in an emerging economy. *Corporate Governance (Bradford)*, *19*(1), 80–101. doi:10.1108/CG-02-2018-0080

Ortiz-Martínez, E., Marín-Hernández, S., & Santos-Jaén, J. M. (2022). Sustainability, corporate social responsibility, non-financial reporting and company performance: Relationships and mediating effects in Spanish small and medium sized enterprises. *Sustainable Production and Consumption*.

Osobajo, O. A., Oke, A., Lawani, A., Omotayo, T. S., Ndubuka-McCallum, N., & Obi, L. (2022). Providing a Roadmap for Future Research Agenda: A Bibliometric Literature Review of Sustainability Performance Reporting (SPR). *Sustainability (Basel)*, *14*(14), 8523. doi:10.3390u14148523

Otley, D. T. (1980). The contingency theory of management accounting: Achievement and prognosis. *Accounting, Organizations and Society*, *5*(4), 413–428. doi:10.1016/0361-3682(80)90040-9

Otley, D. T. (2016). The contingency theory of management accounting and control:1980–2014. *Management Accounting Research*, *31*, 45–62. doi:10.1016/j.mar.2016.02.001

Ottenstein, P., Erben, S., Jost, S., Weuster, C., & Zulch, H. (2022). From voluntarism to regulation: Effects of directive 2014/95/EU on sustainability reporting in the EU. *Journal of Applied Accounting Research*, *23*(1), 55–98. doi:10.1108/JAAR-03-2021-0075

Overesch, M., & Wolff, H. (2021). Financial Transparency to the Rescue: Effects of Public Country-by-Country Reporting in the European Union Banking Sector on Tax Avoidance. *Contemporary Accounting Research*, *38*(3), 1616–1642. doi:10.1111/1911-3846.12669

Oyewo, B., Tawiah, V., & Hussain, S. T. (2023). Drivers of environmental and social sustainability accounting practices in Nigeria: A corporate governance perspective. *Corporate Governance (Bradford)*, *23*(2), 397–421. doi:10.1108/CG-09-2021-0336

Özbay, D. (2019). Türkiye'de finansal olmayan raporlama ve gelişim trendi. *Uluslararası Yönetim İktisat ve İşletme Dergisi*, *15*(2), 445–462.

Özcan, G. (2021). *Yeni tüketici açısından kurumsal sosyal sorumluluk yaklaşımının kurumsal itibar ve tüketicilerin tavsiye etme niyetine etkisi üzerine bir araştırma* [PhD thesis].

Pacelli, V., Pampurini, F., & Quaranta, A. G. (2023). Environmental, Social and Governance Investing: Does rating matter? *Business Strategy and the Environment*, *32*(1), 30–41. doi:10.1002/bse.3116

Palazzo, G., & Scherer, A. G. (2006). Corporate Legitimacy as Deliberation: A Communicative Framework. *Journal of Business Ethics*, *66*(1), 71–88. doi:10.100710551-006-9044-2

Pan, D., Fan, W., & Kong, F. (2022). Dose environmental information disclosure raise public environmental concern? Generalized propensity score evidence from China. *Journal of Cleaner Production*, *379*, 134640. doi:10.1016/j.jclepro.2022.134640

Panwar, R., Paul, K., Nybakk, E., Hansen, E., & Thompson, D. P. (2014). The Legitimacy of CSR Actions of Publicly Traded Companies Versus Family-Owned Companies. *Journal of Business Ethics*, *125*(3), 481–496. doi:10.100710551-013-1933-6

Paoloni, N., Mattei, G., Dello Strologo, A., & Celli, M. (2020). The present and future of intellectual capital in the healthcare sector A systematic literature review. *Journal of Intellectual Capital*, *21*(3), 357–379. doi:10.1108/JIC-10-2019-0237

Parker, L. D. (1986). Polemical themes in social accounting: a scenario for standard setting. *Advances in Public Interest Accounting, 1*, 67-93.

Park, S. R., & Jang, J. Y. (2021). The Impact of ESG Management on Investment Decision: Institutional Investors' Perceptions of Country-Specific ESG Criteria. *International Journal of Financial Studies*, *9*(3). doi:10.1016/0361-3682(92)90042-Q

Pazienza, M., de Jong, M., & Schoenmaker, D. (2022). Clarifying the Concept of Corporate Sustainability and Providing Convergence for Its Definition. *Sustainability (Basel)*, *14*(7838), 1–21. doi:10.3390u14137838

Peak, M. H. (1990). The Alaskan oil spill: Lessons in crisis management. *Management Review*, *79*(4), 12–22.

Pedersen, L. H., Fitzgibbons, S., & Pomorski, L. (2021). Responsible investing: The ESG-efficient frontier. *Journal of Financial Economics*, *142*(2), 572–597. doi:10.1016/j.jfineco.2020.11.001

Peng, Y. Z., & Tao, C. Q. (2022). Can digital transformation promote enterprise performance?-From the perspective of public policy and innovation. *Journal of Innovation & Knowledge*, *7*(3), 1–8. doi:10.1016/j.jik.2022.100198

Pérez, A., & Rodríguez del Bosque, I. (2013). Measuring CSR Image: Three Studies to Develop and to Validate a Reliable Measurement Tool. *Journal of Business Ethics*, *118*(2), 265–286. doi:10.100710551-012-1588-8

Perifanis, N.-A., & Kitsios, F. (2023). Investigating the Influence of Artificial Intelligence on Business Value in the Digital Era of Strategy: A Literature Review. *Information (Basel)*, *14*(2), 1–42. doi:10.3390/info14020085

Perks, R. W., Rawlinson, D. H., & Ingram, L. (1992). An exploration of ethical investment in the UK. *The British Accounting Review*, *24*(1), 43–65. doi:10.1016/S0890-8389(05)80066-6

Perrini, F. (2006). The practitioner's perspective on non-financial reporting. *California Management Review*, *48*(2), 73–103. doi:10.2307/41166339

Petkov, R. (2020). Artificial intelligence (AI) and the accounting function—A revisit and a new perspective for developing framework. *Journal of Emerging Technologies in Accounting*, *17*(1), 99–105. doi:10.2308/jeta-52648

Petrescu, I. (2018). Social responsibility in modern management. *Review of General Management*, *28*(2), 5–15.

Pflugrath, G., Roebuck, P., & Simnett, R. (2011). Impact of assurance and assurer's professional affiliation on financial analysts' assessment of credibility of corporate social responsibility information. *Auditing*, *30*(3), 239–254. doi:10.2308/ajpt-10047

Pham, H. S. T., & Tran, H. T. (2020). CSR disclosure and firm performance: The mediating role of corporate reputation and moderating role of CEO integrity. *Journal of Business Research*, *120*, 127–136. doi:10.1016/j.jbusres.2020.08.002

Phillips, J. (2023). Quantifying the levels, nature, and dynamics of sustainability for the UK 2000–2018 from a Brundtland perspective. *Environment, Development and Sustainability*, 1–22. doi:10.100710668-023-03370-2

Phillips, S., Thai, V. V., & Halim, Z. (2019). Airline value chain capabilities and CSR performance: The connection between CSR leadership and CSR culture with CSR performance, customer satisfaction and financial performance. *The Asian Journal of Shipping and Logistics*, *35*(1), 30–40. doi:10.1016/j.ajsl.2019.03.005

Picchiai, D., & Ferreira, A. O. (2019). Gestão de micro e pequenas empresas: estudo em restaurantes da região metropolitana de Campinas. *DRd - Desenvolvimento Regional Em Debate*, *9*, 454-477. . doi:10.24302/drd.v9i0.2117

Pimonenko, T., Bilan, Y., Horák, J., Starchenko, L., & Gajda, W. (2020). Green Brand of Companies and Greenwashing under Sustainable Development Goals. *Sustainability (Basel)*, *12*(4), 1–15. doi:10.3390u12041679

Pistoni, A., Songini, L., & Bavagnoli, F. (2018). Integrated Reporting Quality: An Empirical Analysis. *Corporate Social Responsibility and Environmental Management*, *25*(4), 489–507. doi:10.1002/csr.1474

Pizzi, S., Del Baldo, M., Caputo, F., & Venturelli, A. (2022). Voluntary disclosure of Sustainable Development Goals in mandatory non-financial reports: The moderating role of cultural dimension. *Journal of International Financial Management & Accounting*, *33*(1), 83–106. doi:10.1111/jifm.12139

Pizzi, S., Rosati, F., & Venturelli, A. (2020). The determinants of business contribution to the 2030 Agenda: Introducing the SDG Reporting Score. *Business Strategy and the Environment*, 1–18. doi:10.1002/bse.2628

Plieninger, T., Fagerholm, N., & Bieling, C. (2021). How to run a sustainability science research group sustainably? *Sustainability Science*, *16*(1), 321–328. doi:10.100711625-020-00857-z PMID:32863971

Politis, D., & Romano, J. P. (1994). The Stationary Bootstrap. *Journal of the American Statistical Association*, *89*(428), 1303–1313. doi:10.1080/01621459.1994.10476870

Politis, D., & White, H. (2004). Automatic block-length selection for the dependent bootstrap. *Econometric Reviews*, *23*(1), 53–70. doi:10.1081/ETC-120028836

Porter, M. E., & Kramer, M. R. (2006). The link between competitive advantage and corporate social responsibility. *Harvard Business Review*, *84*(12), 78–92. PMID:17183795

Porter, M. E., & Kramer, M. R. (2011). Creating shared value. *Harvard Business Review*.

Pospischek, V. S., Spinelli, M. G. N., & Matias, A. C. G. (2014). Avaliação de ações de sustentabilidade ambiental em restaurantes comerciais localizados no município de São Paulo. *Demetra: Food, Nutrition & Health/Alimentação Nutrição & Saúde, 9*(2). Advance online publication. doi:10.12957/demetra.2014.8822

Pratama, A., & Padjadjaran, U. (2017). Company Characteristics, Corporate Governance and Agressive Tax Avoidance Practice: A Study of Indonesian Companies. *Review of Integrative Business and Economics Research, 6*(4), 70–81.

Preston, L. E. (1975). Corporation and society: The search for a paradigm. *Journal of Economic Literature*, 434–453.

Procházka, P. (2020). Jurisdictions with lowest effective tax rates in the post-BEPS landscape: CbCR evidence and implications. *European Financial and Accounting Journal, 15*(1), 33–52. doi:10.18267/j.efaj.231

Pryshlakivsky, J., & Searcy, C. A. (2017). Heuristic Model for Establishing Trade-Offs in Corporate Sustainability Performance Measurement Systems. *Journal of Business Ethics, 144*(2), 323–342. doi:10.100710551-015-2806-y

Puriwat, W., & Tripopsakul, S. (2022). From ESG to DESG: The Impact of DESG (Digital Environmental, Social, and Governance) on Customer Attitudes and Brand Equity. *Sustainability (Basel), 14*(17), 1–15. doi:10.3390u141710480

Quesado, P., Aibar Guzmán, B., & Lima Rodrígues, L. (2018). Advantages and contributions in the balanced scorecard implementation. *Intangible Capital, 14*(1), 186–201. doi:10.3926/ic.1110

Qureshi, M. A., Kirkerud, S., Theresa, K., & Ahsan, T. (2020). The impact of sustainability (environmental, social, and governance) disclosure and board diversity on firm value: The moderating role of industry sensitivity. *Business Strategy and the Environment, 29*(3), 1199–1214. doi:10.1002/bse.2427

Rachev, S. T., Stoyanov, S. V., & Fabozzi, F. J. (2008). *Advanced stochastic models, risk assessment, and portfolio optimisation: The ideal risk, uncertainty, and performance measures.* Wiley.

Ramanathan, K. V. (1976). Toward a theory of corporate social accounting. *The Accounting Review, 51*(3), 516–528.

Rawlins, B. (2008). Give the emperor a mirror: Toward developing a stakeholder measurement of organizational transparency. *Journal of Public Relations Research, 21*(1), 71–99. doi:10.1080/10627260802153421

Rego, S. O. (2003). Tax-Avoidance Activities of U.S. Multinational Corporations. *Contemporary Accounting Research, 20*(4), 805–833. doi:10.1506/VANN-B7UB-GMFA-9E6W

Renneboog, L., Horst, J. T., & Zhang, C. (2008). Socially responsible investments: Institutional aspects, performance, and investor behavior. *Journal of Banking & Finance, 32*(9), 1723–1742. doi:10.1016/j.jbankfin.2007.12.039

Revell, A., Stokes, D., & Chen, H. (2010). Small businesses and the environment: Turning over a new leaf? *Business Strategy and the Environment, 19*(5), 273–288.

Reverte, C. (2020). Do investors value the voluntary assurance of sustainability information? Evidence from the Spanish stock market. *Sustainable Development (Bradford), 29*(5), 793–809. Advance online publication. doi:10.1002d.2157

Reynolds, S. J., Schultz, F. C., & Hekman, D. R. (2006). Stakeholder theory and managerial decision-making: Constraints and implications of balancing stakeholder interests. *Journal of Business Ethics, 64*(3), 285–301. doi:10.100710551-005-5493-2

Richey, L. A., & Ponte, S. (2021). Brand Aid and coffee value chain development interventions: Is Starbucks working aid out of business? *World Development, 143*, 105193. doi:10.1016/j.worlddev.2020.105193

Rigdon, E. E. (2012). Rethinking Partial Least Squares Path Modeling: In Praise of Simple Methods. *Long Range Planning, 45*(5-6), 341–358. doi:10.1016/j.lrp.2012.09.010

Rio+20 Declaration. (2012). *United Nations: Rio+20 - The future we want*. Rio+20 United Nations Conference on Sustainable Development.

Rivoli, P. (2003). Making a difference or making a statement? Finance research and socially responsible investment. *Business Ethics Quarterly*, *13*(3), 271–287. doi:10.5840/beq200313323

Riyadh, H. A., Sukoharsono, E. G., & Alfaiza, S. A. (2019). The impact of corporate social responsibility disclosure and board characteristics on corporate performance. *Cogent Business & Management*, *6*(1), 1647917. doi:10.1080/233 11975.2019.1647917

Roberts, J. A. (1996). Green consumers in the 1990s: Profile and implications for advertising. *Journal of Business Research*, *36*(3), 217–231. doi:10.1016/0148-2963(95)00150-6

Roberts, L., Hassan, A., Elamer, A., & Nandy, M. (2021). Biodiversity and extinction accounting for sustainable development: A systematic literature review and future research directions. *Business Strategy and the Environment*, *30*(1), 705–720. doi:10.1002/bse.2649

Robin, C. F., Pedroche, M. S. C., Astorga, P. S., & Almeida, M. M. A. (2019). Green Practices in Hospitality: A Contingency Approach. *Sustainability (Basel)*, *11*(13), 3737. doi:10.3390u11133737

Rocha, R. T., Introvini, R. F., Caldana, A. C. F., Krauter, E., & Liboni, L. B. (2019). Gestão sustentável – motivadores, barreiras e percepção de micro e pequenos empresários. *Gestão & Regionalidade*, *35*(106). Advance online publication. doi:10.13037/gr.vol35n106.5121

Rockafellar, R. T., Uryasev, S., & Zabarankin, M. (2002). Optimisation of conditional value-at-risk. *The Journal of Risk*, *2*(3), 21–41. doi:10.21314/JOR.2000.038

Rockafellar, R. T., Uryasev, S., & Zabarankin, M. (2006). Generalised deviations in risk analysis. *Finance and Stochastics*, *10*(1), 51–74. doi:10.100700780-005-0165-8

Rodrigue, M., Magnan, M., & Cho, C. H. (2013). Is environmental governance substantive or symbolic? An empirical investigation. *Journal of Business Ethics*, *114*(1), 107–129. doi:10.100710551-012-1331-5

Rodrigues, E. T. (2006). *Organização comunitária e desenvolvimento territorial: O contexto ribeirinho em uma ilha da Amazônia* [Dissertação **de** Mestrado em Planejamento do Desenvolvimento]. Núcleo de Altos Estudos Amazônicos. Universidade Federal do Pará.

Rodriguez, J. (2010). The performance of socially responsible mutual funds: A volatility-match approach. *Review of Accounting and Finance*, *9*(2), 180–188. doi:10.1108/14757701011044189

Romi, A. M., & Longing, S. D. (2017). Accounting for bees: Evidence from disclosures by US listed companies. In *The Business of Bees* (pp. 226–244). Routledge.

Rosa Portella, A., & Borba, J. A. (2020). Environmental disclosure in corporate websites: A study in Brazil and USA companies. *RAUSP Management Journal*, *55*(3), 309–324. doi:10.1108/RAUSP-07-2018-0053

Rosa, C. C., & Cabral, E. R. (2017). Os impactos socioambientais e econômicos do turismo: O caso da ilha do Combú, no entorno da cidade de Belém–PA. *Colóquio Organizações. Desenvolvimento e Sustentabilidade*, *7*, 364–383.

Rosati, F., & Faria, L. G. D. (2019b). Business contribution to the Sustainable Development Agenda: Organizational factors related to early adoption of SDG reporting. *Corporate Social Responsibility and Environmental Management*, 1–10. . doi:10.1002/csr.1705

Rosati, F., & Faria, L. G. D. (2019a). Addressing the SDGs in sustainability reports: The relationship with institutional factors. *Journal of Cleaner Production*, *215*, 1312–1326. doi:10.1016/j.jclepro.2018.12.107

Rosemann, M., & Wiese, J. (1999). Measuring the performance of ERP software-a balanced scorecard approach. *Proceedings of 10th Australasian Conference on Information Systems*, 773-784.

Rosemann, M. (2001). Evaluating the Management of Enterprise Systems with the Balanced Scorecard. In W. Van Grembergen (Ed.), *Information Technology Evaluation Methods and Management* (pp. 171–184). Idea Group Publishing. doi:10.4018/978-1-878289-90-2.ch011

Rosen, B. N., Sandler, D. M., & Shani, D. (1991). Social issues and socially responsible investment behavior: A preliminary empirical investigation. *The Journal of Consumer Affairs*, *25*(2), 221–234. doi:10.1111/j.1745-6606.1991.tb00003.x

Rosenfeld, M. (1984). Contract and justice: The relation between classical contract law and social contract theory. *Iowa Law Review*, *70*, 769.

Rothstein, B. (2021). *Controlling corruption: The social contract approach.* Oxford University Press. doi:10.1093/oso/9780192894908.001.0001

Ruiz-Barbadillo, E., & Martínez-Ferrero, J. (2020). Empirical analysis of the effect of the joint provision of audit and sustainability assurance services on assurance quality. *Journal of Cleaner Production*, *266*, 121943. doi:10.1016/j.jclepro.2020.121943

Ruiz-Barbadillo, E., & Martinez-Ferrero, J. (2020). What impact do countries have on levels of sustainability assurance? A complementary-substitutive perspective. *Corporate Social Responsibility and Environmental Management*, *27*(5), 2329–2341. Advance online publication. doi:10.1002/csr.1967

Russell, S., Milne, M. J., & Dey, C. (2017). Accounts of nature and the nature of accounts: Critical reflections on environmental accounting and propositions for ecologically informed accounting. *Accounting, Auditing & Accountability Journal*, *30*(7), 1426–1458. doi:10.1108/AAAJ-07-2017-3010

Sachs, J. D. (2012). From millennium development goals to sustainable development goals. *Lancet*, *379*(9832), 2206–2211. doi:10.1016/S0140-6736(12)60685-0 PMID:22682467

Şahin, E. (1996). *İşletme-çevre etkileşimi ve işletmelerin sosyal sorumluluğu* [Master thesis]. Selçuk University SBE.

Salmones, M. del M. G., Crespo, A. H., & Bosque, I. R. (2005). Influence of Corporate Social Responsibility on Loyalty and Valuation of Services. *Journal of Business Ethics*, *61*(4), 369–385. doi:10.100710551-005-5841-2

Sancar, O. (2021). *Hastane Çalışanlarının Kurumsal Sosyal Sorumluluk Algısının Ekstra Rol Davranışlarına Etkisi* [Doctoral dissertation]. Marmara Universitesi.

Sandberg, J., Juravle, C., Hedesström, T. M., & Hamilton, I. (2009). The heterogeneity of socially responsible investment. *Journal of Business Ethics*, *87*(4), 519–533. doi:10.100710551-008-9956-0

Santamaria, R., Paolone, F., Cucari, N., & Dezi, L. (2021). Non-financial strategy disclosure and environmental, social and governance score: Insight from a configurational approach. *Business Strategy and the Environment*, *30*(4), 1993–2007. doi:10.1002/bse.2728

Sarkar, S. (2022). Performance evaluation of ESG funds in India – A study. *The Management Accountant*, *57*(3), 40–47. doi:10.33516/maj.v57i3.40-47p

Sarstedt, M., Hair, J. F., Pick, M., Liengaard, B. D., Radomir, L., & Ringle, C. M. (2022). Progress in partial least squares structural equation modeling use in marketing research in the last decade. *Psychology and Marketing*, *39*(5), 1035–1064. doi:10.1002/mar.21640

Sarstedt, M., Ringle, C. M., Henseler, J., & Hair, J. F. (2014). On the Emancipation of PLS-SEM: A Commentary on Rigdon (2012). *Long Range Planning*, *47*(3), 154–160. doi:10.1016/j.lrp.2014.02.007

Sauer, D. A. (1997). The impact of social-responsibility screens on investment performance: Evidence from the Domini 400 social index and Domini Equity Mutual Fund. *Review of Financial Economics*, *6*(2), 137–149. doi:10.1016/S1058-3300(97)90002-1

Saunders, M., Lewis, P., & Thornhill, A. (2009). *Research Methods for Business Students*. Pearson.

Scarano, F. R., & Ceotto, P. (2016). *A importância da biodiversidade brasileira e os desafios para a conservação, para a ciência e para o setor privado. Floresta Atlântica de Tabuleiro: Diversidade e Endemismo na Reserva Natural Vale.*

Schaltegger, S., Gibassier, D., & Maas, K. (2023). Managing and accounting for corporate biodiversity contributions. Mapping the field. *Business Strategy and the Environment*, *32*(5), 2544–2553. doi:10.1002/bse.3166

Schaltegger, S., & Wagner, M. (2006). Integrative management of sustainability performance, measurement and reporting. *International Journal of Accounting, Auditing and Performance Evaluation*, *3*(1), 1–19. doi:10.1504/IJAAPE.2006.010098

Schiehll, E., & Kolahgar, S. (2021). Financial materiality in the informativeness of sustainability reporting. *Business Strategy and the Environment*, *30*(2), 840–855. doi:10.1002/bse.2657

Schmeltz, L. (2012). Consumer-oriented CSR communication: Focusing on ability or morality? *Corporate Communications*, *17*(1), 29–49. doi:10.1108/13563281211196344

Schmidt, A. B. (2022). Optimal ESG portfolios: An example for the Dow Jones Index. *Journal of Sustainable Finance & Investment*, *12*(2), 529–535. doi:10.1080/20430795.2020.1783180

Schramade, W. (2017). Investing in the UN Sustainable Development Goals: Opportunities for Companies and Investors. *The Bank of America Journal of Applied Corporate Finance*, *29*(2), 87–99. doi:10.1111/jacf.12236

Schröder, M. (2003). *Socially responsible investments in Germany, Switzerland and the United States - an analysis of investment funds and indices.* ZEW Discussion Paper, 03–10. doi:10.2139/ssrn.421462

Schröder, M. (2004). The performance of socially responsible investments: Investment funds and indices. *Financial Markets and Portfolio Management*, *18*(2), 122–142. doi:10.100711408-004-0202-1

Schwartz, M. S., & Carroll, A. B. (2003). Corporate social responsibility: A three-domain approach. *Business Ethics Quarterly*, *13*(4), 503–530. doi:10.5840/beq200313435

Scott, W. R., & Davis, G. F. (2015). *Organizations and organizing: Rational, natural and open systems perspectives.* Routledge. doi:10.4324/9781315663371

Seo, H. (2021). Peer effects in corporate disclosure decisions. *Journal of Accounting and Economics*, *71*(1), 101364. doi:10.1016/j.jacceco.2020.101364

Serviço Nacional de Aprendizagem Comercial. (2020). *Formação em Boas Práticas para profissionais da Ilha do Combú.* https://www.pa.senac.br/noticia/formacao-em-boas-praticas-para-profissionais-da-ilha-do-Combú

Shaikh, I. (2022). Environmental, social, and governance (ESG) practice and firm performance: An international evidence. *Journal of Business Economics and Management*, *23*(1), 218–237. doi:10.3846/jbem.2022.16202

Shang, H., Chen, R., & Li, Z. (2020). Dynamic sustainability capabilities and corporate sustainability performance: The mediating effect of resource management capabilities. *Sustainable Development (Bradford)*, *28*(4), 595–612. doi:10.1002d.2011

Shannon, C. E. (1948). A note on the concept of entropy. *The Bell System Technical Journal*, *27*(3), 379–423. doi:10.1002/j.1538-7305.1948.tb01338.x

Sharma, A. K., & Talwar, B. (2005). Corporate social responsibility: Modern vis-à-vis Vedic approach. *Measuring Business Excellence*, *9*(1), 35–45. doi:10.1108/13683040510588828

Sharpe, W. F. (1966). Mutual fund performance. *The Journal of Business*, *39*(S1), 119–138. doi:10.1086/294846

Shmueli, G., & Koppius, O. R. (2011). Predictive analytics in information systems research. *Management Information Systems Quarterly*, *35*(3), 553–572. doi:10.2307/23042796

Sierra-Garcia, L., Garcia-Benau, M. A., & Bollas-Araya, H. M. (2018). Empirical analysis of non-financial reporting by Spanish companies. *Administrative Sciences*, *8*(3), 29. doi:10.3390/admsci8030029

Singh, K., & Misra, M. (2021). Linking corporate social responsibility (CSR) and organizational performance: The moderating effect of corporate reputation. *European Research on Management and Business Economics*, *27*(1), 100139. doi:10.1016/j.iedeen.2020.100139

Skouloudis, A., Evangelinos, K., & Kourmousis, F. (2010). Assessing non-financial reports according to the Global Reporting Initiative guidelines: Evidence from Greece. *Journal of Cleaner Production*, *18*(5), 426–438. doi:10.1016/j.jclepro.2009.11.015

Slišāne, D., Gaumigs, G., Lauka, D., & Blumberga, D. (2020). Assessment of Energy Sustainability in Statistical Regions of Latvia using Energy Sustainability Index. *Environmental and Climate Technologies*, *24*(2), 160–169. doi:10.2478/rtuect-2020-0063

Smith, N. C. (2003). Corporate social responsibility: Whether or how? *California Management Review*, *45*(4), 52–76. doi:10.2307/41166188

Sobhani, F. A., Amran, A., & Zainuddin, Y. (2012). Sustainability disclosure in annual reports and websites: A study of the banking industry in Bangladesh. *Journal of Cleaner Production*, *23*(1), 75–85. doi:10.1016/j.jclepro.2011.09.023

Soderstrom, K. M., Soderstrom, N. S., & Stewart, C. R. (2017). Sustainability/CSR Research in Management Accounting: A Review of the Literature. In Advances in Management Accounting (Vol. 28, pp. 59-85). Emerald Publishing Limited. doi:10.1108/S1474-787120170000028003

Sokro, E. (2012). Impact of employer branding on employee attraction and retention. *European Journal of Business and Management*, *4*(18), 164–173.

Solomon, J., & Maroun, W. (2012). Integrated reporting: The new face of social, ethical and environmental reporting in South Africa? ACCA. The Association of Chartered Certified Accountants.

Spezamiglio, B. S., Galina, S. V. R., & Calia, R. C. (2016). Competitividade, Inovação E Sustentabilidade: Uma Inter-Relação Por Meio Da Sistematização Da Literatura. *Revista Eletrônica de Administração (Porto Alegre)*, *22*(2), 363-393. https://doi.org/ doi:10.1590/1413-2311.009162016.62887

Srivastava, A. K., Negi, G., Mishra, V., & Pandey, S. (2012). Corporate social responsibility: A case study of TATA group. *IOSR Journal of Business and Management*, *3*(5), 17–27. doi:10.9790/487X-0351727

Statman, M. (2000). Socially responsible mutual funds. *Financial Analysts Journal, 56*(3), 30–39. doi:10.2469/faj.v56.n3.2358

Stemler, S. (2001). An Overview of Content Analysis. *Practical Assessment, Research & Evaluation, 7*(17), 17. doi:10.7275/z6fm-2e34

Stevanović, S., Belopavlović, G., Lazarević-Moravčević, M. (2014). Obelodanjivanje informacija o zaštiti životne sredine: praksa u Srbiji. *Ecologica: nauka, privreda, iskustva, 21*(76), 679-683.

Stevanović, S. (2018). Izveštavanje o zagađenju životne sredine: praksa velikih zagađivača i preduzeća u Novom Sadu. In *Pravni i ekonomski aspekti primene principa zagađivač plaća*. Institute of Economic Sciences.

Stock, T., & Seliger, G. (2016). Opportunities of Sustainable Manufacturing in Industry 4.0. *Procedia CIRP, 40*, 536–541. doi:10.1016/j.procir.2016.01.129

Stojanović-Blab, M., Blab, D., & Spasić, D. (2017). Sustainability reporting - a challenge for Serbian companies/ Извештавање о одрживом пословању – изазов за српске компаније. *Teme, 1349*, 1349. Advance online publication. doi:10.22190/TEME1604349S

Stolowy, H., & Paugam, L. (2018). *The expansion of non-financial reporting: An exploratory study*. HEC Paris Research Paper No. ACC-2018-1262, 1-35.

Stolowy, H., & Paugam, L. (2018). The expansion of non-financial reporting: An exploratory study. *Accounting and Business Research, 48*(5), 525–548. doi:10.1080/00014788.2018.1470141

Streukens, S., & Leroi-Werelds, S. (2016). Bootstrapping and PLS-SEM: A step-by-step guide to get more out of your bootstrap results. *European Management Journal, 34*(6), 618–632. doi:10.1016/j.emj.2016.06.003

Suchman, M. C. (1995). Managing Legitimacy: Strategic and Institutional Approaches. *Academy of Management Review, 20*(3), 571–610. doi:10.2307/258788

Su, X., Wang, S., & Li, F. (2023). The Impact of Digital Transformation on ESG Performance Based on the Mediating Effect of Dynamic Capabilities. *Sustainability (Basel), 15*(13506), 1–22. doi:10.3390u151813506

Swanson, D. L. (2021). CSR Discovery Leadership: A Multilevel Framework in Historical Context. In The Routledge Companion to Corporate Social Responsibility (pp. 43-55). Routledge.

Syakur, A., Susilo, T. A. B., Wike, W., & Ahmadi, R. (2020). Sustainability of communication, organizational culture, cooperation, trust and leadership style for lecturer commitments in higher education. Budapest International Research and Critics Institute (BIRCI-Journal): Humanities and Social Sciences, 3(2), 1325-1335.

Szőcs, I., & Schlegelmilch, B. B. (2020). Embedding CSR in corporate strategies. In Rethinking business responsibility in a global context: Challenges to corporate social responsibility, sustainability and ethics (pp. 45-60). doi:10.1007/978-3-030-34261-6_4

Tampakoudis, I., Kiosses, N., & Petridis, K. (2023). The impact of mutual funds' ESG scores on their financial performance during the COVID-19 pandemic. A data envelopment analysis. *Corporate Governance (Bradford)*. Advance online publication. doi:10.1108/CG-12-2022-0491

Tamvada, M. (2020). Corporate social responsibility and accountability: A new theoretical foundation for regulating CSR. *International Journal of Corporate Social Responsibility, 5*(1), 1–14. doi:10.118640991-019-0045-8

Tauringana, V. (2020). Sustainability reporting adoption in developing countries: Managerial perception-based determinants evidence from Uganda. *Journal of Accounting in Emerging Economies, 11*(2), 149–175. doi:10.1108/JAEE-07-2020-0184

Tawse, A., & Tabesh, P. (2023). Thirty years with the balanced scorecard: What we have learned. *Business Horizons*, *66*(1), 123–132. doi:10.1016/j.bushor.2022.03.005

Taylor, J., Vithayathil, J., & Yim, D. (2018). Are corporate social responsibility (CSR) initiatives such as sustainable development and environmental policies value enhancing or window dressing? *Corporate Social Responsibility and Environmental Management*, *2*(5), 971–980. doi:10.1002/csr.1513

TEFAS Türkiye Electronic Fund Trading Platform. (2021). *Fon Detaylı Analiz*. https://www.tefas.gov.tr/FonAnaliz.aspx

Teixeira, P., Coelho, A., Fontoura, P., Sá, J. C., Silva, F. J., Santos, G., & Ferreira, L. P. (2022). Combining lean and green practices to achieve a superior performance: The contribution for a sustainable development and competitiveness—An empirical study on the Portuguese context. *Corporate Social Responsibility and Environmental Management*, *29*(4), 887–903. doi:10.1002/csr.2242

The KPMG. (2020). *Survey of Sustainability Reporting 2020*. https://kpmg.com/xx/en/home/insights/2020/11/the-time-has-come-survey-of-sustainability-reporting.html

Thimm, H., & Rasmussen, K. B. (2020). Website disclosure of environmental compliance management—The case of European production companies. *Journal of Environmental Studies and Sciences*, *11*(4), 648–670. doi:10.100713412-020-00643-4

Thomas, C. D., Cameron, A., Green, R. E., Bakkenes, M., Beaumont, L. J., Collingham, Y. C., Erasmus, B. F. N., de Siqueira, M. F., Grainger, A., Hannah, L., Hughes, L., Huntley, B., van Jaarsveld, A. S., Midgley, G. F., Miles, L., Ortega-Huerta, M. A., Townsend Peterson, A., Phillips, O. L., & Williams, S. E. (2004). Extinction risk from climate change. *Nature*, *427*(6970), 145–148. doi:10.1038/nature02121 PMID:14712274

Tilt, C. A. (2010). *Corporate responsibility, accounting and accountants*. Springer.

Tiwari, K., & Khan, M. S. (2020). Sustainability Accounting and Reporting in the Industry 4.0. *Journal of Cleaner Production*, *258*, 1–14. doi:10.1016/j.jclepro.2020.120783

Torelli, R., Balluchi, F., & Furlotti, K. (2020). The materiality assessment and stakeholder engagement: A content analysis of sustainability reports. *Corporate Social Responsibility and Environmental Management*, *27*(2), 470–484. doi:10.1002/csr.1813

Torslov, T. R., Wier, L. S., & Zucman, G. (2020). *The Missing Profits of Nations*. National Bureau of Economic Research Working Paper, 24071. https://www.nber.org/papers/w24071

Tran, M., & Beddewela, E. (2020). Does context matter for sustainability disclosure? Institutional factors in Southeast Asia. *Business Ethics (Oxford, England)*, *29*(2), 282–302. doi:10.1111/beer.12265

Tran, T. T., & Herzig, C. (2023). Blended case-based learning in a sustainability accounting course: An analysis of student perspectives. *Journal of Accounting Education*, *63*, 1–17. doi:10.1016/j.jaccedu.2023.100842

Traxler, A. A., Schrack, D., & Greiling, D. (2020). Sustainability reporting and management control – A systematic exploratory literature review. *Journal of Cleaner Production*, *276*, 122725. Advance online publication. doi:10.1016/j.jclepro.2020.122725

Tregidga, H. (2013). Biodiversity offsetting: Problematisation of an emerging governance regime. *Accounting, Auditing & Accountability Journal*, *26*(5), 806–832. doi:10.1108/AAAJ-02-2013-1234

Treptow, I., Kneipp, J., Müller, L., Frizzo, K., & Gomes, C. (2019). Práticas de inovação sustentável em empresas incubadas da cidade de Santa Maria, RS. *Revista Metropolitana de Sustentabilidade*, *9*(1), 69. https://revistaseletronicas.fmu.br/index.php/rms/article/view/1649

Tripathi, V., & Bhandari, V. (2015). Socially responsible stocks: A boon for investors in India. *Journal of Advances in Management Research*, *12*(2), 209–225. doi:10.1108/JAMR-03-2014-0021

Tsagas, G., & Villiers, C. (2020). Why "less is more" in non-financial reporting initiatives: Concrete steps towards supporting sustainability. *Accounting, Economics, and Law Convivium*, *10*(2), 20180045. doi:10.1515/ael-2018-0045

Tsalis, T. A., Malamateniou, K. E., Koulouriotis, D., & Nikolaou, I. E. (2020). New challenges for corporate sustainability reporting: United Nations' 2030 Agenda for sustainable development and the sustainable development goals. *Corporate Social Responsibility and Environmental Management*, *27*(4), 1617–1629. doi:10.1002/csr.1910

Tsalis, T. A., Stylianou, M. S., & Nikolaou, I. E. (2018). Evaluating the quality of corporate social responsibility reports: The case of occupational health and safety disclosures. *Safety Science*, *109*, 313–323. doi:10.1016/j.ssci.2018.06.015

Tsang, Y. P., Fan, Y., & Feng, Z. P. (2023). Bridging the gap: Building environmental, social and governance capabilities in small and medium logistics companies. *Journal of Environmental Management*, *338*, 1–10. doi:10.1016/j.jenvman.2023.117758 PMID:36996566

Tsolas, I. E. (2019). Utility exchange traded fund performance evaluation. A comparative approach using grey relational analysis and data envelopment analysis modelling. *International Journal of Financial Studies*, *7*(4), 1–9. doi:10.3390/ijfs7040067

Turker, D. (2008). Measuring Corporate Social Responsibility: A Scale Development Study. *Journal of Business Ethics*, *85*(4), 411–427. doi:10.100710551-008-9780-6

Turkish Ministry of Foreign Affairs. (2023). *Política Externa Empreendedora e Humanitária*. https://www.mfa.gov.tr/surdurullenen-kalkinma.tr.mfa

Tyas, V. A., & Khafid, M. (2020). The Effect of Company Characteristics on Sustainability Report Disclosure with Corporate Governance as Moderating Variable. *Accounting Analysis Journal*, *9*(3), 159–165. doi:10.15294/aaj.v9i3.41430

Ugur, K., & Erdogan, Y.H. (2007). *Remembering Thirty-five Years of Social Accounting: A Review of the Literature and the Practice*. MPRA Paper No. 3454.

Ullah, F., Qayyum, S., Thaheem, M. J., Al-Turjman, F., & Sepasgozar, S. M. E. (2021). Risk management in sustainable smart cities governance: A TOE framework. *Technological Forecasting and Social Change*, *167*, 120743. Advance online publication. doi:10.1016/j.techfore.2021.120743

Ullmann, A. E. (1976). The corporate environmental accounting system: A management tool for fighting environmental degradation. *Accounting, Organizations and Society*, *1*(1), 71–79. doi:10.1016/0361-3682(76)90008-8

UNCTAD. (1999). *Preparing for future multilateral trade negotiations: issues and research needs from a development perspective*. UNCTAD.

Unerman, J. (2003). Enhancing Organizational Global Hegemony with Narrative Accounting Disclosures: An Early Example. *Accounting Forum*, *27*(4), 425–448. doi:10.1046/j.1467-6303.2003.t01-1-00113.x

UNESCO. (2022). *Disclosure, Digitalization, Decarbonization are the three important dimensions of carbon neutrality" asserted at the COP27 side-event*. https://www.unesco.org/en/articles/disclosure-digitalization-decarbonization-are-three-important-dimensions-carbon-neutrality-asserted

UNIDO. (2023). *Definition of CSR*. https://www.unido.org/our-focus/advancing-economic-competitiveness/competitive-trade-capacities-and-corporate-responsibility/corporate-social-responsibility-market-integration/what-csr

United Nations Conference on Trade and Development. (2021). *World Investment Report 2021, Investing in Sustainable Recovery*. United Nations Publications. https://unctad.org/system/files/official-document/wir2021_en.pdf

United Nations Conference on Trade and Development. (2022). *World Investment Report 2022, International Tax Reforms and Sustainable Investment*. United Nations Publications. https://unctad.org/system/files/official-document/wir2022_en.pdf

Upadhyay, N., Upadhyay, S., Al-Debei, M. M., Baabdullah, A. M., & Dwivedi, Y. K. (2023). The influence of digital entrepreneurship and entrepreneurial orientation on intention of family businesses to adopt artificial intelligence: Examining the mediating role of business innovativeness. *International Journal of Entrepreneurial Behaviour & Research*, *29*(1), 80–115. doi:10.1108/IJEBR-02-2022-0154

Ur Rehman, S., Bhatti, A., & Chaudhry, N. I. (2019). Mediating effect of innovative culture and organizational learning between leadership styles at third-order and organizational performance in Malaysian SMEs. *Journal of Global Entrepreneurship Research*, *9*(1), 1–24. doi:10.118640497-019-0159-1

Urbach, N., Smolnik, S., & Riempp, G. (2010). An empirical investigation of employee portal success. *The Journal of Strategic Information Systems*, *19*(3), 184–206. doi:10.1016/j.jsis.2010.06.002

Van der Waal, J. W. H., & Thijssens, T. (2020). Corporate involvement in Sustainable Development Goals: Exploring the territory. *Journal of Cleaner Production*, *252*, 119625. doi:10.1016/j.jclepro.2019.119625

Van Grembergen, W. (2000). The balanced scorecard and IT governance. *Information Systems Control Journal, 2*, 1-3.

Venturelli, A., Caputo, F., Leopizzi, R., & Pizzi, S. (2018). The state of art of corporate social disclosure before the introduction of non-financial reporting directive: A cross country analysis. *Social Responsibility Journal*.

Verheyden, T., Eccles, R. G., & Feiner, A. (2016). ESG for all? The impact of ESG screening on return, risk, and diversification. *Journal of Applied Corporate Finance*, *28*(2), 47–56. . doi:10.1111/jacf.12174

Verhoef, P. C., Broekhuizen, T., Bart, Y., Bhattacharya, A., Qi Dong, J., Fabian, N., & Haenlein, M. (2019). Digital transformation: A multidisciplinary reflection and research agenda. *Journal of Business Research*, *122*, 889–901. doi:10.1016/j.jbusres.2019.09.022

Verma, A. K. (2019). Sustainable development and environmental ethics. *International Journal of Environmental Sciences*, *10*(1), 1–5.

Vial, G. (2019). Understanding digital transformation: A review and a research agenda. *The Journal of Strategic Information Systems*, *28*(2), 118–144. doi:10.1016/j.jsis.2019.01.003

Videnović, S. D., Hanić, A., & Sućeska, A. (2021). Ethically relevant values and behavior of employees in Serbia during the Covid-19. *TM. Technisches Messen*. Advance online publication. doi:10.22190/teme200901023v

Vieira, A. P., & Radonjič, G. (2020). Disclosure of eco-innovation activities in European large companies' sustainability reporting. *Corporate Social Responsibility and Environmental Management*, *27*(5), 2240–2253. doi:10.1002/csr.1961

Vladimir, V. F., Mercedes, N. C., Francisca, C. M. M., & José, M. V. D. (2020). Balanced Scorecard: Key Tool for Strategic Learning and Strengthening in Business Organizations. *Academic Journal of Interdisciplinary Studies*, *9*(3), 1–11. doi:10.36941/ajis-2020-0036

Vos, J. F. (2003). Corporate social responsibility and the identification of stakeholders. *Corporate Social Responsibility and Environmental Management*, *10*(3), 141–152. doi:10.1002/csr.39

Voss, B. (2016). *Discursive constructions of social and environmental accounting in Brazil: the case of Petrobras* [Doctoral dissertation]. Universidade de São Paulo.

Wagner, T., Bicen, P., & Hall, Z. R. (2008). The dark side of retailing: Towards a scale of corporate social irresponsibility. *International Journal of Retail & Distribution Management, 36*(2), 124–142. doi:10.1108/09590550810853075

Waltman, L., van Eck, N. J., & Noyons, E. C. M. (2010). A unified approach to mapping and clustering of bibliometric networks. *Journal of Informetrics, 4*(4), 629–635. doi:10.1016/j.joi.2010.07.002

Wang, F., & Sun, Z. (2022). Does the environmental regulation intensity and ESG performance have a substitution effect on the impact of enterprise green innovation: Evidence from China. *International Journal of Environmental Research and Public Health, 19*(14), 1–24. doi:10.3390/ijerph19148558 PMID:35886408

Wang, J.-S., Liu, C.-H., & Chen, Y.-T. (2022). Green sustainability balanced scorecard—Evidence from the Taiwan liquefied natural gas industry. *Environmental Technology & Innovation, 28*, 1–18. doi:10.1016/j.eti.2022.102862

Wang, S., & Esperança, J. P. (2023). Can digital transformation improve market and ESG performance? Evidence from Chinese SMEs. *Journal of Cleaner Production, 419*, 1–12. doi:10.1016/j.jclepro.2023.137980

Wang, Y. F., Chen, S. P., Lee, Y. C., & Tsai, C. T. S. (2013). Developing green management standards for restaurants: An application of green supply chain management. *International Journal of Hospitality Management, 34*, 263–273. doi:10.1016/j.ijhm.2013.04.001

Warren, J. D. Jr, Moffitt, K. C., & Byrnes, P. (2015). How Big Data will change accounting. *Accounting Horizons, 29*(2), 397–407. doi:10.2308/acch-51069

Warren, R. C. (2003). The evolution of business legitimacy. *European Business Review, 15*(3), 153–163. doi:10.1108/09555340310474659

Wasara, T. M., & Ganda, F. (2019). The Relationship between Corporate Sustainability Disclosure and Firm Financial Performance in Johannesburg Stock Exchange (JSE) Listed Mining Companies. *Sustainability (Basel), 11*(16), 4496. Advance online publication. doi:10.3390u11164496

Wati, Y., & Koo, C. (2011). An Introduction to the Green IT Balanced Scorecard as a Strategic IT Management System. *Proceedings of the 44th Hawaii International Conference on System Sciences*, 1-10. 10.1109/HICSS.2011.59

Watson, A., Shrives, P., & Marston, C. (2002). Voluntary disclosure of accounting ratios in the UK. *The British Accounting Review, 34*(4), 289–313. doi:10.1006/bare.2002.0213

Weir, K. (2018). The purposes, promises and compromises of extinction accounting in the UK public sector. *Accounting, Auditing & Accountability Journal, 31*(3), 875–899. doi:10.1108/AAAJ-03-2016-2494

Werle, M., & Laumer, S. (2022). Competitor identification: A review of use cases, data sources, and algorithms. *International Journal of Information Management, 65*, 1–15. doi:10.1016/j.ijinfomgt.2022.102507

Wesselink, R., & Osagie, E. R. (2020). Differentiating CSR managers roles and competencies: taking conflicts as a starting point. In *Research handbook of responsible management*. Edward Elgar Publishing. doi:10.4337/9781788971966.00044

Westphal, J. D., & Zajac, E. J. (2001). Decoupling policy from practice: The case of stock repurchase programs. *Administrative Science Quarterly, 46*(2), 202–228. doi:10.2307/2667086

Wheeler, Q. D., Knapp, S., Stevenson, D. W., Stevenson, J., Blum, S. D., Boom, B. M., Borisy, G. G., Buizer, J. L., De Carvalho, M. R., Cibrian, A., Donoghue, M. J., Doyle, V., Gerson, E. M., Graham, C. H., Graves, P., Graves, S. J., Guralnick, R. P., Hamilton, A. L., Hanken, J., ... Woolley, J. B. (2012). Mapping the biosphere: Exploring species to understand the origin, organization and sustainability of biodiversity. *Systematics and Biodiversity, 10*(1), 1–20. doi:10.1080/14772000.2012.665095

Wójcik, D. (2015). Accounting for globalization: Evaluating the potential effectiveness of country-by-country reporting. *Environment and Planning. C, Government & Policy, 33*(5), 1173–1189. doi:10.1177/0263774X15612338

Wolff, S., Brönner, M., Held, M., & Lienkamp, M. (2020). Transforming automotive companies into sustainability leaders: A concept for managing current challenges. *Journal of Cleaner Production, 276*, 124179. Advance online publication. doi:10.1016/j.jclepro.2020.124179

Wood, D. J. (1991). Corporate social performance revisited. *Academy of Management Review, 16*(4), 691–718. doi:10.2307/258977

Wood, D. J., & Jones, R. E. (1995). Stakeholder mismatching: A theoretical problem in empirical research on corporate social performance. *The International Journal of Organizational Analysis, 3*(3), 229–267. doi:10.1108/eb028831

Woodward, J. (1958). *Management and technology*. HM Stationery Office.

Wren, D. A., & Bedeian, A. G. (2009). *The evolution of management thought*. John Wiley & Sons.

Wyatt, A. (2008). What financial and non-financial information on intangibles is value-relevant? A review of the evidence. *Accounting and Business Research, 38*(3), 217–256. doi:10.1080/00014788.2008.9663336

Xiao, C., Ye, J., Esteves, R. M., & Rong, C. (2015). Using Spearman's correlation coefficient for exploratory data analysis on big dataset. *Concurrency and Computation, 28*(14), 3866–3878. doi:10.1002/cpe.3745

Xiao, X., & Shailer, G. (2021). Stakeholders' perceptions of factors affecting the credibility of sustainability reports. *The British Accounting Review, 54*(1), 101002. Advance online publication. doi:10.1016/j.bar.2021.101002

Xidonas, P., & Essner, E. (2022). On ESG Portfolio Construction: A Multiobjective Optimisation Approach. *Computational Economics*, 1–25. doi:10.100710614-022-10327-6 PMID:36268180

Xue, S., Tang, Y.-Y., & Posner, M. I. (2011). Short-term meditation increases network efficiency of the anterior cingulate cortex. *Neuroreport, 22*(12), 570–574. doi:10.1097/WNR.0b013e328348c750 PMID:21691234

Yáñez, S., Uruburu, Á., Moreno, A., & Lumbreras, J. (2019). The sustainability report as an essential tool for the holistic and strategic vision of higher education institutions. *Journal of Cleaner Production, 207*, 57–66. doi:10.1016/j.jclepro.2018.09.171

Yang, C., & Fang, H. (2020). A New Nonlinear Model-Based Fault Detection Method Using Mann-Whitney Test. *IEEE Transactions on Industrial Electronics, 67*(12), 10856–10864. doi:10.1109/TIE.2019.2958297

Yanık, S., İçke, B. T., & Aytürk, Y. (2010). Sosyal sorumlu yatırım fonları ve performans özellikleri. *İstanbul Üniversitesi Siyasal Bilgiler Fakültesi Dergisi, 43*, 109-134.

Yasir, M., Majid, A., Yasir, M., Qudratullah, H., Ullah, R., & Khattak, A. (2021). Participation of hotel managers in CSR activities in developing countries: A defining role of CSR orientation, CSR competencies, and CSR commitment. *Corporate Social Responsibility and Environmental Management, 28*(1), 239–250. doi:10.1002/csr.2045

Yilmaz, Y. (2006). Tax havens, tax competition, and economic performance. *Tax Notes International, 43*(7), 587.

Young In, S., Rook, D., & Monk, A. (2019). Integrating alternative data (also known as ESG data) in investment decision making. *Global Economic Review, 48*(3), 237–260. doi:10.1080/1226508X.2019.1643059

Yousaf, I., Suleman, M. T., & Demirer, R. (2022). Green investments: A luxury good or a financial necessity? *Energy Economics, 105*, 105745. doi:10.1016/j.eneco.2021.105745

Yu, P., Luu, B. V., & Chen, C. H. (2020). Greenwashing in environmental, social and governance disclosures. *Research in International Business and Finance*, *52*, 1–23. doi:10.1016/j.ribaf.2020.101192

Yurtseven, H. R. (2011). Sustainable gastronomic tourism in Gokceada (Imbros): Local and authentic perspectives. *International Journal of Humanities and Social Science*, *1*(18), 17–26.

Zampone, G., Nicolò, G., & De Ioro, G. (2022). Gender diversity and SDG disclosure: the mediating role of the sustainability committee. *Journal of Applied Accounting Research*. doi:10.1108/JAAR-06-2022-0151

Zaro, M., Pistorello, J., Pereira, G. S., Nery, C. H. C., & Conto, S. M. D. (2013). Geração de resíduos sólidos em eventos gastronômicos: o Festiqueijo de Carlos Barbosa, RS. *Revista Rosa dos Ventos, 5*(2), 264-279.

Zhang, N., Zhang, Y., & Zong, Z. (2023). Fund ESG performance and downside risk: Evidence from China. *International Review of Financial Analysis*, *86*, 1–20. doi:10.1016/j.irfa.2023.102526

Zhang, Q., Oo, B. L., & Lim, B. T. H. (2019). Drivers, motivations, and barriers to the implementation of corporate social responsibility practices by construction enterprises: A review. *Journal of Cleaner Production*, *210*, 563–584. doi:10.1016/j.jclepro.2018.11.050

Zhao, L., Yang, M. M., Wang, Z., & Michelson, G. (2023). Trends in the dynamic evolution of corporate social responsibility and leadership: A literature review and bibliometric analysis. *Journal of Business Ethics*, *182*(1), 135–157. doi:10.100710551-022-05035-y

Zhong, Y., Zhao, H., & Yin, T. (2023). Resource Bundling: How Does Enterprise Digital Transformation Affect Enterprise ESG Development? *Sustainability (Basel)*, *15*(1319), 1–18. doi:10.3390u15021319

Zhu, J., & Huang, F. (2023). Transformational Leadership, Organizational Innovation, and ESG Performance: Evidence from SMEs in China. *Sustainability (Basel)*, *15*(7), 1–23. doi:10.3390u15075756

Zumente, I., & Lāce, N. (2021). ESG Rating: Necessity for the Investor or the Company? *Sustainability (Basel)*, *13*(16), 8940. doi:10.3390u13168940

About the Contributors

Albertina Monteiro is an assistant professor of Porto Accounting and Business School. Her main areas of research are accounting, entrepreneurship, strategic management, and internationalization. She has published at international conferences and in the Baltic Journal of Management, the Euromed Journal of Business, the Journal of International Business and Entrepreneurship Development, and the Journal of Innovation & Knowledge.

Ana Pinto Borges is a PhD in Economics, Faculty of Economics, University of Porto. Coordinating Professor and Pedagogical President at ISAG - European Business School. Assumes the Executive Coordination of ISAG Research Centre of ISAG (NIDISAG) between 2014 - 2021 and scientific coordinator of the Center in Business Sciences and Tourism (CICET - FCVC), since 2020. Author of more than 40 publications in indexed international scientific journals. Participation in presentations in various national and international congresses and member of the Scientific Committees in academic events. Editor and one of the founding members of the European Journal of Applied Business and Management (EJABM). Former Accenture consultant in the financial area. Economist at the Health Regulatory Entity since 2010.

Elvira Vieira holds a PhD in Applied Economics, University of Santiago de Compostela. Professor, member of the Scientific Council at Institute of Marketing Management between 2007-2009 and Invited Professor at Minho University between 2009-2012. Professor at Polytechnic Institute of Viana do Castelo and Coordinating Professor at ISAG - European Business School since 2009. General Director at ISAG - European Business School since 2012, researcher in UNIAG, scientific coordinator of NIDISAG Research Center (between 2014 - 2021) and of Center in Business Sciences and Tourism (CICET - FCVC) since 2021. Author of several publications (papers and book chapters) indexed to the main bibliographic databases. Editor and one of the founding members of the European Journal of Applied Business and Management (EJABM). 2009 1st prize winner for research of the "Catedra da Euro-región Galicia – Norte of Portugal" and President of the European Grouping of Territorial Cooperation Galicia – North of Portugal, from 2010-2012.

* * *

Muhammad Junaid Ahsan is currently engaged as a guest visiting Ph.D. at CBS (Copenhagen Business School) in Denmark. He is also actively involved in his doctoral studies, specializing in Business and Management studies, under the Department of Economics and Management at the University of Pisa, Italy. Muhammad's research interests revolve around sustainability, leadership, corporate social responsibility, and the field of organization science.

José Campos Amorim holds a PhD in Law. Professor of Tax Law. Member of the Scientific Council of Porto Accounting and Business School, Polytechnic of Porto and of the CEOS.PP. Tax Arbitrator at the Portuguese Administrative Arbitration Center.

Risolene Araújo is a PhD in Accounting Sciences at the Graduate Program - PPGCC/UFPB. Professor of Accounting Sciences at the Federal University of Pará – UFPA.

Beatriz Lopes Cancela earned her PhD in Business Management from the University of Coimbra, Faculty of Economics. She has been serving as an Adjunct Professor at Coimbra Business School and Instituto Superior de Gestão since 2021. Additionally, she holds a research position at CIGEST – Centro de Investigação em Gestão. Her research primarily focuses on sustainable management, with a particular emphasis on sustainable performance, corporate social responsibility, and corporate governance. Beatriz has published in various international indexed journals, showcasing her contributions to the field.

Esin Bengü Ceran PhD at Istanbul University, in the School of Business, Department of Business Administration. She is Research Assistant at Istanbul University focused in the following areas: Research Areas: Social Sciences and Humanities, Management and Management of Enterprises.

Arnaldo Coelho holds a PhD in Business Administration from the University of Barcelona. He is Associate Professor at the Faculty of Economics of the University of Coimbra since 1987 and coordinates different courses in the Business Management area. He is a Researcher at CEBER - Center for Business and Economics Research. He is a researcher in the Marketing field, with emphasis on Relationship Marketing and Branding, Corporate Social Responsibility and Human Resources Management and has publications in several international indexed journals such as the Journal of Business Research, the European Journal of Marketing, the International Journal of Human Resouces Management, among others. He acts, as well, as a business consultant in the fields of marketing and strategy.

Serhat Duranay received his PhD degree in Business Administration from Süleyman Demirel University in 2022. In 2015, he started working as a Research Assistant at Süleyman Demirel University, Faculty of Economics and Administrative Sciences, Department of Business Administration and since 2019 he has been working as a Lecturer at Isparta University of Applied Sciences, Eğirdir Vocational School. Duranay lectures in the fields of Accounting and Finance and research in the fields of investor behavior, sustainable finance practices and financial performance.

Bianca Moraes Fernandes graduated in Accounting at Universidade Federal do Pará (2020). Field of study: extinction accounting. English Level 1 Certificate in ESOL International - Council of Europe Level B2 - Cambridge.

Pedro Fontoura is the Head of Sustainability at EDP Comercial, with over 15 years of experience in the energy sector, including generation, distribution and commercialization, experiencing several roles and responsibilities. Post-doc researcher in the Faculty of Economics of the University of Coimbra regarding

ESG excellence, completed an MBA and a PhD investigating how to boost sustainability performance at organizations, with published articles in peer-reviewed journals, proposing several suggestions to maximize firms' shared value creation. Master's degree in environmental engineering from the Catholic University of Portugal. Focused on developing new ways to do business in a more responsible manner, considering the stakeholder needs and expectations, constantly seeking solutions to deliver more and better results, with ethics at the core of all decisions.

Aida Hanić is a Research Associate at Institute of Economic Sciences, Belgrade, Serbia. Her area of expertise include: Corporate Reporting, Corporate Social Responsibility, Islamic Banking and Environmental protection.

Massimiliano Kaucic received the PhD degree in Financial Mathematics in 2009 from the University of Trieste, Italy, where he is currently an associate professor in Mathematical Methods of Economy, Finance and Actuarial Sciences. His research interests include computational finance, sustainable investments, multi-criteria decision making, and applications of evolutionary computation and swarm intelligence in finance.

Alice Loureiro completed a bachelor degree in Applied Biology at the University of Minho and a master's degree course at Polytechnique Institute of Cávado and Ave: Integrated Management Systems: Quality, Environment and Safety. Obtained an internal auditor certificated training course in ISO 9001, ISO 14001, and ISO 45001 and integrated management systems. Currently working as Occupational Health and Safety Superior Technician and junior consultant at "XZ Consultores". She will start the PhD in Economics in Santiago de Compostela University.

Petar Mitić is a Research Associate at Institute of Economic Sciences, Belgrade, Serbia. His area of expertise include environmental economics, energy economics, sustainable development, economic growth and development and econometrics.

Sónia Monteiro is a professor of financial accounting at the Polytechnic Institute of Cávado and Ave (IPCA). PhD in Business sciences (Accounting), Santiago de Compostela University in 2007. She was the Director of Research Center on Accounting and Taxation. Actually, she is the president of scientific council of management school. She is ambassador of the SDG Portugal Alliance - United Nations Global Compact Network in Portugal, in the SDG 4 – Education. She has been involved in organising international conferences, hosted by IPCA, such as CSEAR conference and SRRNet conference. Author of several articles published in scientific books and journals. Her main research areas are Financial and non-financial reporting; CSR/sustainability reporting, Accounting and environmental management.

Mehmet Özsoy received his bachelor's degree from Istanbul University, Faculty of Business Administration, Department of Business Administration in 2016. He completed his master's degree at Süleyman Demirel University, Department of Business Administration in 2019. He is currently pursuing his PhD in the same field. His research interests include forecasting, clustering, decision support systems, deep learning and machine learning.

Huy Pham is an Associate Professors Doctor with fifteen years of experience working as Senior Lecturer in Public Sector Accounting at the School of Accounting and currently the Head, Department of Public Accounting and Deputy Head of Training Department at the University of Economics Ho Chi Minh City in Vietnam. He also earned his Vietnamese Certified Public Accountant from the Ministry of Finance and accounting and management in public sector. In addition to authoring numerous chapters for the books, he has written numerous papers in numerous journals and presented talks at conferences both domestically and internationally. Huy has extensive knowledge and is an expert in public sector governance, private sector accountancy, and corporate social responsibility. Software engineering, Big data, Blockchain, and artificial intelligence are some of Huy's passions. He has been awarded the Young Scientific Talen in Vietnam issued by Ministry of Education and Training together with Typical Young Teachers in Ho Chi Minh City with six consecutive years (i.e., from 2012 to 2017). Huy is a formidable force at work, inspiring others to put in the effort necessary to achieve with his upbeat outlook and boundless enthusiasm.

Filippo Piccotto received a Master's degree in Statistics and Actuarial Sciences in 2021 at the University of Trieste, Italy. Currently, he is a PhD Student of the Circular Economy Programme, at the University of Trieste. His research interests include computational finance, sustainable investments, behavioral finance, and artificial intelligence applications in financial and actuarial sciences.

Pedro Pinho is a Master student at ISCAP - Finance and Accounting.

Alexandre Rato holds a marketing master degree and works in the sustainability field. He is a researcher at CEBER, at the university of Coimbra.

Verónica Ribeiro is a professor of cost accounting at the Polytechnic Institute of Cávado and Ave (IPCA). PhD in Business sciences (Accounting) from Santiago de Compostela University in 2007. Her research lines are related to environmental accounting and social responsibility in public sector. She is the author and co-author of several papers published in high-quality journals and presented at international conferences in these topics. She is ambassador of the SDG Portugal Alliance - United Nations Global Compact Network in Portugal, in the SDG 4 – Education. She was the director of management school of IPCA.

Rui Costa Robalo holds a PhD in Business Sciences by Faculty of Economics at University of Porto (Portugal). He is associate professor at the School of Management and Technology of the Polytechnic Institute of Santarém (Portugal) and integrated member of the Center for Research in Accounting and Taxation at IPCA, located in Barcelos (Portugal). His teaching has covered various accounting subjects, namely management accounting, management control, financial accounting, nonfinancial reporting, and research methods in accounting and finance. He has supervised several internships of graduate and master students. He has also supervised research from master students, which has covered several topics. He has published research in national and international accounting journals and books. His current research focus on trends and developments in the accounting profession, mainly related with the roles of accountants in digitalization processes of accounting tasks and in nonfiancial reporting practices.

Paola Rossi, PhD, is an Associate professor of Accounting at the University of Trieste. She holds a doctorate in Planning and Control from the University of Florence. She was a Marie Curie Fellow at the Manchester Business School and visiting scholar at the Adam Smith Business School of University of Glasgow. Her main research interests are: integrated reporting, market effects of the non financial disclosure, risk disclosure, impact of adoption of IFRSs in Europe, comparative international accounting. She has several publications in national and international journals.

Nicoly Sousa Santos holds a Bachelor's in accounting from Federal University of Pará.

Gabriele Sbaiz received the Double PhD degree in Pure Mathematics in 2022 at Università Degli Studi di Trieste (Italy) and Université Claude Bernard – Lyon 1 (France). He is currently a Post-Doc Researcher in Mathematical Methods for Economic, Financial and Actuarial Sciences at Università Degli Studi di Trieste (Italy). His research interests include computational finance, sustainable investments, and applications of evolutionary computation and swarm intelligence in portfolio allocation problems.

Adriana Rodrigues Silva is an Adjunct Professor in Management Accounting at the Polytechnic Institute of Santarém. Integrated member researcher of the CICF, School of Management, IPCA, Barcelos, Portugal. Member researcher of the Laboratory of Critical and Interpretive Studies in Accounting (LECIC) at the Federal University of Pará (UFPA). PhD in Accounting from the University of Minho. Research interest focuses on critical and interpretative accounting and accounting history, specifically on themes that give prominence to subordinated voices.

Slavica Stevanović is a Senior Research Associate at Institute of Economic Sciences. Her areas of expertise include environmental economics, corporate governance, corporate reporting, and cash flows analysis.

Giorgio Valentinuz is an Adjunct Professor and Researcher in Corporate Finance at the University of Trieste (Italy). He holds a PhD in Business Administration from the University Ca' Foscari - Venice (Italy). At the University of Trieste, he teaches Corporate Finance, Finance for company valuation and Issues in Financial and Management Accounting. He is co-director and member of the board of the Master's degree in Coffee Economics and Science "Ernesto Illy", where he teaches Trading techniques and risk management. He served for five years as an Independent and Non-Executive member of the Board of Directors of modefinace, the first European Fintech rating agency authorised by ESMA. He is a member of the core faculty at the Master in Insurance and Risk Management and the MBA in International Business, master programmes offered by the University of Trieste with MIB Trieste School of Management. His research interests are ESG investing, company valuation, value creation, dividend policy, entrepreneurial finance, and social investment.

Phuc Vu is currently a Lecturer in the Faculty of Accounting of University of Economics Ho Chi Minh City (UEH), Vietnam. Her research interests are mainly concentrated around accounting and management in private as well as public sector. She also completed several articles as well as studies for international conferences. Moreover, her concerns are also related to publish in various book chapters of reputed publishing house. Her present studies include measuring, recognition and managing performance at different disciplines for both sectors in the global economy.

Index

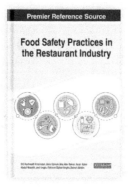
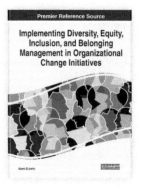

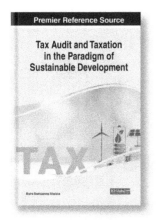

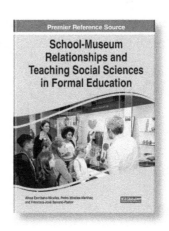
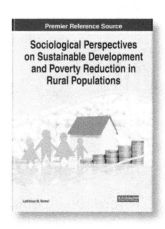

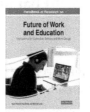

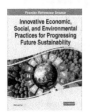

Printed in the USA
CPSIA information can be obtained
at www.ICGtesting.com
LVHW010046021123
762793LV00010B/750